documents, Mr. Redwood concludes
that the mockeries of a few witty skep-
tics interacted with reason and faith to
produce a wide range of opinions,
ideas, books, and controversies on
topics ranging from geology and the
nature of political society to promiscuity and blasphemy. He shows that,
in many ways, the period was more an
age of ridicule than of reason.

Reason, Ridicule and Religion will
appeal to all readers interested in the
the transforming role of intellectual
fashion in history. By focusing on an
important aspect of the advance of
skepticism in post-Restoration England, the book provides an excellent
introduction to an age of sparkling
achievement and rising doubt.

John Redwood is a Fellow of All
Souls College, Oxford.

REASON,
RIDICULE AND
RELIGION

REASON, RIDICULE AND RELIGION

The Age of Enlightenment in England

1660-1750

John Redwood

HARVARD UNIVERSITY PRESS

CAMBRIDGE, MASSACHUSETTS

1976

Copyright © 1976 Thames and Hudson, London
All rights reserved
Library of Congress Catalog Card Number 75–46350
ISBN 0–674–74953–7

First published by Thames and Hudson, London, as
REASON, RIDICULE AND RELIGION

Printed in the United States of America

To Gail

CONTENTS

PREFACE

Seventeenth-century thought was God-ridden. Whenever a man took up his pen and attempted to write about the weather, the seasons, the structure of the earth, the constitution of the heavens, the nature of political society, the organization of the Church, social morality or ethics he was by definition taking up his pen to write about God. Strive as individuals might to remonstrate with their colleagues and contemporaries that they were only interested in writing about the shape of the stamens of plants or the geological formation of rock strata, strain as they might to confine their comments upon republics and kingdoms to comments about political practicalities and the consequences of pragmatism, they always found that they had striven in vain. For, to the many clerics who were seriously concerned about the theological universe they were describing, and to the many laymen who proffered loyalty, obedience and humility to their clergymen and bishops, the world was God's creation and could only be explained within a deist and Christian framework.

Most ages are given over to wrangling and dispute; the period covered by the later seventeenth and early eighteenth century in England was no exception. But it was also an age which felt that it was making considerable advances: an age which could look to the works of a Newton or a Leibniz or a Huyghens and see in their writings significant advances in man's understanding of the universe and the world in which he lived. Newton had revealed the mathematical patterns of planetary motion, Leibniz had developed the calculus, and Huyghens's work on the motion of natural and mechanical objects had all augmented man's grasp of the world of matter, motion and forces. In England after the Restoration natural philosophy, that seventeenth-century combination of philosophical questioning and scientific curiosity, grew in importance both as an extra-curricular activity in the university and as a fashionable pastime in the homes of the gentry and in the debates and lectures of the newly founded Royal Society. This same period was also characterized by considerable activity amongst political theorists: in England explanations were sought for the break-down of the civil wars between 1642 and 1660, when a king had been executed and a whole succession of constitutional experiments had been foisted on an unwilling people. Political theorists following the Restoration in 1660 attempted to find ideological bases for parties or interest groups within the reformed Houses of Parliament or tried to justify attempted coups and revolutions as Whig fought Tory, High Churchman disputed with Low Churchman, and monarchist with republican. Within the Anglican Church itself, despite the threat from dissenters, Catholics and deists, clerics continued to dispute the many contentious doctrinal issues that had for long divided the Christian community. Men disagreed over the exact nature of the Trinity and the importance of Christ's mission, whilst considerable energy was expended in discussing the role of the Church in society and the Church's responsibility to defeat heresy wherever it might be. Most believed that the Church should help the secular power to create stability through rational and devotional support for the existing order of society. Problems only arose when it came to defining the scope of the Church's activities, the action to be taken against non-conformity, and the extent to which the secular powers could intervene in ecclesiastical jurisdiction and doctrinal debate.

There have been many excellent studies of these issues in isolation. There has long since been a historical industry concerned with the natural philosophies of the late seventeenth and early eighteenth century, but it has been an industry largely interested in the growth of mechanical philosophy from the viewpoint of the development of modern science. There has been some interest in the movement of natural religion and the utility of the studies of nature to the defence of God: but there has been no study which has attempted to demonstrate the way in which debates about politics, natural philosophy, theological doctrine, and the social structure were all part of one far greater debate about the defence of the true nature of a Christian community.

It is not enough to discuss Hobbes's contribution to the debate about de facto powers in a state, or to consider Hobbes as the exponent of a classic view of society and a particular view of depraved mankind, without considering the wider context of the debate in which Hobbes had to write. It is not enough to consider Newton's exposition of the laws of planetary motion and his formulation of mathematical variables demonstrating the force of gravity that work in the cosmological mechanics without considering Newton the theologian and Newton the alchemist. Whilst several have discussed Archbishop Wake and Bishop Gibson and their efforts to restructure the Church and have dealt with one or two isolated attacks on particular doctrinal issues, no one has demonstrated the way in which Wake and Newton, Hobbes and Gibson were all participating in controversy about one overriding issue which affected all else: they were debating God's creation and the place of man in God's universe.

It is interesting that in a world where no one would dispute the existence of God openly and in print, much less openly questioned the view that God had made the earth and placed man upon it lower than the angels but higher than all the rest of animal creation, the overruling fear should be of a Godless, mindless world governed by random atoms and created by chance. It is one of those ironies that whilst many of the participants in the debate we describe were serious-minded, honest Christians who had many reasons to believe that their colleagues were similarly pious and law-abiding, there nevertheless sprang up an immense literature concerned about the drift of society towards deism, and even towards atheism.

There was an abundance of tract-writing by contemporary clerical journalists, high-lighting the issues and the debates which were in the minds of many and hinted at in most seventeenth- and early eighteenth-century English books. The work of these men was in part extracted from and in part complementary to that of the great philosophers and apologists, equally if not more concerned with the burning issue of religious orthodoxy and the nature of belief. Amongst the voluminous apologists must be ranked Ralph Cudworth, the Cambridge neo-Platonist of the seventeenth century, and Bishop George Berkeley writing in the second and third decades of the eighteenth century. The tract-writers were hasty to draw attention to all those who seemed to be encouraging the drift towards deism, towards that belief which stripped religion of all but a remote Creator who had left a mechanical universe to its own devices to run in the way He had originally ordained with mathematical precision. The encyclopaedic apologists like Cudworth and Berkeley were scholars attempting to demonstrate the range of the atheist problem in so far as it spanned many issues and disciplines, and they pointed out the way in which the atheist debate was high-lighted in specific controversy or in the discussions of individual natural philosophical and social questions.

When a writer considered geological problems like the formation of the earth or considered matters of political theory he was only too aware of this wider religious debate to which he had to contribute. The clerical Newton, whom many have found difficult to interpret and attempted to ignore, or the seemingly zany Thomas Burnet, the world theorist, were rational participants in live discussions concerning the theological cosmos. Political theorists ostensibly concerned with expounding theories concerning political behaviour and political organization were similarly involved in far wider religious debates. The reasons for the intense hostility which the views of Thomas Hobbes engendered amongst his contemporaries, for example, transcended merely political matters and entered the realm of theological disputes as well. The same is true to a lesser extent of John Locke and is certainly true of James Harrington, John Milton and a host of minor republican authors.

Considerable historical attention has recently been devoted to the fascinating subject of popular faith, and debate and contention over witchcraft and associated beliefs. These, too, fell within the sights of our atheist pamphleteers and encyclopaedic apologists, and in the hands of those contributors to discussions of amulets and charms, or to discussions of providences and apparitions, can be found reference to, and interest in the wider theological universe of the later seventeenth-century world picture. Many rational theologians were willing to argue that if belief in witches and belief in providences were undermined, so too would be belief in other supernatural powers of a less malignant kind. Disputes raged concerning many of the miracles in the Bible, concerning the authenticity of the biblical sources, concerning the nature of the after-life, and concerning Christ's missions and message to mankind. In this atmosphere any man who paused to question the credibility of a particular miraculous phenomenon, or conversely who attempted to magnify and augment the range of miracles by including modern happenings, was thought suspect by the biblical faithful and the Protestant hierarchy. Most intense of all in the later seventeenth century, the cause of many a pamphlet and book in the 1690s in England, was the central issue of the nature of the Persons of the Trinity, and in particular the devotional status of Christ. This dispute, indulged in mainly by clerics eager for preferment, worried about their colleagues or concerned about the doctrine itself, was another of the many creating the uncertainties which generated the fear of irreligion.

The fear of drifting disbelief which raged from the mid-seventeenth century well into the eighteenth was made the stronger by shock administered to the more puritan of consciences by the drift in social mores and standards of behaviour. It was difficult in a Christian society to justify whoring, roguery, trickery and unconscionable display, drunkenness and swearing. Over-indulging the sins of the flesh, or taking in vain the name of God and other holy personages and attributes, were sins abhorrent to every clause of the Bible and every tenet of the rigorous clergyman. Yet, it was undeniable that in coffee houses, the inns and the taverns of the English countryside and particularly of London, the capital city, sins and abhorrences abounded. Following the rejection of the more severe of the Calvinist and Presbyterian demands of the Civil War period, when the Scots and their English colleagues were willing to demand a social regimen aimed at cleansing the nation of sin, it was undeniable that men enjoyed these things more and more and with a greater openness and indulgence than others felt was good for the society in which they all lived. The serious threat posed by atheism was to be seen in the drunken man lying in the gutter or the rake in his mistress's arms. A dissolute society was a Godless society, a society abounding in free discussion and atheist principles was bound to be a society on the verge of collapse, with rotten morals and rotten minds. Such physical and ethical decay brought decrepitude, the decline of marital values, the decline of moral health in the nation, and ultimately in the view of many it brought destruction in the wake of God's vengeance. A nation could not be successful either economically or physically, a nation could not be blessed with victory in battle, if at home it were a den of thieves and sinners rather than an upright and well-governed community of law-abiding Christians. The atheist threat which had been voiced in bad books, and echoed in many a deist's writings, was a threat which was most apparent in the consequent bad morals and bad practices, a process, moreover, that worked no less surely in reverse.

In the later seventeenth and early eighteenth century the two major words bandied about so frequently in debate were the words 'reason' and 'nature'. Reason was the method and nature the high court of appeal for all eighteenth-century arguments: a man's views had to be reasonable, for them to be taken seriously, and the ultimate source of knowledge lay in erecting reasonable suppositions and arguments on the basis of hard fact culled from observations of the natural world. The universe was given, the nature which lay behind it was God's design: God had constructed that universe using superior reason, and man could partake but a little of that rational faculty which he had to devote strenuously to understanding the higher reasoning of the Almighty as an act of worship as well as an act designed to improve the quality of man's life with man and man's life with God. Men believed that by working hard and by praying a little they could hope to unravel some of the secrets of the universe by use of their God-given agent, reason. Belief could not therefore be undermined by making the world more intelligible, because the more the wonder of the world were unveiled, the more man understood the construction of every atom and every particle of the universe, the more he would bow down and worship the power which had brought about that mysterious process of creation, construction, and preservation.

The age which has sometimes been loosely characterized as an age of reason was in many ways no more rational than preceding ages. Men have always used reason to make things intelligible for want of anything better, and most people who write prose or who pretend to think about the larger issues of the world and the universe can lay claim to using some form of reason to help guide their thought and construct their arguments. It is difficult to see that Thomas Hobbes was any more reasonable than Thomas Aquinas, impossible to allege that John Locke's reason was necessarily superior to the reason of Duns Scotus. All that can be said is that later seventeenth- and early eighteenth-century thinkers made rather more use of the word 'reason', and heralded it as an agent with which they could construct the new universe, whilst at the same time amongst themselves implicitly if not explicitly they differed fundamentally about the nature of that reason and the impact of its use. Reasonable men contemplating the same facts, the same nature around them, had come to very divergent opinions concerning the world in which they lived, and concerning the morals and attitudes which they should adopt in the light of that universe. They could come to fundamentally different opinions about the validity of the Bible or about God's dictates to men, just as they could differ fundamentally about whether a republic or a tyranny or a particular kind of limited monarchy or a particular kind of liberty was more or less desirable in the light of God's dictates and in the light of the nature of man and his universe.

Many of these differences can be attributed to a divergent view of the construction of nature, and of what was natural. It was after all a dispute about the nature of man which had been aroused by Hobbes's remarks in *The Leviathan*, about the brutish quality of human life and the savage quality in human nature if abstracted at the time of man's creation, a view which had come into sharp conflict with the view of many a theologian that man was a creature who had to strive for perfection and had only been corrupted at a later stage by evil politicians and by the Devil on earth. It was a difference over nature, too, which had led to the inexorable dispute between the Newtonians in England and the Cartesians and neo-Cartesians in Europe in the later seventeenth century, and it was a dispute over the nature of nature which lay behind many if not most of the controversies in natural philosophy which men of that period engineered. Reason and nature, apostrophized and praised, eulogized if not worshipped, were in many respects more fundamental bones of contention than were the issues they attempted to analyze, and they represent the conflict within the period rather than one unifying force which some commentators have seen in them.

The atheist-hunters could rightly point to a far more insidious growth in English and continental thought than the growth in the importance or at any rate the growing use of the words 'reason' and 'nature'. That insidious growth was the incursion being made by irony, wit, and ridicule. Far more serious in many ways than natural philosophers seeking to explain phenomena which previously had been regarded as supernatural or mysterious, far more serious than the discoveries concerning the formation of the earth in geological science questioning the historical creation described by Genesis, were the remarks of those deists and near-atheists who felt that the whole of theology was a cause for mirth and many of the biblical stories suitable only as the subjects of lampoons. This kind of social irresponsibility, apparent in many a playhouse jest, or many a chance remark in a tavern, reflected the unguarded thoughts of later seventeenth-century gentlemen who were willing in their hearts to doubt a God in order to savour a joke. Where it would take many volumes of argument to determine inconclusively the larger questions concerning the nature of creation or the accuracy of the biblical account, it was possible to make fun of God's cosmos as described by the theologians and the philosophers, in the space of five minutes of theatre jests, or in the odd quip in the tavern or the coffee house. Many of the atheist-hunters were aware of this in their correspondence and many of their pamphlets and works were designed to appeal to an audience which could either convert those who jeopardized Christianity in this way, or could appeal directly to those who attempted to pervert life by seeking cheap enjoyment at the expense of truth and belief in God's universe. It was the age of ridicule which did far more harm to the Christian defences than did the onslaught of reason and nature.

In many ways the Church could and did welcome the natural philosophers as giving more evidence of the beauty of God's creation. In many ways they could even welcome the disputes about political theory, given that many political theorists supported the views of the clergymen and attempted to bolster some place for the Church within the secular framework. In many ways even disputes and wranglings about theological and doctrinal issues were signs of the strength of the Church as well as being illustrations, as they were to some contemporaries, of the dangers of a disunited front. But nobody might allege that it was anything but a bad omen that some people were willing to question whole sections of the Bible for the Christian message by resorting to flippancy. Here then was the breadth of the atheist problem. At a time when the Church and the Christian message were thought to be under pressure, both from a group of men dedicated to discovering truth in the way they thought best through natural philosophy and political theory, and through a group of people who were willing to live the life of a sinner, theologians themselves were disunited and disputing for place, patronage, and for doctrinal supremacy. The Protestant settlement was still attacked by Catholics, and the Protestants themselves still much divided. Fear of atheism was accentuated by the group of thinkers, taking their lead from men like Blount writing in the 1680s, who in the early eighteenth century became known as the Deists and put forward views in favour of a truncated natural religion which to many was but a short step from total disbelief. Deists themselves often genuinely believed that by cutting Christianity down to certain basic essentials, and making these principles self-evident and easy to argue philosophically, they were doing a service to mankind. They had after all made the Christian arguments unassailable in their view, and they had made the defences of religion reflect the tenor of contemporary opinion and debate concerning natural philosophy and politics. Yet, at the same time, more conventional Christians believed that these deviationists had taken out so much of the Christian message and called it into doubt by stripping out many biblical passages and showing that they could be questioned, that it was but a short step towards demolition of the few remaining arguments and the abnegation of the few remaining Christian principles which inhered in the deists' truncated belief. Their view was to some extent borne out by the results of the Darwinian controversy in the nineteenth century. By lodging the defence of Christian principles so firmly upon the argument from God as the Creator and from the perfect design in all natural things in the universe, the Christians had unwittingly weakened their position should anybody offer a credible alternative explanation for the origin and evolution of the world and the life upon it.

These disputes, never as clear-cut as some two-sided representations can lead one to believe, ramified throughout the early eighteenth century in England and built up into an intense discussion about man and his place in the world. The apologists and the self-appointed Christians fought back and refuted every deist book, worming out of every publication possible extensions of rationalist principles which could lead deism inexorably towards atheism. From the presses rushed hundreds of pamphlets, hundreds of books, bolstering the traditional God-ridden universe, and attempting to demonstrate either how the new findings in natural philosophy were part of this God-given world or were another part of the deist threat which had to be hounded out in the interests of social stability and religious orthodoxy. Their doctrinal concerns were social concerns, and their interest centred upon the prize of salvation. Men should not be so foolish as to throw up their chances of eternal life and well-being for the sake of a few errant and disputable philosophical principles, for the sake of a few arid speculations or for the sake of a particular dissolute life style which could follow in the wake of hacking down the Christian citadel.

It is in this context of dispute which existed in the English Church following the settlement of 1660–61 and the end of the civil wars and that period of religious strife and factional struggle, that English intellectual and general history should be viewed. The anti-atheists, the pamphleteers and the apologists were right to fear the undermining of their religion. The natural philosophers and even the deists were in some ways right when they stressed their good intents. But all could agree, deist and Christian, conventional apologist and natural philosopher of a religious turn of mind, that the most serious threat of all to the clerical cause and to the defence of the Church came from those men of wit, those libertines who were all too common in the courts of the later Stuart kings and in the coffee houses and taverns of the early eighteenth century.

INTRODUCTION

The age of reason came slowly and fitfully. There was little agreement about the competence or nature of reason; the rationalist age of the Augustans in many ways continued the reasonable traditions of previous eras. It was an age which could almost openly debate the great questions of the origin of the world and the nature of matter, yet it was an age that found it possible to retreat into an orgy of almost puritan fervour, or into convulsions of national prayer and fasting. Natural happenings were still seen by many as supernaturally inspired warnings and signs;[1] governments still used the rhetoric of divine support and displeasure to cajole their opponents and encourage their followers.[2] It was an age of enthusiasts against enthusiasm, an age which sought to replace sectarianism by reason and which succeeded in ousting civil war and replacing it with frivolity and the acrimony of pamphleteers.

Nevertheless, both the Church and even Christianity itself were under siege. They felt themselves to be so: they saw that the combined forces of ridicule and reason were working havoc with their doctrines and dogmas. Edward Stephens, writing in 1704, perceived three major threats to the Church of England.[3] He felt that the 'knights, gentlemen, freeholders and commons of England' should be warned about the dangers inherent in the activities of Catholic missionaries, Quaker ministers, and Church and State deists. But Stephens need not have worried, for most people in England were conscious of the dangers from these three groups, the one out to undermine the Protestant succession and the revolution, the other two out to undermine the doctrines and credentials of the Church of England. Much of the ecclesiastical and political activity of our period is concerned with attempting to repress their writings, their influence, and their political programme where they had one.

The seriousness of the Catholic position was reflected throughout the period by the activities of successive governments and oppositions: in the reigns of Charles and James to limit royal favour to Catholics and Catholic views, under Queen Anne and the early Hanoverians to prevent Catholic and Jacobite plotting, sedition and rebellion. But their significance was also marked by the voluminous anti-Catholic literature. In 1673 for example a pamphleteer had revived the long-standing attack upon Catholic greed and avarice with his Book of Rates for 'bulls, dispensations and pardons for all manner of villanies and wickednesses', sounding the old trumpet call of the Reformation in case Englishmen were forgetting.[4] Another pamphleteer in 1713 chose to remark upon the recent growth of popery, and offer all Protestants of whatever intelligence and conviction simple arguments to rebut the Catholic advance.[5]

In 1714, with the mistrust of the Pretender paramount in political circles, the virulence of anti-Catholic writings continued. One author reminded his audience that there would be no liberty under a Catholic prince, and stressed the theme of Catholic brutality and butchery.[6] 'Your vertuous Church, for whose sake her sons must wade thro' a sea of blood' conjured up memories of the St Bartholomew's day massacre and the long seventeenth-century religious wars.[7] Another author in 1727 concentrated upon the superior doctrines of the Church of England, arguing that: 'The Church of England keeps close to the Ancient Creeds, commonly called the Apostles, the Nicene, and that of Athanasius: the Church of Rome hath added new articles of faith to these Ancient Creeds, which we reject.' He attacked the Catholic doctrines of the Eucharist, Purgatory and justification.[8] He went on to argue, for example, that the word of God was against the invocation of saints much practised by Rome.[9]

The new sect of Quakers at the other end of the religious spectrum was in many ways as worrying. By 1682 the kind of old Presbyterian Puritan described by John Geree in a short pamphlet was a dying figure. 'He esteemed those Churches most pure where the government is by elders'[10] and he thought of his life as 'a warfare, wherein Christ was his Captain . . . the Cross his banner'.[11] But he was less inclined to do so after the Restoration, and his fire was being stolen by the Quakers and Quietist groups. William Penn and George Whitehead had laid down their essential beliefs, and had been active in leading small groups of discreet Quaker worshippers. Their activities were popularly regarded as a threat to both Church and State.

One of Charles II's early enactments was against Quakers refusing to take the lawful oaths enjoined by the Church of England.[12] Charles and his Parliament feared dire consequences from the 'dangerous tenets and unlawful assemblies' held by the Quakers.[13] Charles Leslie, indefatigable in the cause of right thinking, felt that in 1698 the Quakers were still an errant group of heretics, and he recited for the public a list of their theological deviations.[14] They denied the Incarnation of Christ,[15] the Resurrection and future judgement,[16] they preached in favour of fornication,[17] expressed a contempt for the magistracy and government,[18] and were stiff in taking off their hats and giving men their civil titles.[19] In short, they were to him a thoroughly unpleasant, debauched and seditious crowd.

The Quakers themselves looked to Penn for support and succour. His didactic works went through frequent editions, and he was keen to stress that neither were the Quakers anti-trinitarians,[20] nor were they opposed to the civil government as men like Leslie suggested.[21] They looked to the creed of George Whitehead,[22] they pillaged the works of Fox and his spiritual diaries.[23] Their critics saw them as enthusiasts,[24] as men out to revive dormant ancient heresy. One critic of the sect thought for example that they sought to revive Pelagius's theory that there was no Original Sin:[25] and that they were like Manicheus in being selective in their approach to biblical authorities.[26]

Most commentators agree that outside the activities of the dissenting groups in society, and above and beyond the great activity of the Church and its defenders against atheists and heretics, the state of religious fervour in England from 1660 onwards into the eighteenth century and the early days of the Methodist revival was not happy. Work that has been done on the quantifiable materials available for popular religious history of this period seems to indicate a general lethargy amongst the population, both in church-going and in catechizing. Presentments to ecclesiastical courts demonstrate that many so-called Christians were failing to live up to the standards of their faith, whilst the courts themselves were in a difficult and often ridiculed and uninfluential position. Attendance at church does not seem to have been high in many parishes where returns survive, nor do large numbers seem to have been recorded as communicants where such figures are available. Finally, a great many people seemed to have ignored the Church rites of baptism, confirmation, marriage and even burial.

It should not of course be conjectured that the state of the English Church and its mission amongst the people was any worse between 1660 and 1760 than it had been through the previous five centuries. There is evidence in all centuries of low standards of religious practice, education and understanding, and evidence to suggest that many people did not bother about Christian baptism, confirmation and other rites, either because they were expensive or because they did not regard them as important. Nor should the figures where they chance to survive be taken as representative of other parishes or periods. The figures themselves may well not be accurate, often compiled as they were by men seeking to illustrate a point about their local circumstances and sent to bishops not overworried by the state of Christian belief amongst the illiterate, uneducated or silent members of the society. Bishops feared that men would be misinformed by atheists and deists, and that their words would spread social chaos and disorder in their wake, but it was a breakdown of law and order they feared more than they regretted any deficiency in the standard of theological comprehension in the parishes and hamlets of England.

Many felt that the changes and the lapses of successive civil war administrations had weakened the position of the Church. Between 1650 and 1657 there had been no compulsory attendance in law, and 1653 had seen the introduction of civil marriage. The tithe system, much of the personnel and the parish system had survived the Civil War, it is true, but they survived only after a period of some administrative breakdown as well as theological disruption. Yet administrative tinkering was probably far more damaging than were theological changes, as it had a more direct influence upon the type of religious experience administered to the willing and unwilling poor.

The post-Restoration Church was at least as bedevilled by pluralism, a shortage of vicars, and a lack of services, as its predecessors had been. Often churches held fewer than ten communions a year, and only one service a fortnight. There is some evidence to support the view that after 1714 the trend of the later seventeenth century towards fewer and fewer attending church did continue: the absentees were mainly lower class, and were most numerous in large parishes where they would not be well known and missed. Women attended more frequently than men. There was of course in growing cities and towns, and particularly in London, a shortage of churches to contend with: in country districts there was often a long walk to church, and once people arrived they had to sit in winter in draughty and unheated naves and chancels for the benefit of their spiritual improvement.

It is against this decay or continuance of apathy that the reactions of moralists and High Churchmen have to be measured. They saw direct connections between the sorry state in the average church on the Sunday when there chanced to be a service, and the intellectual currents we examine. To them society needed greater order, conformity and civilization. They regretted the lower orders who swore, drunk, and misbehaved: they hated the artisan who did not labour, the labourer who did not doff his cap, the mechanic who had notions above his station. God had ordained that the rich man should live in his castle and the poor man at his gate: it was in the order of nature, it was part of God's goodness, and the poor always had the chance of entering the Kingdom of Heaven if they behaved. But if the poor disobeyed, and failed to turn up to church, they would miss the good homilies upon the rank and position of men in society, they would escape the moral imperatives it was necessary that they should hear regularly to keep them under control. Bishops were right when they saw their duty to lie in bringing the flock back to the emptying churches.

The Bishop of Bath and Wells addressed himself to the problem of non-attendance in a rather defensive way in 1688, sending written advice from London to his clergy concerning their behaviour during Lent. 'Be not discouraged', he wrote, 'if but few come to the *Solemn Assemblies*, but go to the House of Prayer, where God is well known for a sure refuge.'[27] His defeatism represented a kind of realism, seeking to preserve the faith and courage of those true to the Church in a state of siege from the forces of apathy. Meanwhile, there were those who saw the need for more drastic action, and the projectors and authors of the early Augustan age were full of suggestions and aids for all manner of men to be correctly guided in their faiths. There were simple explanations of the Lord's Prayer and catechism adapted to lesser understandings,[28] and prayer and forms of individual worship recommended to the simple and the lowly.[29] There were other works dedicated to gentlemen,[30] and specialist schemes like that propounded by Robert Boyle for spreading the Gospel in colonial parts.[31] There were lobbies urged upon the influential Society for the Propagation of Christian Knowledge, such as the case put forward by Luke Milbourn that psalms should be more fully incorporated into Anglican worship.[32] Men like Simon Ford perceived the need to emulate the Jesuits and instruct children and youths fully into the way of the Lord,[33] even telling them of the significance of the Articles as well as of the main prayers,[34] whilst men like Dr Claggett attacked swearing and profanities that bedevilled their society.[35]

The rhetoric of pious exhortation kept many printers in business, and acted as a kind of social catharsis for the religious and the reverent to vent their anger and their moral superiority towards their contemporaries and colleagues under cover of helping and educating them into the way of God. The simple duty of explaining the faith, the task of each minister and curate, was aided by those who felt their words were necessary to curb licence and espouse the cause of the good. The testimony to their achievement which remains with us in our libraries provides some evidence upon the poor state of the Church, evidence which is, however, heavily biased against the establishment it pretended to support and help; it furnishes us with more evidence concerning the attitudes of mind of that quite numerous group of clergy and laity who were extremely worried by the irreligion of their times and saw in it social disorder or dire national consequences under some providential reckoning.

Much of the rhetoric of this debate was of course part of the continuing discussion concerning the relative roles of Church and State, as much as it was a serious reflection upon purely religious problems. The cataclysmic changes of the Civil War period followed by the endless debates of Charles's reign over comprehension and toleration, followed by James's efforts to bring back some form of Catholic practice, followed by the Anglican settlement of 1689, strained Church-State relations to the utmost. Religion was a crucial issue in foreign and trading policy as well as the king-pin of any law-and-order programme. Any leaning towards toleration could be construed as a leaning towards the much-hated Catholicism, and towards French alliance. A pamphleteer feared that in 1713 the main danger had and did come from being over-generous towards France, and in his Whiggish way regarded the pro-French policy as being that of the landed interest against the trading interests who wished to stand up to France in the South Seas over trade matters.[36] Religious policy could reflect Tory, landed, pro-French sympathies. Similarly White Kennet's sermon of 31 January 1704 was analyzed by those who sought to defend the royal martyr, Charles I, and to discover the causes of the civil wars.[37] The Augustan age lived under the shadow of the regicides, and many a High Tory and High Churchman would defend the Martyr King against those 'cunning and self-ended men' who had been determined to topple government in 1642-9.[38] These churchmen saw their main role as being the defence of passive obedience, and the condemnation of unlawful rebellion.

Another critic of Kennet attacked him for suggesting that part of the blame for the Civil War rested with Charles I and his poor policies.[39] At the same time Kennet had espoused the theory of passive obedience for James II, and had suggested that this king was above the law: a view also subject to criticism.[40] The Tory doctrine of passive obedience came in for a great deal of criticism during the course of the Revolution settlement, and thereafter there was always the possibility of representing it as disloyal: this was certainly true after Anne's death.

The average Tory was represented as being in favour of Catholicism,[41] as being often a drunkard, afraid of Protestant plots,[42] an exponent of priesthood above sovereignty[43] and an opponent of all free-spirited Protestants.[44] Other writers were willing to see that there could be a distinction between popish affiliations, and mere High Church royalism: this difference can be traced in

the characters of Orthodox, a royalist, and Cacodaemon, in a dialogue of 1678.[45]
In contrast, the Whig was a Low Churchman, a sectarian, a likely rebel, plotter
and spokesman for the irregularities of the succession between 1685 and 1715.
The whole system of preserving the religious fabric depended like the preservation of other laws upon the person of the informer; a man who was ruled less
by his convictions than by his hope for gain from fines. As one writer put it,

> Open prophaneness is imployed to correct suspected heresies: A good cause
> is undoubtedly scandaliz'd by such vile instruments, and could not but blush
> to see those prosecute persons for ceremonial nonconformities who are them-
> selves so much uncomfortable to all the fundamental laws of religion and
> morality[46]

This anonymous writer, who may well have had nonconformist sympathies,
thought it a delightful irony that an informer spent in a bawdy house what he
earned for supervising a Quaker meeting house.[47]

The animus of politics and the way it is an important element in the religious
and sectarian squabbles of the period is nowhere better illustrated than in the
endless debates in the newspapers and pamphlets surrounding the personality
of Sir Roger L'Estrange, the Tory licenser. L'Estrange was rated with the
Devil as one of the two great Tory politicians of his age,[48] and compared to
Pantagruel in a funeral sermon published before he died by well-wishing critics.[49]
Critics saw in him the time-serving avaricious Tory of legend, and remarked on
how

> *Roger even there does earn his pension well,*
> *And brawls for the succession, tho' in Hell.*[50]

Some felt that L'Estrange, a secret Roman Catholic to their mind, banned the
wrong works. He originally declined to license Cole's *A Rod for Rome* against
the Jesuits until the Plot forced his hand,[51] yet he did permit the initial publication
of *Anima Mundi*, later burned by the Bishop of London, which attacked all
religion.[52] Others felt that L'Estrange's view that the press and pulpit should
be controlled was not in accord with men's liberties and Whiggish predilec-
tions.[53]

The debates over the successions of the later Stuart period were as heated as
any that divided High and Low Church, Whig and Tory. The *Observator* had
seemed to suggest that Anne was Queen by revolution or by the abdication of
James: others thought that they had to argue Anne's legitimate descent to counter
these dangerous allegations.[54] For a paper like the *Observator* was to their minds
'a well-wisher to every Rebel and Rebellion, and was born in perdition . . .'.[55]
The Tories detested hints at Protestant and sectarian plots reminiscent of the
Civil War interference with divine right; the Whigs feared Catholic plots: as the
Tory in dialogue in the *Observator* remarked,

> But prithee, because Popish treasons, and massacres are Diabolicall; Are phanati-
> call treasons and massacres ever the more warrantable?[56]

The dialogues and the battles continued into the eighteenth century, with the disputes of the High Church controversy taking over from the divisive issues of comprehension and toleration of the earlier period. The arguments between the *Observator* and the countryman caught the mood of the debate at the time of the Sacheverell crisis. The countryman puts the Whig point of view to the *Observator*:

> I cannot allow these High flyers to be of the Church of England; for methinks their Doctrines tend to the Destruction of all Religion, except that of Rome, which is the utmost consistent with slavery, which thing these men are for.[57]

It is amusing to contrast this with the Whig position in defence of liberty of conscience, stated in the same newspaper some twenty-one years earlier, when the Whig remarked to the Tory: 'Let every man act according to his conscience, whether it leade him to Heaven or to Hell.'[58]

Whig freedom of conscience did not extend to Catholics then, and years later was not even to encompass 'high flyers' from the Sacheverell cohorts of the Church of England.

Tory and Whig positions oscillated back and forth through the issues of clerical practice, Church–State relations, and the authenticity of the succession squabbles, with only one certainty in them, that Whigs and Tories would never agree on anything. The arguments that were deployed ranged over the whole spectrum of the debates we analyse: from geology and the origin of the earth, through doctrine to the management of the Church and the State.

The arguments sometimes included a debate over prescience and the nature of divinity. An author in 1731 recognized the essential elements in this kind of debate when he wrote:

> I shall examine no further than is absolutely necessary whether GOD is *Spirit* or *Matter*, or Both, or Neither, or Whether the *World* is eternal or not; but shall consider *Prescience*, as a *Part* of God's Character, which must be consistent with the Whole of it, and not destructive of *human liberty*.[59]

This same pamphlet went on to review the divergent opinions possible in contemporary debate over the nature of the human soul. It could be viewed as eternal by nature, or mortal, dying with the body, or one could argue that it was mortal by nature, although God could grant it immortality.[60] The author went on to illustrate the difficulties of modern theological dispute, when he noted that

> It is so difficult (not to say impossible) to come at a mathematical Demonstration what the Deity is, that Both Antients and Moderns have found themselves lost in the search. We have no sensible notion of anything besides matter.[61]

This tract reviewed the debates and despaired. It thought that centuries of debate about the soul, God and the universe had only thrown up a number of contradictory and unsatisfactory proposals, and the author in no way trimmed his views to any remaining theological wind. He thought it almost as absurd to say that intelligence has existed from all eternity and created matter, as to say that matter created intelligence.[62] The author ended by arguing a pantheistic case,[63] and shocked the moral perceptions of his audience by arguing that

> . . . with respect to moral evil, I see a beautiful woman, and gain her consent to lie with her; this is evil to her Husband, Father, Brother. But is it evil, in the nature of things, that my eyes should take in a beautiful object, and my sense covet the enjoyment of beauty?[64]

Such was the decay that dispute and difference could lead to; men found all the values accepted by their society to be in doubt, owing to the lack of agreed opinion over the crucial issues of the origin and purpose of the world.

An equally important area of contention lay in the doctrine of life after death, for this was not only the central point of the debate about the nature of the soul, but also supported the whole coercive machinery of the after-life. Asgill was expelled from the House of Commons for writing his work suggesting that men could go to Heaven without passing through death,[65] and for arguing that the present religion of the world founded upon the notion that man is born to die only came true after Adam's fall.[66] Although Asgill knew he would be condemned for his views,[67] he felt it essential to 'shew the insignificancy of death one way or the other, in order to eternal life; and that the death of one man works no change in him'.[68] These were regarded as highly dangerous tenets.

Some contended against infant baptism, another doctrine which the Church felt called upon to defend as a pillar of their educational and baptismal services for young children. John Turner, in 1704 for example, argued that the child could be legally baptised despite his inability to comprehend the doctrine, and despite his being born in sin.[69] Still more critics, as we will see, railed against the Trinity, and provoked long defences, particularly from Charles Leslie who specialized in these juicy controversies.[70]

There were many others who, in their political theories, placed power in the people, an equally abhorrent heresy, seen by George Hickes as the natural outcome of the Epicurus-Hobbes-Locke-Spinoza tradition.[71] Such a theory co-existed happily with an attack upon revelation,[72] the theory that 'omnia est una substantia',[73] and Tindal's view of the state of nature.[74] Hickes saw modern atheists as so many mechanical Prothei,[75] and saw Tindal as preparing the way for Catholicism as well as for atheism.[76]

The deists themselves might well protest with Thomas Woolston that they were moderators and irenicists between competing Christian factions, creeds, and dogmas, looking only for a pure and simple faith;[77] they might well protest their sincerity as Christians with Woolston;[78] but they did so to no real avail. They were judged by conceptions of the truth, and found wanting; their opinions over a multitude of subjects amounted to a view of the world verging on an atheist's. Even the nature of heresy itself was disputed, some suggesting that it was an error of teaching, others that it was an error of will.[79] Men like James Foster argued that one should admonish heretics, against Stebbing's view that one should teach them.[80] Foster believed that heresy originally meant a party, and was not necessarily pejorative in the New Testament, but that it now had come to mean with St Paul's definition 'the work of the flesh'.[81]

Henry Stebbing attempted to clarify the controversy in his reply to Foster in the second letter of 1736:

> The general question is, who are hereticks in such a sense as will justify the Church in excluding them for the privileges of Visible Communion? Mr Foster says, they are those only who make a profession contrary to the Christian faith, in opposition to the sense and conviction of their own minds. My opinion is, that whoever openly impugns the Christian doctrine, whether with conviction or against conviction, whether sincerely or insincerely, is a heretick: and if he reforms not upon proper admonition, may and ought to be debarr'd the privileges of Christian communion.[82]

The differences between them were important ones for the Church to decide, for upon the definition of heresy rested the whole apparatus of censorship, penal laws for dissenters and atheists, and moral and legal restraints placed upon deviant Christians.

The deists of course opposed restraints of any kind upon freedom of enquiry. Tindal laid down his reasons for wishing for a free press, arguing that unless men could arrive at moral and religious views for themselves by rational enquiry, these views would have no influence upon their actions, and therefore fail to achieve their main aim in restraining men in their conduct.[83] Tindal believed that 'there is no freedom either in civil or ecclesiastical, but where the liberty of the press is maintain'd'.[84] Others thought that the press should be confined to turning out good pamphlets against heterodoxy and speculative error: confined to works like *The Deist confuted*,[85] a good example of the genus of anti-deist works pouring from the presses well into the eighteenth century. In this work the author, George Adams, was willing to defend the testimony of miracles as necessary to the Christian faith,[86] and he objected to the way in which the outward ceremonies of religion had been attacked as arbitrary impositions upon men's liberty.[87]

Some preferred to adopt the deists' methods to refute them. One of Asgill's critics burlesqued his argument in a little poem, saying that

> *For, Sir, the liberty to scribble*
> *Allows you not at Church to nibble;*
> *And there I'll leave you in the lurch,*
> *When you plan cannons against the Church.*
> *Such things as these whilome tear yo,*
> *in the late reign of Rogero.*[88]

But others preferred straight attacks upon the pride and sin at the root of all heresy.[89] Some defended the clergy from the virulent anti-clerical attack made upon them: at one remove allegations of atheism were no more than the replies of outraged clerics to the attacks of secular-minded deists upon their profession.[90] Tindal had suggested as much, and in turn the clergy alleged that his attacks upon them represented the frustrations of his career. John Turner, who wrote of the Tindal case, extended his range further and commented on the whole lamentable movement towards secondary-cause explanation. He condemned it roundly:

> The Endeavours of the learned philosophers of this age, to rob their maker of his honour, &c. by tying down all the phenomena of the heavenly bodies to their natural causes, and thereby denying the agency of Providence in all those things, is now grown so scandalous, that they are justly contemn'd by good men, everyway as knowing in those things, as themselves.[91]

Others bolstered Turner's position: another opponent of Tindal attacked those who decried the scriptures,[92] and said that 'reason is against them; for reason openly confesses herself not fully enlightened'.[93] The debates were wide-ranging, and touched upon fundamental issues concerning the nature of knowledge, science, understanding and reason.

But amidst the debates there were disparate but nevertheless strenuous attempts by clerical and secular authorities to repress the deist and atheist side of the argument. When Gibson came to visit his diocese in May 1730, he enjoined that his clergy 'be at least as diligent in maintaining the cause of Christianity, as they [the Tindal deists] are in promoting the cause of infidelity';[94] he did not state that they should repress all deists' views for that was by now impossible. Rather the clergy 'should endeavour to inform yourselves of the true state of the several points in controversy between Christians and infidels at this time'.[95] Gibson had observed the patterns of spread of infidelity: he knew that it was hatched in London, and spread through trading contacts to cities and market towns[96] in contact with the capital.

But Gibson and his enthusiastic colleagues in the Church did not confine themselves to visitation rhetoric urging their clergy to do better. They also had at their disposal the lugubrious machinery of censorship and ecclesiastical courts, as well as having some fitful influence with the civil authorities. Through his diverse correspondence Gibson would hear of the growth of atheism throughout the land. Reports came to him about the prevalence of blasphemy in the Navy,[97] and of swearing and cursing throughout the country.[98] Amongst his papers are records of men accused of sodomy and other sexual offences,[99] whilst information about witches,[100] suggestions about changes in the liturgy,[101] praise for his pastoral letters all arrived for the bishop's attention.[102]

Gibson's views on the relations between the civil and religious power, and upon the duties of religion, would have found a note of sympathy in many eighteenth-century hearts. He maintained that 'no government is wisely contriv'd, in which religion is not consider'd as one branch of the institution'[103] and believed that the civil power had the right to preserve religion from public insult.[104] Gibson acknowledged that ridicule did religion the most harm of all,[105] and ridicule should therefore be prosecuted, otherwise it caused a breakdown of morals and led to apathy.[106] Reasonable and serious arguments against religion, on the other hand, should be met by reasonable arguments on the other side.[107]

Gibson's view bears out the contention that the dangerous elements of the so-called age of reason were not rational at all; it was irony and humour that did most damage. Whiston agreed that it was mockery, not reason, that was disastrous.[108] It was a theme which Gibson had never tired of ramming home. In his 1728 *Pastoral Letter* he had advised: 'When you meet with any book upon the subject of religion, that is written in a ludicrous or unserious manner, take it for granted that it proceeds from a deprav'd mind, and is written with an irreligious design.'[109]

To the bishop the essential rule was to keep a serious regard and reverence in one's mind for things sacred.[110] He realized that it was this reverence, so essential to the well-being of religion, that was breaking down. The consequence of such a breakdown could all too easily be the facile Hobbism of a work like that published by Wildman in 1726.[111] Wildman argued that the world was governed by passion, not by reason,[112] and that self-interest predominated in men's actions.[113]

One way to deal with the problem was through the censorship of unwanted books, and the prosecution of printers violating the laws of blasphemy, libel, and common decency. William Anderton, a printer, was convicted of high treason in 1693 for publishing seditious tracts.[114] Lord Chief Justice Treby had allegedly terrorized the jury into passing such a harsh verdict as guilty of treason by calling the jurors 'ill men, ill subjects, and a pack of knaves'.[115] It must be added that this account of the trial was written by a supporter of James II, and no doubt was not a little biased.[116]

Different works attracted different legal proceedings. Blount's work was taken before the English Parliament, and Toland's condemned to be burned by the common hangman after the Dublin Parliament had debated it. The works of Collins, Tindal and Mandeville amongst others were proceeded against after presentment by a Grand Jury, whilst Milton, Hobbes and Harrington were condemned both by Oxford University and by the Censor. Another way of dealing with impurity was by publishing a refutation, perhaps the most popular technique of all. For example, many sermons evoked responses like those to Joseph Jacob in 1702[117] or to the Vicar of St Aldates in 1731.[118] It may not have had the glamour of a public burning, such as was afforded to a speech intended to be read in the Sheldonian at Oxford in 1713, but it was thought to be efficacious on the grounds that the public would appreciate the correctness of the refutation.[119] Hearne thought a refutation of *Priestcraft in Perfection* necessary as that work invalidated the 39 Articles.[120]

Activities against vice brought their hardship to traders as well as to printers, authors, and clerics. The vintners and whetters who used to trade on Sundays were disrupted by the Queen Anne Proclamation against vice: '. . . who us'd on Sundays to meet on their Parade at the Quaker's meeting house in Gracechurch Street, and adjourn from thence thro' the Tavern back-door to take a whet of white and wormwood.'

They found their activities curtailed.[121] Meanwhile the clergy fought hard to preserve their distinctive calling and the trappings of religious authority. A curate of Wiltshire in 1718 for example defended the succession of the bishops from the apostles, and sought to remind his readers that the clergy were a separate caste.[122] He had to oppose arguments such as those advanced some twenty-three years earlier in one of several dissenting tracts arguing that the partition between clergy and laity was 'erected by Popish and prelatical Pride'.[123]

The journals from time to time urged tougher penalties and tighter controls. Recommendations included prosecuting men as well as women for cases of lewdness,[124] a harsher penalty for whores than merely beating them in hemp,[125] attacks upon bawdy houses that were disguised as coffee houses and alehouses, a clean-up of the magistrates' Bench, a clamp-down on plays[126] and more effective enforcement of the existing legislation.[127] Action should be taken to prevent whores producing a child and arguing that they were married women whose husbands were at sea.[128] But exhort as they might, the *Observator* had to confess that the country was more concerned with factional debate over occasional conformity, than it was with the effective suppression of vice.[129] And so whilst the Church wrangled over the other matters, the massive legislation against misbehaviour proved difficult to enforce amongst a people who would pursue their little pleasures. Too many would have agreed with Rochester's satire upon the Lord's Prayer when he wrote to a mistress:

> If the temptation of seeing you, be added to the desires I have already, the sin is so sweet, that I am resolv'd to embrace it, and leave out of my prayers, libera nos a malo—For thine is my Kingdom, power and glory, for ever.[130]

Against the pressures of such lusts, the Church sadly acknowledged it had few strong weapons, other than recourse to the laws of the land.

Others besides the clergy were aware of the dangerous consequences of ill-life throughout society. In a set of queries from Garronway's coffee house during the reign of Charles II an author asked whether a nation could thrive that was governed by a whore, a pimp and a bastard,[131] whilst another noted how the ladies of pleasure had benefited from the court life of the playhouse, the masque, serenade, balls and revels.[132] Even William Whiston, himself an anti-trinitarian, was concerned about the prevalence of drunkenness[133] and pride.[134] There was no permanent and comprehensive solution: society drifted helplessly to irreligion, and the churchmen and moralists could but bewail it all. As their standards and expectations concerning human behaviour rose, they could but lament what appeared to them to be a serious fall in standards of public religion and manners. Their lamentations have provided the arguments of this book.

The fool hath said in his heart, There is no God. They are corrupt, they have done abominable works, there is none that doeth good.

Psalm 14 v. 1

'Tis utterly impossible to demonstrate there is no God.

Stephen Charnocke,
Several Discourses upon the existence and attributes of God
(London, 1682), p. 41

Chapter One

ATHEISTS ASSAILED
Contemporary Opinions of the Nature
and Causes of Atheism

THE NATURE OF ATHEISM AND ATHEISTS

Atheism was more of a hydra than a Leviathan. It had many heads and many guises; it was not solely the gargantuan animal of Thomas Hobbes's imaginings. For some it was merely the wild pursuit of folly and lust, and the denial of those Christian restraints so out of fashion at court, in the playhouse, or the bawdy house.[1] For others it was a whole way of thinking, a view of the world, which was reflected in the activities of the rake or libertine, but which often had its origins in an all-conceived philosophy. Whilst it was true that many thought that effectively enforcing the existing laws against drinking, swearing, cursing and wenching would be sufficient to solve the problem,[2] others had to admit there was more to atheism than a wandering heart or a voracious stomach. To them it was a disease of the mind.[3] Men like John Toland, the early eighteenth-century deist, would bear out their supposition when they advocated in mock religious language a life of dance, song and wine, amidst their writings on theology.[4]

Some believed that cavilling hordes of atheists were seeking the overthrow of the State. Papist idolators were held responsible for the Fire of London in 1666,[5] the Hobbists were thought by the pamphleteers to be in league with the Turks, whilst the ever more explicit message of the deists was held to threaten subversion of both Church and State.[6] Many men feared these manifestations of anti-Christian feeling, afraid for its impact upon the morals, governance and policies of their country. Many feared that the virtuosi were assaulting the Christian citadel with their natural philosophical speculations, whilst cleric and layman alike saw danger in the life of the debonair gentleman and the sayings of the coffee-house debater.[7] Atheism seemed all of a sudden to lurk everywhere, and everywhere it lurked there were those willing to oppose it. It is one of those ironies that sincere defenders of the faith, in their endeavours to stifle it at birth, often did much to foster its growth through promulgating the ideas they sought to restrain and criticize.[8]

To Johnson an atheist was much the same as he was to late seventeenth-century authors, a man who denied the existence of God. Johnson cited Bentley, South and Tillotson as evidence of this denotation.[9] Nevertheless, Johnson's

strict accuracy occludes the complexity which surrounds the term in vitupera-
tive use. Francis Gastrell, the Boyle lecturer for 1697,[10] is a more useful source
to deploy if we wish to grasp the ramified connotations of 'atheist' in everyday
coinage. The atheist was one who 'says there is no God that governs the world,
and judgeth the earth; there is no God that has appointed laws and rules for
men to act by; there is no God to whom men are accountable for their actions',
for atheism to Gastrell 'is to be considered as a vice, and not a mere error of
speculation'.[11]

To Gastrell and many of his colleagues both as clerics and Boyle lecturers,
the aim of all atheism was libertinism. They thought men were sufficiently
rational to justify hedonism by recourse to irreligious views of the world, but
felt they were insufficiently rational or insufficiently in control of their desires
to see the true force of arguments from natural religious apologia. Men who
denied the system of divine punishments and rewards, thereby justifying their
own sins on earth, were to Gastrell effectively denying value to the Scriptures
and attacking the notion of the soul.[12]

Even more imprecision surrounded the appellation 'deist'. The only agreement apologists reached in defining the activities of the deists, was that they were
less direct in their assaults upon Christianity than were the rantings of the
atheists, but they none the less represented an important step upon the road to
disbelief. A common view was that the deist, whilst acknowledging God,
denied all revelation, all modern miracles, and sought to reduce God to a remote
force, a first cause of a self-perpetuating universe.[13]

Contemporaries when they indicated men of atheism or deism were generally
complaining that the men they accused were violating fundamental tenets of the
Christian doctrine through their lives and works. Allegation and counter-
allegation, reflected the difference in Christian views about the arguments necessary
for persuading men of the Christian faith, as well as reflecting many conflicts of
personality, political disputes and faction squabbles. Most polemicists however
were usually suggesting that the culprit had controverted one or more of the
generally agreed arguments for a Christian world. Anyone who ventured to
attack revelation, miracles, apparitions, the descent from Adam, the Mosaic
creation of the universe, the authority of the Bible, the finite world and the
infinite Creator, the doctrine of the soul, the Holy Trinity, the nature of incorporeal substance, the distinction between things above and things inferred
by reason, the organization of the Christian Commonwealth and established
Church, and the world of spirits, was likely to be decried by ardent pamphleteers.

Whilst the learned theologians strove to counter every false aspersion uttered
from the presses, others, with Samuel Butler, preferred to define the problem
by sketching the personality of the average atheist, portraying the common
cynic in the dining room and the casual Epicurean in the tavern. Butler saw an
atheist as a man who drew a map of nature by his own fancy, ignorant enough
to be prepared to determine a first cause of his own.[14] Butler's sceptic was a
critic who dealt in wholesale,[15] his debauchee a man given over to a life under
the lordship of misrule taking as his creed and doctrine ribaldry and profanation.[16]
Similar characters appear in other authorities upon the atheist problem. Squire

Ralph's presumption in the cabbala arts was another of Butler's praiseworthy attempts to place in verse and personalities the philosophical troubles of his contemporaries: Ralph had

> *first matter seen undrest*
> *He took her naked all alone,*
> *Before one rag of form was on.*
> *The Chaos too he had descry'd . . .*[17]

Where Ralph and his friends could be mockingly described for their attitudes towards the origin of the universe, being only figures of fiction, metaphysicians like Samuel Clarke found life a little more serious. Clarke found that his un-doubted philosophical talents were an impediment to his clerical career, that clerical censorship of his views created difficulties for him trying to support his family and continue his theological and speculative employments.[18] Even William Whiston, sometime friend of Clarke's, harangued him for his excessive concern for metaphysics; a criticism which not only reflected the grief of the wounded Whiston who felt Clarke had been an apostate over the unitarian cause, but also a common prejudice against a form of thought society found increasingly difficult to control.[19]

A similar problem to that which faced clerics of a philosophical bent of mind confronted natural philosophers. Clerics encouraged and praised natural philoso-phers if they worked within the framework of orthodox Christian apologia, strengthening the argument *a posteriori* for God, but the virtuosi were less popular if they ventured new theories and new epistemologies with Hobbes or Descartes or Locke. The world was dominated by a battle for preferment and orthodoxy, yet it was rent by disputes about metaphysical issues of little seeming relevance to the social problems of the Irish and the poor. Satirists like Swift lampooned men for their exaggerated concern over refinements of phrase.[20] Anyone who adopted the difficult profession of metaphysician was naturally suspect to the atheist-hunters; he had to demonstrate his honesty by manfully defenestrating ancients and moderns alike if they were at all errant in their attitudes. Much of the debate over atheism was created by men seeking to convince the public and themselves that they had not exceeded the bounds of propriety in their studies of ancient and modern philosophy.

Francis Bacon, the man who had rung the bell to summon the wits to col-laborative endeavour in natural philosophy, had expressed the much-rehearsed opinion that prodigious learning in philosophy brought great faith; only a little learning was dangerous and led men to irreligion.[21] Yet Bacon, in his Essay on *Superstition*, had hinted at little-canvassed difficulties. He had ventured that superstition was likely to lead to disorder within states, whereas atheism 'leads a man to sense; to philosophy; to natural piety'.[22] Men preferred to foster his Ciceronian belief in the credulity that was represented by atheism, rather than exorcise his suggestion that superstition was worse than a lack of faith.[23] Bacon's words concerning the dangers of superficial study were well borne out in the Restoration court, where smatterers imbibed short draughts of wisdom and long draughts of pleasure. The learned attempted to protest their fervour.

Boyle wrote endless folios praising the universe of his Creator.[24] Power showed the relevance of his microscopical observations to belief in God,[25] whilst John Ray used all his learning in natural philosophy to construct arguments showing the wisdom of God in the works of the Creation.[26] Philosophers praised Descartes for his dualism and used and abused his famous precept, 'Cogito, ergo sum', but were quick to dissociate themselves from his mechanist determinism.[27]

Despite the good intentions of many scientists and philosophers, and despite the large volumes of Christian apologetics that came from the presses, the fear of atheism remained vocal. There was some reason for it to remain so, for by the early eighteenth century there was an imposing range of irreligious views recorded in print. Any potential free-thinker could extract the message of irreligion from the books seeking to refute deism and atheism; any potential deist could turn to the burgeoning library of free-thought.

The literature aimed against the Church was diffuse in its nature. Atheism, it was alleged, could firstly be found in the biographies of those who were held to have supported its tenets. There was the much-discussed case of Vanini, a man who had either suffered for the cause of anti-clericalism, or to the less charitable had justly suffered for promulgating systems of anti-Christian philosophy to the world. Vanini had been burned in 1619 in Toulouse, yet the interpretative literature surrounding his case could be found in England well into the eighteenth century. Details of how he had subverted youth, of how he had led a debauched life, of how he had lied, prevaricated, and at last died in despair, had been patiently catalogued for the literate to consider, enjoy and condemn.[28]

Vanini had crusaded against the critics of the faith, attempting to refute the Epicurean, Stoic and Peripatetic atheists whom he professed to dislike so greatly.[29] Although he worked through a proof of God,[30] although he refuted Ciceronian contentions in favour of an irreligious view,[31] although he mauled Epicurus[32] and defended Providence,[33] he was himself attacked for furthering the cause he claimed to oppose. Despite his professions concerning natural religion,[34] seeing God and his works in the sun, the moon, and the stars,[35] the seventeenth century condemned him out of hand. With Mersenne and Grimmand,[36] and later with La Crose and Schramm,[37] men unravelled the plots that Vanini was supposed to have laid to further the Epicurean cause. Durand could only conclude that Vanini's philosophy was summarized in the couplet

> *Perdutto e tutto il tempo*
> *Che in amar non si spende.*[38]

Durand's view that the *Amphitheatrum* sought to make atheistic philosophers out of its readers, and that Vanini's dialogues were efforts to make men libertines, was not an unusual one:[39] his attempt to deride Vanini's scholarship was a normal form of response to such a fool.[40] Vanini was made atheist by that powerful combination of ecclesiastical disapprobation, polemical pamphlets, fear and legend.

More than one hundred years after Vanini's death an article in the expanded English edition of Bayle's *Dictionary* attempted to alter the record of the condemned heretic.[41] Bayle had not only reprinted the atheist's views, but had also championed the cause of the purity of Vanini's life. Bayle did more to call into doubt his own orthodoxy, already impugned for many other reasons, by this intervention, than he did to alter the popular conceptions of his subject. Most agreed with the standard biographers of Vanini that he had had illicit affairs, that he had revelled in carnal pleasures, and he had committed some undisclosed sin in a convent.[42] He was a priest who had preached a minimal natural religion, who had derided the miracles of Christ by comparing them with the miracles of St Anthony, and by calling all miracles into doubt.[43] He had argued that the Virgin Mary had had ordinary sexual relations with men, that the world had existed from eternity, and that it had been the product of fortune rather than of an all-wise Creator. He had recanted to stall and prevent his execution, but finally spurned the priest when he saw there was no chance of acquittal. He went to his end cursing and screaming.[44]

The campaign against Vanini had developed its own momentum. Atheist-hunters accredited him with the publication of the *De Tribus Impostoribus*[45] and they assumed that he had espoused every anti-Christian position mentioned in his *Amphitheatrum*. There was even testimony to the effect that in private he had denied the existence of God, and that he had denied to the Bible any more value than that accorded to the fables of Muhammed or the tales of Aesop.[46] Vanini was purported to have found the Bible's message inherently implausible, and its text inaccurate.[47]

Atheism was not only found in the biographies of men like Vanini: it could also be found in satire and encyclopaedic form, in the witty and scathing pages of Bayle and his colleagues. Bayle's *Dictionnaire Historique et Critique*[48] often relegated to the footnotes an impressive range of heresies, and the whole work was animated by a critical and sceptical spirit. It is impossible to find a coherent attitude in the Dictionary, although it has a unity of spirit: but even if we could, it would do little to help our understanding of the way in which eighteenth-century men used and read it, complete with their own prejudices and interests. There were many readers convinced of the immorality of the work, although most would have conceded its utility. Courtines has documented the favourable early reception of the Dictionary, and the many editions and enthusiastic correspondence about it demonstrate its influence.[49] A successor to Moreri's Dictionary, Bayle's work was suspect both on internal grounds, and through association with Bayle's other publications.[50]

Whilst the articles in Bayle's work on Vanini, on Eve or on Epicurus gave too much leeway to irreligious views, it was the *Pensées diverses sur le comète* that represented to Bayle's English readers and critics his more sustained attack upon the Christian defences.[51] In the London edition of 1702 Bayle's words became widely accessible, although they had been diffused by repute from reading the French edition.[52] Here Bayle defended the proposition that a community of atheists would live at peace and in as well ordered a manner as a society of Christians, threatening the Christian contention that religion was necessary for public morals and civil obedience.[53] There were those who felt Bayle's questioning of the sense and reason of millions of men from time immemorial, and his doubting their defence of notions connected with the spirit world and the providential importance of comets, was little better than Spinoza's assault upon the argument from final causes and the perfect Creation.[54]

Bayle's invective against idolators, and his scepticism concerning the theodicy of astrology and pagan practice, was read by some as a veiled attack upon the whole Christian tradition for its wars and strife. He condemned pagan practices, whilst pointing out that Christians had taken over some of the pagan festivals.[55] Bayle had aroused fears by asking why men continued to lie, drink, swear and fight when they professed to believe and support Christian tenets.[56]

To some Bayle's view of human nature had hints of Machiavellian and Hobbist influences. He felt that certain humours were the result of birth, education, and circumstance: these humours combined with fear of the laws determined a man's moral conduct whether he were pagan or Christian or atheist. He denied that wits and rakes at court were true atheists: they were rather men of ordinary lusts and leanings, who would later repent and fawn before God in a desperate bid to prolong their own lives.[57] Men did not live according to their beliefs and reason, they were dominated by their passions.[58] These views seemed to denigrate the work of rational theologians who assumed that men would respond in their lives to appeals from reason.

Atheism could be found as a native English growth in addition to the imported strains. The works of Thomas Hobbes of Malmesbury, particularly his *Leviathan*, convinced many a seventeenth- and early eighteenth-century reader that they ought to be banned or virulently opposed. Hobbes had expressed the view that societies were based on fear, and upon men's wish to overcome the internecine war of the state of nature. He had seemed to suggest that morality was based on might rather than on right, was interpreted as denying the existence of right and wrong, and criticized for formulating a secular social science that could analyse society with mathematical and as it seemed anti-Christian precision.[59]

Atheism as a complete philosophical system could be found in the works of Benedict de Spinoza. His pantheism, and the logical rigour of his statements about God seemed a threat to Christians; moreover, Spinoza as a renegade Jew was even more detested than he would have been as a practising Jew, for an orthodox Jew at least accepted a fixed doctrine and view of morality and order, even if it were a misguided one.[60] Spinoza's life and views were circulated in a number of heterodox manuscripts, and in many books and papers purporting to refute him. The best known of these is *La Vie et l'esprit de Mons. Benoit de Spinosa*, a work which circulated in many forms in western and central Europe from the end of the seventeenth century. John Howe's *Living Temple* was dedicated to refuting pantheism,[61] an argument in part aimed against Spinoza as well as against the Quakers and philosophical radicals of the mid-seventeenth-century English revolution.[62]

Atheism was also suspected to lurk in the bookshops of Europe, in copies of infamous texts like *De Tribus Impostoribus*. This work, published in several counterfeit editions, and circulating in manuscript copies, exposed the charlatanism common to Christ, Moses and Muhammed. Its theme reiterated the old atheistic adage that gods and priests have their origins in fear, and retain their influence from the powers of a malevolent State and Church together.[63]

Not only had manuscript and printed copies of *The Three Impostors* proliferated, but the three impostors themselves had been variously interpreted. Kortholt had taken them to be Spinoza, Hobbes and Herbert of Cherbury.[64] The authorities were worried by this spread of blasphemy, if the treatise preserved its original form of criticism of Christ through comparison with charlatans, rather than refuting blasphemy in the manner of Kortholt.[65] English fears are reflected in Smith's observations on the spread of this irreligious doctrine.[66]

By the 1730s these and other routes to atheism had been much augmented. The interpretative literature around figures like Vanini had grown, whilst new rakes and libertines could be added to the lists. The literature surrounding the life and loves of John Wilmot, 2nd Earl of Rochester, is but one of the better-documented examples. There continued to be manifest evidence of drunkenness, debauchery, and evil-doing; many felt that the growth of anti-Christian behaviour could be proven. As more men advanced deist and near-atheist views, so the number of lives of such men could increase, and add to the literature of atheism.

By this decade the work of Bayle and his fellow sceptics had been successfully diffused in English literate society. There were other, native and Classical origins to the sceptical tradition, and these were bolstered by Cartesian doubts,[67] and by the satirical and fashionable scepticism that flourished in post-Restoration London society. Home-grown heretics also burgeoned: there were the world theorists, Burnet and Whiston, there was Charles Blount's gift for parodying the Bible, and there were Coward's soliloquies upon the soul. Locke and Berkeley, striving to be apologists, were not without their critics, sure that they were undermining the faith: the deists, Mandeville, Shaftesbury, Toland, Tindal, Wollaston, Chubb, Morgan and Collins were pouring forth their works and gaining support and followers. From All Souls to the Royal Society there was an outpouring of atheism in print such as the country had never seen before.[68] It is true that there had been a problem of doubt and deism which was at least as old as Christianity itself and much of the late seventeenth-century and early eighteenth-century debate reflects conflicting positions assumed by Classical authors and by the Fathers themselves. It is true that Bacon had feared the atheism of his own day,[69] that Marlowe and his circle had been attacked for their views over the Trinity, and true that during the break-down of the civil wars sectarian atheism had flourished in an unprecedented way.[70] At the same time it remains true that the group of thinkers, satirists and literary figures, as well as the clerics themselves after the Restoration, did more than any preceding generation to threaten the foundations of the Church's intellectual world, and that the Church fought back in a way that was notable for its energy and enterprise if not for its success. As the number of atheistic systems in print increased with the republication of the classical authorities, and as the bookshops began to teem with pamphlets, tracts and broadsheets dealing with the atheist scare, many gentlemen were made aware of this fundamental problem, and took to their closets to study it and write about it themselves. The products of this literary endeavour furnish us with an opening into the conventions and concerns of this great seventeenth- and eighteenth-century debate, to which we now turn.

CAUSES

The causes of alleged irreligion in the later seventeenth and early eighteenth centuries were thought by contemporaries to be many and varied: to the historian they must appear wider still, for the reader of the great atheist controversies of the period must always ask whether there was any justice or novelty in the claims being made by contemporaries concerning the impiety of their own age, and the atheists' debates must themselves be seen as part if not the whole of the problem. It is undeniable that Christian fears and agitation strengthened the popular impression amongst clerics and religious laymen alike that their age was unusually godless despite the advances of its civilization, and that these fears often were used by pamphleteers in their political and literary squabbles to outmanoeuvre their opponents.

Part of the explanation of the renewed intensity of the atheist problem in the decades following 1660 must lie in the psychology of dispute. Clerics squabbling for place and patronage, clerics keen to fault one another for their views, and clerics keen to establish their reputation would all turn to accusing colleagues and enemies of atheistic principles. The charge was bold, it was bound to evoke a response, and it led to embittered and entrenched battles over crucial doctrines. The anti-trinitarian controversy of 1695, smouldering throughout our period; the Bangorian controversy; the Sacheverell disputes; all these are but the most notable, in part contributions to the debate over the piety of the nation, in a long series where authors dug in along battle lines. Once a dispute had produced accusations and counter-accusations, it would then encourage others to polarize their views and enlist. It would also encourage men to a partiality suitable for debate rather than for productive discussion, and disrupt Christian harmony and agreement further.

Political factions tended to associate themselves with such debates, representing their own interests and views. The High and Low Church squabbles of the reign of Anne, the endless disputes over dissenters, the Whig and Tory debates over allegiance to the Crown and the authority of the Church, often impinged on the larger issue of whether policies and attitudes were leading men nearer to or further from God. Political interests, like ambitious or prejudiced churchmen, were only too willing to appeal to the issue of atheism as part of their armoury in their debates and troubles.

The more vacuous commentaries on bad morals and the decay of manners may in many instances have been little more than men reiterating worn phrases concerning the bad times in which they were forced to live; some may have been the old lamenting the freedom of the young, some the puritan envious of the libertine, some the jealousy of the incapable against the frivolous.

Certain books and tracts were written because a literary genre had been created that proved attractive. There seemed to be a ready public to read of the ignorance, pride, folly and immorality of the people at large, and a public avaricious for schemes, projects of reform, and solid reasoned argument for belief in God. The consumer, as well as the producer, had attitudes favourable to the generation of atheist disputes.

Nevertheless, the argument that all the atheist debates can be explained by means of these reductionist theories is unsatisfactory, and the thesis that there was no increase in scepticism and commentary hostile to the Christian cause, difficult to sustain. Some of the disputants rightly feared the growing numbers of irreligious books, and feared the activities of bad men. It is far more difficult to document that contemporaries were correct in their suggestion that society was becoming more atheistic in its practice as well as in its language. Much of this contention was derived from the premise that men would be driven to irreligious practice by seemingly irreligious views, a premise which Bayle and his colleagues in England opposed strongly. To prove it one would need extensive researches on centuries of court cases arising out of allegations of immorality, and even then the number of intervening possibilities – to do with the strictness of enforcement of legislation, the changing of legislation, the success of discovery and the chances of securing a verdict of guilty – would make it difficult to establish any increase or diminution. We propose to leave open the question of the accuracy of vague statements about increases in immorality, although manifestations of the problem as perceived by contemporaries will be discussed.

Contemporaries did not hesitate to ascribe causes to the effects they lamented so prolifically. As with other potential dangers, were they poverty or luxury, innovation or wickedness, atheism was more often than not the product of pride.[71] A man inflated with a sense of his own depth of mind might think that his own observations of the world and nature, and his own distilled philosophical reflections, could suffice him and obviate the need for God. Pride could also rot the moral fibre, permitting worldly values to overtake the inner Christian man, and allowing its prisoner to vent his feelings against the Church through satire and scoffing. Apart from being in itself a cardinal sin, it was pride which inspired the quest for panesciolism, the hunt to explain the world without recourse to mystery or deity, and the love of wit in place of verity. Pride was associated with Rome and anti-Christ;[72] many agreed with John Edwards that this pride was a cover for ignorance.[73]

Some causes, intended by their founders as bulwarks of a purer religion, were rounded on by more conservative contemporaries who saw in change an opportunity for further decay. Whiston, Bull and their friends sought to revive primitive Christianity in England, and return the Anglican Church to the state of religion in the days of the Early Fathers.[74] Their respondents replied that their knowledge of the Fathers was scanty, their new doxologies and services atheistic, and their whole plan yet another attempt to tear apart the Anglican framework.[75]

Swift's satire against revivals was paralleled only by his satire against another much-canvassed cause of disbelief,[76] the rise and growth of commerce and a commercial spirit. Dorotheus Sicurus had propounded the theory that atheism was the product of advancing civilization, peace, and material well-being. Only an age of hardship, struggle and fear would restore notions of divine providence and intervention.[77] E. B. translated the work into English, and in his brutal Preface concluded that the Church and the schoolmasters were responsible for allowing deterioration of the situation, for it was their duty to inculcate morals into the young, and thereby prevent crimes which the law otherwise had to punish.[78] A solution would be provided by encouraging ignorance of scientific pretensions, and instilling fear of adversity from cruel fate. Sicurus noted that Epicurus was persuaded to his system by the arbitrary nature of Providence aiding both the wicked and the virtuous.[79] Others would not have agreed with Sicurus's severe request for harder times; they hoped that reason could lead men back to religion where passions had first led them astray. Writers like William Law confirmed the theory that his own 'polite age' had 'so liv'd away the spirit of devotion, that many seem afraid even to be suspected of it, imagining great devotion to be great bigotry'.[80]

A French tract first published in 1631, available in England, and subsequently translated and reprinted in 1660 saw political and theological strife as the major cause of decline in piety. The battle between Protestant and Catholic dissuaded men from religion in general.[81] The author perceived three sorts of men who regarded the choice of faith as a matter of no significance: those who denied a Providence; those who admitted a Providence, but allowed no express revelation of God's will; and those who whilst accepting the force of natural religion could not see that this favoured any one form of worship in preference to another. This work had some relevance to the English position after 1660, and was read by Englishmen, particularly for its refutation of Epicureans,[82] its defence of the immortality of the soul[83] and the universal consent of mankind in believing in a deity,[84] the regulation of Providence and the nature of Christ as man and God, all central issues in the debates.[85]

Far more popular an explanation than that offered by the war between sects and Churches, was that natural philosophy and the doctrine of secondary causation was leading men away from God. Sir Charles Wolseley writing in 1669 decried the atomic atheism,[86] and saw the denial of miracles and revelations through explaining them by recourse to secondary natural causes, as the worst possible means of attacking the faith.[87] In 1675 when Boyle wrote to Smith, he praised his recent sermon, especially for its not falling foul of philosophy at a time when a great many men thought it a service to religion to oppose studies of nature.[88] Much of the Oldenburg correspondence with Spinoza offered a similar view: in 1665 Spinoza commented on how the theologians were a major impediment to philosophical progress.[89] The Preface to Sicurus had suggested the same when E.B. attacked 'the times in which natural philosophy hath flourished' for allowing men to conclude from their knowledge of secondary causes that there was no First cause, no God.[90] Thomas Sprat when writing his polemical history of the Royal Society felt it necessary to establish that empirical science would not hinder the practice of religion,[91] nor would it endanger prophecies and prodigies in any way.[92]

There was something to recommend both views. Many of the activities of the natural philosophers were harmless from the Church's position. Dr William Croone experimenting with the weight of a carp,[93] or Dr Hans Sloane collecting plants and other specimens and fostering physic gardens,[94] could not be said to be attacking fundamental Christian doctrine by their activities, any more than could Locke be accused of irreligion for collecting his own herbarium with the aid of his pupils and their exercises at Christchurch.[95] Many argued in addition, that natural philosophy was religion's greatest strength, illustrating God's works in all their wonders. On the other hand, there was the inherent danger that the natural philosopher would seek secondary causes to the exclusion of God, and would seek to explain in mechanical and mathematical ways phenomena that had previously belonged to the realm of the spirit. It was also the natural philosophers who had been responsible in large part for the revival of atheistical classical metaphysics, particularly the revival of Democritic and Epicurean atomism.

Connected with pretensions to greater knowledge, and the fear that science was a competing form of explanation hostile to the clerical position, was the pandering to wit that so worried Christians in later seventeenth-century England. Conversation based upon the adroitness of argument and succinctness of repartee, the language of aphorism and apothegm, could urge men to defend any cause for the sake of urbanity and style. The age of Swift and Dryden, of Shaftesbury and their lesser satirical contemporaries, turned the most serious theology into laughter, and the most devastating scientific research into a matter of dirt and worms. It is unfair to suggest that the decline of magic can be proven by citing the number of satires aimed against it during the later seventeenth century, for by such evidence one would have to admit that natural philosophy, religion, politics, the Church and many other important institutions were similarly in decline.[96] It is rather to be inferred that satire and cynicism as literary modes were becoming increasingly popular, and their impact was rightly feared. Shaftesbury was prepared to argue that wit had its place in a well-regulated society as a means of destroying the tyranny of enthusiasm, whilst leaving firm the foundations of the Christian world.[97] Others felt that Shaftesbury's citations of Lucretius,[98] Hobbes,[99] and Rochester[100] revealed his true allegiance and illustrated the dangers of wit. Swift saw ridicule as a way of exposing the follies of everyone, whether they were a Collins, a wicked politician, or a virtuoso.[101]

Those who had follies to defend regretted the impact of satire. With Sprat, they would bemoan the lampooning of their own beliefs and hopes,[102] with many divines they feared that the Church could not withstand the assault of railers. Nevertheless, wit could operate against the free-thinker, as Swift showed against Collins, as well as for him.[103] In general, however, men saw work like that of Mandeville, Shaftesbury, Swift and their colleagues as aiding the cause they might pretend to support, by creating an ambience in which levity and derision thrived.[104]

Some felt that atheism was largely a social problem, spreading fast owing to inadequacies in the clergy and in the administrative structure of the Church. Poor catechizing, non-residence, pluralism, poorly educated or meagrely motivated clergy, the lack of an adequate parochial system following changes in the geographical distribution of the population, the shortage of churches, especially in the large and growing cities, were all suggested as good reasons why the public at large was becoming less religious. Bishop Gibson proposed a thoroughgoing reform of the educational and administrative structure of the Church to deal with these problems, but many of his proposals were lost during his struggle to implement them in the 1730s.[105]

Whilst there was obvious truth in the assertion that lack of belief among the poor and labouring classes in particular could be combatted by more successful catechizing, and by stricter observance of pastoral duties by clergy,[106] it was by no means the case that these problems of neglect were new. It is arguable that the standard of clergy was better than, or at least as good as it had been a century earlier, in terms of its educational standard. It is also arguable that even more necessary than a sound educational and vocational system for the clergy was some better rudimentary education for the people they served. It is interesting that, whereas the administrative and pastoral problems facing the Church in the early eighteenth century were probably the most crucial from the point of view of the long-term interest of Christianity, they on the whole produced the predictable round of bickering, whilst more and more attention of a united clergy wherever such a unity existed was devoted to combatting the small group of intellectuals who appeared to be undermining the Church both from within and without. To the eighteenth-century clergy it seemed more important to defeat a Collins, a Tindal, or a Toland, than to convert the artisans of Manchester and the coal-heavers of Newcastle. To Christianize the country they should have been energetic to achieve both.

The movement of intellectual disbelief was manifested in, if not caused directly by, revivals of ancient philosophies of the Epicurean, Stratovian, Stoical and Lucretian kinds. There were, in consequence, few tracts against atheism that did not rebut the Epicurean premises concerning chance and the formation of the world, the eternity of matter, or the non-existence of Providence.[107] Both deists and churchmen looked backwards as well as forwards; most men thought classical learning was a central consideration in forming their world view. Only the liberated rake and rhetorician hoping to disarm the universities with his vicious pen professed an impartial disrespect for all ancient writers, and even they were forced to accept the relevance and utility of some classical theories during the flurry of debate. Whereas the religious turned to Cicero and endlessly quoted from his *De Natura Deorum*, whilst they thumbed through Ovid and cited their Seneca, their opponents turned to the *De Rerum Natura* or to modern versions of its contents.[108] Creech's translation of Lucretius published in 1700 was heralded even then as the most complete system of atheism in print.[109] The debate over the existence of God was therefore a debate over classical authorities as well as a discussion of physical, moral, logical and philosophical problems. It was in part a corollary of the debate between ancients and moderns.[110]

Attitudes to an ancient like Epicurus were divided. Men of Gassendi's leaning saw the utility of his maxims, particularly with respect to his atomic hypothesis: the Gassendi school sought to make him an accepted part of the Christian natural philosophical canon.[111] Nevertheless, others felt that Gassendi had been wrong to attempt the impossible. To them Epicurus was synonymous with moral laxity; he had advocated a happiness to mankind difficult to divorce from sensual pleasure. The Epicurean injunction to Anaxarchus, for example, 'I summon you to continual pleasures, and not to vain and empty virtues which have but disturbing hopes of results'[112] added force to their case. Many took it as axiomatic that Epicurus was an evil influence. Michelmann hastened to point out Epicurean influence in the works of Hobbes,[113] in disapproving tones. Nevertheless, some laboured on trying to put a favourable face on Epicurus. Du Rondel considered in detail the life and manners of the ancient philosopher,[114] and was on the whole impressed. Digby argued that Epicurus had been misrepresented, that he had meant by pleasure not a 'low lust' but a 'peaceable and quiet conscience'.[115] The same theme emerged from the quotations of Epicurus in Rondel's work.[116]

Bayle's text and footnotes betray the division of opinion well in the article in his Dictionary on Epicurus. The text accepts that Epicurus was responsible for modifying and propagating atomic doctrine,[117] that the friendly harmony of his sect was enviable,[118] but that his religious views had left much to be desired.[119] The notes substantially modified this stark division.[120] Most men did have to consider very carefully the religious views and lives of the philosophers they wished to draw upon, and had to condemn Epicurus and his followers.[121]

Others who looked less far than the philosophers, saw as symptom and cause the organization of a dissolute society. Coffee houses were settings for free conversation and blasphemous dispute, where God could be denied in an afternoon, and the Church destroyed in the intercourse of a week. The tavern, scene of so many unwritten and important happenings in English social, economic and political history, was a place where blasphemous and seditious words could be induced and aided by the sin of drunkenness. Brawls, bawdy scenes, inebriation and lewd practice all often focused themselves on the local pub, in the same way that free-thinking ideas circulated and emerged from the coffee houses. Some insights into this little-penetrated realm of historical enquiry are afforded by the letters, chance remarks and court cases of contemporaries.

The King's Head tavern was in a street called Atheists' Alley near the Royal Exchange;[122] Andrew Allam writing to Anthony Wood in 1680 described the sort of activity that may have surrounded such a colloquial name when he described the summons of sixteen Oxford M.A.'s to Parliament to answer charges of sedition and evil talk following coffee-house and tavern turmoils in Oxford.[123] Richard Bentley acknowledged the seriousness of coffee-house banter in a letter to Edward Bernard. He told Bernard of his plans for his sermons (the Boyle lectures), and suggested that it was not wise to preach against Jews and theists, omitting atheists who were the really serious enemies. Atheism to Bentley had no specific tenets, but it flourished in the talk of the coffee houses. Sermons attacking it therefore had to be sermons against bad morals rather than sermons against bad books.[124] In view of this opinion the format of the final Bentley Boyle lectures, aimed against bad books and atheists' arguments, is a little difficult to understand.[125] Taverns and coffee houses were difficult to control; rumours spread in them, ideas were discussed but not recorded in print, their freedom could be too heady for the liking of the Government and Church.

Others saw the cause of atheism in particular policies or attitudes which they themselves hated, just as men had frequently seen God's hand at work in things they applauded.[126] The cause of toleration was particularly prone to the accusation that it led to licence and atheism. Toleration, to some the natural conclusion to the Protestant doctrine that the individual conscience should be supreme in

religion, was to others likely to lead to a splintering of Church power and therefore of its authority, and a consequent decline in manners and Christian restraints
so necessary to a successful and well-regulated community.

Heated controversy surrounded such an issue, made the more acrimonious
by its being a crucial question of policy between Charles and his Parliaments
throughout the post-Restoration period. The voluminous response to George,
Duke of Buckingham's *Short Discourse upon the reasonableness of Men's having a
religion or worship of God*[127] is symptomatic of the way in which charges and
counter-charges were rapidly generated in the intense political atmosphere.[128]

The argument could be put by the proponents of toleration, that to allow free
choice was not tantamount to legalizing heresy.[129] But their opponents argued
that one should not allow men to select their own faith entirely, in an age when
so many prejudices and passions were abroad to deflect the judgement.[130] One
needed some laws to restrain and guide.[131] The author of *A Persuasive* . . . felt the
only solution was a strong Church of England in order to be able to combat
Hobbist heresies:[132] in such an imperfect world toleration would only permit
atheism to spread all the more rapidly.[133]

At the end of our period there was a strong belief that continued schism between
self-respecting Christians of different sects led to impiety and scepticism,[134] and
the cause of irenicism through reason and an appeal to the Scriptures was often
argued. One tract, in a common vein, argued that dogmatism was the cause of
Christian defeat, reason the basis of Christian strength:

> Let us cease to deify, and idolize our own interpretations, and tyrannically
> inforce them upon others. Let us not vainly imagine we can speak of the
> things of God better than in the words of God: and consequently suffer
> everyone who has Reason to direct him, and a soul to save, to affix what
> ideas he please thereto.[135]

Atheism often arose out of specific works on natural or supernatural subjects.
Charles Blount's *Miracles, no violations of the laws of nature* and *Religio Laici*,
both published in 1683, were seen as works attacking religion because they
attacked the necessity of miracles,[136] a proof often urged for God and his Providence, and because Blount seemed to be arguing in favour of a minimal natural
religion of a layman's making, against the cavils of priestcraft.[137] Critics of atheism
were worried about spreading Epicurean heresies,[138] but also about native attacks
upon providences, miracles and other spiritual phenomena that formed part of
the Christian world picture.[139] Opponents objected to specific theories: Croft
saw in Burnet's work upon the history of the earth a grave threat to the Christian
view. Burnet, besides being a trenchant critic of Moses, had also substantially
modified conventional views of the Mosaic account of the origin of the world,
and was taken to task by the ageing Bishop of Hereford: 'He [Burnet] does so
much magnifie nature and her actings in all this material world, as he gives
just cause of suspicion that he hath made her a kind of joynt deess with God.'[140]

Croft objected to Burnet's constraining God to operate by natural causes,[141]
and for his allowing God to make the whole world out of nothing, yet not
permitting Him to disperse or form the waters as Genesis claimed.[142] Croft

fought Burnet's natural speculations with passages of scripture, in the hope that 'these scripture reasons and examples which I have brought, are far more considerable than his trivial experiments of a mathematical instrument or cubical pot'.[143]

This dispute belongs to that alleged cause of atheism, the rise of natural philosophy. Nevertheless, it also shows how the general cause could be borne out in practice, how individual books and authors generated disputes that often went far beyond the scope of the work that originally produced them, and even in Croft we see the creeping use of natural philosophy in religious apologia. For whilst Croft represents the conservative reaction to natural philosophy, offering a biblical quotation in place of an experiment as evidence, he nevertheless had imbibed enough Bacon to believe that true philosophy aided religion,[144] and enough science to know that spontaneous generation, which he associated with Burnet, was an impossibility.[145]

All students of the atheist problem understood the fundamental unity of speculative and practical irreligion. The interrelationship to most commentators demonstrated the insidious strength of atheism, rather than demonstrating any weakness in their causal argument. Contemporaries strove to see these connections the more clearly in every case that came to their view. There was the example of Scargill, a fellow forced to recant before the Cambridge Congregation for his Hobbist beliefs, who was asked to relinquish his tenure after making public his recantation. The terms of the statement he was asked to make were explicit in showing how his morals decayed as he lapsed into a Hobbist frame of mind.[146] Cardonnel, a fellow of Merton, committed suicide after being polluted by Hobbism.[147]

The drift of men to practical atheism evoked its own voluminous literature. In 1659 Nicholas Clagett had bemoaned the growing irreligion, popery, libertinism and atheism of his own contemporaries.[148] But above and beyond such lamentations, there was a large literature of conversion, aimed at winning back evil-livers to the Christian fold through trite moral judgements, euphoric advice, and self-complacent congratulation in their own rectitude on the ruin of many a dissolute man. It often took the form of a personal account of the tortures of men on their deathbeds, regretting their every deed, and crying for mercy. The most famous and well-advertised case was that of John Wilmot, 2nd Earl of Rochester.[149] Gilbert Burnet's funeral sermon led the barrage,[150] and his *Libertine Overthrown* established wide-ranging consequences from such a notable repentance.[151] William Thomas's account of the death-bed scene spares no detail either.[152] He described Rochester's confession of his atheist's misery and despair,[153] and commented on how Rochester began to discourse of the Last Judgement and future state and even on the advantages of the Christian religion.[154] The manuscript tells how Thomas was acquainted with Dr Radcliffe and Dr Shorter, the two medical men called into the Earl, and tells us how the events of the death proselytized Dr Shorter. Shorter had been a libertine and a Papist: he now professed to be deeply moved by the vision of Wilmot.[155]

The war of attrition against bad morals is as explicit in the *Second Spira*, which gave details of a similar death-bed scene.[156] The torments of the victim's mind and body were stressed by Sault, and the aweful awareness of the dying man that he would be consigned to eternal damnation. The victim repented of exchanging the Bible for Spinoza and the *Leviathan*.[157]

The persistency with which the problem of practical and speculative atheism remained before the public well into the eighteenth century is notable. Irreligion was subject to the great projecting craze, along with everything else from the stock market to the poor; many writers offered their palliatives and panaceas to the nation. A writer in 1730 asked whether Christianity had declined because the clergy were bad, because there were insufficient arguments to support the Gospels, or because manners had been corrupted. These were similar queries to those raised three or four decades earlier.[158]

It was difficult to argue after so many Boyle lectures, tracts, sermons, books and impassioned defences issued in the preceding seven decades, in addition to all those issued since the beginnings of Christianity, that religion lacked arguments to support it. Martin Fotherby was probably guilty of overstatement as early as 1622, when he suggested that the argument he wished to put forward for the defence of God against atheism, was 'the most deserted part of theology'.[159] He could only find writings by Aquinas, Raimond de Sebonde, Bradwardine and Valesius beside the pagan theism of the reverend Tully.[160] By 1730 there had been years of energy expounded on repairing the gaps so apparent to the pioneering bishop.[161]

The author of the 1730 tract neglected to arbitrate between the possible explanations he postulated for the growth of atheism, and instead argued that the Test Act was at the root of the problem, betraying his political affiliations and bias.[162] He felt that the Act by debarring Papists and dissenters from office, but allowing sceptics and infidels to take positions of power, sapped the moral strength of the country. He advocated a reform of manners from above, by exerting greater control over the swearing of oaths, and by checking on a man's sincerity in his beliefs when he applied for high office.[163] He recognized the need to reconcile a free press with Christianity, and saw the possible conflict between liberties and religion.[164]

In a similar vein were the reflections of a writer in 1729. His complaint was that free-thinking had become accepted, so much so that it was apparent in the pages of the *London Journal*, which seemed to decry revelation in every paragraph.[165] In 1731 another author condemned the infidels in his society, whilst defending John Locke from the aspersion that he was the main influence behind the deists.[166] To this author lewdness, coffee-house buffoonery, sceptical principles and the denial of things above reason remained the most pressing symptoms and causes of irreligion.[167] Richardson noted that the late deist arguments were 'but a collection of the old and exploded (and as often refuted as revived) doctrines of the heretics of past ages'.[168]

We may forgive him his breathless prose, for the value of his perception. Collins, Toland and Tindal may well have replaced Coward and Blount by 1731 in contemporary discussion; they had even replaced Hobbes himself in many authors' assessment of the atheist troubles: but the ideas condemned in these different names remained very similar. In 1730 the trinitarian controversy, that had troubled Christianity for so long, was still raging in England as it had been in the 1690s. Waterland replaced Bury and his opponents as a leading protagonist: the issue was little altered.[169] There is a continuity of content in debates about everything from mathematics to matter.

Some feared that the growth of travel literature, and literature describing the customs and practices of other countries in the expanding world, would foster scepticism. A popular atheist argument came from comparative religion: if so many doctrines co-existed in the world how could anyone be sure of any one of them? Many of the books issued were slight, and aimed at demonstrating the unpleasantness, cruelty and absurdity in the customs of other cultures to avoid allegations of irreligion, or because such a view reflected accurately the author's perception of alien cultures. The book published in 1683 entitled *The Strange and religious customs . . .* did not intend for example to make converts to any of the pagan religions it described through its gruesomely illustrated pages.[170] Travellers like Sir John Chardin in Persia could muster a little more objectivity, but their interests were political rather than religious.[171] All professed to admire disinterested curiosity, yet curiosity was often informed by sound prejudices.

Whilst travellers sought to stave off contamination by carrying prejudices in their portmanteaus, at home authors were found in abundance to defend the faith from every chance occurrence of topical significance. Every natural phenomenon, whether it were an earthquake, flood, storm or lightning, produced its own inundation of tracts striving to show from this the workings of God's Providence. Many thought it heresy to deny God's personal involvement with earth tremors or aqueous upheavals, for these were signs of disapproval against a sinful world.[172]

Elevating stories were told of saintly men and women who saw or performed wonders. An anchoress of Norwich had her sixteen revelations published in 1670, dedicated to Mary Blount of Soddington and any others who were still serious enough about spiritual matters not to deride them.[173] The account gave the reader information on the woman's mystical experiences and her vision of Christ's wounds.[174] The tract feared that the number able to believe and benefit from such curiosities was disappointingly small.[175]

There were many practical guides to religion for the popular reader, in addition to these startling proofs of the truth of the faith. Sir Kenelm Digby's translation of Albertus Magnus's *Treatise of adhering to God* was one example of the genre.[176] This advised its readers to free the soul to follow spiritual pursuits, neglecting the temptations of the material life in order to find purity.[177] There was Thomas Adam's exegesis of the basic principles of Christianity, recommendations for those seeking honest religious precepts in plain language for the conduct of their lives.[178]

Many men wrote short practical works of piety.[179] William Allen published such a book in 1678, which rehearsed the nature of Justification,[180] Grace,[181] and Faith[182] before concluding 'how much hath been done by the eternal Father and his Holy Son Our Blessed Saviour, that we might be Justified, Pardoned and Glorified'.[183]

Chillingworth's reply to the Jesuitical arguments in his defence of Protestants had further strengthened the view that Catholicism was atheism, and this too was urged in popular religious works.[184] Other books told men that holiness was the way to salvation,[185] or that all men feared they were imperfect but that need not prevent them from serving God,[186] or from taking Holy Communion.

Besides these direct works, and the necessary task of inciting men to more effective catechizing,[187] there was the need to defend witches, apparitions, spirits, ghosts and other evidences of a spirit world. Recent study has seemed to argue both that magic and witchcraft was in competition with religion, and that by the end of the seventeenth century magic and witchcraft were in decline.[188] Whilst there is some truth in these impressions, the fact remains that it is difficult to document the decline of magic satisfactorily, as well as in some measure the case that a defence of any supernatural or extra-natural phenomena supported the Christian cause in so far as it related to an ambience capable of belief in a spirit world. A tract like *A Whip for the droll, fiddler to the atheist* made explicit the connection between denying witches and assuming an irreligious view. Whilst there were those who saw irreligion in the theological attitudes of those worshipping the Devil, others thought that worship of the Devil at least argued for his and therefore for God's existence.[189]

Besides the many monuments to deism and to the labours of popularized defence of religion, there remained the ever-pressing problem of clerical dissent itself. Many controversies over theological points, particularly over the Trinity, provoked internal allegations of atheism amongst the clergy. The severity of the Socinian problem, it seemed, could only be undermined in the clerical view by a more thorough-going attack from without, such as that launched by Toland in 1696 with his *Christianity not mysterious,* a work which helped to abate the uproar of 1695 over the Trinity.

Bury's *Naked Gospel* had shown the explosive force of the trinitarian question.[190] John Edwards, a voracious polemicist, regarded the Racovians as the fathers of the deists, and the deists as fathers of the atheists.[191] Edwards was not alone in this view.[192] Locke, Toland, Whiston and Clarke were amongst the many notable intellectuals to be caught in the Socinian trap, and had Newton published his theological works he would have been held there too by zealous clergymen.[193]

Such a pamphlet as that considering the charges of Socinianism against Dr Tillotson[194] demonstrated the difficulty of separating High Church debates over doctrine from the general fear of atheism. The author thought that the Arian heresy he claimed to detect in Tillotson was as bad an influence as Charles Blount's *Great is Diana*: he denounced Thomas Burnet in the same paragraph as the archbishop.[195] This tract argued that Gildon and Blount, like Hobbes and Bidle before them, were guilty of the anthropomorphic heresy:[196] they were in favour of toleration, and could be condemned with the Muggletonians and those who asserted the eternity of the earth.[197] Tillotson was accused of 'super-Hobbism'[198] for his alleged belief that religion was nothing but fancy placed in the heads of those ignorant and wicked people ruled by Hobbist fears.[199] The archbishop was attacked for providing the best material for the atheistic wits that year in his sermon on hell,[200] whilst he was supposed to have denied

Revelation with Hobbes, to have laughed at Moses with Gildon and to have supposed that a mother nursing her child was performing a more important religious act than someone in church.[201] He was clearly promoting latitudinarian clergy, corrupting the nation, and showing how worse heresies arose out of Socinian beginnings.[202]

This particular controversy was clearly part of the major debate about the Trinity that produced a mountain of papers in 1695.[203] But dispute over the Trinity did not in any way abate discussion over libertinism and Epicurean influences; if anything it strengthened such debate, for men saw the connections between these topics. A poem like *Religion, the only happiness* sought to expose those who

> *Pleasure alone make their Deity,*
> *Their rules are Epicure's philosophy;*[204]

whilst Ames, writing of rakes, stressed the relations between anti-clericalism, wit, and a dissolute life.[205] In 1688 the mock apogée of the Epicurean cause was reached, with a petition to the King praising him for his toleration which had freed the nation from the bigotries of religion. The author or authors ventured that a king, if he had any religion at all, should be a Catholic, for popery was the most lenient towards human indulgence, and the most conducive to atheism. It was proclaimed aloud that at last there was nothing sacred but trade and Empire.[206]

Occasionally other influences in the supposed atheist tradition were attacked. Paracelsus was little mentioned, save in *The Atheist Unmasked* where the author expressed surprise that such a besotted atheist leading such a vile life should have lived so long.[207] But frequently writers held a consensus view of the dangers, similar views of the causes, and a strong conviction of the importance of defending religion: the refutation of atheism had become the sure and honest foundation of all true religion.[208] Many agreed that Papists, Turks and Muhammedans were atheists,[209] and considerable energies were expended on reminding people of the evils of these divergent religious traditions. The Jews and the pagans were no better than the rank corporealists or Hobbists. In 1680 an author betrayed a plot that he alleged was being hatched between Rome, the Turks and the Hobbists to introduce atheism to England.[210]

The hatred of Jews can be documented from cases like that of Eve Cohan, a convert who was persecuted and tormented by her parents in a bid to prevent her marrying a Gentile and becoming a Christian proselyte. A Christian view of the case is embedded in a lurid account of 1680.[211] It can be seen in Bishop Kidder's long work, which argued that any intelligent Jew had to accept the Christian testimonies.[212]

The Papists were feared as much.[213] Andrew Marvell expressed implacable hatred in 1672,[214] whilst Charles II's policy of toleration and the Catholic bent of James's policy made the hatred so much the more bitter. There was frequent agitation to enforce the laws against recusancy more severely; there were frequent fears that Catholicism would introduce in England wooden shoes and slavery.[215] The pedigree of popery was often analysed to include political oppression, the worship of anti-Christ, and a general tendency towards atheism.[216] The deluge of anti-Catholic propaganda was continued into 1689, and relived a century of post-Reformation anti-Catholic propaganda.[217] Anti-Catholic feeling remained strong in the eighteenth century, whilst the Turks were similarly treated to a powerful combination of political and religious animosity.[218]

There was little new in many of these claims and views. Men had for centuries bemoaned the decay and growing dissoluteness of the world: for years they had wept over the failing powers of virtue and the failing powers of the universe.[219] Nevertheless, after the Restoration in England there was profusion of bad books and bad morals. There came the great reaction against enthusiasm, there came cries for freedom of speculation in the old Carpenter tradition.[220] The Royal Society was a fashionable undertaking, the assault on the Trinity, present in the Marlowe circle, was renewed, as was the assault upon the fideistic universe present in the works of Bruno and Copernicus.

Atheism was caused by the everyday evils of men's lives, and by the permissiveness of high society, just as it had always been. It was feared the more for its revival of old heresies, its affection for ancient philosophies which Cudworth and his colleagues would rather have forgotten. It was feared for its stress upon secondary causes which threatened the heavens, the structure of the earth and the works of Moses. There is some truth in all of the explanations set forth by contemporaries, and the simple view of atheism being bad lives and bad writings goes far to explain the prevalence of so many allegations, tracts and pamphlets, just as it explains the continuous nature of the atheist problem from the days of the primitive Church.

It is the concern of the chapters that follow to trace the charges and counter-charges across the spectrum of intellectual and scholarly debate. Questions like toleration, anti-popery, or English attitudes towards the Turks, the French and other foreign and alien powers are not discussed at length, where adequate treatments can be found elsewhere.[221] For whilst the western attitude to the Jews and Turks, and the English attitude to France are part of the atheist problem, they were in many ways practical manifestations of more fundamental prejudices and premises. It is to these that I now turn.

Whereas these three things are (as we conceive) the Fundamentals or Essentials of True Religion. First, that all things in the world do not float without a Head and Governour; but that there is a God, an Omnipotent Understanding Being, Presiding over all. Secondly, That this God being Essentially good and Just, there is φμοει χαλον χαι διχαιον, Something in its own Nature, Immutably and Eternally just, and Unjust; and not by Arbitrary Will, Law, and Command onely. And Lastly, That there is Something εφ ημιν, or, That we are so far forth Principles or Masters of our own actions, as to be accountable to Justice for them, or to make us Guilty and blame-worthy for what we doe Amiss, and to deserve punishment accordingly.

> Ralph Cudworth,
> *The True Intellectual
> System of the Universe*
> (London, 1677), Preface

... some Professed Opposers of atheism, had either incurred a Suspicion, or at least suffered under the imputation, of being mere Theists, or Natural Religionists onely, and no hearty believers of Christianity, or Friends to Revealed Religion... We had further observed it, to have been the method of our modern Atheists, to make their first assault against Christianity, as thinking that to be the most vulnerable; and that it would be an easy step from thence, to Demolish all Religion, and Theism.

> *Ibid.*

Il faut bien que la chose soit difficile, puisque nous voions tous les jours que ceux qui combattent le plus vivement l'athéisme, lui donnent des armes sans y penser. M. Cudworth et M. Grew très grands philosophes, en sont un exemple.

> Pierre Bayle, *Œuvres*
> (La Haye, vol. 3, 1727), pp. 216–17

Chapter Two

THE ENCYCLOPAEDIC
CHRONICLERS OF ATHEISM

CUDWORTH AND WISE

Behind the works of the many penny pamphleteers who churned out their particular refutations of atheists and near-atheists in reponse to the demands of the minute and the impulse of the hour, lay the much longer and more serious works of the great encyclopaedic apologists. These men were concerned with establishing eternal verities and providing reference works for all those concerned with the defence of the faith on the ground. There was no more skilled or comprehensive a debater of atheist and semi-atheist opinions and heretical onslaughts against Christian doctrine than Ralph Cudworth, the mid-seventeenth-century Cambridge author, tutor and cleric. It was his work which was drawn on by many of the subsequent debaters, and his work which can best provide us with the intellectual framework in which all the debates must be viewed. Cudworth's arguments and prolix scholarship contrast starkly with the racier and more elegant prose of George Berkeley, Bishop of Cloyne. Writing some sixty years after the Cambridge neo-Platonist, Berkeley offered discourse where Cudworth had ventured a barrage of footnotes and detail. Both men, however, shared the distinction of summing up the intellectual scope of the atheist threat for their respective generations; the contrast between them serves to highlight the changes in the content and style of apologia during the passage of years that separates them.

The Cambridge group who flourished in the war-torn university of the mid-seventeenth century were an important force in the debates over irreligion. It was they who most strongly opposed mechanism and its attendant heresies,[1] and it was they who attempted to evolve a system of belief that was rational yet not deistical or mechanistic,[2] that was infused with a true piety yet was not enthusiastic, that was strongly Protestant, yet was not tainted by the terrors of a full deterministic Calvinism.[3] Cudworth and More, reared in the Whichcote tradition, both strongly opposed deviations from Christian belief:[4] their significance in English thought has recently been acknowledged afresh after some decades of comparative neglect.[5] It was from their influence that Shaftesbury later developed some of his reflections,[6] and it is to the Cambridge group that we must look for the important influences of Descartes in English university life in the seventeenth century.[7]

It was among this distinguished body of opinion that the longest and the most revered book of the seventeenth century dedicated to the refutation of irreligion was nurtured. In 1677 the first volume of Cudworth's *The True Intellectual System of the Universe* was published from London for Richard Royson, the royal bookseller. It immediately became a volume which all libraries and all serious theological scholars needed; Henry Godolphin, the Vice-Warden of All Souls, for example, inscribed a copy which he gave the college that same year.[8] Cudworth acknowledged in his Preface to the Reader that his first intention had been to defend free will against the determinist views recently propagated by men like Hobbes,[9] but that he had soon come to see the need for a much longer work to deal with the deep-rooted heresies that underlay the determinist's position. The 'Democritick fate' which argued that all things followed from material necessity, obviating the need for God; 'The Divine Fate Immorall, and Violent' which argued that God was in no way controlled by natural justice, morality or the quest for good in his determination of men's actions; and the Stoical 'Divine Fate Morall and Natural' which accepted both God and natural law, but denied men any liberty anywhere, therefore undermining the role of retributive justice in the world[10] – these were all positions which to Cudworth undermined the essentials of religion which he outlined.[11]

Cudworth was sad that such a volume should be needed at all. Old hypotheses long and best forgotten were being revived. The ghosts of Epicurus, Democritus, Strato and Anaximander were being exhumed. They appeared as part of the confusion of the world in Cudworth's famous engraved title-page, and their theories riddled the many pages of his magisterial work. Cudworth himself accepted with Hobbes that mechanical explanations of material events were the best that we could obtain, and he did not wish to insult the atomists and the Cartesians by denying any validity to their work; but Cudworth did disagree with the more extreme of their protagonists that this entailed a description of universals, incorporeals, spirits, God and providences. Cudworth felt he could attack both Hobbes and Aristotle with impunity, and substitute for the deterministic heresy on the one hand, and the dying Stagyrite tyranny on the other, the Fathers in happy conjunction with Plato, and modern Christianized atomism.

Powicke suggests that Cudworth was foolish to write the book he did. Men accused him of adopting and developing the positions he sought to combat; his work was too big to be read or to be influential. These criticisms seem unfair. The size of Cudworth's book has been a greater deterrent to modern historians than it was to his contemporaries; his influence penetrates a long tradition of tract and sermon writers who paid halting debt to Cudworth when they turned to defending the faith against ancient heresies. He was never thrown to the flames in effigy and his books were never impounded by the clerical censors; instead he was gently promulgated into the following century by his continuator and abridger, Thomas Wise.[12] It is true that men took issue with some of his more unusual interpretations: he suffered attack for his views of the Trinity, where some felt he had given too much to the Socinians in his pursuit of a rational solution.[13] But on the whole Cudworth was esteemed as an influence for the good. It is also true that Bayle strongly criticized Cudworth in 1703–4 but this was related to Bayle's dislike of Le Clerc, who was busy printing extracts from Cudworth's *Intellectual System* as he thought it a fundamental and important work in the defence of religion and the establishment of true philosophy.[14]

Cudworth and his continuator both perceived that the origin of the only complete system of atheism ever propounded in the world lay in atomism and the Democritean view of fate and necessity.[15] The introduction of free will by Epicurus was an incompatible element introduced to no effect: atomism remained an attempt to explain the world in terms of matter and motion propelled by necessity, thereby leaving no role for God to fulfil.[16] Our apologists were convinced of the utility of the atomic hypothesis, but they reasoned that it had been corrupted and atheized by Democritus and Leucippus.[17] In its true state the atomic hypothesis accounted for the world of matter, and forced one to believe in incorporeal substances to explain the soul and God's involvement in the universe. The precept that *nihil ex nihilo fieri posset* could be taken to support the conclusion that God must have powers greater than those of mere nature, capable of creating the world in the first place.[18]

Both Cudworth and Wise argued not only that atomism should be theistic and Christian, but also that in its original form as pioneered by Moshus the Phoenician it had indeed been free from the taint of atheism.[19] They resorted to proving the ancient tradition of atomism as a means of strengthening their case against the Democritean view, attacking it logically and undermining its authority by undermining its antiquity and purity of descent.[20]

Cudworth's defence established that the atomists before Democritus accepted the existence of incorporeal substance and the need for God.[21] He argued them into almost a Cartesian dualist position, needing the world of spirits and mind to be distinct from the world of matter and atoms.[22] He proceeded then to examine the fourteen possible grounds on which atheism could be founded:

1 No man can have an idea or conception of God, and therefore he is but an incomprehensible nothing.[23]

2 Nothing can come from nothing; therefore everything that is must have been from eternity.[24]

3 Whatsoever is, is extended: God is not visibly extended therefore he is not.[25]

4 To suppose an Incorporeal Mind to be the original of all things, is nothing else, but to make the Abstract Notion of a mere accident to be the First Cause.[26]

5 A corporeal God is impossible because all corporeal substance is corruptible.[27]

6 Mind stemmed from the chance arrangement of atoms: atoms were the first thing in the world, therefore the world could not have started with Mind.[28]

7 Reason is only human, and related to flesh and bones: therefore there can be no divine intelligence presiding overall.[29]

8 All living beings are concretions of atoms liable to death and dissolution of their compages: God cannot be eternal and immortal therefore.[30]

9 God is called a First Mover; but nothing can move itself.[31]

10 All action and cogitation is local motion: local motion only occurs from the action of an agent on something; therefore no First Being could be a thinking being.[32]

11 Knowledge is the information of things themselves known existing without the knower, and a mere passion from them: thus the world must have existed before any knowledge or conception of it.[33]

12 The world is so ill made that God could not be responsible for it in all its imperfections.[34]

13 All in human affairs is chaos and confusion: Providence is defective.[35]

14 The ability to order all things everywhere at once is absolutely incompatible with happiness.[36]

Cudworth thought that atheists added to these arguments by conjuring up other fears and doubts. They asked why God left the world unmade for so long, and how God employed his time before the origin of the world.[37] They argued that God removed pleasures from men,[38] and that sovereignty was jeopardised by placing a power greater than that of the civil sovereign above the State, as a court of appeal for rebels and trouble makers.[39]

Cudworth saw the atheist problem in two major ways.[40] He saw that certain sects or groups of opinions had congealed to attack religion: the most serious was atheistic atomism, and the next most serious were the hylozoists under their founder father Strato who argued that there was no God other than the life of nature in matter.[41] At the same time he perceived that these sectaries and their ilk used common negative arguments against God in general and the Christian religion in particular. He set out to strangle both these evil births.

Cudworth's knowledge of the traditions of ancient philosophy also led him to attack the materialist school that developed from the influence of Anaximander.[42] The growth of this hylopathian atheism, a philosophy which recognized forms and qualities rather than atoms but which nevertheless found the origin of the world in chaos and not in God, was an even more ancient growth than the Democritic atheism. A fourth tradition was like the hylozoic in its belief in a plastic nature, but different in that it asserted one universal plastic nature devoid of understanding or sense which ran throughout the universe.[43]

Cudworth himself believed in a plastic nature: he thought there was probably one plastic artificial nature which presided over the whole terraqueous globe, by which vegetables could be formed from a power greater than that of fortuitous mechanism, but lesser than that of the driving Intelligence behind the universe.[44] The atheists were wrong merely in their ascription of supreme powers to a plastic nature that was only a subordinate and pale reflection of the Divine Mind capable of determining the form of the universe.[45]

He replied to each of the atheists' fourteen arguments in turn.

All the pagans had had an idea of God,[46] and the atheists themselves must have an idea of him to be able to deny his existence.[47] Anyone who thinks about the problem of the origin of the universe must be able to form a notion of him.[48] That the so-called pagan polytheist usually postulated One Supreme God who generated or commanded the others undermined the force of the argument that the belief of One God was a recent institution forced upon men by laws and chance.[49]

There were five subdivisions of the argument against the notion of God which Cudworth paused to examine. Some argued that knowledge was dependent upon sense in the Hobbist fashion: we cannot directly perceive God with any of the five senses and therefore he cannot be known or said to exist.[50] Cudworth demolished the argument of 'Nihil intelligere posset quod non prius Fuit in sensu'[51] through the usual devices of challenging the difference between dreams and wakings,[52] the Cartesian problem,[53] and through postulating reason superior to sense which gives us knowledge of God and his effects and organizes raw sense information which is not coterminous with knowledge.[54] This attack was of course an attack on the Scholastics as much as against Locke. Others argued that man cannot understand God and therefore God cannot be:[55] Cudworth retorted that if there was nothing incomprehensible to our minds indeed there would be no need for God,[56] but that was not the case, The moderns, opposing their ancient predecessors, had also ventured to suggest that infinity was an impossibility, for whatever distance or time one cared to postulate one could always envisage a greater or a longer one.[57] But, reasoned the Platonists, if there had once been a time when there was nothing, there could never have been anything: therefore something must have been eternal.[58] All atheists seek to undermine the idea of God by giving an account of why it should have arisen, attributing it either to men's fear, or ignorance of secondary causes, or to the fictions devised by law-makers and rulers to keep them in obedience.[59] The first excuse they offer reflects more upon their own timorousness and their own arrogance in supposing only they understand the nature of the imposture:[60] the second upon their ignorance of reason and the higher principles of intelligence which could never come of bare matter,[61] and their own inability to give a reason for the existence of motion;[62] and the third is absurd for it seems impossible that all sovereigns should simultaneously have discovered the utility of this cheat, and been able to maintain it if it were clearly false.[63]

The strength of Cudworth's case lay in his belief in final causes. He defended these in such a way that they became the model defence for the later seventeenth-century apologist. He forestalled the criticism that because an organ or part of nature performed a function it was necessarily designed for that purpose: and he argued that neither the mechanic causes nor the plastic spirit could be responsible for so fine a design as he saw reflected in the world.[64] He defended miracles,[65] apparitions[66] and prophecies[67] as part of the divine scheme, realities that could not be reasoned away by the atheists' pretences.

Once this ground had been declared in defending the notion of God, Cudworth went on to provide an argument for God's existence. He took the argument of Descartes, expounded in the *Discours sur la méthode*, and attacked it, pointing out both its circularity and its successful establishment of eternal scepticism.[68] He rejected the antipathy to Cartesian metaphysics that had earlier been stated by Henry More, his fellow Platonist, despite their admiration of Descartes's 'mechanical wit'.[69] Descartes had brought into question all our faculties, and had then founded the existence of God on our faculties, and the truth of our faculties on the existence of God.[70] Cudworth felt he had sufficiently established the existence of the idea of God: from this he argued the ontological position.

Major	1	Whatever we can frame an idea of without contradiction, either is or could be
Minor	2	But if God is not, he is not possible to be
Deduction	3	Therefore He is.[71]

An alternative or supplementary argument could be pursued:

1 Something must have existed of itself from eternity

2 This something must have existed necessarily and naturally

3 Therefore whatever existed from eternity must have contained necessary self-existence in its nature

4 Only a perfect being contains such necessary self-existence in its nature.[72]

Cudworth firmly believed that the world had descended from the highest degree to lower degrees; that the greatest perfection had to predate the lesser.[73] Similarly, total knowledge predated man's partial knowledge: the divine knowledge was archetypal from the first original, not ectypal.[74]

He demonstrated that the argument that nothing can come from nothing therefore supported the theist's position, necessitating the prior existence of God and his necessarily self-existing perfections.[75] He recognized that although all atheists are corporealists, not all corporealists are atheists.[76] He then dismissed the next six of his atheists' arguments by an extended digression defending incorporeal substance. To Cudworth there was brute matter, dead, senseless and inert, on the one hand,[77] and soul, thought and spirit on the other which was not extended but nevertheless existed and imbibed life into the dull matter around it.[78] Many ancients like Origen,[79] Plotinus[80] and others were invoked to add weight to this claim. Cudworth defended the abstractions or ideas behind things by saying that the idea of humanity or equinity are merely noemata, or the intelligible essences of things as objects of the mind.[81]

The atheists' arguments numbers 5–8 are dismissed because they all rest upon the premise that there is nothing in the world but material substance.[82] Both the hylopathian atheism of Anaximander[83] and the atomistic of Democritus[84] bring intellect and spirit out of nothing, and are therefore to be condemned.[85] The hylozoists, who argue that every atom has the power to think, had been proved silly by Epicurus.[86] The eighth of the atheists' arguments is also misfounded because it assumes all life derives from dull and corruptible matter.[87]

The ninth argument that there could be no First Mover, rests on the mistaken notion that all action is local motion and that everything in the world is body.[88] Cogitation is not local motion, and thinking beings are not machines in Cudworth's submission.[89] The tenth and eleventh arguments are similarly answered, supported by reference back to the view of the divine mind as archetypal.[90] Hobbes's view that universals are nothing else but names and therefore differ from language to language, is rejected by viewing understanding as a higher plane of perfection than brute objects perceivable by sense.[91]

The atheists' twelfth cavil about the fabric of the world at times confused our not being able to perceive the reason for one particular part of the Creation, with the statement that that piece is ill-made.[92]

The Stoics and others maintained that all in the world below is not made for the benefit of man;[93] but as Plato remarked, the whole was not made for any part but the parts for the whole.[94] Cudworth, however, conceded that most things in the lower world were made principally for men. The thirteenth of the atheists' arguments, that Providence was defective and the irreligious prosper, failed to see that in the long run men were rewarded or punished according to their lives, but God did not intervene at every turn in human affairs.[95]

The queries were also easy to answer. God made the world because his goodness overflowed and strove to communicate to others.[96] God did not make the world earlier in so far as it was impossible that he should have made it from eternity.[97] Atheists were wrong to suggest that incorporeal substance cannot move the world: our souls show that it can move body.[98]

Cudworth closed his great first volume with attacks against the Leviathan doctrine of a debased human nature without natural justice, equity or charity, and against the notion that religion jeopardizes a state's security by jeopardizing the position of Leviathan.[99] He displayed the motive that had persuaded him of the necessity of his task, by devoting his closing pages to defending religion as an important element in social security, and attacking the Hobbist notion of sovereignty and public good.[100]

Thomas Wise was more of a continuator than an abridger. His edition published in 1706 removed some of the prolixity from his master's work, whilst adding to the defence of God additional works of apologia and argument published in the intervening twenty-nine years. Wise felt that the example of Gildon, the follower of Charles Blount who had recanted his former views and rejoined the Christian fold,[101] was a hopeful sign that Christian activity and endeavour might bring back the wavering to the fold.[102] He omitted Cudworth's discussion of Apollonius Tyanaeus,[103] the Sybilline Oracles, the Orphic Trinity, the authority of the Trismegistic writings and some of Cudworth's digressions on the Trinity,[104] and accepted that in places Cudworth had misquoted or misinterpreted the Fathers. He defended his master from the strictures of Bayle[105] who accused Cudworth of wrongly preferring Aristotle to Descartes and for setting up a vital and plastic nature to control the world. To Wise, Cudworth had made quite clear that he did not accept Aristotelian substantial forms, nor had he set up the same kind of hylozoic plastic nature as the one which he had himself so stridently refuted. Wise felt Le Clerc's threat to investigate Cudworth's proof of the pagans' belief in one God was not a sensible one.[106]

Both Wise and Cudworth stressed their belief in the excellence of the true atomic hypothesis as a means of salving the phenomena of the natural world. They both praised the ancient doctrine rooted in the works of Moshus, Pythagoras, Empedocles, Ecphantus, Xenocrates, Heraclides, Diodorus and Metrodorus Chius.[107] They both felt that true atomism led men to seek a First Cause and a First Mover: if it did not, as in the case of Democritus and Lucretius, then the old Aristotelian philosophy was to be preferred. As Cudworth stated,

> Now I say the whole Aristotelian System of Philosophy is infinitely to be preferred before the whole Democritical; though the former hath been so much disparaged, and the other cried up of late amongst us. Because, though it cannot be denied but that the Democritick Hypothesis doth much more handsomely and intelligibly salve the corporeal phenomena, yet in all those other things which are of far the greatest moment, it is rather a madness than a philosophy.[108]

Wise listed rather similar arguments to those of his mentor when he came to state the position he was refuting,[109] and continued Cudworth's analysis of the threats from hylozoism and atomism.[110] There were some cases over which they disagreed: Wise felt Heraclitus was an atheist, but Cudworth had argued that as Heraclitus thought the fiery matter from which the world had originated had been intelligent, he must have been a theist.[111] He shared Cudworth's doubts about Descartes, adding a critique of his own and arguing that intermediary plastic natures were necessary between the mind and matter of the Cartesian universe.[112] Both Wise and Cudworth reflect the general ambivalence of the response to Descartes in England. Descartes, admired for his dualism and by some for his argument for God, was by others feared for his scepticism, his rigid materialism in the world, and his denial of souls to animals.[113] Before Newton there were men like Power and Towneley who found his physics stimulating and his general philosophy of science compatible with their own wishes;[114] after Newton there were few willing to defend the Cartesian vortices or the published sections of *De Mundo*. John Norris, a staunch later English Cartesian, remains a lonely figure in English intellectual life of the period.[115]

Wise also came to the aid of Anaxagoras, Archelaus, Atticus, Pythagoras and Aristotle himself, arguing that these philosophers were not downright corporealists, for they had argued the eternity of some intelligent principle in the universe as well as the eternity of matter.[116] He condemned Philostratus and Blount's revival of his heresies which attacked the divinity and credibility of Christ,[117] and defended Apollonius's claim that he was a monotheist.

Even Celsus, Malchus (Porphyry), Hierocles and Julian the Emperor, all opponents of Christianity, had been monotheists. Wise displayed his learning, drawing on Julian's oration in praise of the sun, and Origen's *Contra Celsum*, an often cited source in the great atheist debates of the later seventeenth century.[118] Similarly, Wise, like his contemporaries, relied heavily on Cicero for his information about pagan belief and ancient philosophy, using the *De Natura Deorum* as a principal text.[119]

Wise added considerably to Cudworth's text when he came to review the atheists' attribution of religious belief to ignorance, fear and cunning politicians. He cited Hakewill's refutation of the popular theory that the world is in a perpetual state of decay;[120] he cited Boyle and Bishop Wilkins to add strength to the argument from natural religion and final causes.[121] Descartes's work on Optics, Scheiner's *Oculus* and a host of others show that the world reflects the wisdom of a contriver, rather than the chance of fate.[122] Bentley's seventh Boyle lecture had successfully demolished the argument of the chance formation of the world,[123] whilst Newton had demolished the quasi-atheistic system of Descartes by the excellence of his physics and mathematical demonstration.[124]

Wise acknowledged that great strides had been made in the previous forty years in bolstering the Christian position. Gibson and Lower had successfully attacked Descartes's theory of the systole and diastole of the heart operating through heat and blood pressure.[125] They had replaced it with a theory more conducive to the wisdom of God. Harvey had shown that a mechanical explanation was similarly inadequate in the reply to Descartes's posthumous *De la formation du foetus*;[126] Wise felt that mechanism would also fail to explain gravity, the diaphragm's motion, and the formation of animal bodies. Bishop Parker's *Tentamina Physico-theologica de Deo*,[127] Bishop Stillingfleet's *Origines Sacrae* against Descartes,[128] the *Voyage du monde de Descartes*, More's *Enchiridion* against Hobbes[129] and his *Antidote against atheisme*,[130] Dr Scott's *Christian Life*,[131] Ray's *Wisdom of God manifest in the works of the creation*,[132] Huet's anti-Cartesian work[133] and Jacquelin's *Dissertations sur l'existence de Dieu* are all discussed or mentioned by Wise in his testimony to the developing tradition of natural theological apologia.

Wise's work shows the way in which the traditions of Boyle, Newton and Ray each added something to the supposed strength of the Christian apologists' cause. Each one added something to the defences outlined by Cudworth in his great seminal work: Ray and Boyle adding detail to the argument from final causes, and showing the way in which natural philosophical evidence could be deployed in religious debate, Newton offering an alternative hypothesis or system to the Cartesian one, overcoming the sceptical and dualistic severities of the French *weltanschauung*. Wise could use a work like Keill's against Burnet against Descartes as well, pointing the way in which Burnet had been influenced by the author of the *Discourse on method*, and criticizing his theories of the world that seemed to attack Providence and the wisdom of God.[134]

Wise was also worried by recent work about witches, and demons. Bekker's view that belief in the Devil as well as God was bitheistic, had been refuted sufficiently by Binet.[135] But Webster's *Displaying of supposed witchcraft* and Coward's *Second thoughts concerning the human soul* had weakened the apologists' positions.[136] Coward's *Grand Essay* was rank Epicureanism,[137] and was merely plagiarized from a tract of 1655 entitled *Man wholly mortal*.[138] Wise brought Cicero's *De Divinatione* and Derodon's *de Existentia Dei* into the debate to counter these influences.[139] Coward's, arguing that the soul was not spiritual, immortal substance, were burned by the common hangman following Parliamentary action.[140] Turner and Broughton both wrote books against Coward.[141]

Wise, like Cudworth, defended incorporeal substance against the materialists, using the evidence of Vergil and Dr Grew to show that there is a principle of life independent of body.[142] Wise opposed Lucretius's theory of sensory perception and knowledge drawing on Creech's notes to his 1700 edition of Lucretius.[143] The Hobbists, who were the worst modern protagonists of the theory that sensation reflects the atomic pressures exerted on sense organs, have been adequately refuted by Tennison.[144] Wise proved mind to be entirely distinct from matter, and here draws on Norris's and Toland's refutation of Spinoza.[145] But Wise was by no means an admirer of Toland's sly refutation of the continental heretic, and he in turn criticized Toland's notion that motion is essential to matter.[146] He also criticized Blount's *Oracles of Reason*,[147] and feared lest acceptance of the Hobbist view of sensation from atomic pressure would lead many insidiously close to pure corporeal atheism. Wise defended the idea that animals' souls were more than mechanical Cartesian devices, and agreed with Mersenne's questions about Genesis over the issue[148] of human souls' immateriality. The Cartesian view of animals had been effectively debunked, but Wise could see no other answer than that animal souls were destroyed on their death in the interests of cosmic hygiene.

Wise defended the idea that knowledge is prior to matter and things, although he was hesitant to fully endorse Norris's view that our ideas are the same as God's though fewer in number. Boethius,[149] Lee's *Anti-scepticism*,[150] and Sir John Davies's *Original, Nature and Immortality of the Soul* aided his argument.[151] Wise, like Keill,[152] Wilkins,[153] and Phillipe de Mornay,[154] saw in the world perfect manifestations of God's concern; even in the disputed climatic zones and scraggy mountains. For without those mountains Wales and Scotland would have been open to invasion. Heaths and sands were essential to prevent overpopulation which would lead to corruption of the air and nature through animal pollution. Wise ended his treatment with a survey of the plentiful anti-Hobbist literature, and some remarks of his own against the great *Leviathan*.[155]

Cudworth and Wise provide us with the most compendial of all those attempts to refute atheism that the fecund seventeenth century produced. Their works show us the way in which the great debate included all the disciplines known to man, and the interrelations between political theory, natural history, theology, biblical criticism, physics, astronomy, and the whole universe of studies. They show us as well the way in which the debates over God and his world developed over the thirty years from the 1670s, with Wise's text including the works of Blount and Toland, Spinoza and Coward where Cudworth had been particularly preoccupied with Hobbes and his sources. Wise also shows us the way in which apologia was thought to have been strengthened by the host of writings of the later seventeenth century using natural history and philosophy, physics and political science to add lustre to the apologists' cause.

Cudworth wrote because he feared the growing incursions of Hobbist and ancient philosophical logic, and because he wished to produce his own scheme over the Trinity and concerning the plastic natures that inhered in things in his effort to salvage the theology of his colleagues against the attacks of the new philistines. He could draw on the work of More and others who had already seen the need for work against atheists, but his distinction lay in the complexity and thoroughness of his treatment, and in his professed intention to keep away from attacking enthusiasts and sectaries who verged upon the atheists in their inclinations in the popular mind. His continuator was undertaking a similar task, but one rendered more complex by the following years of propaganda and dissent in the Anglican cause.

Cudworth also demonstrated the dangers of refutation. To refute, one has to expound; exposition can produce its own insistent logic, and readers could begin to fear lest the author were too sympathetic to the views he was purporting to attack. His fear was well grounded; his prolixity, testimony to his erudition and his concern; the result was ambivalent in its utility in that it fomented the problem with which it dealt so admirably. Its influence is undeniable, and manifest in a thousand footnotes of later writers; but its influence was not confined to strengthening the apologists against their mentors, the atheists and deists of later seventeenth-century England.

The attempts of the Cambridge Platonists, whether it were Cudworth, More, Whichcote, Smith or their friends, earned them the reputation of founding the broad-based latitudinarians, clergy seeking toleration, a reasoned religion, and sometimes with Arminian leanings. No historian has satisfactorily traced their influence on Locke, Boyle or Newton, and the interest that early eighteenth-century men of letters expressed in them is still coming to light slowly. Cudworth, kept alive in the scholarly world after his death by the letters and memories of his daughter, left behind him manuscript notes and writings, some later to be published by eighteenth-century editors.[156] Henry More continued to influence contemporaries through the activities of the Conway circle.[157] He was keen to refute allegations made against him and Cudworth, and commented in a letter to Lady Conway on how after the Restoration, 'They push hard at the Latitude men as they call them, some in their pulpitts call them sons of Belial, others make the Devill a latitudinarian, which things are as pleasing to me as the raillery of a jack-pudding at one end of a dancing rope.'[158]

He and Cudworth thought that their reasoned religion stood against enthusiasm, and against atheism. They regretted those who mistook their piety for deism.

BERKELEY

The genre which Cudworth had begun with such prolixity became transmuted by the pressures of the Augustan age. Through Cudworth's continuator[159] and people like Nicholls and his *A Conference with a theist*,[160] the compendial tradition was kept alive; but with Berkeley we see it changing into the age of the dialogue, the age of the witty, the urbane, and the well written. Berkeley's *Alciphron* was by no means the only one of the dialogues published in the early eighteenth century that took as its theme the growing irreligion of the deists,[161] and the creeping social contagion of evil life; but it was the most complete and the most sophisticated, outstanding for the quality of its arguments and the subtlety of its style. It inexorably exposed the dangers of libertinism and scepticism through the refutation of Lysicles and Alciphron, two free-thinkers, in debate with Crito and Euphranor.

Berkeley was interested in considering 'the free-thinker in the various light of atheist, libertine, enthusiast, scorner, critic, metaphysician, fatalist and sceptic'.[162]

Alciphron was a man of intelligence, whose thought has led him from deism to atheism.[163] He detested prejudice,[164] believed that the relativity of religions damns them all,[165] hated priestcraft and priests,[166] and saw man as a creature of appetite, passion and sense who should follow the way of happiness in Hobbist manner.[167] The eighteenth-century passion for the natural, the enthusiasm of the minute philosophers for some basis of brute fact culled from their observations of the world, had led Alciphron to search for something certain; a something which he found like Hobbes in the appetites and senses of humanity. Unsure of even reason and the powers of deduction, Alciphron and his friends were left with Lear's poor bare forked animal, man.[168] Cicero had thought such a view contracted and degraded men; the free-thinkers found it liberating.[169]

Lysicles was a less thoughtful person. An ardent follower of fashion, he loved to feel free of the irksome duties of reading and scholarship, to feel free to pursue good manners and good breeding alone. He hated dull and dusty scholars bent blind over books; he loved the new philosophers who observed things, not words, and saw man as he was, an active creature, an animal of passion and fashion.[170]

Lysicles in a crude and exuberant way reflected two centuries of controversy over the nature of rhetoric. He believed, in sympathy with the Royal Society's motto of *Nullis in verba*, that the study of things, not words, was the way to enlightenment.[171] Lysicles saw the old scholarly languages as outmoded, their terms leading to a dry and futile debate unrelated to the world as he saw it about him.[172] His departure from the Baconians and the empiricists only came with his suggested remedy for the defects of a book-ridden education: a remedy which maintained that in the words of Alciphron 'proper ideas or materials are only to be got by frequenting good company'.[173] Lysicles had as his favourite sport satirizing clerics, and believed that there was more truth in a glass of port and gentle conversation, than in the tomes of an Aristotle or a Pliny.

'Method, exactness, and industry' were to our philosophers a disadvantage.[174] They had no need of the skills of bibliophiles and bibliographers, nor had they any sympathy for the political arithmeticians traversing the bills of mortality with the zest of a Petty or the application of a King.[175] They went further with a cup of chocolate and the fey wit of the *Freethinker* than they did with the folios of the schoolmen or the quietness of a country retreat. Nevertheless, men had written in the cause which Lysicles and Alciphron held dear: the progress was quite startling:

CRITO: Moschon . . . hath proved that man and beast are really of the same nature . . . Giorgias . . . man to be a piece of clockwork or machinery: and that thought or reason are the same thing as the impulse of one ball against another. Cimon . . . conscience for his actions than a clock is for striking. Tryphon hath written ir-

> refragably on the usefulness of vice. Thrasenor hath confuted the
> foolish prejudice men had against atheism, shewing that a republic
> of atheists might live very happily together. Demylus hath made
> a jest of loyalty, and convinced the world there is nothing in it.
>
> LYSICLES: But the masterpiece and finishing stroke is a learned anecdote of
> our great Diagoras, containing a demonstration against the being
> of God.[176]

Berkeley's use of names has caused scholars grave problems in identifying
them, and has aided the growth of the printing industry no little in putting
forward their differing views.[177] Some argue that the names are important for
their associations with characters in the work of classical authors like Plato;
others that they have a mere etymological significance; whilst others still espouse
the idea that each classical name corresponds exactly to the name of one of
Berkeley's contemporaries. It is clear that these competing theories can be
reconciled; Crito is a name which reflects the character of the man it describes,
whilst the positions adopted by Moschon and his friends do bear a great similarity to the views of particular minute philosophers. Moschon himself could
have been Hobbes or Blount; Giorgias could have been Coward. Tryphon
seems like Mandeville, Thrasenor like Bayle, and Crito like Berkeley himself.
The whole effect of this passage is to show how the works of contemporaries
were all to Berkeley's mind the product of one united movement; a movement
attacking the fundamentals of all religious belief. Where Cudworth had seen
the connections between atomism and irreligion, Berkeley could see connections
between certain economic and social doctrines, mechanism, fatalism, and Hobbist
views of man, and the life of Lysicles, the Epicurean insistence upon happiness,
and the reversal of all traditional moral standards and values.

Lysicles praised vice, because it circulates money in the economy and conduces
to the prosperity of the nation;[178] Euphranor did not attack the commercial
premise, but merely argued that sober and virtuous men circulate more money
than vicious ones because they live longer.[179] Lysicles rejected the authority of
Plato and Seneca:[180] to him virtue is a politic contrivance not adding to men's
real happiness. Where Euphranor saw money as a means to an end,[181] Lysicles
thought men could be happy with money and without virtue.[182] Lysicles saw
man as a machine, rendering virtue and vice meaningless appellations:[183] he
met the retort that men have reason to distinguish them from brutes, and are
free from the bondage of mere mechanism.[184]

Crito's replies condemned the English rake as a person 'neither brute enough
to enjoy his appetites, nor man enough to govern them'.[185] The minute philosophers led men to despair and suicide.[186] Education, fashion and company un-
fairly prejudiced men against religion in this age, under cover of freeing men
from prejudice. Minute philosophy encouraged children to laugh at the old,
and to despise their parents, whilst it persuaded all men to scorn their government:[187] the free-thinkers were like a fifth column of Jesuits, for if they could
destroy the Church of England as they intended the people would be unable
to accept the liberty they offered, and would turn to Rome for succour.[188]

Lysicles's arguments as a rake had merely enforced Crito's belief of the need for religion to promote order in society. Alciphron therefore changed the tack of their argument, and suggested that atheists could have a sense of beauty, virtue, honour and order without the coercive fear of an after-life.[189] Men, said Alciphron, had a natural sense of morality without God or prejudice forcing it upon them.[190] With Aristotle, he suggested that if a man is only good owing to restraints, he is not truly good.[191] Alciphron failed, however, to answer the objection that the free-thinkers only convert by ridicule,[192] although he staunchly defended the idea that there should be no embargoes placed upon truth however unpalatable that truth might be.[193]

The fourth dialogue is the central dialogue about God. Alciphron refused to be persuaded by the form of metaphysical argument which Cudworth would have enjoyed, ruling out of court all arguments taken from the idea of an all-perfect being, or from the absurdity of an infinite progression of causes, and declined arguments from authorities, or from the utility of the notion of God. In return Alciphron agreed not to argue against the wishes of God from anything that may seem irregular in the works of nature, nor to object against the justice and Providence of God from the evil that befalls good men.[194] They fell to a long debate about the nature of vision and audition;[195] Euphranor argued that from motions you infer a mover, and from reasonable motions a rational mover, thereby proving the existence of God as a superior mind.[196] He added that just as words and sounds make a language, so do colours and lights make a visual language of God's creation:[197] this argument being an unusual Berkelian argument deriving its force from Berkeley's earlier writings and researches.[198] God was proven, for he 'speaks himself everyday and in every place to the eyes of all men'.[199]

Crito developed the argument, and attacked those mechanists who think that God made the world like a clock and then left it to run in its own atomic and predetermined way after the fashion of Descartes and Leibniz.[200] Crito affirmed that God intervened through Providences and this is proven by his visual language of the Creation.[201]

This argument was criticized by Lysicles, who felt that the use of analogy by theologians was specious. Too many divines accepted that words like 'wisdom' and 'goodness' had a different meaning when applied to God, which to Lysicles was tantamount to denying God and these attributes altogether.[202] Crito responded that this opinion came from Dionysius the Areopagite,[203] and had long been discountenanced by serious scholars.[204] The schools distinguished the metaphorical kind of analogy—the attribution of a finger to God—from the proper kind—the attribution of knowledge to God where His is to ours as infinite is to finite.[205] This salving of analogy combined with the argument from God's visual language ensured once again that Berkeley's religious protagonists had the better of the debate.

The fifth dialogue deals with the possible similarity of the free-thinkers and the druids,[206] before considering Lysicles's contention that morality and order can exist without heavenly oracles.[207] Crito defended the Church from the allegation that it fosters wars and vices, by illustrating that all these problems predated the Church.[208] Alciphron retorted that clerical debate is unpleasant,[209] that the universities nurture prejudice and corruption,[210] and that Shaftesbury's style has shown how debased the prose of the Church is.[211] Alciphron saw the Church as an enemy of English liberties,[212] Crito saw Protestantism as the keystone of English freedom.[213] Alciphron looked forward to the end of political tyranny dependent for its force upon Church religion.[214]

Alciphron's hostility to traditions is explicit in the sixth dialogue[215] where he ventured that men are foolish to trust the priest, magistrate, printer, editor and translator, for none of these men are divine.[216] He thought that the Bible is too badly written to be divinely inspired,[217] although he accepted that some of its books may be genuine.[218] He found parts of the Bible, like the 49th Psalm, to be nonsense: Euphranor preferred to see it as Hebrew idiom,[219] and defended the style of the Bible.[220]

Lysicles heard from a chemist friend that the soul is animal spirit consisting of subtle oils, and puts this forward:[221] Crito condemned these essays to make intelligible things unknown by seeing them as similar to things known.[222] Alciphron turned to denying prophecies, revelations, and other such phenomena,[223] and indicated that the Mosaic writings do not agree with Chaldean, Chinese and Egyptian records concerning the history of the world, which indicated that the world is more than 6,000 years old.[224] Crito defended the Mosaic account by pointing out that the Jesuits had shown the inconsistency of Chinese writings with the Ephemerides,[225] whilst studies by Joseph Scaliger and Sir John Marsham had posed doubts about the value of Egyptian sources.[226] Boyle, Locke and Newton, great scientists as they were, had all agreed with Moses.[227]

Alciphron's use of Celsus, Julian and Porphyry[228] failed to impress Crito who believed Celsus to be full of contraction,[229] and thought Holsteinius's *De Vita et scriptus Porphyrii* to have shown Julian and Porphyry to be far from authoritative.[230] His argument that the different sects of religious belief brought the whole into doubt drew Crito's reply that the divisions between the dogmatists, empirics, Galenists and Paracelsians in medicine did not disprove the circulation of the blood.[231] Crito felt it would be better if Alciphron and his ilk devoted their talents to solving the problem of longitude or perpetual motion rather than to finding silly errors in religion.[232]

In the seventh dialogue Alciphron used the arguments of the linguistic philosopher, stating that Christians use words as signs for nothing.[233] Yet Euphranor established that we can form with Locke some idea of a triangle,[234] even though a perfect triangle can never exist in nature.[235] He added that the notion of grace to which Alciphron objects is no more difficult than the notion of force.[236] No idea can be formed of force apart from body, motion, and outward sensible effects: Berkeley drew on his reading of the Leibniz-Papin debate in the *Acta Eruditorum* about the proportion of forces, and used Torricelli's work.[237] Similarly, there were difficulties in forming an adequate notion of chance or fate which the atheists say formed the world;[238] whilst defining human personality is as difficult as defining the three persons of the Trinity to which the minute philosophers take most violent objection.[239]

Crito's summing-up regarded the essence of free-thought as being the denial of God's existence.[240] He thought doctrines like those of Spinoza were absurd, resting on arbitrary definition of concepts like making natural right to be natural power.[241] Men were not machines, miracles were not allegory, vice was not to be condoned.

Berkeley's dialogue provides an excellent summary of the state of debate in the great cause of God and his world in the 1730s. In probably the finest literary piece produced by the debates, Alciphron incisively characterizes the shifting positions of the free-thinkers and penetrates the superficial mentality of some deist and atheist thought. The book handles its theme not with the crude dogmatism of the tract writers, nor with the patient and prolix earnestness of Cudworth's scholarship; it instead belongs to an age of wit and clings to the guise of equity and permissiveness. The book allows the free-thinkers to gain no victory in the course of the argument, but yet it manages at times to sustain the sense of expectation that they might be able to stir Crito and Euphranor from their own beliefs. It is difficult to know what motivated the work. Berkeley probably saw it as a necessary part of his career as a churchman to combat what many took to be the leading evil of the age, in the days when the works of Collins, Toland, Tindal, Chubb, Woolston and others were freely discussed. It might have been the natural result of the piety he professed, which Pope remarked upon. It might have owed something to his philosophical interests, where he brought his knowledge particularly from the *Theory of Vision* to bear upon one of the most important speculative problems of his day. It may also reflect Berkeley's undoubted concern about the drift of society towards less wholesome standards and morals. It may well be that all of these thoughts were somewhere in his mind as he sat in America writing the book.

There has been sufficient Berkeley scholarship not to need lengthy review of his career or other philosophical writings here.[242] Critics have often remarked upon the mixed reception Berkeley's works have received: seemingly the champion of orthodoxy, Berkeley far more than Cudworth, was attacked as a sceptic, an innovator, a deist in disguise. From the Berkeley of the *Dialogues between Hylas and Philonus*,[243] through the Berkeley of the *Letters to the Guardian* in 1714: from the *Essay towards preventing the ruin of Great Britain*,[244] an attack upon luxury, to *Alciphron*, we have the works of a dedicated apologist who saw it as his mission in life to refute scepticism, loose living, and atheism, in all its guises. Yet as Bracken has shown, Berkeley by 1733 already had a reputation as a fool, an atheist and a sceptic.[245] Mill thought Berkeley had made the refutation of free-thinking 'the leading purpose of his career as a philosopher',[246] and Sillem has shown that he produced a cogent set of arguments proving the existence of God, some of which we have analyzed above.[247] Others disagreed, and felt that in his attempt to develop and alter Locke's philosophy, a philosophy which had already been developed in dangerous ways by Toland, Berkeley had gone too far towards scepticism and the doctrines that Hume was to foster.

Gueroult sees in Berkeley the programme of Trinity College, Cambridge: 'renover l'optique, la géometrie, le calcul infinitesimal et renforcer les pieux sentiments'.[248] J. O. Wisdom less convincingly sees tensions and psychoses manifest in Berkeley's writings and his belief in the utility of tar water as a medicine.[249] Johnstone draws upon the notebooks to trace the development he sees in Berkeley's thought.[250] Olscamp joins in the hunt for the men represented by Berkeley's classical names, and gives informative study of Berkeley's relations with Shaftesbury and the deists.[251] Amid all this work there remains only Pucelle's introduction to the French translation of *Alciphron* which is wholly concerned with the most perfect of his dialogues, and even this fails to analyse the arguments in detail or place them in their literary and intellectual context.[252]

The contrast with Cudworth is interesting. Berkeley gives far more to wit and style, and far less to authority: more to logic and scepticism, to repartee and debate, than to the heavy erudition of convoluted argument. He seems less worried by the range of ancient heresies Cudworth noted and saw reflected in a few modern authors venturing to support their ancient predecessors, and seems far more worried by the passing of these arguments from the Cudworth collection, and from modern debate, into common language and discussion. Where Cudworth chose to ignore the atheism of the tavern and the brothel, Berkeley centred Lysicles's character around the many fashionable rakes of his own day, and treated his threat to Christianity with great seriousness. Lysicles is a character of extremes: a youth who believed the age of Hobbes had been an age of compromise with the civil magistrate and the secular Church. He is all that a rake should be, all that a man of fashion had to be, intent only on the truth of passions and liberated pleasure.

It is to Alciphron that we must look to discover the speculative heresies that Berkeley most feared. Berkeley is determined to show that atheism is not a unified world view, that it is not as precise and positive as one of the four great heresies propounded by Cudworth and Wise. It is rather a set of trifling objections and mannerisms that lead men from deism to atheism. Berkeley perceived the disease of the time to be the illusion that reason's writ ran everywhere, and that reason was represented by the trifles that free-thinkers spoke of in coffee houses. Deists came to scorn miracles as being akin to dreams and fancies; to scorn Providence because natural philosophy seemed to show that the world was a well-regulated and self-perpetuating machine; to question the immortal soul from physiological studies, and to doubt rewards and punishments from a temperamental arrogance and a virulent anti-clericalism.

Berkeley's free-thinker turned naturally to the arguments proposed by those men the Bishop and his friends most feared. He turned to Hobbes for his linguistic attack upon the idea of incorporeal substance: and to Hobbes for his attack against popery which he extended into an assault upon all established Churches. He used Coward to attack the immortal soul, and Toland for his references to the druids. Travel literature provided information for the sceptical argument from comparative religion, and Spinoza furnished him with pantheism. Leibniz and Descartes were behind mechanism and the attack upon Providences after the first Creation. The literature against witches and apparitions, against miracles and revelations was all used by the free-thinkers who denied the value of books or authorities.

The evidence of natural philosophy was invoked by both sides. Crito believed that Boyle, Locke and Newton were sufficient proof, if proof was needed, of

Bacon's contention that depth of scientific enquiry leads to religious belief. Crito sides with Clarke in the Leibniz–Clarke debates, whilst the deists side with Leibniz.[253] Leibniz had begun the debate with the intention of discrediting the Newtonian hypothesis, arguing to Queen Caroline that it derogated from the wisdom and power of God by calling upon him to intermeddle in his Creation so frequently. Clarke had countered that it was Leibniz who did God more injustice by making him so remote and the universe so mechanical. Berkeley sympathized with the Newton-Clarke position.

The English tradition adhered faithfully to Newton against Descartes and Leibniz. They had some use for Descartes's dualism, but never agreed on the whole with the severity of his mechanical hypotheses. They were beset by the image of God as King, well regulating his subjects and his country. This difference between English and continental speculation was as much a theological and religious difference as it was a scientific one over the nature of the universe.

The free-thinkers not only espoused differing views of the world and its formation. They also took a more cynical view of politics, championed particular causes like those against the clergy, tithes and the universities, and advocated the new economics of vice and luxury. The free-thinkers to Berkeley believed happiness to be a thing of this earth, to be pursued by Machiavellian dealings; to the Christians happiness consisted in a well-ordered and harmonious society pursuing salvation in the world to come for all its members.

Berkeley's main argument for God came predictably from his own work on vision, and in a novel argument to the apologists' repertoire. The language of God, the language of sight, could not to Berkeley's mind be explained by any atomic or effluvial theory. The philosopher seemed to try to make a new gravity out of light, a new force which was neither strictly occult nor intelligibly mechanical, a force capable of sustaining a new mathematical and impregnable proof of God. He seemed little concerned to expose the errors or discuss the merits of the two conflicting theories of light offered by physicists of the preceding century, asserting neither Huyghens's wave theory nor the rival geometrical theory.

Lysicles's chemist friend is an example of Berkeley's subtlety in building up a character and damning him at the same time: he damns him for questioning religion on the basis of theories half understood and glibly passed on by word of mouth. Crito has no real answer to the quibble on a scientific basis, and shows how Berkeley saw science as hostile to his cause if materialist, but otherwise friendly and useful, if it left open areas of divine competence as Newton had done, and as Berkeley felt he himself had done with his treatment of optical matters. The dissension between Leibniz and Papin was a useful conflict for Berkeley, who illustrated from it the way in which sciences craving certainty only managed to find uncertainties and quibbles. He was pleased to show that so-called scientific principles were as dubious as theological ones. But in this respect Berkeley leant heavily towards pyrrhonism, for his reasonings brought both theological and scientific concepts into doubt, rather than directly helping to strengthen the former. Such a treatment gave more credence to the view of Berkeley as an apostate than to the view of him as a faithful apologist.

Alciphron is a delightful example of good intentions going astray. Its intent was probably genuine, to strengthen true religion; its reception was equivocal. The idea of the dialogue was Classical, the impact to some minds subversive. Unlike a tract or a sermon, the dialogue gave the free-thinkers the right of reply, even if that reply were restricted by the inexorable logic that inevitably leads to the demolition of their case. It was that little concession to the free-thinkers, and the wit and raillery Berkeley deployed on their behalf that reflects the difference between the atmosphere of 1677 and the atmosphere of 1732, and explains why Berkeley was more strongly criticized than Cudworth had been. The world of 1732 was nearer judging itself by free-thinkers' standards than the world of 1677 had been. Imperceptibly philosophical argument led men astray, and Berkeley's logic, to him reaffirming God the more successfully, to others seemed to open the way to Hume. Men would have done better to have shared Whiston's scorn for metaphysics, than to have pursued more philosophical and more modern arguments. For as *Alciphron* said, it began to seem inevitable that 'as men abound in knowledge they dwindle in faith'. Besides this, Crito's acid remark that 'In the present age thinking is more talk'd of, but less practised than in ancient times' seemed but a vindictive response.

If kingship was never established, what was I beseech you? Had we no government? Nor could it be, you say: also then for your ready, and easie way to establish a free commonwealth, what will become of your standing council? If no certain form of government can bind our posterity (as you affirm) then is it free at any time for the people to assemble, and tumult, under the colour of a new choyce.

Sir Roger L'Estrange,
No blinde guides
(London, 1660), p. 11

1 Populus est fons et origo Potestatis omnis civilis.
2 Inter principem et subditos pactum semper expressum vel tacitum intercedit, et si Princeps desit officio suo, subditi pactione sua non amplius obligantur.
3 Si justa et legitima Potestas migret in Tyrannidem, aut seciis geratur, quam ex lege divinâ et humanâ oportet, omisso omni jure ad imperandum, abrogatur.

The first three articles of
the 1683 Oxford denunciation
(Univ. Oxon. Arch T B 28)

Not that I am in the least of Opinion with those, who hold Religion to have been the Invention of Politicians, to keep the lower part of the World in Awe, by Fear of Invisible Powers; unless Mankind were then very different from what it is now: For I look upon the Many, or Body of our People here in England, to be as Free-thinkers, that is to say, as staunch Unbelievers, as any of the highest rank.

J. Swift, *An Argument to prove
that the Abolition of Christianity in
England, may, as things now stand, be
attended with some inconveniences*...
(London, 1708) from Swift's
Works, edited by H. Davis
(Oxford, 1939), vol. (ii), p. 34

Chapter Three

ATHEISM AS A POLITICAL CAUSE

The fear of atheist principles, as Cudworth and Berkeley acknowledged even more comprehensively than the frantic pamphleteers and journalists of their respective generations, ranged across all the disciplines adopted and fostered by human enquiry. Following the restoration of Charles II in 1660 many of men's energies were directed towards understanding the causes of the political and social break-down, and towards taking evasive action against intellectual and physical disturbances of the peace. Their efforts were made the more strenuous by the succession of political theorists and practising politicians keen to question if not to topple the shaky framework of the reformed body politic.

Perhaps the most widely detested and feared thinker in England in the later seventeenth century was Thomas Hobbes.[1] Men wrote book after book against him, and not merely against his general determinism, atomism and materialism that we have already seen condemned. They were also annoyed and worried by the political theory that inhered in the *Leviathan* and to a lesser extent in his work on the laws of nature.[2] The terms of the Oxford denunciation of 1683 were concerned with the way Hobbes seemed to found sovereignty upon the people; a range of critics thundered disapproval against Hobbes's tyranny, his amorality, his grounding of human nature on fear and baseness, his mistaken view of political activity, and his argument from expediency rather than from morality.[3] Their interpretations have received support and evoked hostility down to the present generation of Hobbes scholars. But Hobbes was not alone in being able to upset the precarious balance of the post-Restoration polity by his political, moral and social theories. He and his fellow radicals managed here, as elsewhere, to evoke storms of protest. In their critics there was a common mistrust of motives; there was a precarious alliance between Toryism, Anglicanism, social conservatism, the new orthodoxy of the Revolution and the Lockian establishment against subversion from all sides. The old guard and the young men out to make a reputation often wrote to defend the Church. Against a background of the struggle of Whig and Tory, against pamphleteering which reached a peak over the Popish Plot and the cause of the Exclusion, and another peak over the Revolution, the banishment of James and the foundation of a new constitution and monarchy limited and balanced by other powers, there was a constant barrage of opposition to those who carried their Whig views to such extremes that they verged on anarchism; against those who were so foolish as to argue for a republic or a despotism, or who were atheistic enough to argue for a method and science of politics divorced from the theological and moral restraints that still usually operated upon it.

There were those who with Milton refused to acknowledge the flood of royalist sympathy engulfing the country; men who continued to praise the constitutional experimenters, the men who sought a new way in place of the old monarchical system. Milton, unlike many of his contemporaries, did not hasten to trim as the Restoration approached; instead he rushed to condemn his colleagues, friends and compatriots who seemed determined to accept a restored king. Milton attacked virulently the royalist ethos[4] of Griffiths's sermon, preached before the Restoration: in a pamphlet of 1660 he espoused the 'good old cause'[5] and demanded that England and Englishmen remained free of the expense and the tyranny imposed by royal bondage.[6] Even after the Restoration, despite the Proclamations against the regicides and the hostility of the King to the remaining republican politicians, Milton continued his opposition bravely. He faced the strictures of Sir Roger L'Estrange,[7] and was later to have his name canvassed in the great debate about the authorship of *Eikon Basilike*:[8] he soldiered on to the end as a man advocating a dangerous and discredited cause.

The Restoration government took Milton's radicalism seriously: amongst the frequent proclamations against seditious works, his were frequently cited. Milton's cardinal offence was his vindication of the regicides, a vindication of bloody crimes perpetrated by traitors and debauched men.[9]

The animus of the post-Restoration decades against religious and political doctrines that might be inimical to law and order is reflected in a collection of 1663 that collated the dangerous views of Calamy, Baxter, Jenkins, Caryll, Case, Mashall and others; views that had been expressed over the preceding two decades.[10] The editor felt that Baxter had made the people judge the incapacities of the Prince[11] and had denied the English monarchical system of government.[12] White had argued in favour of the dispossession of unlawful princes,[13] whilst Calamy had suggested that all the royalists had fought to subvert religion and liberties.[14] All these had to be condemned.

Running as a repressed refrain through the whole debate was the fear of Nicolo Machiavelli.[15] Machiavelli[16] offended tender consciences by penetrating political hypocrisy, and turning to analysis of what he considered to be the real motives of politicians: the wish for power, ambition, and the satisfaction of glory and riches.[17] He set himself against the mirror for magistrates' tradition,[18] he was unwilling to reiterate time-worn phrases exhorting princes to moral good and just policy unless it were expedient to adopt such factors. Many of the arguments against Machiavelli had been long canvassed: Campanella's book of 1636 was in part aimed against the Florentine.[19] Running behind the debates concurrently was the dislike of Hobbes's denial of the independent existence of good and bad beyond the existence of the words themselves,[20] and his idea of words as counters for reckoning with, not to be valued on the authority 'of an Aristotle, a Cicero, or a Thomas . . .'[21] His old Stoical notion of government as an imposition of an arbitrary kind contradicted the more acceptable view of government as ordained by God, a necessary pillar of order, even a natural phenomenon that had to function as well for the good.

The whole nature of political and social theory had been profoundly influenced by the Civil War. The outpourings of revolutionary millenarists and radical Presbyterians had had their effects upon the intellectual climate, whilst the signs of dissolution and decay, the evidence of butchery and disorder, had genuinely frightened the generation that lived through the period 1641–60.[22] The Restoration itself brought not only the revolt against enthusiasm, soon in the popular mind to be accredited with all the ills of the period as sole or prime cause, but also a conservative revitalization. As students of the Restoration have remarked,[23] politics and religion were characterized by a revival of the Laudians and their recapture of the Church machinery from the Presbyterians; what has not often been noted however is that a similar attempt was made to revamp an ideology of the establishment and to banish for good the intellectual excesses of Levelling and declaiming that had gone before. For whilst it was eminently possible to put the clock back and to regain control of local society through the purses and prejudices of the county squires, whilst it was possible to redistribute Church patronage, to bring forward a strongly traditional Cavalier Parliament and to see the land once again as the prerogative of a social élite qualified by education, birth, wealth and stature to rule, it was more difficult to erase from memory the utopian schemes and radical ideas thrown up by the Revolution. Yet it remains true that the old Leveller schemes and Digger dreams, republican imaginings and sectarian hopes were forgotten or dismissed in all but a few isolated cases.[24] Press licensing and the self-imposed censorship of the gentlemen and landed proprietors ensured that there would be no return to 1642, despite the Whig cries over Exclusion, and the armed Oxford Parliament.

Nevertheless, not all could be forgotten. When the Restoration period opened there was a great work to be put on foot, a work of explaining and assimilating the events and ideas of the past hectic nineteen years, to make sense of them, and to order them for the benefit of society, or to remind men of their glorious Protestant heritage. There was a flurry of historical writing, at its most magisterial in Clarendon, but works by Sprat, Hobbes and others were not without their value;[25] Burnet a little later added yet another classic that was to prove a most popular book.[26] Thomas Sprat, Bishop and fellow of the Royal Society, urged a competition for the best historical narrative and analysis of the Interregnum and wars. Hobbes's *Behemoth* suggests that its author felt historical account was a necessary concomitant of philosophical analysis, and a useful addition to his defence of *de facto* powers and his political theory expounded in *Leviathan*.[27]

As theorists and historians tried to sift the rubble left by the civil wars, some to save their own reputations, some with a more laudable grasp of political realities and a higher sense of intellectual vocation, their theories became subject to that usual process of scrutiny by their colleagues. Men as always were ready to pounce on the slightest deviation from an unagreed consensus in order to stifle their views or their reputations, and to point the dangers that often inhered in too radical a view of the political process. The two that most evoked a storm of protest were Thomas Hobbes of Malmesbury, and the republican and pamphleteer, James Harrington. It is one of those sad ironies of history that Harrington, far more influential than Hobbes in his treatment and explanation of the Civil War, should have been neglected whilst modern studies burgeon with book after book on Hobbes. For both these men were significant political theorists; Hobbes was more of the philosopher, Harrington more of the meddler in affairs and the pamphleteer. Both of them shared the dubious distinction of being regarded by many of their contemporaries as atheists.[28]

Hobbes worshipped sovereignty on earth rather than the powers of heaven. He saw that religion led only to dissension; that priesthoods were merely tiresome threats to the laws and the order imposed by the King; that any claim to a supernatural power and his dictates here on earth could disrupt the peace of the commonwealth. Hobbes was not prepared to tolerate such disruption. Even if a ruler were an infidel, the subject should obey him;[29] for faith in Christ and obedience to the secular laws are the only two essentials for salvation.[30] The effect of his early reading of Euclid, his love for the logic of mathematics in political science, and his fear of civil disorder, persuaded[31] Hobbes that an undivided sovereignty was essential; this necessitated a rigidly erastian state.[32] His contemporaries could but think this was immoral; and worse, that it undermined the foundations of all true government, which had to be based upon the powers of the divine ruler.

Hobbes later attempted to claim that his book, which seemed at the time to defend *de facto* powers, was a work of apologia for monarchy and even for the Church of England. With the hindsight that 1680 could bring, and with the friendship that John Aubrey could offer, Hobbes could then say, 'a book called *Leviathan*, was written in defence of the King's power, Temporal and Spiritual, without any word against episcopacy, or against any bishop, or against the public Doctrine of the Church'.[33]

He was strictly correct; he chose his words with great care but with little efficacy. His works were still a kind of contraband; friends and foes alike traded in them, and they seem to have circulated widely. We know that Aubrey was circulating Hobbes's life in November 1673 when he sent it by ox wagon,[34] and he tells us that in that year Hobbes was published at Amsterdam.[35] England was getting the works of its greatest philosopher from across the heretical seas.

The attributions of atheism made by many against the few are written off as unimportant by Raab. He suggests that

> To ask whether Harrington (or Machiavelli, or Hobbes) was an atheist is to ask a false question. The point about God is not that he is non-existent, but that he is irrelevant. The theme of this whole work has been the retreat from God in the realm of politics, and in this campaign Harrington was an important figure.[36]

There is some truth in this view for the student of political theory alone, but Harrington's difficulties with his critics do reflect the much larger debate to which political theory was thought to contribute.[37] John Rogers, for example, argued that Harrington sought to free men from the restraints of God and the King in order to rule the people himself. Rogers thought this akin to the kingdom of anti-Christ on earth.[38] It is in a sense an unimportant question to ask whether deep down Harrington, Machiavelli and Hobbes were atheists who nightly and daily denied God, but it is not a false question; the distinction Raab draws between non-existence absolute and simple, and 'the retreat from God in the realm of politics' is not as easy as he implies; for still remained there the threat of a retreat from God in economics, social studies, natural philosophy and even in theology itself. To contemporaries it was a vital question to know whether or not a man were an atheist, because if he were he had no morals and therefore his views could never be trusted.[39] It was even more vital to read everyone's works with an eye not to the truth in Raab's sense of the limited truth about politics deducible by secular theorists, but in the sense of the overall truth of the world picture and the theology that the views reflected. It is impossible to agree with the categorical assertion that the generation of Halifax thought only in terms of 'interest' and never in terms of divine justification.[40]

An idea of the working of the political system in terms of interests and pressures did not preclude at least moral maxims about oughts and shoulds for the political process, nor did realization that interest lobbied and effected the process preclude a view of overall divine plan. Secularization was a long process, and was by no means attained by the age of Halifax. For the age of Halifax was also an age of the defence of Providence, divine laws and cosmic plans. It was still an age that moralized over every earthquake, and feared the debauchery of the kingdom meant an imminent end to its fabric. It was an age that does not allow facile characterization.

Thomas Hobbes's desultory progress through the anti-atheism literature of a century has been studied in part by Mintz, but as we have seen, it continued long into the eighteenth century. The arguments raised against Hobbes were aimed against four prevailing errors that men perceived in his works; those of determinism, ethical relativism, pessimism and scepticism. He was pessimistic in that he thought men were motivated by fear and greed; he implied that they did not therefore operate on the basis of Christian principles and that the whole Christian framework was a sham. He was cynical about the role of the magistrate, seeing him imposing a religious code for social convenience as he saw fit to keep the people in order, and was not intrinsically correct or upright. He was a materialist who saw the world determined by the nature within it, and not overruled in its day-to-day operation by any moral powers. His scepticism, expressed through his linguistic philosophy threatened so many clerical positions, asserting as it did that a statement had to have empirical evidence to support it if it were to have any meaning. This made of revelations, apparitions, ghosts, witches, and other spiritual presences so many fantasies and false notions; it endangered hell, heaven and so much else. This was telling destruction for one man to wreak, and accounts for the violence of the reaction against him.

Few of the attacks upon Hobbes stopped at pointing out the worst possible consequences of his intellectual positions; many did not even stop at pointing out the way in which Hobbes shared views in common with Spinoza, Blount, Gassendi and the atomists.[41] Men also alleged that Hobbes was evil-living, that he demonstrated the inevitable consequences of materialism and moral relativism, the decline of personal standards of life. It was a rare friend like John Aubrey who had the courage to straighten the record, and show that Hobbes lived a good, even a church-going life.[42]

What men feared most from their politicians and from their political theorists was conspiracy or the suggestion of revolution. They feared, perhaps genuinely, perhaps for political and social convenience, that atheists from Warsaw to Lands End were in secret league aimed at the overthrow of all government, order and religion. They feared having to deal with men who accepted no rule of life and morality other than expediency. They feared the renewed turmoil of society, disrupted as it had been by the sectaries of the civil wars, sectaries who were to many no better than atheists. Contemporary pen portraits stressed the connections between atheist, deist, Socinian and enthusiast, and thought the theoretic atheist a loyal ally and companion of the drunkard, the debauchee, the ranter and the extravagant enthusiast. Every society needs its witches to hunt and denounce; Restoration society was particularly prone to this kind of social animus, living as it did under the terror of civil strife. Men feared toleration, for many Churches seemed coterminous with no one strong Church and therefore with no one, and perhaps with no religion. They feared the whole ambience of social deism (the concern of a later chapter). They above all feared that atheists within a state would capture and hold power by wicked means, and using Hobbes's *Leviathan* and Mandeville's *Fable of the Bees* as sacred texts, would endorse the collapse of the moral and social order. Society, they reasoned, would be remodelled on the lines of an anarchy, or on moral despotism. These fears were often serious; it was not wise to treat them lightly.

The rhetoric of disapproval remained strong well into the eighteenth century, although after the Hanoverian accession the complaints and the recriminations take on more and more the air of social duty, whilst the number of voices dissenting from the great tradition of pious and often platitudinous paranoia increased greatly with the hey-day of the deist movement and the settlement of the Newtonian universe in an Augustan and Classical age.

Political theory too settled down into a Lockian sloth; a sloth that looked two ways, a position that could be represented as liberal or conservative, limited or radical according to taste and fashion. Before the Restoration, and at the time of the Glorious Revolution, even during the reigns of Charles II and James when divine right had still been a dying issue rather than a dead one, political theory had rather more significance than it did in the early decades of the following century. During the Interregnum, theorists were constitution-makers; they were vindicators, they were planners, they were visionaries. They sensed their vital role in forming and developing the political life and form of the Commonwealth. Some new Utopia of Atlantis could be more than a mere pipe dream, more than an argument over the right to rebel, more than some tired vindication of the status quo; they could construct from the rubble of the monarchy some great new edifice of inspiration and planning.

James Harrington was a theorist who perhaps did less to herald or build a new state, than he did to satisfy contemporaries as to the reason of the collapse of the old. His achievement as an idealist should not be displaced, however, by any references to his undoubted skill as an exponent of economic determinism in political affairs.[43]

Harrington's famous agrarian laws asserted that power followed property.[44] Harrington decreed a balance in the State, and thought that if this balance of property ownership were ever upset, then the State would be overthrown, the superstructure replaced with confusion, until such time as a new form of organiza-tion could be developed that would reflect the new balance of property in the State and could balance the constitution anew under the Agrarian Laws.[45] Given the redistribution of land ownership in England and given the break-down in the monarchical framework despite Elizabeth's temporizings, the only solution was to accept the power reality and begin again. Harrington suggested the division of the people into different groupings according to criteria regarding their quality, their age, their wealth and their place of residence.[46] There were to be those who were over thirty years old, to be the elders and the standing garrisons, and those between eighteen and thirty who were the marching armies.[47] There was a division between those owning assets and property to the value of more than £100, and those below that line, called respectively the horse and foot.[48] Geographical units of the parish, hundred and tribe further divided the people.[49] The horse elected to the Senate, the body for discussion and proposal, the foot and the horse together elected to the Chamber of Representatives, who ratified decisions of the Senate to make them law. Priests were to be con-trolled and educated in particular ways, their tenure depending upon the ballot of parishioners, and elaborate checks ensured that the country would not be overthrown by priestcraft and superstition.[50] There was to be no national religion, but toleration was afforded to anyone who did not directly threaten the Christian faith.[51]

Harrington's theological difficulties arose at almost every point in his theory, and extended far beyond his anti-clericalism which could even at times prove extremely fashionable. There was his favourable attitude towards the work of Machiavelli, and his interest in Hobbes whom he sometimes affected to admire.[52] Whilst he continuously stressed his hatred for Levellers and anarchists, he was deeply associated with the Republican movement and this was scarcely the best pedigree he could have found.[53] There was his attack upon the idea of good and bad government, and his far-reaching revision of the Aristotelian view of politics, particularly of the Aristotelian classification of constitutions, removing the category of perversions from the language of theoretical politics. His view of society was deterministic; governments could never be absolutely bad or good, they could merely reflect to a greater or lesser extent the substructure of the societies they ruled, and thereby prove themselves more or less stable, more or less efficient and long-lasting. Any such analysis of policy in terms of power, and society in cynical terms of brute forces was a radical movement away from a politics grounded on principles and Christian morality. There were finally his particular recommendations in ecclesiastical policy, and especially his far-reaching toleration; this was criticized on the grounds that it may even have included Muhammedans and Catholics, and it was therefore an invitation to licentiousness, and in the end to the decay of good government and organized religion. The case against Harrington appeared as irrefutable as it was wide-ranging.[54]

Harrington was the leading figure in an important political club that met on the eve of the Restoration to discuss constitutional matters.[55] Nevill and Wild-man were members of the Rota, which met between November 1659 and February 1660 at Miles's coffee house in New Palace Yard, Westminster.[56] In January Pepys attended the meetings, along with several other London society men and politicians. The club seems to have been dominated by Harrington himself and his theories: when they came to consider Milton's *The Ready and easy way to establish a commonwealth* Harrington put his own objection forcibly that 'there is not one word of the ballance of property, nor the agrarian, nor the rotation'[57] in Milton's theory. Others preferred to attack the main theme of Milton's republicanism, asserting that 'you believe liberty is safer under an arbitrary unlimited power by vertue of the name commonwealth, than under any other government how just or restrain'd soever if it be but call'd kingship'.[58]

Harrington brought his own commonwealth to the club for debate under the resolution of December 20th 1659, when it was agreed that a model of a free State should be debated.[59]

Here the club members debated the proposition that the balance of property was at the heart of the power in the State,[60] and progressed to discuss toleration,[61] religion[62] and military affairs.[63] Harrington developed through his writings and through the discussions of his club all the facets of his theory and all the arrange-ments of the State he wished to establish. Decrees and orders of the Committee of Safety were drafted:[64] decrees which the reader of the Bodleian copy summed up in the words 'a piece of roguery'. The ways by which a free and equal com-monwealth could be introduced suddenly were explained in graphic detail;[65] the ballot was introduced for voting in the Rota meetings and its efficiency extolled for the benefit of the future Oceana.[66] Harrington was careful to avoid the taint of Machiavellianism, although by his references and his way of writing he hinted at it frequently and mocked and derided those who condemned his master.

> Certain it is, that where any private citizen or free man might not (some way or other) propose, there never was a well ordered commonwealth.
>
> . . . So went it in the Protector's time, in every revolution since. La fortuna accieca gli animi de gli huomini, but that is atheisme, that's machiavel.[67]

Harrington was one of those leading protagonists in the great debate about republicanism and the constitution that occurred in pre-Restoration England.[68]

It is most instructive to compare Harrington's theory with the Christian commonwealth of one of his staunchest critics, that ubiquitous divine in the realms of learning, Richard Baxter. In 1659 Baxter sent his own political tractate to the press, and along with the usual noises against Hobbes and his *Leviathan*, there appeared in it many pages of specific refutation of Harrington's position and suggestions.[69] The list of indictments provides us with an interesting guide to what a critic, starting from entirely different premises and interests from those of Harrington, could make of his work. Baxter, a keen exponent of a commonwealth created to worship God and his wonders, an advocate of the rule of the godly, and of the approximation of the rule on earth to the rule of the saints, disliked everything about Harrington's model for sure government which attempted merely to find a system of devolving power in such a way that a quiet State could be created. Religion to Harrington was basically another possible source of disturbance, and so it was to be neutralized by the policy towards the clergy, and by the toleration of differences within certain limits or norms of acceptability.

Baxter's *Commonwealth*[70] lost little time in turning to refute the commonwealth of his fellow theorist. The Puritan turned to extrapolating from Harrington's model to see what logical deductions followed from the theories propounded. The logic of Harrington's view was

> *1* The world by dissenting may make God no God, that is, no Governor, of the world; and so he holdeth his government on our wills. *2* If his doctrine be true, the law of nature is no law, till men consent to it. *3* At least where the major vote can carry it Atheism, Idolatry, Murder, Theft, Whoredom, &c. are no sins against God. *4* Yea no man sinneth against God, but he that consenteth to his laws. *5* The people have greater authority of government than God. *6* Rebellion is the sovereign power in the multitude. *7* Dissenters need not fear any Judgment or punishment from God. *8* Cannibals and atheists are freemen, as not consenting to God's government. *9* Men owe not any subjection, duty, or obedience to God at all unless they make themselves debtors by consent. *10* ... No man need not be damned if he will but deny to be a subject of God.

Such startling deductions as these did not please the trim and godly Puritan divine. To Baxter the fundamental of life was knowledge and apprehension of God the Creator,[71] and of God the sovereign ruler of man;[72] his main consideration was how to erect God's kingdom on earth in a satisfactory way.[73] From this central truth political aphorisms could be deduced, on how to make a State suitable to the ideal of human nature and conduct represented by Christian ideals.

Much of Baxter was virulent anti-popery. He hated Harrington for putting Venice forward as a model of an ideal commonwealth, for in Venice whoredom and Papistry abounded.[74] Much of it was virulent hatred for allowing men to choose freely for themselves, for the Puritans knew well that democracy was not the answer until a wholesale reform of manners, and a complete change in human nature had occurred to create the perfect society. Baxter allowed himself to say how the people, permitted to choose rulers in Harrington's model, would choose bad men and not good 'as if we knew not what hard, and scornful and censorious thoughts the vulgar have of Nobility, learning, and all that is above them'.[75] In Baxter's commonwealth the wicked were to be debarred from choosing governors,[76] and a perfect theocracy was to be established[77] beneath God the universal sovereign and his elect on earth.[78] Baxter therefore attacked Harrington for allowing bad men to choose bad and for failing to further his own ideal. Following the Restoration, the works of Baxter became as unpopular as the works of Hobbes or Harrington, only for different reasons. Thus in the Oxford denunciation of 1683 Baxter was condemned for his theories on five counts for his views. Firstly, because he thought of the King as having merely a co-ordinate power that could be overruled by the other two main powers in the constitution, the Lords and the Commons. Secondly, because he suggested that sovereigns who became tyrants forfeited the right to rule. Thirdly, because he thought that power and strength gave men a right to govern, and illustrated the way Providence had favoured and vindicated their cause. Fourthly, because he had suggested that should men dispossess unlawfully their sovereign and then covenant one with another, they would then have to honour their latter covenants. Finally, because he thought that Charles I had made war on his Parliament and therefore forfeited the right to be King.[79] Harrington's work was not condemned in this decree: he had, however, been examined in the Tower of London after the Restoration concerning his republican contacts and schemes.[80]

This proscription of the works of Baxter serves to illustrate the strength of the Tory retrenchment and counter-attack after the Rye House Plot, when streams of loyalist pamphlets poured from the presses, and when the Whigs found themselves in complete disarray and displeasure. It also serves to show the way in which critics of others often were themselves feared by the extreme conservatives, even if they had quite correctly pinpointed the objectionable and the unsavoury in those they were criticizing.

Baxter, in 1683, was certainly in distinguished and varied company, suffering as he did the strictures of a reactionary University determined upon a last fling of loyalism to the Stuart House. For with his book good old favourites like the *Vindiciae contra Tyrannos*, as well as Julian the Apostate, Bellarmine, Cartwright and Travers lay condemned. Amongst the more modern were Milton, Hobbes, Goodwin, Dolman and Hunt. It is interesting that as late as 1683 men were still concerned about anti-monarchist, or even monarchist literature in favour of curtailed royal powers written up to a hundred years earlier. That they condemned Baxter in the same breath as the Elizabethan Puritans or the civil war theorists such as Owen and Goodwin illustrates the way men feared that works outlived their immediate setting, and remained an everlasting testimony to opinions and troubles that were past, but perhaps also to come. The Glorious Revolution did not make heroes of men overnight, but it did something to mitigate the severity of judgements against them.

TOLERATION AND CENSORSHIP: TWO CRUCIAL DEBATES

Whilst theories were subject to debate and discussion as men feared their practical implications, and feared in particular the ways in which they legitimized power, and the ways in which they suggested governments could be changed or could cease to hold popular approval, there were other questions which seemed to have even more immediate consequences; these were the great causes of press licensing, and toleration.

The legislative framework for press censorship up to the end of the seventeenth century was hammered out in Parliament, and consolidated by the work of Roger L'Estrange following the 1662 Act. Parliament was concerned both in regulating the trade and production of books as an economic exercise, and in monitoring the content of books published. Presses were to be licensed, and all books had to be submitted to one of a number of authorities for approval, depending upon their subject matter.[81] Philosophy, religion and natural philosophy, for example, were the prerogative of the Bishop of London and the Archbishop of Canterbury; matters of lineage and arms, for the Master of the Wards; history and politics, for one of the Secretaries of State.[82] L'Estrange began his regime of hounding out unlicensed presses; quaysides were rummaged for illegally imported works, and official imprimaturs became essential to the orthodoxy if not to the well-being of any book abroad in England. Opposition to the Press Acts came from many sides. There was the sullen opposition of unemployed journeymen, printers and illegal masters setting up illicit presses; there were the authors like Charles Blount whose works were printed by trick or illegality; and there was finally the campaign mounted against the whole idea of the Press Acts, a strange alliance of deists, radicals and honest men unconvinced that the present Act was working, tainted as it was with a high Toryism scarcely appropriate after 1689. Charles Blount is a good example of a man who combined the causes of radical Whiggism, free thought, and a strident belief in freedom of expression. Here was a man who had first written on political subjects in 1679 when he had added to that deluge of pamphlets and tracts at the time of the Popish Plot,[83] which feared the joint imposition of popery and tyranny.[84] He had frequently been in trouble with the Censor for his works, although he was to find his triumph when he cheated the unhappy Bohun into publishing a treatise arguing Queen Mary's and King William's right from conquest rather than legitimate succession and the abdication of James. By playing on Bohun's high Tory susceptibilities Blount was able to overthrow the Tory cause and substitute the freedom of his Whig principles. For as the Commons Journals say, this publication was sufficient to remove Bohun.[85] It also aided the cause of those opposed to the licensing laws.[86] Blount helped the repeal in addition by his literary activities, borrowing phrases and inspiration from Milton's *Aeropagitica* urging freedom of the press, and reviving part of the good old causes.[87] Blount personified the fears of the Tories;[88] a man who unfortunately combined nascent atheism with a wish to loosen the restraints of society on the press, marriage, and radical Whig politics.

As late as 1731 the Bishop of Asaph was willing to argue to the Societies for the Reformation of Manners, that the only way to succeed was to stem the tide of evil books from the presses; a palliative Walpole was to try in order to trim the political views of his opponents.[89] But the bishop did not have the best of the argument, and his critics were able to maintain without fear of controversion that the liberty of the press was a right which naturally belonged to men.[90]

Free-thinkers were normally in favour of liberty over the press: Tindal the jurist had gone so far as to argue that if the press were restrained so should the pulpit be;[91] but he basically believed in the need of rational creatures to be permitted to think freely on all issues.[92] Archbishops and bishops were usually on the other side. They were more willing to consider the kinds of reasons urged on Sancroft in a paper in the Tanner collection, where the adviser made it clear that a rigid control over presses, printers and apprentices was essential in the joint interest of controlling content and watching carefully for heresy and sedition.[93] They were supported by ardent or loyal royalists, who argued with Atkyns that 'the liberty of the press, was the principal furthering cause of the confinement of Your most Royal Father's Person';[94] although not all agreed with Atkyns that the trouble with the Stationers was that they were too weak in imposing their controls over the outpourings of the presses.[95] Atkyns wished to return to the patentee monopoly system that had operated under Elizabeth; he clearly hoped for gain himself from this system,[96] and chose to ignore the outrage which monopolies had caused both to Elizabeth and the early Stuarts.[97]

Many of the figures debating the atheist question naturally expressed views about freedom of the press. Locke favoured total liberty, both because the Stationers' monopoly was against the economic interest of the public, and because the principle of gagging men was undesirable,[98] when policy was renewed in 1695.[99] Blount, Toland, Tindal, Milton, all sought a freedom from any embargo upon ideas and a free trade in books. Their involvement often strengthened prejudices against them as free-thinkers.

L'Estrange set the tenor of argument for the proponents of licensing in 1663, when he reviewed the necessity of censorship,[100] and listed a host of treasonable works published over the preceding couple of decades in England.[101] Those on the other side were like Philopatris scathing about the paternalism of the censors:

> Every acute reader upon the first sight of a pedantick license, will be apt to misinterpret the word [imprimatur] and think it signifies no more but that, this book is foolish enough to be printed.[102]

Philopatris reiterated many other common arguments against the system of controls.

James Harrington, when he contributed to the debate in 1692, saw the force of arguments in favour of some kind of control, on the grounds that if there were no Press Acts, the government would have to construct a law of libel, there would be an increase in the number of lawsuits about piracy and copyright, and Dutch printers would be enriched by allowing free imports.[103] Harrington was prophetic of the legislation that had to come in the early eighteenth century, but his argument to continue the existing Press Acts is sufficient to prove that not all supposed atheists would support a removal of embargoes upon ideas, for whatever motive.

It was not only the works of the free-thinkers, however, that necessitated legal action. Catholic books like Austin's *De Devotione* had to be checked: a warrant to impound all the available copies was issued by Sunderland and the books delivered to the archbishop.[104] Medieval works were carefully checked by the College of Physicians under delegated powers:[105] the physicians were keen to control all aspects of their trade for economic as well as for moral reasons. Some, with Philopatris, could see in the designs of those who believed in censorship, designs akin to those of the Catholics themselves, whose cause only thrived on ignorance, an ignorance that could only be guaranteed by curbing the output of the presses.[106] The fever of the Popish Plot brought a cry for a free press, so that the ways and means of the Catholic conspirators could be exposed once and for all without the troubles that they faced with L'Estrange, the licenser. Philopatris invoked the holy name of Milton, and considered the case of Galileo, as an emotional example of the worst Papist impositions that could be made upon true learning.[107]

The cause of toleration evoked similar lengthy debate among men of letters, connected as it was both to theoretical issues of importance, and to practical questions of everyday politics. There were those ready to suggest that any movement in the direction of the tolerationists and the latitudinarians threatened the belief of all, whilst the converse could as readily be stated, that toleration was necessary to peace and prosperity within a state, and an acceptance that there were certain things which only the individual conscience could answer.[108]

The endless invocation of freedom in late seventeenth-century debates could represent either the view of the radicals or of the conservatives. Most accepted the need to limit the monarchy somehow, for there were few genuine exponents of tyranny. There remained only dispute about the extent of the limitation, and the people who were to wield the effective power in the balanced constitution. On the one hand it was dangerous and unfashionable to be republican, unfettered on the other hand divine right theory had little credibility left.

Toleration had not had an easy course during the hectic decades of Reformation, or even under the tutelary spirit of the Elizabethan settlement. Few countries could opt for it as a practical policy in the late sixteenth century and seventeenth century: it had floundered in Poland, and only survived on any scale in territories adjacent to or under Turkish control. Elsewhere partisan feelings were too strong, the issues of principle too deeply entrenched. But in England the abortive attempts of Charles II to introduce greater freedom were forgotten amid the tyrannical leanings of James II's policy. Those who favoured at least a measure of latitude whilst at the same time maintaining their hatred of Catholics and Catholicism came after the Revolution to the fore of politics. The year 1688 represented the triumph of the Lockian view, even accepting the doubts that Laslett has thrown on the date of composition of *The Treatises of Civil Government*.[109] It was a victory over Filmer, and a defeat for the high Tories.[110] Gone for ever as it seemed were claims of absolute divine right, and gone too were the crude defences of de facto powers such as Hobbes had made. The new men looked to property, to liberty, to representative institutions and to control over the executive by a watchful group of land-tax payers. Such a view, whilst not without its critics, evoked little substantial challenge in the political theory of the late seventeenth century, and evoked little hostility in the great debates over irreligion. Men had begun to accept the need for a commonwealth to be organized for purposes of taxation, regulation, order and liberty, without necessarily expecting the commonwealth to fulfil the aims of the godly on earth, or the rule of the saints. The shift in expectations passed unnoticed by the pamphleteers against irreligion, who were concerned only to avoid allegations of enthusiasm and fanaticism against themselves, claims only too easily made if they ventured to construct plans for an ideal society.

Locke's position over toleration was limited, but none the less it made a great impact upon his contemporaries, and was thought by many to be far too liberal even though it excluded Catholics, Muhammedans, atheists and other irreducible schismatics. Locke believed that everyone had the individual right to decide for himself in matters of religion and conscience, but he did not think that political considerations were irrelevant to religion as a more modern tolerationist might venture to suggest.[111] He believed that a government is only established to protect worldly goods, and that therefore men should not follow its religious dictates blindly for they were not guaranteed to provide salvation,[112] but if religious doctrines involved subversive claims then they must be subject to proscription. Locke's theory was answered by the usual pamphlet battle; in particular by Proast who brought allegations against Locke's idea of freedom and against his too liberal a position.[113] But on the whole Locke's views were timely, and they were sufficiently well backed by modern scholarship and the current of opinion; his political ideas were especially fortuitous in the circumstances of 1689, whilst his other general claims in the *Essay on human Understanding* or in the letters on education and toleration were ushered into a world that was almost ready for them, and prepared to adopt him as the new establishment of reason, with a modicum of faith, of order, with a modicum of Whiggish principles, of propriety, with a hint of liberalism.[114] Locke's view of human nature did not attract too much censure. Unlike modern critics in the tradition of Strauss, few of his contemporaries thought of him as a Hobbist.[115] In the euphoria over the Revolution Locke's idea of the growth of property and wealth, his theory which was similar to the labour theory of value, coupled with the pragmatic endorsement of what had become the status quo, was ignored in favour of his social contract, his stress on the role of property ownership, his careful advocacy of a Utopia of liberal Toryism. It was to him that men looked for their interpretation of a balanced constitution and a suitably fettered monarchy. That Locke's state of nature seemed to become more and more like that of Hobbes, that Locke modified his original optimism with more and more pessimism of the very kind for which Hobbes was condemned, often escaped notice, or passed without remark. Locke could do little wrong in political theory; it was to his *The Reasonableness of Christianity* that men turned if they wished to condemn him. It was for his views on reason in religion that he was suspected of parenting the deists; not for his politics that seemed heaven-sent after 1688.[116]

SHAFTESBURY AND THE EIGHTEENTH-CENTURY AMBIENCE

After the settlements of 1688 and 1701, after the abatement of fears of the Great Rebellion and the seventeenth-century crisis, the debates of the early eighteenth-century political theorists had a different, less feverish tone to them. It is true that there was still a Jacobite threat, and still extremists who seemed to want the total dissolution of society, but basic questions had been altered. Where before the understanding of the nature of man had contributed to a study of political obligation, later the main questions centred not on obligation but on the aims and purposes of society. Fear as a motive and as a controlling passion necessitating tight moral or expedient theories of duty and consent was replaced by the pursuit of happiness; the two varied themes existed somewhat uncomfortably together in authors of the late seventeenth century. The tenor of discussion was to relate social theory, ethics, aesthetics and political theory to a general debate in a religious context about the nature and purpose of social organization, devoid of those point-by-point plans for reform of the body politic that had characterized books and pamphlets some fifty years earlier.

One of the greatest figures of the new age was that of Shaftesbury. He extracted from fine and sensitive observations of the world conclusions concerning the aim of societies and the nature of good and evil. Shaftesbury stood between two traditions; convinced on the one hand that good and evil had a real existence which he proved from elaborate consideration of perception and beauty, yet on the other a convinced sceptic about the world. He was a man who sought to establish reason as King where before prejudice would have ruled. He was not as severe as Boyle or Hobbes; his view of human nature was not so pessimistic. Nor did he share the strange mixture of pessimism and optimism that characterized the enthusiasts and radical Puritans who found man irredeemable and deep in sin, yet thought he had every chance were he of the elect to gain eternal salvation.

Shaftesbury illustrates the growing popularity of the argument from aesthetics in his *Philosophical Rhapsody*. He reasoned that there were three orders of beauty. The first was represented by things formed into suitable and pleasing shapes by others. The second and higher order of beauty consisted of the forms that formed such beautiful objects: and the third was God, the form that formed the form that forms.[117] Beauty to Shaftesbury never existed so much in matter, as in the mind that perceived it. Philocles the sceptic was made to agree with this notion of beauty after long argument, and this was extended into the realm of good to establish its innate existence in the minds of beholders.

As Philocles was forced to agree, 'there is no real good but the enjoyment of beauty',[118] and this beauty which is in the mind partakes of the divinity of God who is the supreme beauty presiding over all and making the forms that created beautiful forms.

To Shaftesbury
Every one, of necessity, must reason concerning his own happiness; what his good is, and what his ill. The question is only, who reasons best: for even he who rejects this reasoning or deliberating part, does it from a certain reason. . . .[119]

The mind, the reason, must and does tell what is beautiful and therefore what is good, what is ugly and therefore what is evil. This much is easy to comprehend: the difficulties arise only when men equally deploying their reason find different answers.[120]

In the rest of his better-known work, *Characteristicks of Men, Manners, Opinions, Times*,[121] Shaftesbury had less in common with Berkeley of the dialogue of *Alciphron*. The connections between the arguments of the dialogue of Shaftesbury in 1709, and *Alciphron* some twenty years later have been little remarked upon, but are none the less interesting. Some of the arguments, and much of the style of interruption, division, and scenery wherein the discussions occur, display a certain common spirit.

The *Characteristicks* is one of those literary masterpieces which drew hostility and acclaim for what it professed to do. Attempting as it did to narrate a set of perceptive observations concerning men and manners, to some it appeared to be making of the trite and obvious a high-flown art, a philosophy, which it did not justify or sustain. To others, better disposed, it is a wholly engaging work, setting forth a number of views of men and their world which no one else ever had the courage or the talent to record in print. Shaftesbury's contemporaries did not think that literary criticism was confined to issues concerning the quality of the prose and the depth of the thought and experience: they believed it also had to take into account the general world picture and the quality of the theology inhering in Shaftesbury's or any other author's book.

Shaftesbury retained some views culled from the moral tradition of his contemporaries in his consideration of the State and its nature. He would not accept the Sophists' and Hobbists' theory that the State was a set of artificial conventions, a belief which tended to undermine the whole notion of good,[122] but nor would he agree to what he considered debased Christian theory couching morality in terms of rewards and punishments to be expected hereafter, a normal argument in an age of hell-fire and damnation preaching, which was becoming less popular in the Augustan enlightenment of the Shaftesbury circle. Shaftesbury could not agree with Hobbes that interest and selfishness alone ruled the world: but the other ingredients he introduced were not particularly helpful to Christianity. To aver that passion, humour, caprice, zeal and faction also ruled was to be a little too close to the truth for comfort.[123] Shaftesbury's morality was idealistic: he felt that all men had perforce to court a Venus of some kind,[124] that riot and excess were to be condemned, and that beauty, truth, and honesty were what men should strive towards.[125]

Shaftesbury's position over political theory and the aims of man was less of a difficulty for clerics than his views on wit and social manners, which seemed more conducive than his idealism to dissolution of morals.[126] He committed some other sins; he was one of that tradition that, following Blount and the early deists, insisted on revising common misapprehension concerning Epicurus. He illustrated how the highest good and pleasure to the Epicureans lay in temperance and moderate use, not in riotous excess latterly associated with them.[127] He questioned the whole anti-atheist endeavour through the sceptic Philocles in the *Rhapsody* and went so far as to aver that

. . . 'tis notorious that the chief opposers of atheism write upon contrary principles to one another, so as in a manner to confute themselves. Some of them hold zealously for virtue, and are realists in the point. Others, one may say, are only nominal moralists, by making virtue nothing in itself, a creature of will only, or a mere name of fashion. 'Tis the same in natural philosophy; some take one hypothesis, and some another.[128]

The comparison Philocles drew is interesting: to argue that hypothesis in natural philosophy has the same epistemological status as premise and argument in theology demonstrates the impact of natural religion, and the danger that the clear association of the one to another would lead to such arguments by analogy which previously would have been unacceptable. It was not previously agreed that an inference from a lesser science concerning methods of proof could be transferred to a higher science, especially to the highest of all. To argue that those who opposed it on different grounds thereby increased the disrepute concerning religion was also an interesting view. For whilst theologians recognized that differences between sects weakened religion, it rarely concerned seventeenth-century apologists that their arguments were not compatible one with another, even in the same book. Philocles here expected a degree of consistency between men that one man often could not muster, or even thought desirable. Men like Cudworth and Bentley must have believed that the more arguments and the more possibilities were discussed, the stronger religion would be through sheer weight of learning and opinion.

Philocles and Theocles made their position clearer by demonstrating how apologists introducing innovations into Christian argument invariably came to grief. To them innovation involved incompatibility with what had passed before. They saw that new arguments were regarded as dangers, and perceived the 'common fate of those who dare to appear fair authors' giving some credence to atheist positions.[129] They passed on to consider Cudworth, who suffered for the equity of his views: an equity not always so apparent to later readers, but an equity apparent to conservatives of the day, for Cudworth had dared to express atheist views and even give them some measure of cogency.[130]

Philocles, the critic, was therefore making subversive claims when he denounced inconsistency of principle between defendants of the Christian cause, for what were inconsistencies to some were proof of great versatility and strength to others. The claim that innovation and exposition of antagonists' views was dangerous was a common one, and represents a fair summary of the chances that befell Cudworth, Bentley, and later, Clarke and Berkeley.

Shaftesbury's views were taken up and defended by Francis Hutcheson who was swift to point out those fundamental distinctions between Shaftesbury on the one hand and Mandeville and Bayle on the other.[131] Whilst Shaftesbury shared some of their cynicism and savoir faire, he had defended the ideas of good and bad more clearly than Mandeville had managed, and with the help of his defendants such as Hutcheson he came through less scarred than Mandeville. Hutcheson tried to 'introduce a mathematical calculation in subjects of morality'[132] as many predecessors had, but he also sought to show the ancient philosophers had established the existence of innate moral properties or even entities.

Whilst Shaftesbury was busy with his moral and aesthetic theories, attempting to find a middle way between atheism and the old-fashioned credulity, his contemporary, Bernard de Mandeville upset the world of precious theological conformity with his writings on a range of social and economic matters. His *Modest defence of public stews* had a bad enough title to invite condemnation by all serious-minded thinkers, whilst his open advocacy of profligacy in the *Fable of the Bees* was far worse.[133] Here Mandeville put forward an economic theory that was to remain intolerable morally for many years, until Keynes made a virtue of activity to compensate for unemployment, and again revived the Mandeville position.[134] Mandeville's view was that private vices were often public benefits; that contrary to public opinion which saw the dissolute individual as a threat to the security and well-being of the whole community, the dissolute individual was a positive asset because he injected wealth into the commercial life of the nation.[135] As Phillip Harth suggested in his introduction to the most recent edition of the *Fable*, Mandeville rapidly became to the eighteenth century what Machiavelli had been to the Elizabethans, and Hobbes to the age of Charles II.[136]

It was not surprising that contemporaries reacted as they did. The average verse would proclaim the value of vice aloud:

> *Thus vice nursed ingenuity,*
> *Which join'd with time, and industry*
> *Had carry'd life's Conveniences,*
> *Its real Pleasures, Comforts, Ease,*
> *To such a height, the very Poor*
> *Lived better than the Rich before;*
> *And nothing could be added more.*[137]

whilst the Moral hammered home the message wilfully:

> *Then leave complaints: Fools only strive*
> *To make a great an honest hive.*
> *T' enjoy the World's conveniences,*
> *Be famed in War, yet live in Ease*
> *Without great Vices, is a vain*
> *Eutopia seated in the brain.*
> *Fraud, Luxury, and Pride must live,*
> *Whilst we the benefits receive:*
> *Hunger's a dreadful plague, no doubt,*
> *Yet who digests or thrives without? . . .*
> *So Vice is beneficial found,*
> *When it's by justice lopt and bound;*
> *Nay, where the people would be great,*
> *As necessary to the state,*
> *As Hunger is to make 'em eat.*
> *Bare virtue cannot make Nations live*
> *In splendour; they, that would revive*
> *A golden age, must be as free,*
> *As acorns, as for honesty.*[138]

Mandeville owed a heavy and scarce-mentioned debt to Pierre Bayle; a debt which permeated the whole work of his in answer to Bishop Berkeley's *Alciphron* Dialogues, and his work on religion and the national happiness, receiving scant praise in the Preface and on page ninety-three of Mandeville's book.[139] Nevertheless, he managed to provide a searching and penetrating critique of contemporary views of morality and the nature of man, whilst attempting to clarify the incompatibility between his idea of Christian virtues such as peace, humility, and toleration, and the aims of a nation such as England's embroiled in war, colonial enterprise, and the pursuits of profit. His good intentions and his wisdom about the way of the world are both eloquently expressed in his later works, which take the form of apologias and explications of the *Fable* and the lesser satires.

Mandeville was under no delusions about the nature of the reactions to his books, and his analysis was here sound if cynical. He remarked that to have a book condemned by a Grand Jury nowadays was 'the wrongest way in the world to stifle books, it made it [*Fable of the Bees*] more known, and encreas'd the sale of it',[140] whilst he saw the whole attributions of evil to the work as a scandal invented by journalists peddling their wares and pushing their circumstances.[141]

As rational or as well-meaning as Mandeville seemed, he still bore too care-lessly the marks of the tradition of Hobbes and Machiavelli. He thought virtue to have had its origins as manliness, necessary in a state of nature, and dismissed the claim that virtue came from God in the following argument:

> There is no virtue that it has a name, but it curbs, regulates, or subdues some passion that is peculiar to humane nature; and therefore to say, that God has all the virtues in the highest perfection, wants as much the apology, that it is an expression accommodated to vulgar capacities, as that he has hands and feet, and is angry. For as God has not a body, nor anything that is Corporeal belonging to his essence, so he is entirely free from passions and frailties.[142]

He went on to suggest that Christianity could not flourish as a discipline for an army; that only a perverted doctrine purporting to be religious could instil the necessary bestiality for war. The confidence that bad Christians take in the idea of divine inspiration for their bellicose actions was a grotesque misreading of the Christian message.[143] This was extremely reminiscent of Machiavelli's remarks that Christianity was a feminine religion, scarcely useful for instilling martial values into predatory armies.[144]

The whole of Mandeville's case rested on a naive wish for happiness and irenicism, a sense of the true nature of the Christian ideal, and a mordant wit and cynicism which saw the way the world perverted and then justified its view of the Christian message.[145] It was an irenicism and humility of spirit that urged that the doctrine of the Trinity,[146] the nature of the creed, and the question of free will be left as adiaphora or unknowables; that men be granted a wide measure of latitude in their beliefs, and certainly a toleration for all Protestant sects, including the Socinians.[147] Mandeville combined this opinion with a long attack upon the excesses of the priestcraft, and the way in which the English clergy and other Protestant divines had proved as power-loving and as wealth-seeking as their Catholic pre-Reformation colleagues and ancestors who had first caused the Reformation outbreak.[148]

Here was that very same strand of anti-clericalism, and that rational realization that strife, bitterness and abnegation of Christian values could only be curtailed by a wide toleration, that led almost all his contemporaries to see him as yet another of those dangerous subversives, using the ideal of primitive Christian love and happiness to subvert Church, States, and morality as men knew them. Protest as he may that he was being misrepresented, there was little let-up in the hordes of material pouring from the presses fulminating against him, of which Berkeley's *Alciphron* was only one of the better and later literary masterpieces.[149] Its argument summarized a couple of decades of righteous indignation, journalistic extravagance and clerical fear.[150]

The age of deist politics and the debates about aesthetics was also an age of continuing debate about those aspects of political theory that had so perturbed the critics of Hobbes, the men that had condemned Locke and feared Spinoza. Tindal exemplified the deist political theory at its most heinous,[151] and shows us how in the eyes of his contemporaries it was but Hobbes and Spinoza rolled into one. A typical critic of 1709 attacked his state of nature which was a war of man against every other man;[152] he condemned his making of justice and injustice as an artificial thing that depended upon human contracts and was not divinely inspired;[153] he disliked reason being the only guide in Tindal's idea of religious practice;[154] he hated Tindal's grounding all political power in the people;[155] he associated Tindal's views with Spinoza's, making God to be the whole universe;[156] and thought his institution of civil society out of a state of nature to be an atheist's doctrine.[157] The same connections were still feared; that society should be devoid of divine domination, that morality should be the product of chance and contracts, that the gospel of Epicurus, Hobbes and Spinoza should replace that of the Bible. The debates show great continuity as well as discontinuity: as our critic of Tindal noted, Cudworth had refuted all his views before he had stated them![158]

The debates that these men and works illustrate were complex, but they do express a certain unity of argument and discussion. A man's attitude towards human nature clearly affected his view of the social contract; his view of good and evil affected his attitude towards the aim that the State ought to follow. His view of the clerical profession and the role of the Church reciprocally affected his attitude towards the political commonwealth and the tension of harmony between Church and State, whilst his wishes for the type of political power a State ought to be ruled by reflected both his basic conception of human nature, and his idea of the purpose of civil communities. Similarly, an attitude towards the nature of beauty, and the functions of sense perception, aesthetic judgement, and mental process could also be represented as having relation with natural law, divine rule, and the argument from the Creation and its wonders. The economic thought of a man was integrally related to his attitude towards vice and social purpose, whilst an attitude towards behavioural patterns in society was a contribution to whether men could be trusted, and whether they lived their lives in accordance with principles, innate ideas, and natural law imperatives.

Wherever a man ventured an opinion, he was venturing an opinion concerning the whole debate, and strive as he may to isolate branches of study he was expected to take responsibility for the full consequences of his attitudes.

The traditions we have studied demonstrate the pitfalls that men saw before them in discussing these problems, and show how the various traditions interplayed to shift the consensus of opinion. It is, for example, possible to find the pursuit of happiness as an aim in pre-Restoration writers, but there is not the universal agreement comparable to that which one meets in the second and third decades of the eighteenth century. The nature of man becomes more and more subject to analysis of perception, mental process, and curious natural enquiry; his nature becomes more and more reasonable, less and less subject to the fears and depravities which the Hobbists, or independently the Puritans and sectaries, often believed. The stress on confusion and struggle in human affairs, and in the constant confusion created by providential intervention is replaced by more orderly conceptions.

There were basically four positions which anyone could adopt concerning the nature of man. They could argue with Hobbes that without force and secular coercion man fought and struggled; that he was mean and selfish. They could argue with the idealism of Locke and the more Christian naturalists that man in a state of nature was more amiable evidence of the divine Creation, although this argument could not be taken too far, for its logical conclusion was that of Rousseau that civil society had therefore corrupted him by a confidence trick of the few to enslave the many. They could argue like Hobbes that man was nasty and selfish, but that he was subject to divine retribution and Providence, that special provision was made for all us sinners, and that the elect and reprobate were pre-ordained. Such enthusiastic views were to suffer a marked decline in our period. Finally, they could argue a more prevaricating position, the kind of implicit position taken up by clerical opponents of Hobbes, and opponents of the deistical tendencies of the Lockian type of natural and moral law, that man was a sinner, but that he had redeeming features, and that biblical and miracle evidence showed him through his reason the path to morality and salvation. Man, to those, was neither wholly corrupt nor wholly good: he was an undefined person who reacted to the stimulus of God's goodness.

Further divergencies arose over the nature of good and evil. Just as it was wrong to argue that man was totally and utterly corrupt, whether from the sectary's or Hobbist's position, so it was incorrect to suggest that good and evil were mere names, connected with likes and dislikes, and reflecting social attitudes. Competing theories included that which believed good and evil were natural, and inhered in things, and the more conservatively Christian which thought that God imbued acts and things with good and evil, and with beauty and ugliness. The movement in debate as the period advanced was from discussion of good and evil in response to the Hobbist contentions, to discussion of the nature of aesthetic beauty and the perception of it: a beauty which became coterminous with good, and connected with truth. This long tradition stretched from the early eighteenth century and such writers as Ashley Cooper, through to the classic statements of Keats on his Graecian Urn.

When it came to practical political organization, the debate was conducted within circumscribed limits. Harrington and the surviving Republicans were not respectable: nor were Hobbists and extreme Royalists who favoured unlimited monarchy. Debate continued over the extent and nature of the limitations to be imposed upon a monarch's power. To err too far towards either a Republic or a tyranny was undesirable. Extreme Whiggism, connected as it was with a free press, toleration, and greater liberty, was un-Christian under the Stuarts, but gradually won more and more ground into the eighteenth century, until the cries against it seem little better than hollow rhetoric like that flexed against party in political organization, or become the rantings of the extreme conservatives exerting little influence.

When it came to economics, it was men like Mandeville with their cynical view of human nature who were most heavily castigated. It was unpleasant to argue too strongly in favour of luxury, especially for the poorer members of society: for this threatened social order, at the same time as it allowed theoretical puritans to fulminate against bad manners and corruption. Even explicit and brash commercialism was reprehensible for its hold was certainly never weakened or questioned in economic, political and social debate. When it came to discussing social provision, workhouses, economic regulation, trade and commerce, there were few enough Christians willing to attack the whole premise of thought on these subjects. It was a great indulgence to complain about them elsewhere when the whole society rested on the very kind of operations Mandeville analysed.

What Mandeville most disliked, like Bayle and Machiavelli before him, was hypocrisy. It was the same with Swift who, like Machiavelli, chose irony to expose it wherever he saw it; and it was their exposure of such a prevalent attitude amongst their well-fed, complacent contemporaries, who were willing to muster pious phrases over port and profits from the plantations, that probably did much to stimulate the virulence of the criticism aimed against their work. They were un-Christian for their analysis: there was no question whether they were accurate, and whether they were un-Christian merely because in strict terms they were describing an un-Christian society.

None of those pregnant metaphors like the grumbling hive or the absence of the good husbandman in society saved them from abuse; for it was dangerous to describe any economic and social system that was reminiscent more of the atheist's community of Bayle than of the ordered and comely Christian kingdom. To suggest that all political power was a cunning plot of politicians was unforgivable: political power should or did reflect some kind of natural law and pre-ordained order, and the ruler or rulers, whoever they were, should have a judicious Christian sense animating their legislation and rule, as long as this made no severe inroad into social stability and commercial success. The kingdom of God becomes the kingdom of gentleman, trader, and governor, and the Great Chain of Being survived as a truncated expression of social cohesion, and defence of the powers and privileges animating the English Revolutionary Settlement. To dissent was to err: to be a radical was dangerous; to be a Hobbist, a realist, a cynic or a sophist was to destroy the fundamental of the Christian community and its support for the English gentlemen with their proprietary Church.

Some few, whose lamp shone brighter, have been led
From Cause to Cause, to Natures Secret Head;
And found that one first principle *must be:*
But what, or who, that UNIVERSAL HE;
Whether some soul incompassing this Ball
Unmade, Unmov'd; yet making, moving All;
Or Various Atoms interfering Dance
Leapt into Form, *(the noble work of* Chance;)
Or this great All *was from* Eternity;
Not ev'n the Stagirite *himself could see;*
And Epicurus Guess'd *as well as He:*

from Dryden, *Religio Laici*
The Poems of John Dryden
(J. Kingsley ed. Oxford, 1958),
vol. i, pp. 311–12

But some men will not bear it, that any one should speak of Religion, but according to the model that they themselves have made of it.

J. Locke, *A Vindication of the*
Reasonableness of Christianity, as
delivered in the Scriptures
(London, 1696 ed.), p. 8

We are, from his works, to seek to know God, and not to pretend to mark out the scheme of his conduct, in nature, from the very deficient ideas we are able to form of that great mysterious Being. Thus natural philosophy may become a sure basis to natural religion, but it is very preposterous to deduce natural philosophy from any hypothesis, tho' invented to make us imagine ourselves posest of a more complete system of metaphysics, or contrived perhaps with a view to obviate more easily some difficulties in natural theology. We may, at length, rest satisfied, that in natural philosophy, truth is to be discovered by experiment and observation, with the aid of geometry, only; . . .

from Colin McLaurin, *An Account*
of Sir Isaac Newton's Philosophical
Discoveries (London, 1748), pp.
90–1

Those who describe this one determin'd Course
of pondrous Things to Gravitating Force,
Refer us to a Quality occult,
To senseless words, for which while they insult
With just contempt the famous Stagyrite,
Their schools should bless the World with clearer light.

Sir Richard Blackmore,
Creation (London, 1715), pp. 8–9

Chapter Four

THEORIES OF MATTER AND THE ORIGIN OF THE WORLD

The most difficult and important issue confronting later seventeenth-century natural philosophers and theologians was the question of the origin of the universe and the place of man within God's cosmological framework. It was to this debate that the English philosophers, Sir Isaac Newton and John Locke, were to make their distinctive and important contributions. Their intrusion into the preserves of the theologians and the ancient philosophers caused considerable discussion and controversy, as their contemporaries struggled to assimilate their novel ideas and assess their relationship to the God-ridden universe of their education.

When Diderot, d'Alembert and their collaborators came to publish their encyclopaedia of mathematics in 1789, there were few amongst the intelligentsia of western Europe who would have disagreed with their firm endorsement of Newtonian principles. The Laplacian programme of physical researches was to maintain the broad perspectives of the Newtonian scheme,[1] and even Maxwell in the mid-nineteenth century was in the Newtonian tradition when he advocated as a 'new' method the use of analogy to supplement deduction from phenomena.[2] The system of classical physics had reached its apogee in the fine prose of the French writers: they could force Europe to accept what had been controversial some eighty years before when they stated that the system of Physics established by Newton was now received favourably by all the 'philosophes'.[3]

In their analysis of the Newtonian tradition the French contributors to the great Dictionary recognized the divergent attitudes towards matter, motion and gravity behind the conflict that had occurred between Aristotelians, Cartesians and Newtonians, and they acknowledged the importance of Cotes, Clarke and Gravesande to the spreading and development of the English philosophy. In their account of these ideas they failed to stress the difficulties encountered by so many struggling for a new view of the world, and a new theory of matter and of the origin of the universe. Their excellent narrative concealed the objections that confronted the Newtonians on the publication of the *Principia* and the need to integrate its findings in the classical and theological universe of its contemporaries.

Some hundred years earlier Bentley and Newton had been engaged in an important correspondence that began the efforts to gain general acceptance for the new cosmological ideas. The decades of philosophizing and popularizing that were to follow owed much to the questions and naive requests of Richard Bentley, and the patient replies of his master. No natural philosopher interested in the mathematical problems of force and gravity could afford to omit some general account of the applicability of his ideas to the God-filled world of his contemporaries. If he preferred not to, there would have been many who were all too willing to construe his meaning unfavourably. Newton was aware of the danger, and fought to allay the fears of clerics and reactionaries, both in his general scholia, and in his letters to the First Boyle lecturer.

In Newton's opening paragraph to this published correspondence can be found his often quoted remark that he hoped his theory would be useful to Christian apologists.[4] His later remarks gave early expression to ideas that passed through Bentley as Boyle lecturer,[5] through Cotes's Preface to the second edition of the *Principia*,[6] through Clarke's Boyle lectures for 1704–5[7] to his correspondence with Leibniz in the second decade of the eighteenth century.[8] It was only through this conscious and concerted work that the Newtonian theorists were able to consolidate the position of their ideas at the centre of English metaphysics and science; it was only through a programme of successful popularization and concern with the wider ramifications of the theory that Newton became an important part of the argument from design, able to add weight to the wisdom of God and his world.

Following Derham's efforts to popularize Newton in the early eighteenth century,[9] the task became relatively easy, as poets and prose writers, poetasters and dilettante scientists all strove to celebrate the renowned genius of Newton. They would, like James Thomson, write poems dedicated to his memory on his death in 1727, rejoicing in his victory over the Cartesians:

> *The heavens are all his own, from the wide rule*
> *Of whirling vortices and circling sphere*
> *To their first great simplicity restored.*
> *The schools astonished stood; but found it vain*
> *To combat still with demonstration strong . . .*[10]

and would with Blackmore render in verse the beauties of God's wonders against the Cartesian system propounded in Europe.[11] Desaguiliers would extend the system, and demonstrate its wonders as a model for government, using analogy to show how Newtonianism had favourable social implications.[12] Whilst the battle to establish Newtonian orthodoxy continued, the poets and men of fashion converted in large numbers. A poet like Blackmore, however, would add critical caveats to his praise, lest he be construed as endorsing Epicurean elements in atomism.[13]

Bentley sought Newton's mathematical and cosmological expertise to aid him against infidelity. In reply to Bentley's many queries about the various possible theories of the formation of the universe Newton patiently explained that if the matter of the universe were equally scattered in particles through a finite space then all such particles would gravitate to the centre and form one large mass there, following the laws of innate attraction. If the world were infinite then similarly arranged matter would form many worlds or masses. The atheistic theory that matter united by chance under the impulsions of gravity was not, however, a plausible one: for it was impossible that all shining matter would fortuitously come together to form a sun, and all other particles adhere to form opaque bodies like the earth. Cartesian mechanism similarly failed to satisfy the English empiricists, a mechanism which evolved comets from suns, and planets from defunct comets. The disposition of the universe argued instead an intelligent cause and Creator.[14] Newton's argument thought that deterministic explanations were fallacious, whilst chance could only have produced worlds of chaos and formless configuration.

Bentley's second question produced a similar response. Comets move erratically, and therefore there was nothing innate to all matter that could have made the planets move as regularly as they did. Only a divine mechanic could have set them in such a perfect motion.[15] When Bentley sought a theological deduction from the inclination of the earth's axis, Newton was more hesitant in his reply. He suggested: 'I see nothing extraordinary in the Inclination of the Earth's Axis for providing a Deity, unless you will urge it as a Contrivance for Winter and Summer, and for making the Earth habitable towards the Poles.'[16]

In this respect he tempered his scientific judgement with his wish to aid the Christian cause as much as he could. He said enough to vindicate the excessive anthropocentrism of subsequent Anglican apologia, and enough to show that his first reflection was more impartial and detached.

Newton's second letter underlined the difficulties of Bentley's hypothesis that matter began evenly spread out in particles in the universe.[17] He attempted to define the problem of the infinite in which Bentley had become embroiled. Nobody could hope to discuss the question of the origin of the world, time and matter without deciding whether the world or the universe was infinite or finite. Bentley was in error, said Newton, in regarding all infinites as equal, for the infinite number of units into which a foot may be divided were twelve times as numerous as those into which an inch could be divided. He adopted Wallis's attitude that one must allow proportion even in infinities.[18] It was impossible to decide whether in a strict interpretation infinities were either equal or unequal, but for mathematical purposes they had to be treated as proportionate.[19] Bentley had also been silly to attribute the idea of the innateness of gravity to Newton: the philosopher contradicted him, and added that he did not agree with Blondel for suggesting that if planets were dropped from a distance towards the sun, they would rotate around that body with their present motions.[20] The forces involved necessitated God to turn the planets aside from their course as they dropped towards the centrifugal point.

Newton's third letter explicitly rejected the Epicurean and materialist view of the world. If the materialists were right then gravity became absurd, for it was operation at a distance: but Newton was convinced that gravity acted as if it were a force, and therefore recourse to some immaterial principle was perhaps necessary.[21] Although Newton equivocated, as always, upon the exact nature of gravity, hinting that it could be either material or immaterial, Bentley and his followers read Newton as giving sanction to immaterialist views.[22]

His letters to Bentley are evidence of Newton's concern for the metaphysical consequence of his theory. They show Newton the cautious experimenter and mathematician warning his followers against committing him to too exposed a philosophical and theological view, as much as they show the Christian virtuoso concerned for the cause of his religion. They also illustrate that Newton was prepared to endorse and censor the works of those who sought to popularize his message; he was only too ready to show Bentley where he had been in error over the idea of evenly spread matter, or over the question of infinites, just as he criticized Bentley's failure to prove that the world as we know it had not grown out of older decaying worlds. The letters are instrumental in setting the tone for much of the subsequent debate between the Newtonians, and their antagonists on all sides.

The success of the Newtonian system was assured by the vigour of its exponents as well as by the delight of many Englishmen that they had discovered native mathematical talent to rival and outshine their French and Dutch rivals. It was assured by the dictatorial position of Newton in the Royal Society, by his caution over general and philosophical issues, and by the intricacy and complexity of the arguments of the *Principia*. Followers found it easier to read the book with his advice in mind, often skipping the more difficult passages. Critics found it impossible to fault the basic mathematical logic of the proofs and lemmae. As a corpus of Newtonianism passed into print, it became axiomatic to youth and age alike, and was learned with the catechism and the Christian message. Newton was promulgated in the Schools at Cambridge by the Lucasian Professor of Mathematics, who later published some of his expository lectures on the subject.[23] Successive Boyle lecturers told their congregations of the miracle of Newton's heavens, and hastened their words into print to reach an ever larger audience. By 1728 a printer and publisher had been found for Newton's own simplified version of the *Principia*, which he had studiously withheld from publication. Now that two decades had passed in which the Newtonian theories had been discussed at an elementary level of philosophical and theological interest, there seemed little point in withholding Newton's own simplified scheme which he had reticently kept in his closet.

The Preface to the English translation which appeared simultaneously with the Latin text, announced that Newton had originally planned to publish such a work, but had abandoned the scheme, confining his metaphysics and general reflections to the third book of the *Principia*.[24] Whiston seized the opportunity to hammer home the message by printing a few short extracts from the *Principia*, the work on chronology, and from the *Optics*, in his little book published the following year.[25] Whiston chose his extracts to show how Newton enquired and enquired into the nature of things until he reached the One first cause. He rejected the Cartesian system Newton had so ably demolished, and gave Newtonian examples of the final cause arguments at their best.[26] He thought it silly to believe that the world could have arisen from chaos by the 'meer laws of nature',[27] and he agreed with Newton that 'God without Dominion, Providence, and Final Causes, is nothing else but fate and nature'.[28] To Whiston, Cotes's Preface represented a culmination of Newtonian science in its self-appointed role to defeat atheism.[29]

Newton and his colleagues were well-established members of a respectable English tradition by the time that Berkeley chose to refute fluxions, and to find in the mathematics of infinitesimals black arts hostile to the Christian cause.[30] The Newtonians had fought off the Cartesian threat from the continent, and had managed a long debate against Leibniz to defend themselves from allegations of irreligion and to justify themselves before the Queen. They had become part of the fabric of Anglican apologia by the time of Berkeley's criticisms in 1734.[31]

Berkeley's Queries, aimed against Newton in 1734, reflected a general feeling of unease about mathematics that had been manifest in sixteenth- and seventeenth-century thought. But it was also an attack upon Newton's whole method of procedure, an expression of latent fears about the drift of the world to deism through natural theology. Berkeley asked whether 'it be not a juster way of reasoning, to recommend points of faith from their effects, than to demonstrate mathematical principles by their conclusions?'[32] and 'if certain philosophical virtuosi of the present age have no religion, whether it can be said to be want of faith?'[33]

These propositions shocked many into replying, and a long controversy ensued, where men rushed to the defence of the divine Newton, now established in a body of prose and poetry as the man who had unfolded nature's secrets.[34] The controversies between Berkeley and Jurin and Walton forced others into the fray.[35]

Through his study of ancient philosophy, theology and the classics, Newton had managed to concern himself with the whole gamut of contemporary intellectual problems: by careful and cautious publications he had preserved a reputation not only as a natural philosopher, but also as a Christian. No major allegations were made concerning his anti-trinitarianism, but at the heart of Newton lay a fundamental belief in the power and wisdom of God, an omnipotent, interventionist Deity who influenced everyone's lives.[36] Other Newtonians like Clarke and Whiston, shared many of their teacher's attitudes; they like him were so keen to stress the power and wisdom of the Divine Being, that they fell prey to the Arian heresy.[37]

Newton had been wiser than Whiston, in remaining an outward conformist for most of his life. His rewards came in the eulogy of men on both sides of the Channel, who could echo Fontenelle in saying that Newton had been an honest Christian for most of his life.[38] Fontenelle's *Eloge* was a fitting and accurate tribute: he commented on how 'Sa philosophie a été accepté par toute l'Angleterre', and how Newton had lived to see his own apotheoesis, unlike Descartes who had died too soon to see his own greatness. In comparing the philosophies of the two, Fontenelle gave due credit to Newton's criticisms of Descartes, which were so powerful especially to English minds, but with some rough justice he noted the similarities between the Newtonian position and the scholastic, between the English solution, and the system that Descartes had ousted: 'L'Attraction et le Vuide, bannis de la Physique par Descartes, et bannis pour jamais selon les apparences, y reviennent ramenés par Neuton, armés d'une force toute nouvelle dont on ne les croyoit pas capables, et seulment peut-être un peu déguisés.'[39]

Fontenelle's judgement was undoubtedly tempered by a little reluctance that Newton was not a Frenchman, and was tempered by the realization that much of Newton was not new. He understood the contribution that Kepler had made to the bases of Newton's mathematical astronomy, and acknowledged the debt Newton owed to Flamsteed's patient calculations and observations. Fontenelle had grasped the expertise of Newton's mathematics, gave him full credit in the dispute with Leibniz over the primacy of discovering the method of fluxions, and praised his work on optics and astronomy highly. His treatment of the importance of Newton's work benefits from incisiveness of mind, and a tinge of scepticism that is lacking in some of Newton's more avid English supporters.

Fontenelle pointed to the relevant in Newton in much the same way that we might from a perspective interested in the development of natural science. He found: 'Deux principales dominent dans les *Principes Mathématiques*, celles des forces centrales, et celles de la résistance des milieux au movement, toutes deux presqu-entièrement neuves, et traités selon la sublime Géométrie de l'auteur'[40] and discovered in the *Optics* that 'Cette différente refrangibilité des rayons rouges, jaunes, verts, bleus, violets . . . est la découverte fondamentale du Traité.'[41]

The praise that Fontenelle gave is important not merely for its reflection of balanced standards of criticism, but also for its reflection of a pattern of interpretation that was to become more and more common in Newtonian studies through to Brewster and the nineteenth century: the view that Newton the scientist, Newton the improver of telescopes, Newton the Master of the Mint, was a man at once comprehensible and praiseworthy, whilst Newton the alchemist, Newton the theologian, Newton the incarnation of God's revelation to the world was altogether less intelligible, even embarrassing. The darker side to the Newtonian cosmos, and to the theological world of his successors, is only recently receiving more sympathetic understanding.[42]

It is also interesting in one reared in the Cartesian tradition. In England the activities of men like Wallis, proponents of Newtonianism and critics of the Cartesian scheme, similarly supported the Cambridge mathematician. As early as 1675 Wallis had taken for granted the existence of gravity,[43] and the presence of vacua in nature, whilst continuing Descartes's *materia subtilis*.[44]

The contribution Newton made to the scientific and cultural heritage of his England and his Europe was destined to be most hotly disputed in the realm of metaphysics, theology, and philosophy. His work on chronology betrayed his own interest in these matters, and although he refrained from publishing, the manuscript subsequently became available in Paris and was hustled into print. This work aroused a storm of protest for its unorthodox treatment of biblical chronology. Leibniz attempted through this and other means to associate the whole of Newton with an atheists' plot to subvert the world of learning and then the world of political stability. It was the cry of atheism which threatened the new synthesis.

Newton's published theology was limited to his work of exposition of the prophecies of Daniel and the Apocalypse of John. His exegesis in this work is fairly conventional, associating the four beasts of *Revelations* to the four great empires, two beyond the Euphrates, and two, the Greek and Roman, on this side of the great divide.[45] His chronology made more radical changes. He brought the Argonauts forward by five hundred years, through re-assessing the date of Chiron from old astronomical observations. Newton used contemporary observations and deduced from them that, given the known movements of the fixed stars, Chiron had been incorrectly charted by previous writers.[46] Whilst Halley confirmed the astronomical computations, the French took up the pious cause of refuting them for their upsetting effects on the whole scheme of chronological theology as they conventionally viewed it. John Conduitt had no such scruples. As a close friend of Newton's and his successor at the Mint, he was tainted with the English philosophical heresy, and wrote in his edition of Newton's work how wonderful it was to see 'Astronomy, and a just observation on the course of nature, assisting other parts of learning to illustrate antiquity'.[47]

The occult in Newton that has so disturbed students for decades, was little known to all but a few of his contemporaries. His work on chronology was cited as proof of his wide-ranging talents, but was not on the whole taken too seriously. His essay on prophecy was cited to demonstrate his Christian disposition, and was an especial recommendation in one who was pre-eminently a mathematician with all that that implied. His alchemical work was little known and less discussed. The Newton of the early eighteenth century was Newton the cosmologist, not Newton the Rosicrucian.[48]

Newton's incursion into cosmological debate had a great impact on his generation in England. Before he wrote they argued out the Cartesian universe, and rejected its mechanical self-sufficiency and its dualism of mind and body. They sought solutions in neo-Platonism, empiricism, partial scepticism, and 'the cool candle of the Lord'.[49] After Newton an English orthodoxy settled on the early Augustan age, accepting most of Newton's theology and much of his physics. They took his evidence of a wilful interventionist God as proof of the Creation, and as comment on the origins of the world around them. The orthodoxy did not preclude humane studies. It was no triumph of a genius of science against the follies of the age. Newton's re-writing of the notes to the *Principia* to establish his doctrine on the basis of ancient authorities was not an aberration of his peculiar mind. It was a sincere attempt to make the doctrine acceptable to the classically trained who had insufficient skill to decipher the mathematical lemmae and proofs of the *Principia*, as well as an acknowledgement of the impact of classical learning upon Newton the man and the scholar.

Newton provided an answer to the perplexing problem before the generations after Cudworth: he satisfied men that he gave a mechanical and scientific answer to the problem of the Creation and continued existence of the world without falling prey to the deterministic heresy. He avoided the atheists' position that chance and blind matter produced the world, motion being an essential ingredient of atomic particles. He avoided the heresy which Spinoza and his English disciple Charles Blount were guilty of encompassing, he evaded their contention that matter and motion were coterminous and made motion the agency of God manifest in the world. The Cambridge Mathematician did not travel along the road which Toland and some of the later deists were to follow influenced by Spinoza's and Blount's views. Newton's works were revered where Blount's, Spinoza's and Toland's were burned and criticized virulently.

Where Newton managed through his pre-eminence in matters scientific to avoid any great criticism for his theological irregularities, many of which remained unpublished, his fellow philosopher John Locke was less fortunate. Newton himself originally thought Locke a Hobbist, attacking 'the root of morality' in his *Essay*, but later repented of this view in a letter to Locke.[50] Locke read Newton's *Principia* enthusiastically,[51] and soon became an admirer of its precepts, despite its mathematics which he found abstruse.[52]

Locke's philosophy had given Newton and many others some grounds to fear. They had felt that Locke's statements on morality, and the grounds of good and evil being in pleasure and pain, smacked of Hobbism.[53] They had feared that his strictures against insignificant language, and comments upon the need for ideas to be grounded in the firm reality of observed nature, were similarly Hobbist in their implications,[54] as was his plea for a morality as firmly based as mathematics, Hobbes's own intention in the *Leviathan*.[55] But it was not only the whole form of the *Essay*, or its statements upon the sensitive area of morals and government that had led to this charge: it was also Locke's attitude towards the spirit world and his advocacy of certain sceptical hypotheses.

Locke had, for example, considered the possibility that the senses deceive us: something considered by Bacon, Hobbes and many others. He had concluded that the certainty of corroborated evidence from the senses was all that men needed: a reasonable, common-sense refutation of extreme scepticism,[56] which has more often been attacked for being unhelpful, rather than for being intellectually untenable.[57] He had further argued that all our knowledge came from sense evidence and ratiocination upon these simple observables.[58] It was feared that his clear distinction between faith and reason, and his subsequent argument that faith anyway always had to be reasonable, left too little leeway for religion.[59] These allegations were not entirely fair. Locke had strained to propound the Cartesian view that we know we ourselves exist, and we can prove from this that God exists.[60] He had stated clearly that 'we have an intuitive knowledge of our own existence; a demonstrative knowledge of the existence of God; of the existence of anything else, we have no other but a sensitive knowledge, which extends not beyond the objects present to our senses'.[61]

He had issued a caveat that if God had decreed certain definitions for moral terms then he was not suggesting these were misuses of those terms.[62] He had distinctly noted revelation as a method of perceiving ideas.[63]

Locke had also been aware of the importance of the origin of the world to the proof of God. His attitude here had been conventional and Christian. He had argued that nothing can produce from nothing: therefore something must have been from eternity, a something which could not have been matter or motion or even the two together, for these could not have produced intelligent beings.[64] The First Being must have been cogitative, all-powerful and eternal.[65]

Locke read the *Principia* soon after its publication, and hastened to review the work, demonstrating its force in demolishing the Cartesian vortices and the excellence of its epistemology.[66] Along with the reviews in the *Acta Eruditorum*[67] and the *Philosophical Transactions*,[68] Locke's review was the most easily accessible exposition of Newton's achievement in the *Principia*. Locke was soon convinced that Newton provided an answer to many pressing contemporary intellectual problems but his own enquiries, of equal significance to political theory and the study of human nature and philosophy, were less enthusiastically received when their theological consequences were deduced. Some of his contemporaries hastened into print to prove that Locke was tainted with the deist way of reasoning, even if his direct statement of being was Christian, and this tradition has received some support from Leslie Stephen, from Crous, and from their followers.[69] Hefelbower has come to Locke's support and has suggested that the deists drew their inspiration not from Locke but from Herbert of Cherbury, that Locke himself merely shared a general sensibility in which reason and nature were of fundamental importance.[70] In this he stands against that pusillanimous pamphleteer of the late seventeenth century, John Edwards, who saw Socinian tendencies in the works of Locke, and against John Leland's characterization which believed that Locke had much in common with the minimal natural religion of the works of Shaftesbury, Woolaston, and Chubb.[71]

If we assume that Locke read the books he bought and housed in his library, then we can be sure that he knew of the great atheist debates. He owned Sault's *A Conference betwixt a modern atheist and his friend*,[72] his *Second Spira*,[73] Bentley's Boyle lectures[74] and Lany's refutation of Spinoza.[75] He participated in them in his replies to Edwards, and refers to them by implication in his philosophical works.[76]

The case of Locke rested on his treatment of the demonstration of the existence of God which forms the centrepiece of the fourth part of his *Essay concerning Human Understanding*.[77] His influence was wide and not in England alone; as far away as Italy his reasoning influenced the whole tenor of discussion over the nature of God and truth and human reason. Whilst Locke at home was subject to attack for his irreligion, and even his pupil Berkeley who was both his admirer and his critic was not immune for being a bishop and for becoming a stalwart defender of the faith, abroad his fate was similarly discussed. In 1732 Paolo Mattia Doria spent two volumes in elaborating the very problems of truth and reality in commentary on Locke's *Essay* and Berkeley's *Theory of Vision* that had perturbed early English readers of these works.[78]

Locke's metaphysics were important for they laid down general rules concerning standards of proof and the role of reason which lay behind much of the debate conducted on both sides of the issue over the origin of the world and the nature of matter and motion. It seems likely that Locke was not a serious deist of his own volition, but that his philosophy influenced deists and Christians alike in the early eighteenth century. His *Reasonableness of Christianity* did not go so far as the deists were to wish, but it deployed some arguments that could be construed in their favour. Toland claimed that his *Christianity not mysterious* was a precocious pupil of Locke's own work, a claim which Locke strained to deny but which made his own moderate position much more difficult to maintain with any conviction.[79] Locke hastened to stress arguments from miracles and revelations as well as from reason, in an attempt to dissociate himself from the new liberal school following in the wake of Herbert of Cherbury.

Crippa's interpretation here seems satisfactory. He shows the connections between Locke's ethical idea of the law of nature, and his proof by revelation and providence of such natural laws and codes of conduct that have nevertheless been found out by natural reason.[80] Crippa also discusses the trends of religious thought that help explain Locke's publication of the anti-atheist translation: he suggests that polemics against libertines and fanatics became a way of reasserting the highest realities of the faith.[81]

This view is substantiated by the sympathy which Locke clearly expressed for the views in the *Discourses* which he published in 1712,[82] views aimed against atheist arguments over the nature of matter and the origin of the world. These *Discourses* note how the assault of the atheists upon the immortality of the soul and the Being of God had forced those of a contrary party to have recourse to natural reason and common principles which their adversaries would not deny, in an attempt to refute them satisfactorily.[83] The *Discourses* rehearsed in customary fashion the arguments against matter and motion being coterminous, against the eternity of matter in the universe, and against the idea that the world was the product of chance.[84] They deployed the Cartesian argument of the incapacity of matter to produce reasoning processes, and deduced from this that our souls must therefore have come from a Divine Being since they were capable of functions above the mere prerogatives of matter and motion.[85] The world was such that it must have been the product of a Divine Creator.

Locke's involvement with this work could be seen as a sop to the conscience of his generation, just as his difficulties and his prevarications over his attack upon innate notions thereby also denying the innateness of the idea of God, could argue a Politique intellectual development for the English philosopher. Such a view would be unfair. It is undeniable that Locke's metaphysics and his human understanding, and especially his *Reasonableness of Christianity*, left him open to misunderstanding.

This latter book was attacked by John Edwards for allegedly arguing a Socinian position.[86] The book had stressed the importance of belief in Jesus as the Messiah[87] and had left certain hostages to fortune in statements like 'a great many of the truths revealed in the gospel, every one does, and must confess, a man may be ignorant of, nay, disbelieve the truths delivered in Holy Writ'.[88]

He had said that men did not have to understand many points of the Christian message, for Christianity was not designed for philosophers alone.[89] Despite Locke's detailed and excellent replies, the damage had been done, and his earlier book had been construed against him.[90]

But it is also more probable that he, with the best of his contemporaries, was entirely conventional over matter, motion, determinism, and the origin of the world, and that he believed the line of anti-atheism implicit in the *Port Royal Discourses*. There is nothing incompatible with an attitude against atheism in the rest of his thought, not even the halting signs of interest in the superficially attractive rigour of deist logic. Locke thought he was serving best the cause that some felt he had subverted. Locke's position over matter and motion, like Clarke's and like that of the Boyle lecturers, set the tone for the refutation of heresy in the faction-rent age of early eighteenth-century clerical politics and argument.[91] The similarity of Locke and the Boyle lecturers is striking: they were the new élite, the new logicians of the clergy and theology, the new natural philosophers with the enlightenment of anti-atheism in their pens and minds. It is to the Boyle lecturers that we must now turn, to see the strength of the case against atheism with respect to matter and motion.

THE BOYLE LECTURERS

The Boyle lecturers deserve their own place in any history of the theology of matter and motion, for their lectures more than anything else wrestled with these problems from their inception in 1692 until well into the middle of the following century.[92] The tone for them had been set by Richard Bentley, who used his opportunity as the first lecturer under Boyle's will to expose the errors of Hobbes, Spinoza, Descartes and their followers, not only over the issues of motion, matter and thought, but also over the origin and frame of the world. Bentley sought to reconcile his plea for liberty of philosophizing and the cause of the moderns, with established Christian apologetics.

His theses received a generous accolade of praise. Their usefulness was recognized by all those who further chose to write of the debates, and most agreed with Evelyn who was present as a trustee of the will, that they had erected a very imposing case for the Christian cause.[93] We may discount White's recent criticism that the first lecture was an unworthy piece of raillery unbecoming to his hero,[94] and extend Monk's view of their importance from being merely the integration of Newton into the Christian cosmos, into a commentary upon a set of seminal debates in the relations between religion and science.[95]

Bentley shared Cudworth's passion for amassing every conceivable argument in support of his own, without worrying too much about their mutual compatibility. He refuted his opponents by number and quantity, with hypothesis and empirical evidence, with logical deduction and inherited prejudice. He seemed nurtured on the spirit of Petty and Plato, on political arithmetic and heavenly geometry. He computed willingly the amount of matter required to fill the space in the universe, and demonstrated the vacuum and its necessary existence from differences in specific gravities. He made of Newton's gravitation a personal force used by God to keep the world in being and the planetary system in revolution. He spent page after page working through problems of matter, motion, perception, and the beginning of the world.

In Bentley's work those connections between world views and the underlying theory of matter are explicit. He laid down a tradition, himself probably borrowing from Cudworth, which was to be perpetuated by Gastrell, John Harris, and later Boyle lecturers. He wove a careful path through vitalism and mechanism, through the materialist theory of perception and of the origin of the world, through the theory of blind chance and the theory of fate, through determinism, through dualism, and through the relation of souls and spirits to the material world. He sought to adopt a Christian atomism, to consider hylozoism, and to arrive at the perfect Newtonian providential scheme, which was mechanistic, but allowed God a noble role, which was atomistic, but which had nothing to do with an arbitrary world formed out of the innate propensities of matter. He sought to find that solution to these problems over the nature of matter, which run below the wider debates we here consider, a solution which later Christian Newtonians tempered with some of Locke's metaphysics could all accept.[96]

Bentley was keen to demonstrate in his first lecture the errors of Epicurus. Like many, he relied upon Lucretius for his statement of the Epicurean position, and he extracted from it the materialist theory of perception which he thought to be absurd.[97] This was the very doctrine which men thought Hobbes had set out in the early chapters of his *Leviathan*, and was one which mechanists feared was becoming increasingly popular with the revival of atomism. Baldly stated, it argued that thought and sensation were only so much matter in motion. Light waves or sound waves were motions in particles pressing on sensory organs, and thence on nerves to the central nervous system. Anything perceived was therefore a physical reality emitting atoms which caused an image in the mind. Such a theory, taken as crudely as Bentley took it, was clearly ludicrous. For, said Bentley, given this view Epicurus and Lucretius themselves would be forced to accept the existence of gods, for men had images of gods in their mind. The materialist would have replied concerning the nature of dreams and apparitions, made out of sense experience in the material world, by motions within the nervous system: but Bentley was not to contend with any such refinements.[98]

Bentley's second lecture was dedicated to refuting the proposition mentioned in his first, that motion and matter can think of their own, without needing to resort to God, soul and spirit in Cartesian fashion to explain the rational and spiritual world.[99] The faculties of the soul were too fine to be explained by matter alone; St Paul provided Bentley with a guide, for his was the invective that attacked the Epicureans for their carnal affections, and his the polemic which had inveighed against the Stoics for their pride, presuming as they did to declare 'that a Wise Man of their sect was equal, and in some cases superior to the Majesty of God Himself'.[100] The world could neither have resulted from a fortuitous concourse of atoms, nor could it have existed from eternity. This position was a common one: we find it reiterated in Cotes's preface, where he bemoans the herd of thinkers who argued in this way,[101] and it can be found in many of those pamphlets and discussions which formed the substance of our introduction. Bentley was more of a systematizer than an original mind.

Bentley displays as well as any the value of Cartesian dualism to contemporary religious apologists. While as we have seen the reception of Descartes was somewhat equivocal,[102] and he often had to be defended from atheism for his mechanical world system, nevertheless his and Augustine's dualism was central to Christian thought, as it always had been. The debt Descartes owed to the Jesuits for his theological training, and for the logic of the Catholic Schools, extended deep into his philosophy of science and his basic metaphysics.[103] Many in England were quick to see the use of the *Cogito, ergo sum* argument for God, and chose to remain ignorant of, or to ignore completely, the argument of Descartes's critics who with Arnauld pointed out its circularity.[104] Such a critique was rare in England, where criticism of Descartes, where it fell most heavily, was directed against the fictions of his physics, and his world system, largely from empirical and Newtonian studies.

Bentley set out to prove that 'there is an immaterial substance in us, which we call Soul and Spirit, essentially distinct from our bodies: and that this spirit doth necessarily evince the Existence of a Supreme God and Spiritual Being'.[105] It was largely a premise of Bentley's that thought and will could not be explained by means of matter and motion considered alone; the rest followed at leisure. Bentley reinforced his argument more by wit than by evidence, and asked dryly whether or not we would account it 'a strange and miraculous thing' if the flint and the steel, instead of a few sparks, should chance to knock out definitions and syllogisms.[106]

Bentley was not to be accused of blind Cartesianism, however; he soon returned to criticism of the Cartesian position.

> The Ideas of thought and matter are absolutely incompatible. And this the Cartesians do themselves allow. Do but convince them, that Brutes have the least participation of thought, or will, or appetite, or sensation, or fancy; and they'll readily retract their opinion. For none, but besotted atheists do joyn the two Notions together and believe brutes to be rational or sensitive machines.[107]

His criticism saw the weakness of the dualism with respect to animals: for they too had some emotional and responsive capacity, rendering their being automata most unlikely, or making the distinction between brutes and men more questionable, thereby threatening men with the possible fate of becoming Hobbist machines.

Bentley's conclusion to this lecture offered fatherly advice to his audience. Atheists he thought would be better advised to deny God outright, on the grounds that they cannot see Him, or they should similarly deny the existence of the soul. They should dispute that they are sure there is no God, for if there were a God he would strike them as atheists with lightning. Such arguments Bentley thought more robust than meddling with atheistic atomism.[108] That his atheists did not do so is interesting: it implies that all feared the fifth column of atheism from ancient and modern theories of the structure of matter, more than they feared the fool who forthrightly swore and atheized his thoughts. The atomist, as Bentley well realized, was more dangerous because he was insidious, and difficult to refute: his life would have been easier had the atheist openly denied God because he could not see Him.

Bentley's final three lectures are also worthy of consideration, for they meticulously recited the principal arguments of those who fought the atomistic and Aristotelian natural philosophies for their attitudes over the problem of the origin of the world, and matter in motion.[109] Integral to this argument were the arguments of natural religion and final causes: the beneficial planning of the universe which Bentley continuously stressed, was the finest evidence of all against the origin of the universe being the product of chance, or against the idea that material things had existed eternally.

When Aristotle was subject to late seventeenth-century attack for suggesting that the matter of the world had existed from all eternity, the problem arose over the nature of infinity. Most had to wrestle with this, as we have seen Newton doing.[110] Bentley attempted to formulate an answer satisfactory to his case. He suggested that a thing may be eternal in time, although the time were terminated at one end, but he hastened to add that there was a 'vast difference between the false successive eternity backwards, and the real one to come'.[111] To allow the former was to allow the possibility that the world had existed from eternity, to allow the latter was necessary to permit souls to be eternal. Bentley sought a formula that did not involve him in denying theological imperatives, but which ruled out the possibility he was refuting from the premise he adopted.

The argument between Hobbes and Wallis, one of the most celebrated of seventeenth-century mathematical disputes, was also addressed to this problem of infinity and the origin of the world. Wallis sought to prove that the world had a beginning, by arguing that if Hobbes accepted that there was an infinite number of years in series before he was born, then there must have been a greater number than infinite in the series of years to the present date. This was blatantly absurd, reasoned Wallis, and therefore Hobbes had to accept that the world had a beginning.[112] He here deployed the problem of the completed infinite, comparing it with the uncompleted infinite. Hobbes retaliated by saying that the same argument could prove that God must have had a beginning, and concluded: 'Thus 'tis when men intangle themselves in a Dispute of that which they cannot comprehend.'[113]

Locke tended to Hobbes's view, arguing that perplexities and contradictions were the natural consequence of such an incomprehensible thing.[114] and venturing that

if these men are of the mind, that they have clearer ideas of infinite duration, than of infinite space; because it is past doubt, that God existed from all eternity, but there is no real matter co-extended with infinite space: yet those philosophers, who are of the opinion, that infinite space is possess'd by God's infinite omnipresence, as well as infinite duration by his external existence, must be allow'd to have as clear an idea of infinite space as of infinite duration; tho' neither of them I think, has any positive idea of infinity in either case.[115]

Locke seemed to cast aspersions upon both conceptions of infinite; a scepticism which some cruder minds could construe as anti-Christian.

Bentley examined also the perplexing problem of the proposition that nothing can be made out of nothing.[116] This phrase, taken from Lucretius, had become a crucial one in late seventeenth-century debates about these questions, and it was often examined closely to see whether, as some thought, it supported the idea that matter must have been from all eternity, or whether as the Christians stressed, it demonstrated the need for an omnipotent God to create all. Bentley, worried by this ambiguity concerning atomic doctrine, returned to consider it in the second of his three lectures on the origin and frame of the world.[117] He reasoned that God was necessary to the Epicurean system to make sense of its otherwise pointless materialism ruled by blind chance. He reasoned that much of the atomic doctrine could be proved satisfactorily on a scientific basis, but that the metaphysics that previous atheistic wits had placed behind the atomic theory failed to make sense. It was true, undeniably, that matter was atomic in structure, that there were vacua, and that gravity was the force which held matter in being in its rotations and movements. It was true because the divine Newton had demonstrated much of the Epicurean theory, and recognized his debts.[118] Nevertheless, it was not true to say with the Epicureans that gravity was caused by a property in matter itself, for it seemed beyond disbelief that gravity should come from anything but the wisdom, power and providence of God. Mere matter could not act upon mere matter without contact; if we admit an occult property such as attraction at a distance it requires the supernatural to explain it.[119] Bentley saw in Newton both the light of revelation, and the logic of the mathematical initiate.

Francis Gastrell shared many of Bentley's beliefs.[120] He too attempted to out-flank the materialists by resorting to an even more severe materialist theory of perception. For, he reasoned, if we hold notions of the infinite, the eternal, and the omnipotent, these must have been created by the reality itself forcing the perception upon our senses. This can be further supported by the argument from universal consent, for even the Hobbist, the Sadducee and the deist admit a God.[121] Gastrell recited the Bentleian problems, with less precision, and with more tired prose rhythms. He saw that either God must have created the world, or else matter had to be eternal, whether formed into the shape of the present arrangements from the beginning, or changed during time by the motion of matter.[122]

Gastrell, however, turned not only to his predecessor's Boyle lectures, when he was drafting his own; but also to Cudworth, although he admitted neither source in his text. He lifted verbatim much of Cudworth or took his arguments from Bentley who himself owed a large and unacknowledged debt to the Platon-ist. Gastrell even used Cudworth's philosophical argument concerning the necessary existence of a perfect Being to infer the existence of an eternal and perfect God, stating as Cudworth himself did that the argument would probably not obtain universal acclaim.[123]

Dr John Harris similarly took up the cudgels against the materialist theory of perception when he came to refute atheism in its various guises.[124] He took Hobbes's *Leviathan* as the most important work of this genre, and read it to say that we can perceive nothing that is not the object of sense. Harris ridicules Hobbes for this belief, for seeming to say that therefore men with long noses and acute eyes were more intelligent than the rest of us. Harris failed to distinguish between Hobbes's belief that men ratiocinate on the grounds of their sense perceptions, and the sense perceptions themselves, which by no means formed the sole content of the Hobbist mind. Harris did not wish to understand the anti-scholastic, and as some thought anti-Christian, distinction Hobbes was making between true empiric reasoning, and false knowledge taken from some other source than the mental evaluation of empirical information.[125]

Harris used Locke's metaphysics and the arguments of Cudworth to prove the existence of God, in their adaptation of the Cartesian proof. Locke was used for the argument from authority, and the argument from our own Creation: Cudworth and Descartes for arguments centring upon the certainty within us that we exist, and from this the certainty that others exist, and that God necessarily exists as well. Similarly, Harris borrowed from his predecessors the notion that we could form an idea of God if he did not exist. He cited Locke with approval, to articulate the notion that 'people whose thoughts are so immersed in matter, and who have so subjected their Minds to their senses, that they seldom reflect on anything beyond them, are apt to say that they cannot comprehend a thinking thing'.[126]

The fault was all with the materialist: it was his limitation that he refused to see the separate existence of spiritual entities, and his own particular obtuseness that refused to acknowledge the argument *ex hominem ad Deum* ('from man to God').

The Boyle lectures were perhaps the best sustained of all the attacks upon those who erred over matter and motion, but they were not wholly concerned with this cause. Where Bentley and Harris, Gastrell, Samuel Clarke and John Hancock would spend most of their time refuting the *Deus est res extensa* of Spinoza or the doctrines of Toland and Blount, where Harris would seek to vindicate the mechanical philosophy from unfair aspersions, and where all of them would borrow from Locke, Cudworth and Descartes to help prove their metaphysical cause, their colleagues would be concerned with very different problems.[127] John Williams thought that Moses threatened to become another Gospel;[128] Samuel Bradford felt it necessary to prove the credibility of the Christian Revelation aginst deist allegations;[129] and Offspring Blackall joined his cause at the turn of the century.[130]

But the seriousness of the atheists' threat through the works of Epicurus, Democritus, Spinoza, Blount, Hobbes and Toland was not underestimated by the lecturers or by their fellow pamphleteers. They were only too well aware of the trouble that the ideas of Lucretius could cause, and the way in which natural philosophy misdirected could lead to irreligion. If they often borrowed one from the other, and if their position advanced little on that of Bentley who in turn did not add a great deal to Cudworth, they can be forgiven. It was not that they were bad at their task, but that Cudworth, Bentley, and later, Samuel Clarke, were so comprehensive, and provided so adequate a treatment of the debates that centred around the origin of the universe.

ATHEISM IN MIND AND MATTER

Beneath any attitude towards the formation of the world and functioning of the universe there was always a precedent theory of matter. It was difficult to argue about the causes and nature of attraction, the existence or non-existence of the void, or the nature of the movement of matter, without thinking of some uncompounded irreducibles which would facilitate discussion. Similarly it was impossible to think constructively concerning the relation of thought to sensation in the material world, without some understanding both of spiritual and physical things themselves. Competing theories here as elsewhere characterized the seventeenth-century experience. One set of criteria that had to be applied to them, in addition to critical criteria concerned with evaluating their scientific merits, was concerned with their theological acceptability.

The importance of atomism in seventeenth-century physical sciences cannot be overestimated. Atomism in one form or another was an essential part of both the Cartesian and the Newtonian worlds: it was there in Gassendi, Boyle, Clarke and many lesser scientific and philosophical thinkers.[131] Variation was both possible and manifest: Boyle's idea of corpuscular motion[132] differed greatly from Willis's view of life as a 'subjugated flame'.[133] Nevertheless atomism, Christianized but with suspected atheistic leanings, was a dominant influence. As McMullin has shown, a theory of matter is crucial to any philosophical system: it is as important to theories of the origin of the world and the nature of physics, as an understanding of the nature of man is important to a political theory.[134] Boyle's earnest efforts to expose the errors of atomism, both for the weaknesses of the argument[135] and for the exclusion of God,[136] illustrate the fears and the fascination. The wisdom of God was manifest, to Boyle, in the smallest of atoms,[137] but the atoms of Epicurus and Hobbes could not have come together to have formed a world.[138]

Gay has thought that there were roughly three competing positions concerning the relationship between matter and mind in the late seventeenth century: Cartesian dualism, Spinozist unified substance, and the intermediate Newtonian–Clarke position believing that matter is separate but subordinate to spirit.[139] There is a measure of truth in this oversimplification. More importantly, there was the growth of a certain consensus in favour of one of many possible forms of a basically atomist view of matter. It is a misinterpretation to see in the rise of mechanism a ready and inevitable progress of Epicurean atomism from ancient and heretical sources. McGuire's work has demonstrated rather that fundamental to Boyle, Locke and Newton was the idea of the analogy of nature and the Great Chain of Being, thereby offering a classical Platonic and medieval origin for the metaphysics of post-Restoration science.[140] His crude contrast between the continental scepticism of Bayle and Leibniz towards the material universe, and the English empiricism which believed in use of analogy to travel from the observable to the unobservable, is too simple; but there is value in his scholarly findings in connection with Newton's use of analogy in the third rule of the *Principia*.[141] It is also salutary to remember that scepticism could be as serious a threat to natural philosophy as to religion.[142]

The fortunes of a broadly atomic doctrine, whether directly derived from ancient authors, or whether arrived at by way of analogy, or even through logical imperatives, waned and prospered alternately during the century, but the movement was probably generally strong in their favour. In the early seventeenth century it was the face of Democritus which most affected the contemporary philosophy. Bacon was impressed by his works, and lesser men of letters took up the Democritean cause. Democritus gave to Bacon the style of the aphorism as well as temporarily a doctrine of matter.[143] It is with Gassendi and his English epigone Walter Charleton that we see the more marked influence of Epicurus: Democritus died after the flourishing of pseudo-Democritean literature, the euphoria of the Renaissance scholars, and the brief interlude of influence over the Lord Chancellor of English wits.[144]

Gassendi's great *Syntagma* became one of the most important source books for atomism. It was aimed at an erudite audience and sought to prove that Epicurean doctrines could be Christianized: in England it was diffused by various thinkers not least of whom was Walter Charleton. His work entitled *Physiologia Epicuro-Gassendo-Charletoniana* has as its sub-title *A Fabrick of science natural, upon the hypothesis of atoms*. Published during the Interregnum, it was an important work for the dissemination of Epicurean ideas in England.[145] After the Restoration Epicurean atomism remained theologically dangerous, tainted as it was with the sybaritic life and the idea of a deterministic explanation of the universe. Men read Lucretius with greater and greater interest; others attacked the whole fabric of the world seen through these ancient eyes, as being wicked and immoral. But despite the antagonism still manifested against the underlying metaphysics, and against the associations of the sources, the general idea of a universe of atomic matter in motion within a large vacuum of space grew more influential amongst natural philosophers. Boyle's work on the air pump and hydrostatics seemed convincing enough to the English scientist.[146] The vacuum was an undeniable, almost tangible, reality. Within this context the rejection of Leibniz's monads, and the derision poured on the Cartesian universe, is intelligible.[147]

Atomism remained a broad framework of reference. It could include thinkers as diverse as the near-Cartesians of the Power and Towneley circle, and the middle-way Newtonians. It included the corporealism of Boyle, so called in a desperate bid to make the doctrine acceptable theologically, and the downright materialism of the Hobbists.[148] It was difficult to think of a rival hypothesis that could maintain its ground by the last quarter of the century. Hylozoism, plastic natures, world souls all seemed to be dead.

The success of atomism was by no means new, or even sudden. Its early successes have been pointed out admirably by Mr Kargon, who shows how the Raleigh group and the Great Tew circle before the Civil War both flirted with it, whilst the connections between Hobbes and Charleton on the one hand, and Gassendi and the Paris circle on the other during the mid-century troubles further strengthened its support.[149] The Gassendi group took the battle against the Cartesians into the heart of the enemy's camp, and tried to convince them that there was only one form of material particle, and not three different types as the Cartesians liked to suppose.

It became axiomatic that matter was formed of an infinite number of indivisibles. Such a view fostered the growth of mechanism, and men sought to explain all events in terms of the action and movement of particles. All that remained was to define the nature of the irreducibles; for such a definition affected the whole metaphysic that could be based upon them. Some thought that atoms were only invested with the properties of indivisibility, hardness and elasticity. Then there were those who wished to add motion to the innate characteristics, while yet others wished to add gravity or some other attractive or repellant force. The inclusion of these latter two could give rise to allegations of an atheist's plot: for if matter could move or could be acted upon mechanically, what need was there of God? Could not the world have been formed through the actions of such innately determined materials?

The Newtonians modified the atomic mechanical orthodoxy, aware of both its inadequacies in explaining the world, and its theological deficiencies in leading the unwary towards determinism and heresy. They introduced something of the Stoical view, and attempted to argue that forces other than those created by the collision of particles operated upon the atoms. The Toulmins see this as a complete refurbishing of the atomic doctrine in the light of changed experimental circumstances. It was also a significant one in the relations between atomism and religion.[150]

Those who sought to make motion an attribute of matter came in for the roughest criticism. Gastrell, for example, borrowed from Bentley and Cudworth to suggest that there was an important distinction to be made between motion, perception and will on the one hand, and solidity, extension and figure on the other. Gastrell thought that motion was completely distinct from matter, and impressed upon it from outside. If matter were coterminous with motion, then it must follow that every particle of every piece of matter must always be moving. Such an idea seemed preposterous.[151] Gastrell managed to combine a certain Aristotelian common sense in his physics, which saw that many bodies and particles were at rest, with a belief in Cartesian dualism that kept the world of motion and mind apart from matter and mechanism. He did not conceive of motion of a particle within a seemingly hard and resting body; if the body did not move, then neither did the atoms within it.[152]

Harris re-echoed this view. His common sense managed to find cause for laughter when he suggested that he could as well conceive of a bullet when it lay at rest, or of a stone when it lay idle, as he could of a bullet projected through the air, or a stone thrown as a projectile. Harris ignored the relativity of motion which meant that even his stationary stone or bullet was moving continuously within the planetary system.[153]

Anyone who adopted the Spinozist position was even less well off than those adopting Toland's idea of matter and motion being conjoint.[154] If substance were both cogitative and extended, then the logical deduction would be that each atom of matter could think independently of the rest. Bradford replied that 'then there must either be no God at all, or else every particle of matter must be a distinct God by itself'. He preferred the orthodox view that the human soul was both immaterial and immortal in that it partook of parts of the divine nature.[155]

Samuel Clarke consolidated the Christian Newtonian position.[156] His logic brought to a successful conclusion all those arguments that Bentley had begun; he summarized the debates in propositions and lemmae about matter and motivation, motion and perception, that had worried his generation incessantly. Opposing Hobbes, opposing materialism, opposing Spinoza, attacking Blount and hounding out pantheism, Clarke found that he could defend liberty against blind chance, fate and determinism. He reasoned out a Newtonian Christian atomism, whose central theme was the divine attributes and the Being of God. With this mighty synthesis there were those that felt the work of apologia complete. Others dissented, and saw in Clarke nascent deism.

Anyone looking back to the work of Cudworth would be impressed by the width and penetration of his scholarship, and would admire his tireless energy against atheists. But he had not been blessed with life in Newton's England. Cudworth may have dictated the scope and nature of the problem of atheism to subsequent generations, and shown them how error in any small branch of learning could grow like a cancer to trouble the rest, but he did not dictate the solution. His theory of intermediary plastic natures or principles mediating between spirit and matter, between God and atoms, was to prove a short-lived expedient in the rapidly changing literature of Christian apology. In Bentley and Clarke gravity replaces plastic presences, and matter co-exists with thought in almost Cartesian fashion. Descartes had become an illustrious man: scorned for his physics in England, he was none the less praised for his Augustinian canons on matter and thought. Whilst his cosmology was derided, his metaphysics was probably more influential surreptitiously in the 1690s, than it had been explicitly in the 1650s.

When Derham came to record his views, he gave full exposition to the ambivalence concerning Descartes in England. Whilst attacking the Epicurean hypothesis, and the Cartesian account of matter in motion offered as an explanation of the rational soul, he added:

> Although I charge here the folly of the atheist, that perverts the Cartesian scheme . . . yet I am far away from charging the great Cartes himself with atheism; who, as foreseeing what might be charged upon him, or perversely drawn from his principles, seems to have taken particular care, to let the world know he was far enough from being an atheist: that in treating of natural things, although for the sake of free philosophising he doth (not deny but only) exclude the consideration of final causes, and of God the supreme cause (that being rather the business of a Christian divine than philosopher).[157]

Derham here developed a mature distinction between two different types of scholarly enterprise, and realized that they both needed a separate vocabulary and method of treatment. Such a view would have been all the more radical or impossible some thirty years earlier. The defence of Descartes on the grounds that if he did not express himself in any derogatory way towards the faith then he was not expected to be an apologist was surprising. For many the whole method of seeking out secondary causes in place of primary ones was inimical to religion. It led to a changing vision of rational explanation, away from divine interventionism, away from divine control, towards a concatenation of secondary causes from pre-existent dull matter. Derham's wish for philosophical liberty was very fine, but could have the dreadful consequences many opponents feared.

Derham's unfortunate slip in implying that final causes were not the preserve of the philosopher was not taken very seriously either by himself in his self-appointed dual role as theologian and natural philosopher, nor by his English contemporaries. His equivocation was also theirs; Descartes had had many fine perceptions and some of his metaphysical and methodological views were important for the growth of true knowledge. He was therefore not to be condemned, but excused for his other opinions, on the ground that liberty of philosophizing was highly commendable.

If Descartes could be reasonable in some respects, there was even the suggestion that Epicurus, Lucretius and others were not as bad as they appeared at first glance. Some theologians saw the way in which their ideas were capturing the hearts and minds of their generation, and therefore sought to Christianize them rather than atheize their followers. John Leng struggled with this conclusion through worrying over the efficacy of the argument from the universal consent.[158] If all men had believed in a God and this gave us the best proof of his existence, then Epicurus could not have been at all influential among his contemporaries. He was not prepared to go so far as to make Epicurus harmless, as Gassendi had done, but he sought to make Epicurus a solitary fool amid a universe of religious men.[159]

Others of a more radical mind would seek to vindicate the more seemingly atheistic of the Epicurean views. They thus hoped to outflank the disopprobrium of atheism in a way different from that pursued by the Newtonians and the Boyle school, who sought to modify atomism to take it beyond its atheistic associations.

The necessity of Christian views channelled and restrained natural philosophers in their thoughts over matter, motion, and the origin of the world. It could be argued that the restraints were productive, and the theological as well as the logical need and the empirical wish to go beyond Epicurus and Lucretius,[160] Democritus and their later exponents, aided the development of Newtonian thinking over gravity and action at a distance, while it forced men to go beyond the sterile mechanical form of their later seventeenth-century conclusions. It could equally well be argued that the theological restraints alone did no more than deter men from publishing certain views, or involve them in acrimonious controversy if they did publish them; that it did not substantially affect their scientific opinions. This is to erect hard and fast lines of division where the seventeenth-century mind would not make them, and where people like Derham in the eighteenth century would only make them as part of a radical move to free science from the restraints he obviously felt did operate. To Newton and the Newtonians the idea of a theory of matter and of the origin of the universe apart from consideration of the nature of God would have made little sense. Their natural philosophy did everything it could to strengthen the intervention of God in what was very much his Creation.

Few would doubt the first creation of the universe by an all-powerful God. Few could accept the Spinozist pantheism, and move with Blount and Toland towards some favourable reception of his ideas. Many would dispute the nature of the world God had created, and the way he kept it in being. It was in these debates that a general atomism settled as a conventional view, but a view that allowed much freeway.[161] In England Descartes suffered from criticism, but made up some lost ground at the end of the century when people selected passages from his books and used these for their own purposes. Even Maclaurin, writing in 1745, felt Descartes was very influential, though his work was dedicated to illustrating the superiority of the Newtonian system.[162] Anyone who thought motion an attribute of matter was condemned, but the Newtonians were permitted to argue for attractions and repulsions operating at a distance on particles, with major attacks only coming from the continental Cartesians.[163] Anyone who thought all things of the spirit as well as of matter to be one substance varied in an infinite number of ways was guilty of the Spinozist heresy.

Apart from these deviations men were comparatively free to discuss the world, in the light of their agreed knowledge that it had been designed and created by God. All that remained for them to argue was how best it had been arranged to reflect his glory, so that apologia could come naturally from free philosophizing. The dawn of the eighteenth century was the dawn of a great age of minimal consensus, when to everyone the arguments of natural religion were of telling power, but all else was cause for great controversy as to whether it strengthened or weakened the faith. Many took these pragmatic considerations to be the best means of assessing the relative truth or falsehood of scientific opinions.

Ah! my loved God! In vain a tender youth
Unskilled in arts of deep philosophy,
attempts to search the bulky mass of matter;
To trace the rules of motion; and pursue
The phantom Time, too subtile for his grasp!
Yet may I, from thy most apparent works,
Form some idea of their wondrous Author:
And celebrate thy praise with rapturous mind!

From James Thomson,
*The Works and Wonders of
Almighty Power*; Thomson,
Works (OUP, 1965), p. 483

Chapter Five

THE ORIGIN OF THE EARTH

Atheism in Genesis and Geology

To the seventeenth-century biblical chronology, the account of Moses, and the science of geology were all part of the same world of learning. No one seeking to enquire into rocks or minerals, into earth history or the formation of the earth's configuration could afford to ignore or deny the value of his primary source, the Bible.[1] All that men could and did strive to do was to reinterpret the Mosaic account in accordance with their own understanding of the biblical text, and with their own findings from non-biblical sources, mainly from the evidence of fossils.[2] On all sides there was a desire to reconcile scripture and natural philosophy, for there was the growing feeling that the miracles and wonders of the Creation provided the best of all arguments to prove the existence and being of God. Authors of natural histories could point to the excellence of each plant and animal, to the beauty and utility of its contrivance, and deduce from this the wisdom of the Creator. It was these arguments which John Ray and Bishop Wilkins perhaps did more than any others to foster: but their works are only the best of the studies of nature and of the philosophical deductions made from these, representing a tiny fraction of the work being done all over England by a host of collectors, dilettanti and clergymen.[3]

By the early eighteenth century the enthusiasm was such that Sloane from his central position in London attempted to direct massive local researches all over the country into the flora and fauna. Letters survive illustrative of the volume of correspondence and hopes that was engendered by this enterprise, letters mainly to and from country clergymen telling of their plans and their imperfections in the task of gathering information.[4]

Dr Hans Sloane was one of the greatest collectors and men of scientific curiosity: a man who represented on a large scale the interests of many lesser gentlemen, vicars and country experts on natural philosophy. Sloane used his position as Secretary of the Royal Society and his knowledge as a doctor, his knowledge of herbs and of the human anatomy, to fulfil his wish to collect and compare the botanical and zoological specimens of many countries, counties and climes. He compiled lists of Indian and Japanese curiosities;[5] he kept a cabinet of minerals,[6] and received such works as the *Historiae Plantarum Helveticarum* from a correspondent in Switzerland who dedicated this compilation of Swiss plants to him.[7] He noted the growth of various kinds of fungi in places like the Bishop of London's garden at Fulham,[8] and kept a catalogue of the seeds sent to Dr Breynius for his use.[9]

Correspondents often sent Sloane materials for his collections and his interests: '2 strange sorts of water insects' came in a bottle of preservative with other insects from one friend[10] who cared to remain anonymous: whilst the large fly, the artificial flower, 'a sort of root growing in Siberia in a place called Shamansky' and the other things sent by Mr John Bell came on the express condition that Bell's name be recorded in the list of donors to the Sloane collection.[11] Sloane loved to record the growth of his own collection; in one manuscript we can see him carefully adding up 1850 specimens, and then placing them into different categories. He boasted at this stage some 95 types of bee, 17 kinds of water bugs, and 31 father long legs.[12]

Sloane and his colleagues were not merely collectors of rarities and banalities, however. They also directed the effort of the Journals like the *Philosophical Transactions* in reviewing and advising on the books of theory and practice that could bring order out of the bric-à-brac of their cabinets; the order of under-standing to add to the meticulous order of their catalogues and indexes. About the year 1695 a review of Scilla's book on marine fossils was drafted, as the author felt that this book, though old, had not been sufficiently read and noted with its views on the fossil problem.[13] Similarly Woodward's book was recommended to readers as being an interesting account of the history of the earth.[14] A man like Catesby would be employed to write a natural history of Carolina for the Royal Society,[15] and the *Catalogus Plantarum Horti Academici Argentinensis* was reviewed favourably.[16] Sloane's library,[17] his interest in the contents of the Leyden physic garden,[18] his correspondence with men from all over the globe on Royal Society business, made him as important a scientific intermediary as Oldenburg had been. The interest in Sloane is merely that he exemplified in a later decade the spirit of the collector, the spirit of the men who provided the evidence, the rarities and the information, out of which our geological theorists had compiled their grand theories of the earth. It was this basic work of corres-ponding, digging, walking and hiking, of pillaging the countryside and collect-ing foreign remnants of the ancient earth, that fired the theorists, and provided them with their captive audience, keen to read of the great movements of the world that produced these different rocks, minerals, animals and fossils.

It is true that Sloane was not the first of the collectors, nor is it fair to suggest that where Oldenburg would have solicited views on the vacuum or on a recondite mathematical problem Sloane would have preferred a catalogue of plants. For the age of Oldenburg was also the age of Aubrey; the age of Huyghens was also the age of collecting mania at court and in the country. Just as the antiquarians under James I had sought salvation through manuscripts and books, and with Cotton had joined the fervour for great libraries, precedents, and fine judicial points, so the age of the Restoration brought with it the mania for rarities of a different kind. Plot pillaged Oxfordshire; Lhwyd was keen on augmenting the Ashmolean collections; public and private concerns built up their supplies of rocks and animals. Aubrey wrote a natural history of Wiltshire,[19] and was anxious to record the superstitions of a by-gone age, as he did in his *Remains of gentilisme and Judaisme*.[20] It is interesting to see how this tradition of comment developed into Toland's history of druids, and the deist movement against priestcraft as ignorance. These raw materials collected by a thousand gentlemen at home, and by the Societies and dedicated men of learning in the capital, were transmuted by the physico-theologians into a new form of religious apologia. As John Ray acknowledged, the argument from final causes had been frequently used before, but its clarity, simplicity and beauty had been obscured by too many arguments from biblical texts, from miracles and presages, apparitions and spiritual presences. Its clarity had been equally obscured by the limitations of men's inquiries into nature. But now that Cudworth had written his great *True Intellectual System* refuting atheists, now that More had used the final cause argument in his *Antidote against atheism*, now that the microscope had revealed a new finesse in the natural world unmatched by the rough products of human artifice, the moment seemed ripe for a re-affirmation of the importance of the final cause argument.

Ray could turn to Boyle and his disquisition on final causes;[21] he could turn to the activities of the preceding generation of Cambridge Platonists who had become increasingly interested in this argument the more sceptical they grew about Descartes's theistic mechanics. He could assert with confidence that the new statement of this old argument would penetrate deep in society, reaching the most vulgar of understandings: God's existence and wisdom was sufficiently proved 'by every pile of grass or ear of corn'. The first verse of Psalm 19 was to be hosanned across the pages of science: 'The Heavens declare the glory of God, and the Firmament sheweth his handy-work'.[22]

Ray was supported equally by men like the Bishop of Chester, whose *Treatise of Natural Religion* had illustrated the importance of the discoveries of the new science to the development of final cause apologia. His own book went through twelve editions between 1691 and 1759 and produced many lesser and greater emulators:[23] it often formed the basis for the Boyle lecturers, men of the calibre of John Harris, DD and FRS, and Dr Samuel Clarke, whose second series of Boyle lectures in 1705 represent a high point in this form of religious argumentation.[24] The new theologians were men more at home in their gardens than at their altar-rails; they agreed with Tillotson that a mother suckling her child was in many ways the most pious and important act that could be imagined; they thought in terms of natural religion, which they considered irrefutable, and bound to succeed in the war against infidel and atheist alike.

This seemingly whole-hearted movement to bolster the best Christian argument of the new age, was not without its critics, nor its subverters. Whilst Ray and his followers pressed for the harmony of Moses and man, Charles Blount and Thomas Burnet mocked the biblical text and suggested that it was only allegory, not to be taken seriously.[25] Later at the turn of the eighteenth century Dr John Woodward was subject to clerical criticism for his ill-timed attempt to reconcile Moses with fossil evidence, whilst Whiston, anti-trinitarian and a staunch Newtonian, was helping the cause of those out to undermine Moses.[26]

Where a man like Edward Lhwyd could undertake serious geological work without falling foul of so many clerics and clerical positions, and hold his post as Superior Bedel of Divinity at Oxford, Blount, Burnet and Whiston could only stir up more and more antagonism.[27] Lhwyd was influential and respected; his copies of Whiston's and Woodward's works remain today in the Bodleian, interleaved and heavily annotated in the hand of the Keeper of the Ashmolean. His own interests were more heavily concentrated in the fields of comparative etymology and philology: he compiled several dictionaries of Celtic languages,[28] wrote much in Welsh and Irish, and was particularly keen on travelling through the Celtic regions of Britain collecting materials and things of interest.[29]

John Ray and his followers saw themselves in the tradition of Cudworth, More, Boyle and Stillingfleet.[30] They attacked Descartes's theory that the universe was indefinitely extended,[31] and attacked Cartesians for thinking they could find out all causes, thereby banishing final causes which were at the centre of Ray's world.[32] More's *Antidote* had shown how well equipped the mole was for his life;[33] other examples of God's providence and provenance abounded.[34] Ray did extend his studies into the field of world-theorizing, and argued from the Genesis text that waters of the deep and rain joined together to cause the Flood:[35] his work owed something to the radical theorists contemporary to him, and he did accept that great changes had been made in the surface of the earth since the general deluge through the activity of volcanoes and water erosion.[36] Ray was admired for his natural religious apologia, however, much more often than he was attacked for wandering too deep into the problems of the origin of the world.

Perhaps the most wide-ranging of the geological revolutionaries was Thomas Burnet, a man who set out to establish a new and complete theory of the earth with an explanation of all earth history from the Creation to the present troubled world. His view was pessimistic, his tone antipathetical to the conventional wisdom of the apologists.

William King brings to us a popular ballad common at the time of Thomas Burnet's work, which captures the mood in which his great theory of the earth was received:

> *That all the books of Moses*
> *Were nothing but supposes ...*
> *That as for Father Adam*
> *And Mrs Eve his Madam,*
> *And what the devil spoke, Sir,*
> *'Twas nothing but a joke, Sir,*
> *And well invented flam.*[37]

To many later commentators Burnet has been seen as an eccentric of little significance, a man who wasted most of his time writing and defending an absurd scheme of the formation and history of the earth. Basil Willey, who has edited Burnet's text, is guilty of this error, even though he does try to place Burnet in the intellectual tradition of the physico-theologians.[38] Burnet was probably sincere in thinking that he had contributed to the fundamental problem of reconciling biblical with other evidence; his critics were equally sincere in thinking they had found in him nothing but scorn for Genesis and for the classic Christian acceptance of the six-day theory of the Creation.[39]

Burnet's theory envisaged the earth created first as a perfect globe without blemishes in the form of mountains and craggy wastes, without deserts or tundra, ruled by one equable climate from one region to another. The earth was upright, not tilted on its axis, so that all areas of the globe received an equal spring weather. The rich and fertile soil that covered the whole globe brought abundance anywhere. It was only the dissolution of the moral world down to the days of Noah which necessitated some commensurate revolution in the physical world. The great geological upheaval came as the Flood. The crust broke. The waters beneath the crust erupted on to the surface, and their violence created seas and continents, mountains and valleys, and the tilting of the earth's axis. The crisis emerged not from direct divine intervention, but from natural causes, causes that God had set in train at the Creation to result in a broken world following the degradation of man through his own moral errors.[40]

The theory was therefore deterministic, but it attempted to grant God the role of Creator and designer of the whole cosmic plan, who made the earth as part of his own perfection. The whole future lay in progress towards the last great conflagration which would naturally come to pass through the surface heating up to ignition point; the time of this would coincide with the time of the Last Judgement.[41]

Contemporary critics found many things they disliked in this sweeping general theory. They disliked his self-confessed animus against Moses: for he proclaimed that he was persuaded to theorize through the inadequacies he found in the Mosaic account. They disliked the logical inevitability of the system, the tone of biblical criticism, the search for allegorical or unusual meanings in Scripture, and the presumption of the work.[42] Nor did it help Burnet to have a letter from C.B., without doubt Charles Blount, published in his defence as a preface to the 1736 edition of his *Archaeologiae and Theory of the Visible World*.[43] One critic saw a straight choice for Burnet between Christianity and his theory of the earth:[44] if he chose the latter he would lead men to hell.[45]

Burnet thought Moses inadequate. He cited the impossibility of the waters above the heavens being sufficient to inundate the earth through the force of rainfall in forty days alone. He calculated the necessary volume of water to drown the earth including the peaks of the highest mountains, and found his answer far in excess of the maximum volume that could possibly have fallen in forty days of rain. This led him to assume that some other cause of the deluge must have been operable, and made him suggest that the mountains were an after-effect of the deluge, for their pre-existence would have necessitated a much larger volume of water to drown the whole earth than if it had been flat at the time. He thought it unlikely that God would have planned so ragged and tattered an earth in his original cosmic design, and found many difficulties in the alleged organization of six days' work that God took to produce the whole universe.[46]

Burnet's creed was based upon a sincere desire to find the truth by reason, with some limited deference to the biblical source most relevant. He sought fidelity to the spirit of the text rather than to the letter; he argued that his way was the true Augustinian way, and impressed the Fathers into his cause. As he maintained in *The Sacred Theory*, Scripture could give conflicting testimony, and here discretion was essential:

> So for instance, if there was one place of scripture that said the earth was mov'd, and several that seem'd to imply, that the sun was mov'd, we should have more regard to that one place for the motion of the earth, than to all the other that made against it; because those others might be spoken and understood according to common opinion and common belief, but that which affirm'd the motion of the earth, could not be spoke upon any other ground, but only for truth and instruction sake.[47]

Such statements as these were not aimed at endearing him to critical clerical audiences. There followed on publication an endless debate, refuting first this part then that part of the great theory. The elaborate diagrams, the political arithmetic of the rainfall, the illustrations showing just how the collapse occurred when the crust fell into the abyss were all ignored or forgotten amidst the paranoia of the atheist-hunters, who sniffed irreligion in Burnet's general tone, in his Scripture criticism, in his whole philosophical understanding. Burnet replied with his *Archaeologiae Philosophicae*,[48] seeking to outflank criticism by showing that his theory best accorded with ancient theories of the nature and formation of the earth. Just as Newton rummaged for a prisca philosophica to prove anew his *Principia*, so Burnet sought proof for his view that Moses gave an inaccurate account suited to the ignorance of the times in which he lived. He suggested that given the enlightenment with which the later seventeenth century was blessed, men should be able to distinguish the essential true religious message of Moses, from the errors with which he supported it to make it acceptable to the primitive science and understanding of his contemporaries.

Burnet was a strong critic of Aristotle's theory that the world had existed from all eternity. He preferred to substitute the general received idea of formation by God out of the chaos, and thought this had been well established:

> Mundum nostrum, sub eadem forma et apparatu quo gaudet hodie, semper et aeternum extitisse, praeter Aristotelem, et non nullos forsan, Pseudo-Pythagoricos, nemo aperte asseruit. Sed id totum quod terrae Globum appellamus, orbemque habitatilem, in formam olim fuisse massam, turbidam et indiscretam, Chaos dictam: mundi orituri quasi redimentum; omnes sapientes uno ore tradiderunt.[49]

Burnet was better disposed towards the atomists than towards Aristotle, and was especially interested in Epicurus at the expense of Democritus and Lucretius.[50]

But more damning for him than this attempted defence through recourse to ancient and dubious sources which he often criticized, was his insistence in setting himself against the tenor of contemporary anthropocentric and world-centred apologia. His statement that 'to say . . . that this earth, the Dregs, the meer scum of Nature, is the Supream head of all things, and as it were the first born product of the whole creation, cannot be without abuse and scandal'[51] caused more trouble still. He had denied that the world was as old as the rest of the universe, denied that in its present state it was well designed, denied that God had made it and left it as it is, denied the truth of much of the Mosaic account, and violently twisted the rest. He had then backed this up with citations from the ancients, dubious appeals to the authority of Augustine, and a challenging theory of biblical criticism and its place in relation to reason and science. His work which today appears to be yet another floundering attempt of a would-be geologist lost in the turmoils of seventeenth-century theological debate and rancour, appeared to his contemporaries as a challenging heresy, seeking to suggest that much of the Bible was no better than a pack of lies. Burnet's effort to say that lying was essential to put the Old Testament message across to the early and stupid populace did little to mitigate his cause in the eyes of his severest critics. Burnet continued unabashed to demand that everything should be examined in the first instance with respect to its truth, and only the false should be examined to see whether it were prejudicial to religion or no. He thought it extravagant to be alarmed at every new theory to be propounded, without independent rational enquiry, for this seemed to bring into doubt the credibility of the religious cause more than anything else.[52] Croft preferred to argue when he came to attack Burnet in 1685, that 'This way of philosophizing all from natural causes, will make the whole world turn scoffers.'[53] Many shared his fears.

Charles Blount's letter to Gildon defended Burnet from some of the strictures brought against him, and was subsequently published in his collection, *Oracles of Reason*. The Preface to this medley assortment, besides including a long digression in favour of the lawfulness of marrying one's dead wife's sister, gave a defence of reason as a sufficient force to provide for all our happiness.[54] He sought to associate restriction of judgement in matters of reason and truth with the arbitrary governments of tyranny and popery, and he suggested that fiery zealots did far more harm to the Christian cause than did 'all the attempts of professed atheists'.

The letter to Gildon defends Burnet's view of Moses as a pious allegory. He draws support from Browne's *Vulgar Errors*, showing that Browne too had doubts about the validity of all the Bible stories.[55] Blount argued in two ways; firstly that others besides Burnet have doubted the Scriptures, an argument that is of no particular help to his cause; and secondly, that Burnet is anyway probably quite correct in his interpretation. Macaulay's plagiarist and hack pamphleteer then issues into a long attack upon the inherent implausibilities of the Mosaic account, drawing on Burnet's seventh chapter.[56] He gives his famous farcical rendering of the conversation between Eve and the serpent, asking how the snake could speak; he asks how Eve could have been made out of one of Adam's ribs, when there was clearly not enough matter in one rib to make her whole body; and asks if Adam was a hermaphrodite before Eve's creation. With the aid of Burnet's eighth chapter he examines the hexameron, and reiterates the inconsistencies which the *Archaeologiae* had found in the work.

Blount's spirited defence of Burnet did Burnet's reputation more harm than good. Blount, already a scandal for his writings and alleged Hobbist creed, seemed to point Burnet's message in just the way all feared it was tending; towards flippancy and ridicule of the Bible. It was a defence which incriminated rather than helped Burnet.[57]

There were other writers, less ambitious and less far-reaching, or less challenging in their presentation, who nevertheless aroused troubles in their treatment of geology and earth history. William Whiston was one such author who made a substantial contribution to geology and chronology, who at the same time ran into troubles with the reactionary clerical lobbies.[58] William Whiston was before 1711 an imposing figure in the new establishment, the respectable man of science and of learning who had been Lucasian Professor of Mathematics at Cambridge, Boyle lecturer in 1707, and author of a new theory of the earth that was not so virulently anti-Mosaic as Burnet's.[59] Whiston sought to place earth history in the context of Newtonian thought, and sought to show yet again that the Newtonians offered a rational and a Christian solution to the whole gamut of arts and sciences.[60]

A staunch critic like John Keill would concede that Whiston's theory was preferable to Burnet's, but he still complained that Whiston like Burnet sought a mechanical explanation which could never be found or proven.[61] He agrees that a comet may well, as Whiston supposed, have passed at the time of the Flood, but he does not agree with Whiston that a comet colliding with the earth was therefore the sole or major cause of the disaster. Only God could have brought about such a flood by his direct intervention.[62]

William Whiston displays the wide-ranging talents and interests of contemporary men of ability. He wrote on mathematics, biblical chronology, on the defence of the faith and the Apostolic Constitutions, on charity schools and natural philosophy.[63] These wide interests were not haphazard companions, but were illustrative of the way a lively mind could travel in the early eighteenth century: from mathematics to Newtonian ideas, from there to the question of faith and Scripture evidence, from there to practical charity and ecclesiastical reform, and then back again to Scripture, natural philosophy, and mathematics. Whiston's drift to hostility against the Trinity, his friendship with Clarke urging him to become an Arian, and his general abilities make him a fascinating figure.[64]

Whiston realized when writing his theory of the earth that the account of Moses was the starting point for any such discourse. He discussed with himself whether the Mosaic account was 'a nice philosophical one', or whether it was an exact historical representation of events as they had occurred: he concluded that it was the former. He found that 'The notions they have entertain'd of the Nature, Stile, and Extent of the Creation of the World in six days, are false, precarious, and no less contrary to the Holy Scripture themselves, than to sound reason and true philosophy.'[65] For whilst he accepted the rule that one should never depart from the literal text of the Scriptures save when absolutely necessary,[66] he felt that it was manifestly obligatory to do so in the case of the six days ex nihilo theory of the Creation.[67] The Mosaic account in this matter applied only to the formation of the earth, and not to the other planets as well.[68]

He felt that the division between the ascription of final causes, and the analysis of mechanical ones was a difficult one to define, but he veered in favour of the scientific determinism of the mechanists. As he himself explained, 'if a miraculous power be allow'd in a needless case, we shall ever be at a loss how far to extend it, and where mechanical causes ought to take place'.[69]

Whiston intruded the mathematical and Newtonian method into chronology as well as into earth history. In a set of propositions and lemmae he managed to combine Newtonian logic with a style reminiscent of Petty's political arithmetic:

> The computation of the present numbers of Mankind on the earth, and of the space necessary for their amounting to such a number, according to the usual proportion of their increase and doubling, do's alike confirm that chronology, which the Hebrew text of the Old Testament do's exhibit to us.[70]

His two works combined represented a brave attempt to find a way out of the impasse; the impasse of needing a new theory of the earth, without upsetting received clerical and religious opinion by departing too violently and explicitly from scriptural authorities. Whiston departed less than Burnet; he therefore suffered less abuse and criticism. He also managed to shelter beneath the reputation of Newton, and present his findings as yet another ramification of the growingly ubiquitous orthodoxy established by the Cambridge mathematician and fellow of the Royal Society.

John Ray had given a great stimulus to the wisdom of God manifest in the Creation movement which looked back to his seminal work.[71] It was he rather than the deists who had most influence over Dr John Woodward, a man who became Gresham Professor of Physic in 1692[72] and a fellow of the Royal Society in 1693.[73] He began his studies with the problem of marine fossils found far inland all over the world, and sought an explanation for these that harmonized both with Moses and with scientific analysis. He therefore wrote a complete theory of the earth, paying especial attention to the universal deluge.

His argument put forward the contention that the fossils of animals were originally formed in the sea; that the universal flood had seen the dissolution of the frame of the world, and the re-formation of it with the fossils falling down amidst the sand and mud and gravel particles which formed the continents. The deluge had been over the whole earth, and was not confined to a local phenomenon in Israel as some had suggested; it had been affected by waters in the abyss which could repeat the performance if the necessary first cause so decreed.[74] He included in his work some papers to 'assert the superintendance and Agency of Providence in the natural world: as also to evince the Fidelity and exactness of the Mosaik account of the Creation, and of the Deluge'.[75]

Woodward maintained that he had subjected Moses to the same tests as he would have applied to any other historian, and had found him accurate. He had widely used the empirical method, himself observing fossil types all over England, and drawing on evidence from abroad through his correspondence.[76] He discarded all of the possible explanations of the presence of marine fossils on land put forward by other writers, with the exception of Burnet's universal deluge theory. He could not accept a whole series of local floods, nor could he agree that there were no truly marine fossils ever to be found inland. The idea that these remains were the cast-away bones of animals fished out of the sea to be eaten on land was equally unconvincing. The earth before the deluge had been incredibly fertile;[77] at the deluge all had dissolved in the great waters, and had settled in a very different pattern.[78] It was not until the Flood that the curse placed on Adam at the Fall was put into effect, and the soils of the earth were made difficult to till: the world was no longer a place for the ease and profligacy of men.[79] Woodward agreed with Burnet that only in the abyss beneath could there have been water enough to drown the earth; rainfall would have been insufficient. He promised a further book to demonstrate this mathematically.[80]

Despite this heavy influence of Burnet, Woodward departed from the text of his master. He denied that the Flood, over which they in substance agreed, was the product of natural causes. To Woodward it was rather the act of God.[81] It was this modification which made Woodward less of a target for those worried about theological respectability. He was careful to denounce Charles Blount, saying of the *Oracles*

> ... for my part I see nothing in it but what we had long before from Vaninus, Spinoza etc; and what hath been over and over refuted and exploded. The author since ye publication of it, hath shot himself, and is dead of ye wound.[82]

Woodward revered Bentley, not Blount.

Woodward explained the formation of rocks and minerals in strict corpuscularian and mechanist terms. Following the commotion in the waters, the metal particles and other pieces of matter came to coagulate one with another.[83] The shapes of the stones and mineral deposits were decided by the two simple principles of 'the configuration of the particles whereof they consist, and the simple motion of the water to bring those particles together'.[84] Woodward also applied his theory of the particulate structure of matter to questions of meteorology. To him thunder was caused by the rising gases emerging from caves and pits under the impulse of the sun's heat extracting vapours and exhalations from the deeps.[85] Fogs too could be explained in this way.[86] This theory led to a denial of the possibility of alchemy or other transmutation jugglery, for it rested upon the premise of the fixity of the particles that formed a particular kind of substance through the coagulation process.[87]

Woodward dissented from Burnet's view in one other major way. He thought that the antediluvian earth was not flat and perfect as Burnet had supposed. There had been oceans, tides and storms, whilst the axis had always been tilted as it now is tilted.[88] For proof of this Woodward gives equal weight to geological evidence and to the testimony of Moses.[89] For example, biblical evidence can convince us that there were seasons before the torrents of the deep were opened.[90]

John Woodward did not belong to the Burnet–Blount connection. He chose his friends more wisely, being a correspondent of Thomas Hearne and Bishop Moore.[91] He was a religious man carrying out respectable researches into fashionable nature. He defended Providence wherever he could,[92] and saw God's hand at work in the major events of biblical history, and natural creation. Unlike Burnet, who some have suggested was one of the many parents of the deists and was connected with the free-thinkers, Woodward was free even of the imputation that he wished to attribute everything to mechanical causes.

Woodward's interests were varied, and his life comparatively free of disputes over his writings. It was as a physician that he entered his major pamphlet battle following the publication of his *State of Physic* in 1718.[93] His dispute with Curll in 1712 was a more private affair. One of the most interesting documents to have survived it is Woodward's letter to Hearne making a plea for his own honesty, and decrying Curll's treatment of him.[94]

He was interested in a wide range of problems in natural philosophy, which could have brought him more trouble had he ventured them into print. He wrote to Hearne about Friar Bacon, asking whether this disreputable cleric had first observed the motions of the loadstone and had invented the mariner's compass; a question that offended the patriots of Gresham College as much as it worried those who thought of Bacon as an evil genius best left without any credits to his name.[95]

Woodward did not escape without critics even given the careful modifications of Burnet's theory embodied in his own work. Although he was more sympathetic to Ray's movement, Ray hastened to criticize him, as did Arbuthnot who compared his work unfavourably with Steno's.[96] In all his explicitly empiric and scientific works Woodward's interests were led inexorably to and from his theory. As his library grew more and more comprehensive in the earth sciences,[97] and as his collection of fossils developed, he began the hard work of cataloguing and systematizing his findings. In this he was like many men of his generation, led to natural philosophy through the craze for collecting exhibits. He was in that long tradition of men working towards a complete compilation of nature's wonders, men who from the heroic days of the Royal Society's project on the history of trades, through all those who sought to compile histories of providences, sought to classify and summarize nature.[98] Woodward merely differed from the humdrum and the humble antiquary and naturalist in his perception of the value of his collections to wider theoretical debates; he departed from strict Baconianism in his drive to theorize.

Like many of his generation Woodward thought that in natural matters the 'only sure lights' were histories 'of fact, and observations'.[99] But these had to be thought about and led to deductions, for 'a like censure would be his due, who should be perpetually heaping up of natural collections, without design of building a structure of philosophy out of them, or advancing some propositions that might turn to the benefit and advantage of the world'.[100]

He likened the pure empiric collector, the Baconian, to the storer of building materials who failed ever to build an edifice; a metaphor similar to the extended one used by Descartes in his *Discourse on Method*; an attack similar to that made by Hooke against some members of the Royal Society who demanded a pure and high Baconian line from fellows.[101]

Woodward accepted exhibits from all over the world and all over Europe in particular; he wrote to Dr Scheuchzer at Zurich and Dr Leopold at Lübeck,[102] to the Abbé Bignon, Dr Jussieu, and Agostino Scilla at Rome,[103] seeking from them rock specimens and any other interesting curiosities they could manage to send him. He read Scilla's *I corpi marini petrificati*,[104] and criticized Lister and Plot.[105] He fought with Lhwyd[106] and attacked Dr Buttner,[107] both with the aim of vindicating Moses at the same time as successfully interpreting Moses in accordance with his views on the history of the earth and the deductions offered by fossil evidence.

It is his refutation of Dr Buttner which most readily betrays Woodward's interest in preserving the Mosaic framework as he saw and understood it. Buttner's theory that coralloids dug up on land are antediluvian remains he refutes by arguing that if this were so there 'interven'd no dissolution; or at least, that it was not universal'.[108] He cited Genesis at the foot of the page as additional evidence, but continued his scientific case from his theological premises. He thought the whole of Buttner's book to be dangerous, both for its failure to understand the true nature of the deluge, which he, Woodward, had revealed, and for its view of certain land fossils as comparable to marine fossils.[109] Woodward shows us a common feature of the debates over irreligion, that of a man slightly suspect himself hitting out against others who he genuinely believed had done more damage to the cause than he had himself. His work also shows us the patient toil of a man who struggled to support the Christian view whilst at the same time being himself an innovator: a difficult but not entirely untenable position to adopt.

Woodward's construction of questionnaires and of methods to systematize unruly collections, reflects the atmosphere of Gresham and the Royal Society.[110] The problems he raised concerning the earth, its minerals and its soils, arose from contemporary scientific disputes as much as they did from Woodward's own generalized interests in the history of the earth. He asked enquirers to 'search carefully in all places for shells, and other marine bodies but more especially at or near the tops and highest parts of rocks and mountains'[111] and he solicited those interested in mines to be sure to ask whether the miners had ever seen any evidence of minerals growing in the depths.[112] He was like many of his contemporaries particularly intrigued by the difficulties of explaining the presence of marine fossils on land, and the presence of the remains of species unknown in the region where they were found, especially the giant elephant skeletons found in England.[113] All these questions permitted only one solution; the Woodwardian theory of dissolution and reformation of the earth at the Flood.

A natural line of thought took Woodward to the other vexed question of the origin of peoples and the migrations that led to the settlement of the Americas before the arrival of the Europeans.[114] He accepted the Genesis reference that Tubal Cain knew of iron,[115] and he took the evidence that the American peoples on the eve of the conquest knew nothing of iron or brass, and saw that this created difficulties for the idea that the American peoples were descended from biblical figures and ultimately from Adam. The solution had logically to be a catastrophic flood, which not only destroyed most people, but also all knowledge of metals. The American founding fathers then could have left the tribe descended from Noah before these people re-discovered the nature and uses of iron.[116]

America had to be peopled from the common stock for the orthodox view to prevail. Woodward therefore sought other arguments to bolster his view. Stone arrowheads found everywhere from the Straits of Magellan to the soils of England showed a similarity of pattern. Woodward dismissed technological determinism as an explanation, and saw in the similarity of complex patterns in these weapons a further argument for peoples deriving from a common origin.[117] Woodward worked faithfully and well, expounding theories and amassing proof, working all the time within his view of the Christian framework to make Genesis not only the most rational but also the most plausible of scientific hypotheses concerning marine fossils, differing species of trees and the American peoples.

Woodward's library was well stocked with the controversial literature surrounding Thomas Burnet, which would have acquainted him with the theological difficulties Burnet had encountered.[118] He was also acquainted with those other works besides that of Scilla, published towards the end of the seventeenth century, notably those of Henry Sheers, and T. Robinson.[119] He would also have known the entries in the *Philosophical Transactions* for January and February 1696, when these issues were discussed generally.[120] Woodward is a good example of a man educated in the earth sciences at the end of the century, well-read and conscious of his duties both scientific and theological. He owned books by Bruno,[121] Blount,[122] Bayle,[123] and Bentley.[124]

It was Woodward who most impressed John Harris when he came to write his entries on the history of the earth for his great *Lexicon Technicum*. He perceived the distinction which had to be drawn when defining fossils, between 'such as are Natives of the earth' and those that were 'adventitious, and reposited in the earth by the universal deluge'.[125] He copied his list of such fossils from Woodward's work, and complimented Woodward's theory for its dependence upon fossil evidence, and for its assumption that the rock strata looked like sediment deposited after the Flood.[126] Harris would have nothing of Burnet, nor would he tolerate partial deluge theories.[127] Harris, himself a Boyle lecturer and a keen advocate of natural religion, involved in the movement for topographical and natural studies of localities, was an important influence in the spread of Woodward's views.[128]

Whilst Woodward, Whiston and Burnet represent three of the most important figures in the attempts to place the history of the earth on a sure and wide-ranging general footing, there were many others equally interested in this field of research who were content to make substantial contributions that were not so ambitious, or contributions that did not offer so much contentious theory as Burnet or Whiston. Everyone from the meticulous Ray to the scurrilous Scriblerians could enter the ranks in the controversies, everyone from Edmund Halley to Leibniz. The debates were as large as they were important, as far-ranging as they were crucial to the defence of God and his world.[129]

Where Burnet would claim to complete a theory of the world, Hooke and Lhwyd would be content to concern themselves with specific problems over the nature of fossil development and earthquakes. Where Robert Plot, Martin

Lister and William Cole would tend to doubt the organic origins of fossils,[130] suggesting they were *lapides sui generis*, Woodward would boldly assert the organic principle. He would even more radically argue that all were placed following the dissolution of the flood through their specific gravities affecting the depths to which they sank in the surrounding chaos of matter. Where Ray would contradict the organic principle drawing on the work of Redi, Malpighi, Swammerdam and Lister about spontaneous generation, Whiston would loudly proclaim his Newtonianism and invoke a comet to solve the whole problem. Where Ray would faithfully adhere to the six-day theory of the Creation, Burnet would pick holes in it.[131]

The fate of these three most ambitious of theorists was mixed. Burnet, a follower of Descartes, a dabbler in mechanical causes, and the most trenchant critic of Moses, was feared the most, yet he had a great influence and evoked a great deal of critical response which demonstrates that he was taken seriously and read widely. Woodward, a follower of Burnet, modified his theory in important ways to make it more palatable, and correspondingly was considered less of a direct threat to the Christian cause. Woodward admired Ray, but was criticized by him for they disagreed over several crucial matters. He was earnest and sincere in his wish to help the Christian case, and sought to place Moses in a favourable light: although he realized that he had to use the same kind of scientific evidence that Hooke, Plot and others had popularized. He was not prepared to be so explicit about the relative significance of scriptural and other evidence as Burnet when he said, 'I know no other guide but one of these three, Scripture, reason and ancient tradition; and where the former two are silent, it seems very reasonable to consult the third.'[132]

Many would have agreed with this innocuous-looking comment out of context, but when they read Burnet's work he seemed not to wait for a silence in the Scriptures before he started looking elsewhere for reasons and evidence to support his own contentions. To Woodward there was almost a duty to make the evidence fit the Genesis view, and yet there was a strong element also of making Genesis fit with Burnet and his theory.

Whiston differed from the other two by virtue of his strong Newtonianism. He submitted his manuscript draft to Newton, Wren and Bentley,[133] and was to have it praised by John Locke.[134] Whiston consciously sought the patronage, protection and ideas of that group of men so confident that their new mathematical vision was sent by God to enlighten the world and strengthen the religious cause; men confident that minds were won by arguments, and that minds were the essential battle-ground for religious success. Whiston like Woodward sought to uphold Moses, yet he too was unhappy if Moses did not accord with the trajectories of Newtonian comets, and if secondary causes did not seem to play a mammoth part in determining the timing of the Flood and the future of the earth. Whiston's subsequent drift to theological error came over the Trinity, to be followed by years of wandering towards the Baptists' fold.[135] He found the Moravians, Wesley's inspiration, too enthusiastic; in this he was a true child of the Glorious Revolution, not a revolutionary against the times.

This period of profound discussion of the earth sciences, history and chronology, was sure only that the Bible text was an important departure, and even a prime determinant of geological study. For the sake of a quiet life a theorist had to explain and gloss the biblical text as if it were true in every chronological and scientific detail. To deal in allegory was dangerous; to hint at ridicule was fatal. A theorist had also to remain pure in his contacts, his references, and his friends: Burnet suffered from the Blount connection. Whiston suffered later in life because his theology began to taint the reception of all his works. The moderation of the initial theory was then of little help in evading pamphlet conflagrations.

At the same time that theory had to be dominated by a deference to Moses, a great cataloguing and collecting movement was afoot. Sloane and Savile, Ashmole and Ray, Lister and Plot and a host of others were comparing and classifying flora and fauna, and digging up fossil remains in every available chalk pit, mine and quarry. It was the kind of work the average gentleman would understand and indulge in on a trip around the estates, or on the grand tour in Europe as a young man. It was encouraged by the Royal Society, encouraged by the fashionableness of natural philosophy, encouraged by the ease of the task in comparison with serious study in the closet. It was fanned by the controversies, which aroused interest and spread the names of Whiston, Burnet, Keill, Woodward, Ray and others even more widely out from London to the counties as men and books travelled the roads of England. The sales of each edition may not have been large, but the number of editions and the number of different books is testimony to the financial advantages and the reputation that could accrue to authors as well as testifying to the interest and the serious study involved in the debates as a detached intellectual exercise.

This great pillaging of the mines and rape of the countryside, this movement which burdened every substantial house with lumps of rock and insignificant bric-à-brac had its implications for geology. Serious cataloguing brought to light the glaring differences between the types of fossil found, and the types that one would have expected assuming a fixity of climate and earth structure since the Creation. Archaeological remains, so popular in the Augustan drive to dig up all that remained of antiquity, also threatened the descent from Adam and the one-race theory of the peopling of the world. Observations of mountains, rocks, strata and the disposition of continents by the geographers, cartographers and adventurers had also been intensified since the fourteenth century, and their results had some slight influence over the world makers of the seventeenth century,[136] and their related distant cousins, the world theorists.

Nevertheless, all this new information did not lead to any great change of theory, away from the pattern of the Mosaic Flood and chronology. Theorists preferred if anything to strengthen the importance of the Mosaic Flood, albeit at the expense of departing from the literal sense of the text in the interests of scientific rigour, rather than postulate other theories for the making of mountains, the depression of seas, the flooding of the globe, and the migration of peoples. All theorists differed in their elaboration of the Mosaic account, and in their willingness to depart from it; but they were all fundamentally influenced by it, by its theory of the Deluge, and the descent from Adam.

In some ways the work of Hooke was a more serious worry for the Church than was the work of any of our three great cosmogonists. For Hooke had ventured to theorize on the possibility of species dying out, whilst others adapted to a worsening environmental situation.[137] Taking inspiration for the theories of the decay of the world from Ovid and later writers,[138] Hooke stressed the importance of earthquakes and tremors in effecting changes in the form of the earth,[139] and moved towards a theory which jeopardized the once-and-for-all Creation of the world by a beneficent Creator.[140] Where Burnet precipitated trouble by his rendering of Moses, Hooke studiously turned his attention to natural rather than biblical evidence.

Once the organic theorists of fossils had won their case against those who did not see fossils as animal remains, there remained the problem to explain how they came to be in the places they were, and to explain why some had no living counterparts.[141] Few were willing with Hooke to argue that species had disappeared for that was an assault upon the wisdom of Providence. It was Steno who had argued that the history of the earth could be read in its present configuration.[142] This was to be an important departure, and consolidated an increasingly implicit premise of seventeenth-century thought about geology.

Burnet's alleged atheism was not so much the product of a conflict between religion and science, nor even of the perhaps stronger philosophies: it was almost no more than an error of biblical criticism, together with a petty and hectoring lack of reverence for the Mosaic text. Theories of the earth were still expected by many to attribute a great deal to direct divine intervention, and any hint of determinism such as could be found in Burnet's theory was guaranteed to upset clerics and conservatives alike. There was a school of thought which wished to defend each book of the Bible, each verse, each dot, each comma, in its allegedly strict literal sense. There was a much stronger school which wished to defend God's direct and personal involvement in his universe, and keep him as a Father rather than as a remote intellectual necessity. There was another opinion which wished to stress primary causes, and fight off the growing logic of secondary causes they attributed to the new science and to its supposed allies, the nascent deists. To some Burnet had therefore been a parent of the deists in his love of mechanical determinism, of secondary causation. All his arguments about God's overall regulation of the world process, all his pious talk about the coming conflagration and his Cartesian arguments about the moral and physical worlds being synchronous, failed to impress. Woodward learned the lesson, and invoked final causes for the Flood, although maintaining an idiosyncratic deluge that upset others, especially on scientific grounds.

When the men of the early eighteenth century came to review the hectic activities of the geologists and theorists of the preceding four decades, they would probably have had sympathy with the view that Harris expressed in his great *Lexicon Technicum*, that Woodward was the man who had done most to advance the cause of true learning with respect to fossils and evidence for the earth sciences; that Woodward's speculations were fascinating and worthy of consideration in so far as they offered an explanation of how the events Woodward described could have occurred; and that Burnet had raised many questions which were irrelevant if not dangerous. Harris's view reflected that of the new physico-theologians; the view of the Boyle lecturers, the view of the Boyle and Clarke school of the mutual relationship of science and religion in the perfect Christian virtuoso. This view would still be challenged by the more dubious of clerical reactionaries, men who thought there was better proof of God in a Providence than in a weed, or by men who thought the need to prove God's existence at all threatened the whole precious political and religious structure of society. It would also be challenged by men of the ilk of Burnet and Blount, men more willing to question and ridicule Moses openly, men who felt that secondary cause explanation should be stressed above or beyond final cause apologia.

But both these groups were unpopular in the decade of the 1710s. It was the heyday of Ray's movement, it was the age of the country parson commenting on how the mole was perfectly designed for his life of digging and burrowing, the age when every known detail of the human body would be described and its remarkable suitability for its purpose expounded. It was this conscious anthropocentric apologia that triumphed; but the doubts of others lingered on and appealed to the wilder spirits of questioning young men.

The early attacks upon spontaneous generation and other problems connected with the origin of non-human life did not have so great an impact immediately.[143] The progress recorded by Joblot, was not to be carried forwards until Needham and, finally, Pasteur.[144] The idea of spontaneous generation, over which there were divided opinions in the seventeenth century, did not give rise to theories prepared to suggest that the origin of human life was other than from the Creation. The lesson to be learned for any theorist was that many of his contemporaries, as late as 1710, were not going to respond warmly to mechanical determinism, nor to any great departure from the chronology and eschatology of the Bible. The materials collected and the doubts sown by the flurry of activity of the seventeenth-century earth scientists, were to take years to come to full fruition.

And since all Miracles are banish'd,
And Holy Inspiration vanish'd,
What need have we of laying on
Of sweaty paws of mitred Don?

Mr Bowman's *Visitation sermon*
(London, 1731), p. 19

Some modern zealots appear to have no better knowledge of truth, nor better manner of judging it, than by counting noses. By this rule, if they can poll an indifferent number out of a mob, if they produce a set of Lancashire noddles, ... to attest a story of a witch on a broomstick ... they triumph in the solid proof of their prodigy.

Anthony Ashley Cooper,
Characteristicks of Men, manners,
Opinions and Times, pp. 147–8

How we came to translate *spirits*, by the word *ghosts*, which signifieth nothing, neither in heaven, nor earth, but the imaginary inhabitants of man's brain, I examine not: but this I say, the word *spirit* in the text signifieth no such thing; but either properly a real substance, or metaphorically, some extraordinary *ability* or *affection* of the mind, or of the body.

Thomas Hobbes, *Leviathan*
(ed. M. Oakeshott, Oxford)
Part 3, Chp. 34, pp. 259–60

Reason therefore here, as contra-distinguished to faith, I take to be the discovery of the certainty, or probability, of such propositions, or truths, which the mind arrives at, by deduction made from such ideas, which it has got by the use of its natural faculties, viz by sensation, or reflection.

Faith, on the other side, is the assent to any proposition, not thus made out by the deduction of reason; but upon the credit of the proposer, as coming from God, in some extraordinary way of communication. This way of discovering truths to men we call revelation.

John Locke, *Works*
(6th ed. London, 1759),
vol. i, p. 330

Chapter Six

WITCHES, APPARITIONS
AND REVELATIONS

Supernatural phenomena excited debate and interest in the seventeenth century. God's presence was to many an imminent, interventionist one: God could send signs, inspire dreams and revelations, warn men of future events and help forecasters through providences and prognostications. There were those who felt such practical manifestations of the Deity, along with other supernatural phenomena and the practices of witchcraft, were incredible or things of the past. Others contended that a witchless world, a world bereft of ghosts and apparitions, was akin to a Godless world. The natural philosophers used their skills in evaluating the true nature of repeated happenings; the biblical critics added their reflections upon the supernatural events of the holy testimonies.

The role of revelation and of apparitions was in considerable doubt from the middle of the seventeenth century until the end of our period. A substantial change in the priorities of Christian apologia was undermining the importance attached to such phenomena: the changing nature of a reasonable explanation placed a higher premium on the argument from universal consent, natural religion, final causes, and philosophical necessity of a first cause and first mover, than it did on the tangible world of spirits and poltergeists. There were those comparatively neglected thinkers who decried the great deist attack upon revelation, and there were those who still felt that no spirit meant no God: but these gradually lost ground to the thinkers who argued for reason and nature, who sought certainty in moral and scientific subjects from logic and natural studies. The development and triumph of Laudian positions, and the success of the Hammond circle's views influenced the post-Restoration theological ambience.[1]

More was under review than merely the questions posed by the old superstitions, and more than one of the previously central arguments for God and his spirit world. It was even more than a whole cosmology that was assailed: for the very nature of the human soul, part of the questioned spiritual universe, was under lengthy review. So too were the questions of revelation, biblical evidence and credibility, and the nature of proof for theological and natural philosophical statements.

The long debates over providences, apparitions, witches, comets, presages, cures, magical charms, amulets and the like have been patiently chronicled until the end of the seventeenth century by the recent proliferation of studies of witchcraft and its related beliefs.[2] There have been excellent local studies like that of Dr Macfarlane, seeking to show the connections between social pressures, economic environment, and witch beliefs in the provinces and village communities, representing a significant contribution to our knowledge of social history and anthropology.[3] There has been less study of the intellectual problems surrounding these beliefs in relation to the wider theological and philosophical issues arising out of them, and little appreciation of their connection with the general problem of atheism and irreligion as a social and intellectual movement feared by many.[4] Douce's list of works on the subject illustrates that the volume of printed works remained sizeable into the eighteenth century. The whole gamut of Christian experience was thought to be at stake in discussions which ranged widely from revelation to biblical criticism, and from witches to the role of Christ and the soul of man. The deists were feared as a group for bringing nearer the evil day when all revelation and much of the Bible would be dismissed as superstition, fit for ridicule, and all that would remain would be the *a posteriori* argument of natural religion, urging all men to belief in a God, but no man to follow any particular tenets of morality other than his own liberal view of the laws of nature. What to many a philosopher seemed a surer way of guaranteeing human consent and a unified system of practice, through invoking the divine imperatives of natural laws formulated by their own pens, was to others nothing more than casting away the whole basis of Christian sanity, throwing aside rewards, punishments, hell, damnation, terror, sin, the immortal soul, Christ's words, and the spiritual appearances and interventions once so common in daily life.[5]

Those who challenged this system of spiritualism which permeated Christian experience and argument before the Augustan age were many and diverse. They range from Webster and the fiery preachers of the Interregnum, who nevertheless opposed the idea of witches, through to William Coward whose doctrine of the soul aroused storms of protest. It includes all the usual figures in our debates, ranging from Hobbes's often quoted remarks upon incorporeal substance and spirit worlds, through the pantheism of Spinoza and the ridicule of Blount, to the natural religion of the truncated Christianity of the deists and their social colleagues. Revelations and miracles were under attack: it was the cause of many clerics to defend them.[6]

When Offspring Blackall, like his predecessor Dr Bradford, came to give his Boyle lectures he perceived that amidst all the debate of matter, motion and natural philosophy, amidst the attack upon Jews and atheists, the central question of biblical evidence and the credibility of Christian revelation had been strangely omitted from discussion. Bradford aimed his attack against the deists, those 'who are not sunk so much below humane nature, as to call into question the Author of their Beings, or to deny that Providence by which the world is governed . . . but yet pretend to disbelieve, or at least doubt concerning the Christian Revelation'.[7] This definition he shared in common with Gastrell, Blackall, and many others influenced by these works.[8]

Bradford recognized that to convince the sceptic and the deist who nevertheless accepted natural religion was an easier task to perform than to convince the out-and-out atheist. It was also a necessary task for the one led to the other, whilst the unwillingness to accept duties and rules for this life from the words of Christ the Mediator was certainly far from orthodox Christianity, and remote from genuine religious experience. The deist had to concede that men possess an immortal immaterial soul[9] whilst the body resides in sin, death and misery: therefore he should also concede that God is likely to want to help the soul, which is part of his divine nature. Christ had come into the world as a Mediator,[10] and urged men to heaven, where they would find 'the complete and everlasting happiness of an innumerable company of intelligent and reasonable creatures'.[11] Christ's love was our revelation: Christ's mission refuted the deists' myopia in seeing only natural religious arguments at the expense of the vital message of Christianity.

Bradford's great weakness in his argument was his wish to resort to inter-Christian bickering at the expense of the Catholics and the High Anglicans in favour of honest middle-of-the-road Protestantism. He constantly reiterated the phrase of Boyle's will to the effect that the Boyle lecturers should refrain from such a descent to squabbling, but he nevertheless often found himself doing neither less nor more.[12] He urged the utility of revelation in laying down our duties and in aiding the repression of our passions by means of the control of the Gospel,[13] and by means of the Gospel through the life of Christ giving us a perfect example of how to live.[14] The value of the whole message was assured, through the proof afforded to its statements by prophecies, miracles, and the wonderful success of its propagation.[15]

Bradford's argument is in some measure a representative statement of the conservative clerical cause. Almost oblivious of the advances or regresses in natural philosophy, theology and natural studies, all that Bradford admitted to understanding was that deism represented decay and irreligion. He was willing to argue the good old cause from all those testimonies of the Bible, of our Saviour, and of spirits and presences, in a way which remained untortured by secondary causes or philosophical niceties, unsullied by the new world of nature and reason. In an appendix Bradford added an answer to the atheists' objection that God had left the world untended until seventeen hundred years ago, when he had sent Christ, and even then had confined knowledge of him through Christ to small areas of the world where the message could be propagated.[16] It was essential both to prove that the Bible was the message of Christ, and that God had taken every precaution to ensure that men should hear and receive the Gospel from God.

Offspring Blackall endorsed Bradford's suggestions by reiterating some of his clerical views against deists, and by adding a far fuller exposition of the virtues and value of the biblical text. He sought to show that the Holy Scripture gave men sufficient doctrines for leading a good life, and that it gave us reasonable motives to induce us to lead this life.[17] From this basis he argued that we have reasons to suppose the books of the Bible were written by their alleged authors, to suppose that they were accurate in their account of historical fact, and there-fore to believe the divine revelation in the books as well. Blackall argued from the mundane to the divine, and thought that to vindicate the verifiable parts of the Bible, at the same time as agreeing the authorship by contemporaries and apostles of Christ, was sufficient proof of all the rest of the holy books.[18]

Blackall's justification of his arguments was a little more tenuous than the rigour of their initial exposition. He thought it adequate to establish authorship through the general acquiescence of Christians in the common ascription. By such a method we can be as certain of the authority of religious books as we can be that any other ancient book was written by him to whom it is attributed.[19] This argument was dangerous in the age of Bentley and criticism of Aesop and Phalaris: but Blackall justified it by an appeal to the fear of anarchy, for if we doubt the Bible we have also to call into question the 'authority of all books and truth of all history'.[20] This was exactly what some men were prepared to undertake, and grounding the credit of the Bible on analogies with secular literature could hardly even have endeared Blackall to clerical authorities any more than it endeared him to deists.

Blackall led an unusual attack upon the idea of mathematical certainty in religious argument which ranked him, like Bradford, amongst the conservatives. He reasoned that Christ said to Thomas that those who believed without seeing his wounds would be much the more admirable than the doubting ones who needed such basic proof as Jesus's hands. Blackall felt this applied similarly to those who needed taut logical argument to persuade them of the existence of God rather than belief from the often inadequate and scrappy testimonies readily available.

In Blackall's first lecture he had considered the possibility that the Gospels were not written by the apostles, the unlikely contention that the apostles had lied, or the chance that the apostles themselves had been deceived.[21] Blackall used a similar argument here to the one he used in his appeal to the consequences of believing the opposite in the third sermon cited above. He reasoned that if we object to miracles and revelations 'then there is no such thing as certainty in this world; then they that make the objection can be no more certain of what they themselves see or hear than other men can be'.[22] Analysis of objections against the Gospels has led Blackall to the Cartesian problem of doubt and the nature of dreams and waking, a problem which he answers not by resorting to the Cartesian circularity, but by a recourse to the joint argument from the dread consequences of such doubt, and from plain common sense that tells us whether we are seeing things aright or not.[23]

Blackall is tainted to some extent by the common prejudices of his generation, despite his stance against the scepticism, innovation and new metaphysics that so cursed or blessed his age. He adopted some of the shallow optimism of eighteenth-century thought, and reasoned that happiness is the aim and purpose of men, and that the Scripture enforced us to obey it through convincing us that it is in our interest to follow its word.[24] Blackall felt no qualms about using a crude form of reward and punishment theory, related directly to Pascal's wager argument that it is far better to forgo a few pleasures here in case failure to abstain from these should lead to the eternal damnation of hell-fire.[25] After proof of the historical record of the Bible story[26] Blackall finalized his argument with comment upon the proof offered by Christ's divine mission,[27] by the prophecies of John the Baptist,[28] by the power of miracles, prophecies, and the resurrection from the dead.[29] There would be no new revelations for the ones we have to date are sufficient for their purpose;[30] any new ones would probably be unsuccessful in their aim of conversion anyway, for the whole purpose of sending us into this world was to prove us and try us, tempting our faith.[31] Blackall concluded that 'our prejudices and our interest are both for Christianity; for we suck'd it in with our mothers milk, and we found it the establish'd Religion of the country where we were born'.[32] God is thus far kind to us in helping us choose the right way, but He 'is resolved to deal with us as with men, to incline, not to determine our choice; to persuade, not to force us to be happy'.[33]

Blackall feared for new revelations especially in view of the growing powers of the virtuosi. Any more miracles would

> . . . only serve to set the philosophers' wits to work to invent new forms of matter, and new laws of motion by which to solve them; and any solution of them, tho' never so improbable, tho' only by occult qualities, would serve turn, and be thought better than to recur to an Almighty power.[34]

Blackall's opinions are worthy of such prolix attention for they represent a pragmatic churchman aware of the dangers of the general trend of English thought, yet fighting for the old way of apologia, convinced that the new arguments from natural philosophy and theology were weakening the central message of Christianity. What was the use, thought Blackall, of discussing matter, motion, the origin of the world, the nature of political society, if the very message of Christ as the Mediator, Christ as salvation for sinners was to be forgotten amidst all this new learning? Was this not far on the way to irreligion if only by default? Did not the deist, the virtuoso and the others, the metaphysicians and the new logicians, merely undermine the faith by seeking to prove God's existence beyond all doubt, thereby doubting all the more, and at the same time taking away the test from Christian faith by virtue of making the whole certain? These views were in substance correct, but Blackall's plea, and that of Bradford and other like-minded men, was able to do little to stop the precipitate rush to reason, nature, and general and metaphysical argument. The deists and the speculators were winning.[35]

The problem of the role of revelation and its relationship to reason was one element in the larger dispute about the world of the spirit and authority in comparison with the world of reason. The arguments for and against the importance of revelation centred upon the nature of acceptable proof,[36] the tradition of the Scriptures,[37] and the relative force of human knowledge and understanding.[38] Even Blackall's comparative conservatism was influenced by the prevailing rhetoric and standards of debate. He discussed miracles in terms of evidence, proof and testimony, and attempted to persuade the 'reasonable man' of their value. He believed that men were motivated by the wish to further their own interest, and to attain happiness and freedom. His statement concerning this could have been written by virtually anyone of his generation, and was not entirely the best argument imaginable to defend the motives for Christianity:

> The arguments that do most strongly persuade us to anything, are from interest; from the profit and advantage we shall reap by doing it; from the tendency it has to make us happy; and Happiness consists in being perfectly free from all pain and trouble and Vexation; and in the full and free enjoyment of whatsoever is pleasing and delightful to us.[39]

Even the stauncher defendants of the faith had imbibed a theory of man and his motives far from that prevailing in the days of the primitive Church and the Fathers, far even from the days of an ardent belief in dispute between Satan's kingdom and the Kingdom of God predetermining all else in this world.

Against this kind of argument for God and his world a whole range of works can be placed. Blount and his ridicule of the early books of the Old Testament was not directly equalled by any attack upon the works of the apostles, but there were those who were opposed to revelation, to argument from direct biblical sources, to doctrines of the soul and to the explanation of comets, witches and other such phenomena by anything other than anthropological and natural philosophical means.

It is informative to compare the hopes of Blackall and Bradford with the fey wit and social affectation of the *Freethinker*, one of the many journals that sprang up in the relatively liberated and free years of the second decade of the eighteenth century. The journal combined the flippant with the occasionally serious and could range from discussing revelation and miracle to defending or attacking the latest fashions, and airing the merits of hooped petticoats with an air of seriousness that betrayed the style of *The Rape of the Lock*,[40] although in poor counterfeit.

The journalists of this magazine could write quite happily that presages and omens were only the 'phantoms of a distempered imagination',[41] and could suggest that mankind's great frailty, in addition to his propensity to vice, was in the strong inclination of his mind 'towards everything, that is mysterious, Dark, and incomprehensible'.[42] The writers believed strongly that such religion was nothing better than rank and unsavoury superstition, deployed by the leaders of the religious group for their own advancement. The Heads of such a creed

> . . . are never for stinting mankind in pretended mysteries and miracles, suitable to every age and complexion; which, though they would be of weight sufficient to sink a good cause, with people of common sense; yet with minds duly prepared they pass for undeniable arguments in favour of the superstitions they are forged to support.[43]

The whole idea of eclipses as omens was merely the fables believed by French troops: how much better it was to explain such phenomena by natural philosophy for that would not frighten the ladies in the way in which the presage scheme did.[44] *The Freethinker* extolled the virtues of scepticism, and appealed to Descartes to support the value of this universal method, although doubt was not to be applied to such self-evident propositions as those mathematical relations that argued that two plus two make four.[45] The journal had taken Descartes and his worst theories concerning the uncertainties of human knowledge without acknowledging his strong fideism and belief in God. The journal never tired of showing the evil effects of superstition and prejudice, and the favourable ones of scepticism and reason:

> Where superstition prevails to any great degree, we generally see arts and sciences, and everything that depends upon Judgement and Understanding, languish and die away. The Reason is plain: the habit of submitting the understanding to nonsense and contradiction in one sort of subjects, must in time bring it to base compliance in others.[46]

Here was the classic statement of the deist, the sceptic and the pure natural philosopher: here was the cry of the man of reason against popery, tyranny, priestcraft, superstition, and the uncultured clerical society, the puritan theodicy or the Calvinist theocracy, as much as against the whore of Rome and the French Versailles of religious oppression. Here was that very statement that Blackall and Bradford had most feared would come to pass.

Another of the most feared attacks came upon the nature of the human soul. Everyone dreaded general scepticism and the abuse of Reason, but when Coward published his work there was the usual virulent response to one who dared to challenge a fundamental specific point of the Christian faith. It was much easier to attack and to define an opponent who directly addressed himself to a theological issue than it was to analyze the errors of growing scepticism, laxity of life, wit, and manners,[47] and it was easier to respond to a clerical view than to a general ambience of debate and standards of proof which even in the case of such as Blackall and Bradford was as we have seen affecting orthodox defendants of the faith as well as atheists and innovatory apologists. Coward was one of that line of men, like his anti-trinitarian colleagues, who gained notoriety not because he was necessarily the worst offender against orthodox Christianity but because his position was easily recognizable, and assaulted a major fortress of the Christian defences.

By the time Coward came to publish his *Second Thoughts concerning the human soul* in 1702[48] there had already been a long literature from the days of the early Church upon this subject. Coward's aggressive title page, however, prejudged him in the eyes of many of his readers, asserting as it did that it could prove that

> . . . the notion of Human Soul, as believ'd to be a Spiritual Immortal Substance, united to Human Body, to be a plain Heathenish invention, and not consonant to the principles of Philosophy, Reason, or Religion; but the ground only of many absurd, and superstitious opinions, abominable to the reformed churches and derogatory in general to true Christianity.[49]

Here was a work purporting to refute the central argument of the apologists, and the central argument of the Cartesians: the whole frame of debate concerning the universe, the world and man which rested on dualism, the supremacy of spirit, and man partaking of the divine nature. Coward took his arguments against the psychomuthists[50] from the nature of life, for to him life was the essence of man, and there was no need of a soul even according to the Holy Scriptures, let alone according to reason and natural philosophy. To him life was properly the human soul, and 'this life will to the Righteous be chang'd into life everlasting at the day of the general Resurrection'.[51]

When Coward published his *Grand Essay* which continued this line of speculation further, complaint was made in the House of Commons.[52] He followed it up with a medical work, *Optithalmoiatria*, which ridiculed the idea of the soul existing in the pineal gland.[53] His natural philosophy and his theology were not appreciated, and a long debate involving Clarke, Collins, and a host of lesser men began.

In 1705 *The Just Scrutiny* sought to analyze all doctrines it perceived to be in common debate.[54] In this work which Coward probably wrote (the title page bears the initials W.C. and the name of Merton where he was a fellow) he discussed the two possible major theories: firstly his own which the Scriptures vindicate, that the soul is the breath of life, not immaterial substance; and secondly that the soul is a principle naturally mortal but immortalized through its union with the baptismal spirit, according to the Platonism then common in Christian thought. This work represented the letter Coward addressed to Clarke in reply to his strictures, and made reference to the theories of Coward's longer work, the *Grand Essay*.[55]

This book illustrates yet again the recurrent and interlocking nature of all these problems we have been studying. For here at the root of Coward's attitude towards the soul is not only a view of the Scriptures and a piece of classical scholarship exposing as he sees it the false Platonic interpolations of the Christian message, but here also is a theory of matter and mind, an answer to Broughton's *Psychologia* and an attempt to answer problems over the relation of matter, motion and thought.[56] To Coward matter had in it an innate propensity or quality to move or of motion, which must give rise to thought. As a result, his idea of the soul became subject to attack for Hobbism and materialism. Coward found it impossible to preserve his distinction between the breath of life, and mechanistic materialistic motion in his prime matter despite his efforts to defend his position. He conceded, unlike Descartes but like some of his critics, that brutes may have reason, for even 'the souls of brutes were created . . . by breathing'.[57]

Coward's work did give a patient analysis of the Platonic, Socratic and Pythagorean ideas of a soul with their discussions of the soul as thought, immaterial substance, part of the aether, as an incorruptible, and of the brain as its 'hegemonick',[58] and avowed firmly that he had returned to Moses. Others were not so willing to follow him there. Much of his knowledge of the Greek philosophers and their doctrines of the soul was taken from Stanley's latin lives of Pythagoras and Socrates. Some of his more personal remarks, and his correspondence with a range of friends covering this and other subjects, bore out Coward's conviction that the Christian doctrine had been corrupted by infusions of Classical writings, and that it needed revision to return it to the purity of the apostles and the Bible.[59]

Whilst Coward was in trouble for revising Christian doctrine on so fundamental a point,[60] and seeming to do so less in accordance with the Scriptures
than with rising materialism, the general movement towards reason and empiricism in approaches to the world of spirits, comets and revelations was progressing
rapidly, despite the protestations of the clerical conservatives. As. E. E. Worcester
has shown, in the religious writings of John Locke it could be argued that the
inclusion of evidence taken from revelation and miracle was merely a device
to retain clerical approval for what was primarily a rational empirical theory.
The law of cause and effect, and the dominance of the final cause argument in
Locke's proof of God and his deductions concerning beliefs were to some the
nodal points of Lockian theory. There are others who would be more sympathetic and see in Locke that eclectic wish of many seventeenth-century writers
to deploy as many arguments as possible in favour of their cause.[61]

The deists were busy working along the same lines as some suppose Locke
to have been doing. Among the Toland manuscripts there is many a plan for
a book exposing superstition, for reviving sceptical tracts or for casting doubt
upon the whole cosmology of witches, spirits and miracles. One such abortive
project carries the following aim on its scrawled title page:

> Superstition unmask'd: wherein the nature and effects of this vice in all re-
> ligions are fairly display'd; containing I. Plutarch's admirable Treatise of
> superstition, with concise notes: II. The Preliminary Discourse of the celebrated
> . . . and III. A Letter on the same subject, Principally distinguishing Super-
> stition from Religion, by Mr Toland.[62]

Toland in print developed some of these ideas as far as he dared. His *Letters
to Serena* published in 1704 took up the cudgels against the stupid impositions
of custom and nature upon men's ideas and attitudes.[63] He attacked the system
of education which made men believe that the principles they received arbi-
trarily from their schooling have divine or natural sanction behind them and
thus make them the only tenable ones. He combined with this analysis an
attack upon the attitudes so common towards hobgoblins and spirits: 'They
terrify us with storys of spirits and hobgoblins, making us believe that all lone-
some places are haunted. . . .'[64]

To Toland all was priestcraft, all was a cunning plot by able men perpetrated
on idle credulous populations unable to perceive the way in which they are
being imposed upon. Apart from the priests, the 'rest, being the bulk of mankind, are retain'd in their Mistakes by their Priests. . . . [The] joys of Heaven and
the torments of Hell . . . [are] impressions of Hope and Fear, which yet are ever
founded in Ignorance.'[65] Toland would have had no sympathy with the fears
of those at the time of the 1652 eclipse, so vividly described in a letter in the
Ashmole collection. People feared 'strange lights and monsters' as well as the
heavenly activities.[66]

The second letter of this philosophical collection returned from the general
problem of superstition to the problem discussed by Coward: the origin of
Classical ideas of the soul, and their relation to Christian doctrine. Scholarship
had proceeded along the path of textual commentary, and intellectual history

as a discipline seeking to expose influences, traditions, and revolutions through a study of texts was as it had been for so long impressed into the service of truth, in relation to Classical and Christian claims. Toland described how Aristotle had related that

> The most ancient Greek philosophers did not dream of any principle or actuating spirit in the universe itself . . . but explain'd all the Phaenomena of Nature by Matter and local Motion, Levity and Gravity, or the Like.

Toland narrated how Anaximander and Anaximenes had taught that the universe was infinite and matter eternal, and how Anaxagoras had added the principle of mind to matter.[67] Pherecycles was the first amongst the Greeks to commit the immortality of souls to writing.[68] It was the Egyptians who had been formative in adding the immortality of the soul, heaven, hell, visions, spectres, necromancy, and divination to philosophy.[69]

Toland's views are well represented by his *Letters to Serena*, one of his more delightful and explicit philosophical works. He continued in the third letter to discuss the origins of idolatry and the reasons for heathenism. To Toland all superstition originally resulted from funeral rites,[70] and he gave an anthropological explanation of the rise of magic and other such beliefs, through the growing power of the clergy which he so disliked: 'The people . . . believing those Gods to correspond with their priests, who they thought might as well foretel any other secret as they did eclipses, consulted them about all they dreaded or wish'd.'[71] Against this growing mythology Toland juxtaposed the new science which realized that there are no special places in the universe, a view which disparaged the whole idea of heaven and hell. Tyrants began to use God-given attributes to further their control over the people, thus renewing the old allegiance of absolutism and unjustifiable divine claims,[72] while men began to describe things in terms of the Gods' pleasure and anger, forcing them to seek methods to appease or placate them.[73]

Toland concluded his anthropological analysis of the origin of Gods with comment on the proliferation of them, and their use by the poets: 'Alia quoque ex ratione, et quidem physica, magna fluxit multitudo Deorum, qui, inducti specie humana, fabulas poetis suppeditaverunt, hominum autem vitam superstitione omni referserunt.'[74]

These letters, purportedly to the Countess in need of instruction in matters of physical and natural speculation, demonstrate the connections between the attack upon certain mysteries and practices common in the medieval Church which had continued through to Toland's day, and the anti-priestcraft movement, natural philosophy, and Spinoza's philosophy which so affronted Toland's contemporaries: something which would affront them even more when he came to publish his last and most flagrantly provocative work, his *Pantheisticon*.[75]

Where atomism and free speculation led Toland to pantheism and to becoming a devout disciple of Spinoza, it had led some hundred-and-twenty years before in the works of Giordano Bruno to aggressive prose, seeking to shatter the theological cosmos which he saw before him. Bruno's attack was first written in 1584, but it still had some value at the end of the seventeenth century. It took far longer than his own generation for his opposition to the Great Chain of Being and the Elizabethan world picture to become acceptable. Many of Bruno's ideas which stemmed from his manifesto of intent were still heretical in the early eighteenth century, and some like the plurality of worlds were endlessly debated.

Bruno had written all those years before of the need to

> ... convince our minds of the infinite universe ... Break and hurl to the earth with the resounding whirlwind of lively reasoning those fantasies of the blind and vulgar herd, the adamantine walls of the primum mobile and the ultimate sphere. Dissolve the notion that our earth is unique and central to the whole.[76]

Much of this programme it is true had been achieved: but the theological adjustments necessary to accept the new Brunoistic world picture, of infinite space, a multitude of worlds, and the absence of spheres and graded hierarchies, had involved continued accent upon anthropocentrism. The adjustment had involved changing from considering the earth as alone, to considering the earth as a particular masterpiece of art, and considering man as the meeting of the world of spirit and the world of flesh through his given faculty of reason.[77] Fontenelle's speculations concerning the possibility of men or rational beings existing on the moon did little to upset this.[78] The ridicule of the satirists who saw the Royal Society putting men on the moon through having mice in their telescope tubes did considerable damage to Fontenelle and his sympathizers.

Such isolated problems as comets are reflected in the intensity and attitudes of the literature of the period. The later years of the seventeenth century saw many a tract and pamphlet arguing that comets represented a world in which God intervened and showed his will through such providences. In 1681 the signs of the times were thought to include a comet, the sighting of three suns, and the presence of three dead tower lions.[79] In 1673 the blazing star that had recently been sighted was viewed as a rod and warning by God against the beastliness of our sins.[80] In 1680 a student of astrology was still proud to recommend his trade on the title page of an account of a comet,[81] whilst a writer in 1664 had assumed that stars exerted influences, and decided the question at discussion was merely what kind of influence they exerted.[82] In 1662 a compendium of signs, not untypically, linked the sighting of a blazing star with monstrous births[83] and the raining of blood in two towns in Buckinghamshire.[84] There were times when these works had more than a passing astrological significance. One collection published in 1681 was a contribution to the campaign to persuade people that L'Estrange was a Papist. It described the 'pourtraiture of Sir Roger' seen at mass in the Queen's chapel,[85] as well as throwing in such apparitions as that seen by Lady Grey to preserve the compendial form.[86] This work also sought some pretence to scientific explanation and language for the 1680 comet.[87] There were other occasions when the spirit that animated them was less than serious, as in the tract which took the theme of the extravagance of the periwig and the threat of England becoming choked by hair, and related it to cometal influences and the prevalence of 'atheism, whoredom, and desperate swearing'.[88] Spirits too were from time to time defended or attacked, and reference made to the great religious debates of which they were part.[89]

By the early eighteenth century works so lavishly illustrating the providential importance of comets do not appear so frequently in library catalogues or in footnote references in books. The argument became increasingly confined to the books of refutation and apologia, to the works that sought to purge the land of the growing volume of deist heresies. Perhaps the attitude of the pamphleteer in Dublin in 1680, who was interested more in measuring and tracing the course of the comet he observed, was becoming increasingly typical.[90] Perhaps the scientific work of Newton and Halley was having its effect.[91] More likely the works of Bayle and his satiric *Pensées diverses sur le comet* were having their surreptitious but whole-hearted impact. Perhaps the whole tenor of contemporary thought was influencing this particular problem as it was influencing others, and the deists and natural philosophers were driving home the significance and competence of natural causes to their literate audiences.[92] Certainly there were plenty of books and articles that were telling in this direction:[93] yet even Flamsteed's observations of the 1677 comet had appeared to them forecasts of danger for the King of Spain, Don John, and the Imperial dynasty.[94]

The great debate of the new age became whether there had been only a general providence, a providence of God laying out and regulating the mechanisms of the world, or whether there were or are specific providences still deployed by God as warnings or interventions.[95] Current was running strongly in favour of the deists' position by the 1720s. The feeling was implicit in all those arguments from Locke and Clarke with their carefully worded statements in favour of reason, to the explicit statement of the attack on revelation that could be found in Toland, Tindal, Chubb and Morgan. Chubb thought that 'reason either is, or ought to be, a sufficient guide in matters of religion',[96] and dismissed all irrational presences as pagan or superstitious.[97] Tindal was similarly concerned to banish superstition, and to found religion on right reason and the 'nature of things'.[98] He did not rule out revelation,[99] but thought that it had to agree with and could not augment the logic of nature:[100] 'The Religion of nature was so perfect, that nothing cou'd be added to it; and that the Truth of all Revelation was to be judg'd of it by its agreement with it.'[101]

He was prepared to go further and counter-attack those who thought the argument from reason irreligious, and sought to associate them with pagans, infidels and enthusiasts, the common polemic opinion of deists and deist sympathizers: 'They who magnify revelation, weaken the force of religion of reason and nature, strike at all religion; and that there can't be two independent rules for the governing of human actions.'[102]

Tindal was worried about a dual allegiance to reason and revelation, and felt that only by making reason supreme could men escape the chance of circumstances of their birth, education and socially determined beliefs.[103] It is fortunate that Dr Waterland's lavishly interpolated copy of Tindal survives in the Bodleian; Tindal does not survive in his own old College, who disowned him and only bought the refutations of his work for the benefit of posterity working in the Codrington. There is a brief letter in the College archives in which Gardiner exposed Tindal as the author of *The Rights*, and Gardiner offered his services to prove that this was the case. There is otherwise an uncanny silence, although there is information about the dispute between Tindal and the College over the question of his taking orders.[104]

It is in the Waterland copy of Tindal that the basic divide between the deist and the anti-deist camp becomes explicit. Both shared a certain premise, the premise that the criterion to be adopted was the criterion of what argument of belief would lead most men to, rather than from, the faith. Their disagreement was really one of tactics. Where Tindal asked:

> What reason can the bulk of mankind have to prefer one religion before a number of others, on the account of such things, as, upon Priestly authority, are believed to belong to every one of them; such as Visions, Dreams, trances, extacies, Inspirations, conference with spirits, traditionary reports concerning miracles & c.[105]

Waterland replied:

> More easy to judge of these, than to judge of abstract reasonings, and long deductions of the law of nature.
>
> They must have some guides for one, as well as for the other; and so the objection of implicite faith in guides is as strong in one case as in the other.
>
> The question in ye result will be, whether such guides as Toland, Collins, Tindal & c. are to be chosen, or such commissioned guides as God had appointed, and the wisdom of ye nation approved.[106]

Tindal espoused the cause of Clarke and used his Boyle lectures to further his own argument,[107] and ended by defending the equity of nature[108] as opposed to arbitrary revelations.

His critic, Foster, argued that the liberty of England which had permitted Tindal to publish, would soon allow a host of defences of revelation.[109] He was not concerned by Tindal's argument that revelation could only reflect the findings of natural religion already known to men.[110]

By 1738 Chubb and his friends could openly appeal to common sense to reject the whole providential framework. They argued against an interventionist deity of a Newtonian kind on the pragmatic ground that evidence from divine revelation would be no assistance in converting reasonable infidels,[111] who would not accept revelation at all as a part of the debate, and by dint of an appeal to man's innate rationality 'that God should be frequently and almost perpetually immediately interposing as aforesaid, is a supposition that is greatly unlikely in itself, it is void of proof, and is grounded only on mere presumption'.[112]

Chubb could re-echo more than two decades of the deist attack on men's ideas conditioned by superstition, prejudice and error, and set himself up as the protagonist of the rising rationalist cause.[113] He was even prepared to attack the notion of original inherited sin.[114] This attack was countered on the grounds amongst others, that it could not be vindicated by Scripture,[115] and that original sin was necessary to persuade men that their hearts were the origins of all iniquity.[116]

The pressure had been such that Edward Ballard felt it necessary to stand up in the Oxford University Church of St Mary's on Sunday 2 September 1733 to reiterate arguments that showed that the existence of many and divergent heresies did not nullify the truth of the Christian religion or even of the Anglican view.[117] He took as his text St Paul's 1st Epistle to the Corinthians, Chapter 9 verse 19: 'For there must be heresies amongst you, that they which are approved, may be made manifest' and he reasoned that the apostles frequently fell into error and yet that had not undermined their authority.[118]

By 1733 there were certainly heresies enough to worry any serious cleric. Added to the works of Tindal and Chubb attacking revelation came the book of Thomas Woolston against miracles. Woolston began his enterprise about miracles in an irenicist spirit; intervening in the dispute between William Whiston who had turned from geology to imputing that the miracles of Christ should be taken allegorically, and his clerical opponents.[119] Here he had argued that all prophecies and testimonies in the Old Testament prefigured Christ, and set out to demonstrate the 'wonderful harmony of opinion between the old Jews and the apostles and fathers of the Church'.[120] But his method was to suggest allegorical interpretations, calling on Origen, that staunch opponent of Celsus whom everyone condemned in his words, to support his cause.[121]

> For not only Origen tells us, that literal commentaries on the scriptures, would run the Church into infidelity; but the jews say, that even atheists themselves would be converted by cabalistical divinity, or allegorical interpretations.

The Moderator wound up his case with an excessive condemnation of Whisston's position, and a side-swipe at Clarke's intrusion into the discussion.[122] Shortly afterwards Woolston produced a set of discourses on the miracles he had become embroiled with in the Whiston controversy, discourses destined to provoke even more trouble than the Whiston view had fostered.

He set out to show that

> . . . the Miracles of healing all manner of bodily diseases which Jesus was justly famed for, are none of the proper miracles of the Messiah, neither are they so much as a good proof of his Divine authority to found a religion[123]

and instanced each of the miracles of Christ in this and subsequent discourses, examining what the Fathers thought of them, and construing them in an allegorical sense. He was pleased to be able to show that Augustine himself had owned that 'Possunt Infideles istam vocem delatam de Caelo, per conjecturas humanas et illicitas Curiositates ad magicas Artes referre.'[124]

He succeeded, at least to his own satisfaction, in finding that most of the Fathers did support his allegorical bent, and went on in his second work to question even more directly the miraculous foundations of the New Testament. He asked whether there was any evidence about the degree of lameness that Jesus cured and whether there was proof that cure could not have been equally well effected by a doctor or by nature.[125] He blandly asserted that the Church should be glad he was exposing silly stories before the infidels did, for his doing it could only strengthen rather than weaken religion.[126] He looked intimately into haemorrhage stories,[127] and into the case of the adulteress.[128] Nothing was to be sacred from his rational critique.

It was not long before the replies and the condemnations of these and of the subsequently published discourses came pouring in. John Sherlock attacked Woolston in the company of Collins and Tindal, in the form of a court-room drama trying the cause they had espoused.[129] That Muhammed was an impostor did not imply that Jesus was also one;[130] that 'the priest only continues what the nurse began' was an unsatisfactory explanation of the spread of Christianity, for by what force did it spread originally?[131] Woolston's council vainly asserted that miracles were inappropriate in this age,[132] and that young men seen at the sepulchre were an apparition in a time of ignorance.[133] In the summing-up Woolston's guilt was manifest.[134]

Particular critics defended particular miracles: a pamphlet of 1729 like that of Sherlock defended the Resurrection, and buyers and sellers of the temple,[135] the water into wine[136] and the infirm man at Bethesda.[137] Nathaniel Lardner defended the raising of Jairus's daughter, the case of Lazarus and other evidences of the resuscitatory arts in the Bible.[138] For whilst Lardner was in favour of reason and freedom leading men's religion,[139] and cited Sprat on the free converse necessary for truth,[140] he felt that Woolston's fifth dialogue had gone too far. Henry Stebbing joined Lardner in defending the alleged resurrections of biblical figures,[141] only to call forth a reply by Woolston that same year to some of his stauncher critics.[142] The following year saw Stebbing return to the fray with a more substantial work,[143] and saw a humble clergyman in the country venture into print against the notorious infidel,[144] who advised Woolston to eschew allegorical interpretation and ridicule.[145] Much of the work was repetitious, for a man like Thomas Ray had already gone through three editions of a detailed refutation of Woolston by the time the more sluggardly came to publish,[146] just as William Harris's treatment of the Lazarus question had been detailed in his 1729 appendix to his pamphlet.[147]

No less a man than Bishop Gibson had by this time become greatly concerned about the spreading infidelity, and in a series of Pastoral Letters he warned the people of his diocese about the dangers of a Tindal, a Toland, a Collins, or a Woolston. He saw Woolston's scriptural interpretation as harmful in the extreme.[148] Amidst the general directives to men to be concerned about the controversy, Gibson preached at the faithful to hold fast to the old proofs and the old ways, and not to venture with a Mandeville or a Woolston into ridicule or new arguments. He assured men that any book written 'in a ludicrous or unserious manner' was depraved;[149] that reason without revelation was a most insufficient guide and that men were not to be misled by this;[150] and that the old 'lain and direct proofs of the truth of Christianity' should not be relinquished.[151] Gibson exerted the full powers of his competent administrative mind to the problem of the great fear, and the problem of spreading disbelief in town and country-side under the deist impact.

When Thomas Stackhouse came to review the two-year flurry of activity against Woolston, the debate on miracles was seen to have been as extensive as it was acrimonious, and as crucial as it was wide-ranging.[152] Stackhouse could cite the works of Gibson and Chandler, Smalbroke and Sherlock, Drs Rogers and Pearce, Stebbing, Lardner and Ray. But the survey of the controversy was really but one more damnation, and stories of how 'when he [Woolston] was born, hell first broke loose'[153] were given some prominence, whilst a constant refrain was Woolston's pride,[154] an essential attribute of any atheist.[155] Woolston stood condemned by his own works; his trial merely confirmed the universal judgement against him,[156] and argue as he may that allegory was the best long-term defence of the Bible, to most he appeared to be making fools, impostors and dunces of them all. Both ancient prophets and modern priests seemed condemned by Woolston's fervour for the faith.[157]

One pamphleteer thought Woolston had expressed an inveterate spirit of hatred towards all revealed religion.[158] He felt that the deist ought to be incarcerated,[159] for his doctrine led to the rape of women in the streets and the defilement of churches.[160]

The full-bodied attack on miracles, and the immediate and prolonged response to it from senior churchmen, shows something of the danger and strength of the deist cause. Woolston was arguing a position that was to become more and more popular as particular parts of the Bible were brought into doubt by advances in natural science and in historical understanding, but it was a position that senior clergymen were quick and correct to perceive as fundamental to the whole notion of Christianity as they knew it. Miracles were needed as testimony of Christ's divinity; without them the unitarians had a chance of swaying opinion. Miracles were needed to attest essential doctrines; without their proof the whole fabric of New Testament Christianity seemed unstable. Miracles were necessary as part of the spirit world, part of a world of providence and magic, of amulets and interventions by the Divine Being; miracles were necessary as proof of God's powers, as proof of God's concern, as evidence of revelation. The kind of shorn religion of reason, illuminated only by man's own paltry researches into nature, seemed to Gibson as to many of his colleagues to be a terrifying prospect that would lead the ignorant flocks of parishioners into straight disbelief. For he who could comprehend a miracle story was not thought capable of refined metaphysical argument, nor was such a man likely to be swayed by a chain of deductions and reasons. In attacking miracles Woolston had touched on as uncomfortable and as crucial a point as any that an eighteenth-century cleric could find.

Woolston's evil genius was to be reinforced and perpetuated by Thomas Chubb, who urged scepticism about the credentials of any miracles,[161] and who considered and dismissed Stebbing's attack upon his and Woolston's position.[162] Chubb was also willing in an Appendix to inquire further into the whole notion of a life after death, and to challenge Dr Warburton who was a keen defendant of this idea.[163] Conyers Middleton was also anxious to press home the attack against many spurious or ridiculous miracles. He denied any occurring after the days of the apostles, and launched into an onslaught on those like Chapman and

Waterland who defended miracles from the fourth or even fifth century after Christ.[164] Middleton raised the topical case of the Abbé of Paris who died in 1725 amidst rumours and claims of miracles, which Englishmen and Protestants had spent much time and paper denying, and suggested that

> Let our declaimers then on the authority of the Fathers, and the faith of history, produce if they can, any evidence of the primitive miracles, half so strong, as what is alleged for the miracles of the Abbé de Paris.[165]

Any foreign miracle was likely to precipitate Catholic–Protestant squabbles over its authenticity and meaning.[166]

There were many others willing to further the cause of reason and a notional natural religion in England; but there were continental influences too that were not without significance.

Whilst major changes were being effected in the whole cosmos and our view of it, in Europe as in England debate continued incessantly over the question of the spirit world. The influence of works like that of Binet was considerable, and the conflict between Binet and Bekker was one that crossed the Channel in packet boats from France to England where it was read avidly. Binet's work which criticized Bekker,[167] argued in the now popular way of intellectual history, attempting to find the historical origins of certain views. Binet's avowed purpose, like so many others, was to use intellectual history to vindicate the argument from general consent for belief in God or spirit worlds, and to contradict Bekker's argument that the opinion of daemonic activity had descended from the Babylonians to the Reformers.[168] Binet argued that 'les payens en général, ont bien reconnu que les démons étoient d'une nature spirituelle, quoique moins pure et moins parfaite que celle des Dieux'[169] and impressed the best of the Ancient Fathers, including Lactantius, and Origen to support his arguments.[170]

Binet's argument for universal consent illustrates well the kind of compromises that this back-to-history approach to religion necessitated for the Christian cause. It meant that one had to concede that men had always believed in differing Gods, even in a plurality of gods, and it meant that doubt could thus be cast upon the validity of any one of those religious systems. The critics of the Christian cause were seen to be merely associating the Christian religion with that of the heathenish pagans, full of superstitious practice on everyone's admission and thereby discredited. It illustrates well also the fervent wish to ground religion upon Classical and ancient learning, to ground it upon the pristine authorities of the early Christian Fathers, and to regress to the original arguments deployed against the pagans in the struggle both to bolster the waning confidence of the Christians in a new world of comparative affluence and sophistication, and to strengthen the cause against the growing numbers of infidels daily more apparent in social and intellectual life in the capitals and even in the country-side and the universities.

The new learning and the old learning were jostling to find their relative positions in the new scheme of Christian defence and apologia. Derodon's *De Existentia Dei*,[171] a moderately influential work in England after the Restoration, demonstrates well the balance the new theologian had to find between general arguments, natural religion, new science, Classical learning, and the Ancient Fathers. This work was a long and complete one which attempted to expound a philosophy in the three major areas of metaphysics, logic, and theology. Whilst Derodon's logic owed something to Aristotelian categories, and whilst his definition of philosophy was far from novel, his work was influential in its concentration upon the argument for the existence of God, and in the comprehensive nature of its treatment.

Derodon viewed logic in terms of the problem arising over predicaments, substances and accidents, definitions, divisions and arguments.[172] This is not to say that Derodon was by any means purely Aristotelian, nor that he was slave to the logic of Aquinas and the schools. His criticisms of both these authors were at times perceptive and far-reaching; in particular his attack upon Aristotle's doctrine of universals.[173]

Passing on from these three formal divisions of philosophy Derodon treated the subjects of physics, in relation to metaphysics and theology. He developed the influential argument for God per creationem,[174] and argued against the possibility of infinity and the eternal world.[175] Here were all the favourite arguments for God neatly related to the large compendial work of philosophy. Derodon gave lengthy exposition to the argument from universal consent,[176] to the argument from the Scriptures,[177] to the order of the universe,[178] and to the great excellence of the First Being.[179]

Derodon's great synthesis of philosophy perceived the unity in study that ranged from physics to theology and from natural philosophy to logic: Derodon's work, involving a critique of Aristotle, nevertheless showed how much of the Aristotelian framework of study remained as crucial as ever; but it also showed how modifications of the old spirit-world picture, amidst a coherent philosophy, and how modifications of the Aristotelian logic and metaphysics, combined in one work to produce a view of the world satisfactory to the clerical cause, and to the best of ancient and modern learning. From spirit worlds and apparitions Derodon travelled through the whole gamut of intellectual experience, seeking reconciliation between empirical philosophy, new logic, and God.

Moving out from such general philosophical frameworks as Derodon could provide, the lesser English writers of the seventeenth century turned to endless debates of particular phenomena and particular scriptural problems, attempting to use techniques of biblical criticism and empirical philosophy to make sense of difficulties either in everyday experience or in biblical stories. Great empirical controversies would range over the status of a ghost or a haunted house, long disputes would be undertaken concerning the status of prophets and disciples, the role of revelation and the credibility of miracles. Typical of such literature which abounds in any seventeenth-century library catalogue is a tract written in 1679 concerning the spirit of prophecy.[180] Addressing himself to Locke and Hobbes, the author set out the conservative cause that reason was not enough, that the divine authority of the Christian religion and of the apostles' words, deeds, and prophecies, were not explicable by reference to reason and nature, but that they entailed faith and belief in the Holy Scriptures. The author was prepared to argue that it was silly to expect a philosophical demonstration of God,

> . . . for such a demonstration must be either *a priori* or *a posteriori*; *a priori* it cannot be, because that supposes causes precedent to the first, viz. God himself, and so implies a contradiction. Nor can it be *a posteriori*, because the generations. . .[181]

Here some thirty years before Waterland's strictures of Clarke, and some twenty years before the *a priori* and *a posteriori* arguments were the highlights of English culture, comes a critique commonly propounded against rational theologians that they were wasting their time. They were seeking proof of something essentially beyond human powers of proof, and seeking to destroy the heart of the Christian message, and prophecy, mystery and the powers of the apostles and Christ: 'the faith of the Gospel is a sort of Supernatural Doctrine, which cannot possibly be demonstrated by the light of nature, and for that reason (were there no other) it is unreasonable to demand it, and senseless to reject the Gospel for the lack of it'.[182]

The anonymous author has with many others come to the root of the cause between rational exegesis of Christian doctrines in the light of nature and empirical philosophy, and the more conservative defendants of the faith, who felt a world of mystery, of spirit, of ghosts, of fear and superstition, of poltergeists and witches, was an integral part of all religious belief and practice. The vindication of prophecy undertaken in the body of the work was one part of the general clerical defence of all these mysteries, and was reason enough why Locke's *Reasonableness of Christianity* and Toland's *Christianity not mysterious* were sufficiently daring in their titles to offend many a conscience. Proof was forthcoming that Christ's prophecies were both true and right;[183] did not they have to be thus, if any credence were to be given to the whole Christian framework? Reason alone was idle and insufficient.

Besides prophecy and spirits there were essential doctrines from the life of Christ that many felt the need to defend. Some were impelled to give special support to the doctrine of the Resurrection. Addison for example had defended the Resurrection in his poem upon old Fuller's altarpiece at Magdalen College, Oxford. Addison's poem had a specific twist, however, which did not make it merely another work of conventional apologia for the doctrine of the Resurrection against natural explanations, for the poem was concerned with the atomic theory, and with giving a natural philosophical jargon to the story of the altarpiece, making an interesting essay in mixed metaphor and intents.[184]

There was much mixed feeling, and many mixed metaphors, in the discussions of the late seventeenth and early eighteenth centuries in England. It is difficult to classify thinkers into the conservative who defended a whole range of apparitions and happenings, against the rational progressives or the empirics who argued primarily from the *a posteriori* and *a priori* positions, who thought God's existence could be proven like any other logical proposition or any other induction from observable phenomena. The positions adopted were too complex for that. It has often been remarked for example how surprising it is that Glanville, a staunch sceptic in matters of natural philosophy, would support witches so vehemently: but his is just one of many cases where the division, if attempted, breaks down.

The conservative clerical cause saw that its interests would never be furthered whole-heartedly by stressing the final cause argument and its exaggerated anthropocentric conclusions at the expense of all else. With Stanhope, Blackall and Leng, with the other Boyle lecturers, the need was perceived to champion revelation, and to stress the miraculous as well as the wonderful in the biblical story. With a host of lesser writers supporting spirits, ghosts and other apparitions there were those who saw the need to defend the old order of a spirit-animated world, evidence they felt necessary to the whole notion of Good and Bad, of God and the Devil, of rewards and punishments, of heaven and hell. Without this order there could be no motive for belief, there could be no ordered Christian cosmology. There was the need also to defend the Resurrection, to stress the role of Christ as the Messiah, and to defend prodigies, divine interventionism, and prediction. The whole universe needed to be mutually dependent, and all needed to reflect divine caprice and satanic subversion.

This coherent world picture was in disarray by the end of the seventeenth century. The attacks that came upon it were from those who hated priestcraft, with Toland and his deist friends; those who hated superstition, and sought nature and reason as their satisfactory explanations; those who had recourse to secondary cause theories; and those rational theologians who believed in a theology other than the interventionist spiritual cosmogony of their forbears.

The middle position was now the rational and natural position: the clerical views of those who with the more conservative sought to defend the old medieval cosmology were being defeated by attribution, fashion, and changing social and intellectual standards. The work of the tradition through Webster to the attack upon witch beliefs, tracing its origins from Scott's *Discoverie*, made it increasingly difficult to argue intelligently that witches existed. The long debates over the path and trajectory of comets conducted in the persons of figures as diverse as Newton and Bayle began increasingly to work from the premise that comets could and would be explained with reference to a natural cause rather than to direct divine intervention in the scheme of events on earth. With the reappraisal of comets came reappraisal of that whole host of other evidences for prediction, prophecy and warnings so common before. Similarly the miracles of the Christian Church, so prolific in the period through to the Reformation, were now universally accepted to be redundant, of no assistance to a rational age, and unlikely ever to recur. All that was in doubt was the exact incidence of them in biblical times, and some would venture as far with Blount or Woolston as to ridicule or explain away the action of miracles in the Bible. The soul itself was in question: advancing medical studies made it unlikely that the soul could in Cartesian fashion reside in the pineal body, and the age was such that if the soul had nowhere to reside it was difficult to believe in it. Common acceptance was given to the proposition that the soul was coterminous with the brain at least during a human being's life on earth, but dispute raged over whether it could be subject to a mechanico-materialist explanation or not. Such was the advance of scientific materialism.

The decline of hell, of rewards and punishments, of the soul, of the spirit world around us, of the prophecies and personal interventions of an earlier world picture was the result of changing fashions. It was a casualty of the natural philosophy movement, a casualty of the revolt against enthusiasm, a casualty of the extension of the Protestant message to its logical extremes. The movements which had begun with the rejection of indulgences or the breaking of images, the whitewashing of walls and the reduction of ceremony and priestly power, was now proceeding to the reduction of the intellectual paraphernalia of the Catholic universe: reducing theology to reason, and testing previously accepted axioms of behaviour by reference to nature, reason and empiricism. Similarly the movement which had developed through the Oxford and Paris schools and had blossomed in the Academies and scientific periodicals of an expanding seventeenth-century Europe had as a consequence the doubts and scepticism concerning the peripheries of established Christian experience which did little to aid the old-fashioned clerics in their struggle to preserve the heaven, the earth and the hell of their old spiritual worlds. The combined forces of rational Protestant theology, and mathematical philosophy, were too much for the wavering intellectuals. The age of popularized Newton, of a common acceptance of the Copernican model, even some credit given to the universe of Bruno; the age of coffee-house discussion, and of the wish to out-think and out-talk rivals and friends in speculative daring, led inexorably to the rational natural theology that flourished in England after the Restoration, a theology that looked back as well as forward, but a theology which nevertheless amounted to a new world picture, the combined consequence of science, society, political history, and the struggles in the English Church and State. Not to the chance influences of books and men of genius alone should we look for our explanation, nor to the hindsight which has told some historians that the critics were correct and the incumbent defenders of the spirit world in error: for a satisfactory historical solution we must turn to society, politics and culture, as much as to the alleged warfare of science and religion. For much of the change was a spontaneous change in the methods of theological defence, not a reluctant acceptance of error on the part of dull and stupid Aristotelian clerics. The problem we can see is that clergy as well as metaphysicians and philosophers willingly changed their methods of argument as they felt the new ones to be the more secure and impregnable, for they were taken in by the new standards of proof and debate. Only a few of their colleagues, as we have seen, shouted against them, and saw in this a fifth column of great danger. Their cries of fear and alarm were all to no good, for by the middle of the eighteenth century there were few willing to argue God from witches or miracles, whilst there were many coming forward with cabinet collections and the irrefutable logic of final cause apologia.

The *Son* (or *second Person*) is *not self-existent*, but derives his *Being* or *Essence*, and all his *Attributes*, from the *Father*, as from the *Supreme Cause*.

Samuel Clarke,
Scripture Doctrine of the Trinity
(London, 1712), p. 270, Section
XII

There are no such words as Trinity in Unity in Scripture consequently no such Doctrine.

Sherburne's Commonplace book,
Sloane MS 836, f. 61 r.

Chapter Seven

THE PERSONS OF THE TRINITY

It was Gastrell who sagely remarked that no part of the Christian faith had engendered so many different heresies as that of the Trinity.[1] Gastrell felt that the notion of three in one, simple to grasp, should not have been cause of so much dispute.[2] There was much evidence to recommend his view that too many people were concerned with hair-splitting over the doctrine, and many of the anti-atheist positions adopted during our period were concerned with this perennial Christian problem. Hobbes had noted the drift to Arianism on the first page of his discussion on heresy:[3] those who tried with John Foster later in the eighteenth century to argue that the Trinity was not a doctrine essential to Christianity had to fight against a long tradition of apologia which ascribed considerable importance to the notion.[4] Tooll in 1722 was worried about the practical problem of the spread of Arianism amongst the dissenters of western England:[5] his fears followed many decades during which long and bitter controversies had raged about the correct formulation of the Anglican doctrine.

For it was the Trinity that became one of the focal points of doctrinal dispute in later seventeenth-century Anglican theology. The exact nature of the Trinity was important not only to those who held strong theological views about the nature and importance of Christ, but also to those who wished to avoid plunging Anglicanism into pantheism on the one hand, by formulating three gods, or deism on the other in the sense that they believed in only one god with Christ, his son, as a much lesser and relatively unimportant figure. In many ways the essential doctrine of Christianity was here at stake. It was important to define the nature and the person of Christ, and important to understand his relationship with the father. Upon the successful formulation of this doctrine, and the successful reconciliation of a trinitarian view with wider issues of theological, biblical political and social importance rested much of the Anglican and Christian framework. The only problem remained that of reconciling the various diffuse biblical statements about the nature of Christ, with a form of words from the Creed and in the ordinances and statutes of the Church, which could prove satisfactory to everyone without lending credence to heretical doctrine.

In 1690 a dispute flared up in Exeter College, Oxford. There was little new or unusual in this, for college politics then as now could be acrimonious, and the expulsion of a fellow or the indictment of a colleague were matters of the greatest concern for such a xenophobic institution. What was unusual was the publicity afforded the contestants, the lengths to which the embattled Rector and fellows were willing to go, and the scandals which emerged from the whole affair. More was at issue than merely the expulsion of Mr Colmear for alleged immoralities with the women employed to make the beds in the morning: by the end of the matter men all over the country had read depositions and extracts from statutes, tracts and pamphlets which proliferated around the controversy, had seen Trelawny the Bishop of Exeter barricaded out of the college when he came on Visitation, and finally seen the Rector expelled from his own house by the episcopal Visitor. The Rector's book, *The Naked Gospel*, was widely condemned as a Socinian tract, and confined to the flames by an irate Oxford convocation. Internal college squabbles, immoralities that had produced two bastard children among college staff, and the culmination of an anti-trinitarian book, combined to add evidence to the atheist-hunters who sniffed anti-trinitarianism in the air, and knew nothing but ill could come of it.

Dr Arthur Bury, Rector from 1663, is not remembered with affection by the college's Victorian historian[6] and has been remembered by posterity as a man lacking in administrative ability who let his college slide and then precipitate itself into decline and ignominy. Bury attracted the help of James Harrington, republican pamphleteer and heretical political thinker, the man we have already seen condemned for his own works, and for Toland's resuscitation of him after his death.[7] Harrington replied to the calumnies heaped on Bury from Christ Church and London, and attempted to show how pure were both Bury's books and his life. *The Naked Gospel*, widely accused of denying Christ's divinity, was to Harrington innocent in this respect,[8] whilst Bury himself had not enjoyed life amidst the petticoats of the college wenches.[9] Harrington strove to show that the points made against Bury by the author of a tract supporting the activities of the Visitor were libellous.[10] For by 1690 Bury had been accused of the evil life that he had expelled Colmear for leading, and he in turn had been subject to the scrutiny of the anti-atheists seeking to find heresies in his *Naked Gospel*, a work intended as an irenicist programme for the project of comprehension being put before the Congregation. The bishop had descended upon him, had received testimony to the effect that he had written a work tending to undermine the faith, and heard evidence about the maldoings concerning the expulsion of Colmear and the decay of the college under Bury's charge.

Convocation met, and with great solemnity publicly condemned the book and its doctrines. Bury found himself attacked in the very institution which he himself had supported and used over the preceding years. On the 19 August 1690, the following was inscribed in Convocation registers:

Causa convocationis erat, ut Propositiones quaedam falsae et haereticae, pravitate infames, citata et exscripta ex libro cui titulus est, *The Naked Gospel*, quae veritatem Evangelicam radicitus convellunt; ut pote qua servatoris nostri Divinitatem impugnant, aliaque Fidei nostrae mysteria in aeternum *veneranda ludibrio et contemptui habent, publico Venerabilis hujus domo decreto damnarentur.*[11]

The denial of the divinity of Christ, the statement that Muhammed professed all the articles of the Christian faith, and Bury's extended treatment of the Trinity, were roundly destroyed.[12]

Even Convocation felt provoked into something more than mere destruction, however. The same official record contains a history of the rival creeds and rival views of the Trinity in the primitive Church, and argues why that of Athanasius came to prevail. Bury produced a scholarly as well as a tactical response from his critics and judges.[13] He himself later repented, stating that he was ready to repent any unhappy word that may have caused offence,[14] although he remained true to his belief that an understanding of the eternal generation of the Son of God was not essential to salvation.[15]

The controversy generated by the whole enquiry shows well the way in which seventeenth-century debates such as these managed to mix the personal and the trivial with the general and the important, and heap objections against a man from all quarters. Whilst James Parkinson would come to his rescue, and this sometime fellow of Lincoln would defend his next-door neighbour,[16] the bias of opinion was strongly against Bury. Some supported Colmear, with the author of a pamphlet which cleared his reputation,[17] some attacked Bury directly and supported the Visitor.[18] All this debate only served to show that there was an absence of unanimity, and a proliferation of claims and counter-claims, as men wrote defending principles, and amassed testimonies taken from local residents, college staff and fellows. Mr Colmear was cleared from the charge of incontinence by an anonymous writer from London;[19] only to be accused again by protagonists of Bury. The whole affair went to an appeal, the findings of which are summarized in University latin recounting how they were unable to uphold Bury's counter-assertions.[20]

The scandal involved was national, although the concerns, certainly with respect to immorality and internal college affairs, were parochial; the attitudes behind them were the usual ones that led men to atheism, unless they were checked, and the offending books burned. Bury had taken up an attitude towards the spread of the faith, and towards primitive Christianity, which told against the more orthodox conceptions. In his Preface to the *Naked Gospel* he reasoned that the early Gospel spread irresistibly, but that the power of its persuasion declined progressively as more and more interpolations and additions were made to it.[21] He concluded from this, quite simply, that the changes made to the Gospel in later times were therefore the cause of the slower rate of progress. Changes such as those that had exalted the 'dignity of faith above its usefulness' had corrupted the text and the message:[22] the author examined all these deleterious modifications of the text, and used these to prove the basic contention that Christianity was now in decline following its heyday in the early years. The whole of the first section of the work was taken up with faith, which Bury thought to be essential, and the most perverted in the modern Church: although Bury's faith was tempered with elements of natural religion.[23]

Bury's attitude was not unlike that of the Whiston school, to follow later, although his textual criticisms were not so severe or radical as those of Whiston, for his argument was more based upon the observation concerning the spread of Christianity as evidence of its truth and vitality. Bury was bound to be condemned for wishing to undress the Church of all the Councils, decrees and dogmas in his search for purity and style, and like those other well-meaning advocates of primitive Christianity Bury was to be attacked for his sincerity and his warnings concerning the present state of the faith. It was one of those prevailing late seventeenth-century paradoxes that he who genuinely thought himself nearer the true Christian spirit and practice, was the more likely to be regarded as a subversive, than the middle-of-the-road lax occasional Christian who nevertheless accepted the decisions and doctrines of the Church when he remembered to do so.

The drama created by this small episode in University and religious history is testified by the Register of the college, that gives a gripping account of the Visitations and the defence of the college. On 24 July it describes how 'Clause est Collegii janua ne ad visitandum accederunt episcopus, sed cum ab interiore parte rupta esset fera, et turba quominus iterum clauderetur impediret, accessit episcopus in aula ascendens curia celebravit'.[24] And a year later a letter is added from James Harrington illustrating the close role he played in the whole affair. The letter was to the Rector, that is to the new appointee, Painter, and accepted the fact that the college as then formed would have to proceed to new elections of officers as was their regular custom.[25] Harrington had obviously moderated his tone, having lost the pamphlet battle.[26] Acrimony had been great on both sides; the tone of Bury's letter about the excesses of Colmear, when he first managed to have him removed from the college, is only paralleled by the later vituperation against the old Rector.[27]

Replies to Bury's book soon followed in large numbers. William Nicholls and John Long both wrote explicit denunciations of the work,[28] whilst Wallis's great compilation on the Trinity came at a time when it was difficult to avoid making the association between Wallis's keenness on the correct doctrine of the Trinity, and the great uproar caused by Bury's deviations.[29] Wallis, Oxford Professor of Geometry, Chaplain in Ordinary to the King, and sometime preacher at St Mary's Church in Oxford, strongly asserted his conventional trinitarian theology in the troubled years of the late seventeenth century. His essential belief was that 'The true notion of God, including Infinite, Absolute, Perfect and c. must needs also include Unity; for it is inconsistent that there should be many such. So that, in a manner, Polytheism includes Atheism',[30] a belief which he was proud had not been shaken since his early years under the troubled regimes after the fall of Charles I, despite the many vagaries of politics and modes of Christianity.

His additions in the 1690–1 sermons to his 1664 position are mainly additions of counter-arguments taken from supposed Arians and Socinians, all unnamed, placed beside their refutations.[31] He dealt with problems that had arisen more acutely in the biblical and theological wrangles of the past few years, and had an ingenious way of treating the difficulty over the word 'person' which was the cause of much of the trouble that led men to anti-trinitarianism. 'Person', said Wallis, is a word that has been abused in the English language, such that we take it to signify another man, where we need a neutral word to answer the Latin word 'homo'.[32] The whole piece reads as a blurring rather than a clarification of the issue, but it represents an earnest attempt to answer the problem.

Wallis also provides us with an interesting working definition of the difference between an Arian and a Socinian, recorded as his view at the time of intense controversy over the problem, and at a time of immense confusion of the one for the other. To Wallis a Socinian's view of the Trinity went so far as to make Christ a mere titular God, whilst the Arian had more respect and would make Christ Deus Creatus, a true God, but an inferior one to the Father.[33] Wallis was prepared to defend revelation and the inscrutable wisdom of God. For example, he did not think that the objection that the doctrine of the Trinity was unknown to the Jewish Church before Christ had any force. He answered this point by stating:

> If it were not made known to them, it was not necessary for them to know. For matters of pure Revelation, are not necessary for them to be known, before they are revealed, (nor farther than they are revealed) but may be so to us, to whom they are revealed.[34]

The furore aroused in 1690–1 continued for several years; in 1693 Francis Fulwood was still willing to defend the Socinian position over the Trinity,[35] whilst a counter-apologist saw Socinians in the same light as he saw the Papists, seeing in both anti-scriptural fanaticism, and idolatry.[36] Bishop George Bull had involved himself in the affair of Bury and continued the controversy into the mid 1690s. Writing for a scholarly audience in the learned tongues, Bull was already known for his *Harmonia Apostolica* which had sparked off controversy in 1676.[37] Bull soon made himself one of the principal advocates of the Athanasian creed and the Anglican Trinity,[38] arguing strongly against the doctrines of Socinus and Episcopius.[39] It is interesting to note that when, in the 1720s, Bull was translated the translator argued that Bull's work was especially relevant to the debate against Samuel Clarke and Daniel Whitby, for the translator hoped Bull's amassment of references to the authority of the Fathers would redress the balance which Clarke and Whitby had striven to upset by their interpretations of early authorities.[40] One of Bull's main protagonists had been Gilbert Clarke, the author of an explanatory text of Oughtred,[41] who dabbled in theology as well as in the black arts of mathematics.[42] Clarke responded to Bull's *Judicium Ecclesiae Catholicae* and its attack upon the writings of Episcopius,[43] by challenging his interpretation of the Nicene Council, and examining texts prior to the Council concerning the primitive Church's view of the Trinity.[44] Bull's *Defensio Fidei Nicaenae* had placed him in the fore of scholarly apologists: whilst his work on justification had aroused considerable discussion and opposition,[45] his trinitarian stance was staunchly in favour of the prior existence of Christ to his birth on earth,[46] in favour of consubstantiality,[47] and in favour of the Son co-eternal with the Father.[48]

Socinus still haunted many men's minds. John Wallis, our redoubtable protagonist of Anglican orthodoxy, had found him beneath many pernicious doctrines. He had denied the existence of the soul after death,[49] and had denied that the soul was capable of perception of pain and pleasure;[50] he had with his followers exalted reason far above Scripture.[51] This was surely enough to condemn him, and with him all those tri-theists and Arians.[52]

Who were these Arians, Socinians, anti-trinitarians, semi-Arians and tritheists that men like Wallis and Edwards so roundly condemned? For whilst much of the debate in 1690–2 can be laid to the door of Bury, and even to the difficulties of one small Oxford college, there were many others that gave credence to the belief that there were hordes of men laying siege to this essential Anglican doctrine as a prelude to overthrowing the whole garrison of Christian arguments. Part of the problem was created by the revival of past heretics in reprinted editions of their works. In 1691 John Bidle's unitarian work from the midseventeenth century was republished, along with a life of its author asserting that he had not studied Socinian books.[53]

He had drawn twelve arguments from the Scripture from careful study of the divine texts, and had concluded that the Holy Spirit and the Son were distinguished from the Supreme God and could not therefore be regarded as part of Him and His omnipotence.[54] Bidle's declaration of 2 May 1644 was repeated,[55] as was a similar declaration for 1648.[56] Bidle was made out to be a martyr for the anti-trinitarian cause, for he had died in prison in 1662 following his arrest on suspicion.[57] He had been similarly interned under Cromwell for his views.

Some of it came from skilful reprinting of extracts from the Church Fathers who had written before the Athanasian creed had gained full acceptance by the Churches. Fathers like Irenaeus, Justin Martyr and Origen were reprinted in gobbet form in 1691.[58]

Tertullian could be quoted as saying:

Tertius est Spiritus a Deo et Filio, sicut tertius a radice fructus ex frutice.
Et tertius a fonte, rivus ex flumine et tertius a sole, apex ex radio[59]

and his fellow patristic authorities had been just as indiscreet for the heretichunter seeking precedents to enjoy himself to the full.

There was William Frere, a more modern writer, who had challenged Sherlock, and produced his own anti-trinitarian work.[60] There had been a little work providing notes and comments on Athanasius, which saw the whole three-in-one argument as ridiculous in the extreme, and recalled that Athanasius had been condemned by six separate councils as a heretic.[61] Savage's reply to this work had been fighting an uphill battle, and was not overtly successful in clarifying the mysteries of person.[62]

There was Bury's additional work of self-justification replying to the activities of the clergy of both Universities, which openly suggested that Christ had been deified either from the time of the Conception or from the time of the Resurrection.[63] There were the answers to Wallis's great efforts, which ridiculed the whole doctrine, especially its pretension to being reasonable.[64] There was a trio of great men, great writers and thinkers, all of whom were distinctly tainted with this heresy: Milton, Locke and Newton. One of England's greatest poets, scarcely acknowledged by his own generation and the succeeding one because of his political embroilments and his defence of the regicides and the common-wealth ideal, was too a deviant over the Trinity.[65] Milton went so far as to expose the absurdities of the Trinity as he saw them in his last manuscript thoughts on the subject. He failed to see how one could believe in more than One God when Jesus himself had said that this was the case:[66] and if Christ were a Mediator, 'It cannot be explained how anyone can be a mediator to himself on his own behalf.'[67] When he could write 'The Son himself professes to have received from the Father, not only the name of God and of Jehovah, but all that pertains to his own being' the case seemed conclusive enough.[68] The leading philosopher of the period, and the greatest of all scientists were thought to have doubted conventional wisdom over this salient dogma, as was the Archbishop of Canterbury, Doctor Tillotson.

One of the major assaults upon John Locke's *Essay upon Human Understanding* arose over fears concerning the Trinity. Edward Stillingfleet, Bishop of Worcester, attacked Locke's system of ideas from the standpoint that they gave too much weight to the unitarian position, and that they formed the basis of Toland's *Christianity not mysterious*.[69] The bishop was particularly worried by the difficulties of forming any certain notion of substance from the Lockian theory of ideas.[70] Locke replied to these allegations, but the controversy revealed the potential difficulties that could arise over the notion of the Trinity in philosophical works that their authors might like to suggest were entirely divorced from such theological speculations.

Locke's *Essay* was being judged later in the light of his *Reasonableness of Christianity*. John Milner took Locke to task for his suspected Socinian views,[71] leaving it for the reader to decide against Locke by juxtaposing passages of his against those of Socinus or the Racovians. He found that Locke came near to suggesting that there was no prior notion of God in man,[72] that the only real necessity of belief was to believe that Jesus was the Messiah,[73] and that Original Sin did not exist.[74] Milner conceded the case was more difficult over the existence or non-existence of eternal torments and other such problems.[75]

Among the Locke manuscripts there is a bound volume entitled *Adversaria theologica* which shows his interest in the 1690s in the question of the Trinity, and in seeking biblical texts to settle the issue.[76] Locke never proceeded far with his task of collating texts on a wide range of subjects, but he did record a number of references under the heading 'Non Trinitas',[77] whereas he found only two for the heading 'Trinitas'. He filled a page with references against Christus Deus, and found only three for Christus Deus Supremus.[78] Those that he did record can be traced to Bidle's unitarian citations. These last three could not be written off as generally misguided men, for they were not discredited by their political stance. Newton became master of the Mint and President of the Royal Society; Locke became the gospel of the Glorious Revolution; Tillotson's position is self-explanatory. This was worrying, when men so high in popular esteem turned out to be little better than atheists, denying the divinity of

Christ.[79] Their acumen often lay dormant in manuscripts that they did not dare publish.[80]

The case of Tillotson was as heated as that surrounding the Rector of Exeter. There were doubts expressed by contemporaries as to whether Tillotson were a true Arian or no; but the pressures of the campaign against him tended to produce their own validation.[81] Tillotson had suggested that a mother nursing her child was performing a more meaningful act of worship than many in the formal surroundings of the Church; he had urged the utility of natural religion and its arguments, veering towards a deistic form of religious apologia. When Tillotson published some sermons in 1694 men could read in these his arguments which demonstrated the progress of his social and religious thought, demonstrating how since the Restoration he had clearly relied most heavily on natural religion for his own convictions. He argued that 'the Creation is of all other the most sensible and obvious argument of the Deity';[82] he seemed to stress a kind of reason which some would construe as Socinian in its implications.[83]

Charles Leslie led the field in his opposition to Tillotson's Christian views. This avid pursuer of atheists wrote many a tract denouncing infidels and deists: he linked Blount with Tillotson in his first essay on the Socinians,[84] and reviewed the whole controversy later in a useful little work of 1708.[85] Leslie reflects the contemporary passion about the alleged Socinian and anti-trinitarian outburst: he reviewed the position after a decade or more of most intense pamphleteering against errant clerics who had wandered in their opinions concerning the Trinity.

The question of the Trinity became embroiled in the theological and sectarian problems that surrounded the doctrine of transubstantiation. Dialogues between a Protestant and a Papist tried to dissociate the falsehoods of transubstantiation, apparent to the Protestant,[86] from the doctrine of the Trinity.[87] Sherlock opposed a tract that he thought had shown a young Catholic convert persuading a Protestant that transubstantiation was as well based as trinitarian doctrine.[88] Edward Stillingfleet took up the theme, and argued against transubstantiation on several grounds, including the contention that Christ's body could not be in more than one place at any given time.[89] The Protestant in Stillingfleet's dialogue triumphantly concluded that no father affirmed the doctrine of transubstantiation whilst many could be impressed in support of the Trinity.[90]

There was a large literature on transubstantiation, some of it recent in the 1680s. Tillotson himself had written a discourse against the notion, mentioning the commonest argument about the contradictions of a body being in more than one place.[91] William Payne[92] was most worried about the elements of idolatry in works like that of Boileau,[93] whilst Claggett in one of his specific works showed that the 6th Chapter of St John was not a firm foundation for the doctrine.[94] Henry More thought the senses could rightly distinguish objects, including the bread of the Eucharist, when he replied to French advocates of transubstantiation.[95] A book in 1687 attempted to expose the Jesuit arguments for miracles, by suggesting that the case rested solely on miracles,[96] and these miracles were never seen but much talked about by those with an interest in the doctrine.[97] John Patrick was keen to show that transubstantiation was no doctrine of the Primitive Fathers,[98] whilst John Gother was one of those few who had books published in England in support of the doctrine, believing as he did that transubstantiation went back to Christ.[99] Another tract published in 1687 argued that transubstantiation was not part of the doctrine of or the Fathers of the Church, nor Justin Martyr,[100] nor Origen,[101] nor Irenaeus,[102] and that therefore the French clergy should not press it upon the French Protestants.[103]

These are merely examples of the large literature aimed at strengthening Protestantism by opposing this particular dogma of Catholicism. That they soon involved the Trinity in their squabbles is symptomatic of the worries shared by many about the origins of the doctrine, and its true definition. Others, like Sherlock or Nye, kept more particularly to the doctrine of the Trinity itself, although Sherlock was heavily involved in disputes over political questions where he delayed taking the oaths to William and Mary.[104]

Sherlock's contortions over oaths were also seen by some of his contemporaries as part of the problem of irreligion. One critic argued that Sherlock's two years of indecision, followed by a reversal of his attitude, discredited the clergy and weakened the whole position of the clergy and the Church.[105] Others saw in Sherlock's belief that the legal issue of right to the Crown could be separated from the question of whether allegiance were due or not, a potentially dangerous doctrine that could justify any overthrow of the monarchy.[106] Sherlock's argument that princes without legal right could have God's authority, caused him trouble the more he insisted upon it.[107]

South responded to Sherlock's Vindication by arguing that Sherlock's account of the Trinity gave too much leeway to the Socinians,[108] and by arguing that the three persons of the Trinity were not three distinct spirits or independent minds as Sherlock seemed to suggest.[109] That same year Sherlock defended his writings against the Socinians from the allegation that by opposing them he had given more publicity to their views than they deserved.[110] South returned to the fray in 1695 when he reasserted his claim that Sherlock was a tri-theist:[111] amongst other things he thought that Sherlock had confused the words 'person' and 'mind',[112] and that he had not recognized that three infinite minds were contrary to the authority of the Church as expressed in the Athanasian creed.[113]

Sherlock found himself in further difficulties when he published an enquiry into the reasons behind the Oxford decree concerning the heresy of three distinct infinite minds in the Trinity.[114] Sherlock was convinced that the attack was aimed against him.[115] He felt that only a National Synod could rule on a heresy,[116] and felt that the University, by rushing into the difficulty over the Trinity, had succeeded in condemning the Nicene faith and most other formulations of the Trinity.[117] John Wallis could not let this attack go unnoticed, and he replied on behalf of the University and the Heads of Houses responsible for the decree, criticizing Sherlock for the aspersions he cast on the authority of Oxford,[118] and pointing out that Sherlock was not mentioned in the decree.[119]

Sherlock then compounded his crimes in the eyes of South and the University with a sermon in which he spoke of the dangers of corrupting the faith by philosophy. A critic hastened to point out that this was tantamount to saying that the articles of the faith were not consistent with natural wisdom or with experimental knowledge.[120] Sherlock had again demonstrated his belief in three eternal and infinite spirits,[121] and had undermined the weapons of reason and natural religion necessary to the defence of the faith.[122] Jonathan Edwards also joined the assault on Sherlock.[123]

Sherlock's case had exposed differences between the nominal and the real trinitarians, as much as the publications of the unitarians had provoked responses from supposed trinitarians which had shown up differences in the trinitarian position. The real trinitarians were to many no better than tri-theists;[124] the nominal trinitarians, whilst preserving the true doctrine, thought one critic, had innovated in the form of words used to express their belief.[125] Sherlock would not be moved from his view that the divine persons were real substantial beings.[126] Sherlock's hatred of the Socinians had led him into the tri-theist trap.[127]

In the 1680s and 1690s many others wrote on this matter. Daniel Whitby opposed the Arian and Socinian heresies in his work proving that Christ was God, using the patristic authorities as well as arguments from the nature of God.[128] Nye examined the texts brought forward by Milbourn[129] to establish that they did not prove the divinity of Christ.[130] Stephen Nye found Milbourn guilty of simple errors in his reading of texts, alleging for example that he had substituted Christ for Isaiah in the 53rd Chapter of Isaiah.[131] Nye reviewed the whole problem in his *Considerations on the Explications of the Doctrine of the Trinity*.[132] He praised Cudworth for the depth and range of his learning, and applauded the way in which Cudworth had stated that the Son and the Holy Ghost were derived from and created by the Father,[133] but attacked him for not espousing a thorough-going anti-trinitarian position.[134] Nye accused South of being a Socinian, Wallis of being a Sabellian, Sherlock of tri-theism, Cudworth of moderate Arianism, and Hooker of believing in a trinity of contradictions.[135]

Some twenty years after Bury's case, a new dispute of even greater intensity was raging around the ubiquitous learning of William Whiston. Whiston had already published his *Theory of the Earth*, and had been forced to concede that the first edition of that work did not grasp basic principles of hydrostatics necessary to make the system comprehensible;[136] he was already installed as a lecturer on mathematics and Newtonianism: he now turned to a cursory reading of the Ancient Fathers, and began a campaign to return the Protestant Church to primitive Christianity.

Whiston centred his case for revised doxologies, ceremonies, dogmas and attitudes, upon his readings of the *Apostolic Constitutions*. These Whiston asserted, were of equal interest with the Gospels, and their statements which favoured a more Arian position over the Trinity deserved due weight. He was duly attacked by a number of critics for arguing the anti-trinitarian heresy, for suggesting that books other than the Bible ones rivalled the Gospels, for being too selective in his scholarship from the Ancient Fathers, for deriding the decisions of the Council of Nice, for blaspheming against Christ's Majesty and Divinity, and for introducing the Arian reason into the sanity of Anglican belief. Without Christ, without the Fathers, with a revision of basic biblical texts, the world seemed to some to be near collapse; the consequences of atheism were imminent.

Richard Smalbroke was one of Whiston's foremost critics. He began his opposition in stringent style, reminding readers of Whiston's prolix abilities to foster error in every subject of importance.

> It will at last appear that Mr Whiston has made as false steps in his study of ecclesiastical Antiquity, as he formerly did in Natural philosophy. The world is now pretty well convinced, that he pretended to explain the deluge without underlying hydrostatics.[137]

He disliked Whiston for urging men to read the Fathers into the early fourth century, and then to abandon the project when they reached the Fathers of the Council of Nice.[138] Despite all Whiston's assertions to the contrary, he was an Arian,[139] and he had sought to bring a new book through Arab manuscripts into a place of importance it had not previously enjoyed.[140] The criticisms of Styan Thirlby, author of two tracts against Whiston's suspicions, pointed out the unpleasant way Whiston tried to hide behind the use of the word suspicion for his revisions of biblical interpretation, and echoed comments similar to those of Smalbroke.[141] He thought Whiston had been most unfair in his attitude towards Athanasius and his established creed,[142] and he pointed out that if we reject the testimony of Athanasius we have to reject all the collaborative testimony of Socrates and the historians of the fourth century as well.[143] Thirlby concluded with citations from the Fathers all showing venerable doctrine of the Trinity to vindicate Athanasius. Justin, Athenagoras, Tertullian, and Cyprian were the main contenders in this battle of the books.[144] All demonstrated how, with Tertullian, 'Dum Unicum Deum non alias putat credendum, quam si ipsum eundemque Patrem et Filium et Spiritum Sanctum dicat',[145] and how Cyprian's *De Idolorum Vanitate* and *De Unitate* eloquently summarized the truth. The survey of the problem concluded with a critical analysis of Whiston's use of the life of St Antony.[146]

A more patient textual criticism, analysing the sources for Whiston's arguments, came from Dr Grabe. He showed how Whiston left out crucial texts from the New Testament that proved the orthodox trinitarian view;[147] how he had omitted crucial evidence from the Fathers;[148] and how he had even wrongly assigned texts, thinking for example that the sentences of Paul, Tit. ii, 13, were applied to God, when most with Grabe accepted that they applied to Christ.[149]

Around Whiston grew a voluminous literature, and the usual atheist legends. There were allegations concerning his private life, and allegations of a general atheists' plot; such allegations annoyed Whiston immensely, and in his long rear-guard action attempting to persuade his critics to judge him and his work on its merits without prejudice, Whiston rebutted these severe charges, and sought to expose the methods of his opponents.[150] He complained of how they sought 'to misrepresent my friends and assistants, as Socinians at least, if not Deists, or Atheists; to raise or spread idle ill-grounded stories about my private affairs and management' and spoke particularly here against such maltreatment as he had received from Mr Chishull.[151]

Whiston was clearly aware of the dangers of such a campaign as was being waged against him, and was aware of its methods. He saw how men would seek to slander him, not by debating whether or not his statements were true in any absolute sense, but rather would read his work with a notion of what was necessary to the Church and faith they professed, and would accordingly damn his innovations, at the same time drawing from them the most dire consequences imaginable. They would make him part of all the moral, political, social, theological and natural philosophical heresies we have analysed in the preceding pages. Socinianism was, as Edwards suggested, a long way along the path to atheism via deism.[152] Whiston felt aggrieved at the campaign of terror, orthodoxy and misconstruction that he saw aimed against him: his contemporaries were aghast at the lengths to which he would go to introduce novelty and danger, reason and heresy, into the Christian code. He saw that excommunication was heavy sentence, and one which Congregation might in a rash moment impose upon him: he replied before such action, that Congregation should examine the Apostolic Constitutions, and consider his views in full.[153] Here too he tried to counter-attack by suggesting that defenders of the Trinity, such as Dr Allix himself, Bishop Beveridge, and Mr Nelson, had gone too far the other way and had ended up in tri-theism, arguing as they did that Christ had his own necessary self-existent independence of God the Father as part of his divine nature.[154] He also chose to expound on the Constitutions here again, to clarify the manuscripts containing them that we inherited,[155] and referring the reader to Dallee's volume which refers to them, entitled *De Pseudopigraphis Apostolicis*.[156]

Whiston worried at the theological problems he broached in his *Primitive Christianity Revived* over the subsequent decade, and there was seldom a year that passed without further controversy. The question became particularly heated at the end of the 1710s. Tract after tract debated the concrete proposals for reform of ceremony which Whiston had proposed. The Bishop of London was implicated in the dispute, and much of the literary outpouring was an attempt to vindicate the bishop and his stance against Whiston's heresy.[157] Dr Sacheverell interposed, and attempted to oust Whiston from his Church, preaching against him as he did so. This aroused yet more antagonism.[158]

The dispute in usual eighteenth-century fashion diversified further, and soon included no less a figure than the Earl of Nottingham. Men like Higgs were ready to champion the Earl's cause, and did so adducing the Trinity from natural reason, disproving the texts that Whiston had used in his letter to the Earl seeking to show that his primitive Christian scheme was correct.[159] Thomas Woolston joined the fray with his weighty latin, and in particular attacked Whiston's use of the John *Apocalypse*,[160] and he related the Whistonian controversy to that of the Bangorian dispute, equating the two in vehemence and importance.[161]

Woolston's whole work was written as if by Origen against Celsus, and took Whiston to be one of the prime movers of heresy within theological debate. A resounding imperative was given in the course of the work, which served as a manifesto of the anti-Whiston lobby:

Consulite libros Poetarum, Mythologorum, et Philosophorum vetustos. Investigate Fabulas Deorum Gentium, Naturamque Religionis qua Populus Romanus instituebatur; unde discatis, Christum veram Probationem et Revelationem Ejus Divinitatis vulgari hominum captui exhibuisse et accommodasse.[162]

Woolston echoed the plea made by so many authors that Classical scholarship should be used in the service of religious and philosophical enquiry. The poets and the ancient philosophers were to be ransacked, and accurate scholarship would bring fables and truths to light. None disagreed that Whiston should turn to Classical histories and old sacred writings in search of the truth: they merely objected to his findings, which contradicted centuries of ecclesiastical decision and dogma, and contraverted certain crucial and much-rehearsed passages in the Bible and Ancient Fathers. All agreed on the method: men disagreed about the conclusion and the relative weight to be given to differing statements of the position.

Meanwhile the letters to and from the Earl of Nottingham were continuing, and they remained popular into the next decade.[163] The debate with the bishop was also remembered, and Whiston's letters to him were re-published at the same time.[164] Here Whiston had accused the bishop and his Church of being the innovators, allowing the Council of Nice and later decisions to influence their choice of doxology. Whiston maintained his case that his was the old doxology of the primitive Church, and that his critics were the heretics.[165] Samuel Clarke, a friend of William Whiston, an exponent of Newton, related to the Arian circle in London around Emlyn and his acquaintances was in a difficult position. His friends sought him to express his true views on the Trinity, that is their views, and use his influence in the country to expose the trinitarian position. Clarke, ever-conscious of the danger to his career apparent in such an act, and perhaps aware of the complexity of the cause, prevaricated. In 1706 he published a fairly innocuous work of apologia which was conventional over the Trinity;[166] this was not enough to dispel doubts about his opinions, and when he came to his Doctoral viva in 1711 he was heavily questioned over his opinions about the Trinity although this was not the subject he was defending as his exercise for the degree.[167] The clerics of the Cambridge establishment were not entirely satisfied, and Clarke had to swear to abide by the 39 Articles, an oath which Clarke took in order to receive his degree; but subsequently he renounced this oath, and began publishing about the Trinity.

Few of Clarke's own papers survive, but we know of his troubles through the writings of his friends, and his own vindications published subsequently in defence of his action. He began a long debate during the years that the Whistonian troubles were lying dormant, arising out of his major book, *The Scripture Doctrine of the Trinity*.[168] Once Clarke had aroused opposition, attacks against his previous work were not slow to follow, and soon came Waterland's attack upon him for his argument *a priori* expounded all those years previously in the Boyle lectures.[169] This was followed by an exchange of pamphlets and arguments over the Trinity in the period 1719–22, and some of this can be traced through Van Mildert's life of Waterland; the tracts themselves adding nothing to the general debates over the Trinity that we have already analysed.[170]

Samuel Clarke found his clerical career ruined. Voltaire tells how Clarke was considered for the see of Canterbury, but was turned down on Gibson's advice that unfortunately he was not a Christian even though he was the most learned and respectable man in the kingdom.[171] He was offered the Mastership of the Mint on Newton's vacating that position, but after great debate decided that it was too secular a position for him to hold. Despite his precarious finances, despite his large family and the ever-pressing needs of clothing, schooling and food, Clarke continued on his way as closet philosopher to his Queen, eminence grise in English Letters, but unrecognized by his Church, and the centre of endless debate over his own exact attitudes towards the great theological issues of the day.

Those on the side of Anglican orthodoxy clung to the doctrine of the Trinity as grimly and with as much determination as they could muster. Despite the problem that whenever a cleric wrote on the Trinity, even with the best of intentions, there would be those who saw in his unfortunate choice of words too great a leaning towards tri-theism or anti-trinitarianism; despite the defections of growing numbers of leading intellectual figures of the period, the Church remained staunchly trinitarian. A man like Clarke would not be promoted; a man like Whiston would be expelled from Cambridge; a man like Bury would lose his Rectorship of an Oxford college; a man like Jackson, Clarke's protégé and defender, would get no further than the gift of Wigston's hospital where Clarke had once held the position as Master; the force of Parliament and the law would be impressed to aid the cause of the conservatives, which found its bulwark in the Universities.

The great fear lasted for many a long decade: at a height in the stream of worthless pamphlets produced in the 1690s,[172] it was still a leading fear of Archbishop Wake's in the early 1720s, and still a consideration of major importance when John Henley came to establish his Oratory in Lincolns-Inn-Fields in 1726, using the liturgies of Whiston's *Apostolic Constitutions*. When Wake came to draft a bill against blasphemy in 1721, he was full of concern for the authors who have denied 'the divinity of our Saviour, Jesus Christ'[173] whilst those that denied the Trinity were to him in exactly the same category as the members of the Hell-fire Club.[174] John Henley, the pulpit orator, was a perpetual scandal to the generation for the contents of his sermons and the forms of his liturgies; partly it was feared that he too was proselytising to the cause of anti-trinitarianism in the Whiston fashion.

Anti-trinitarian leanings seemed to be indissolubly connected to Newtonianism and to deism. They inhered in the Newtonian scheme, linked as they were to Newton's own passionate belief in the necessary power of the will of the Father, the Creator of all, the One and only God who enlightened the world and Newton through providences, revelation and reason. They agreed with the deist conception where the deist sought a similar order, harmony, and one Prime Mover, the cause of all activity and matter in the world.

These origins are very marked in Thomas Chubb's writings. *The Supremacy of the Father asserted* began with a prayer to the Father as First Cause,[175] whilst the Dedication confirmed a layman's right to apply his reason to religion and publish his views, even if these did not agree with conventional clerical opinion.[176] Christ could not be equal to God, because God alone is the Supreme Cause of every effect we see in the world.[177] Chubb went on to find scriptural and reasonable proofs that God is acknowledged as the God of the Son as well as of the rest of the world;[178] that the Father has authority in commanding the Son;[179] that Christ expressly states that he is inferior;[180] and that the Son debased himself by becoming a man, and is consequently in a less degree of glory after his being a man, than he was in antecedent to that debasement.[181]

Chubb was attacked for his views by Clagett, but he returned to the fray and defended himself in the same year, reasserting eight principal arguments for the inferiority of the Son to the Father.[182] He was not alone: Collins, Tindal, Toland could all be impugned in some degree for their trinitarian position, but they committed other errors which attracted the imagination of their contemporaries more than their waverings over this fundamental doctrine. The anti-trinitarian fears were framed by the extreme deists, but they were the product of the Arians, the Newtonians, the Burys, Whistons, Clarkes and Chubbs of this world.

The intellectual origins of the position could be those found out by reason, by too heavy a dose of natural religion, too great a concentration on the argument from the First Cause at the expense of Christ the Mediator. They could be difficulties arising from scriptural and textual scholarship in the tradition of Joseph Mede and Isaac Newton, scholarship aimed at finding a complete truth by carefully expounding texts together, scholarship that unearthed large numbers of references to Christ that suggested that he was inferior. Whiston's compilation was just one of the most fanatical; many men would have gone through the Bible recording references to the three persons, and then attempted to weigh up the balance of references in favour either of a Supreme Father or three persons of equal significance, co-existent since eternity. There could also be genuine philosophical difficulties about the concept of three-in-one that was at the root of the Trinity which could cause a rational man to resort to logic chopping attributed to the schoolmen to save his orthodoxy; a compromise many were not prepared to make. Vituperation of pamphleteers and orthodox bishops could also make a man appear a worse heretic than he was: a semi-Arian became an Arian, to an anti-trinitarian could be attributed many more Socinian heresies merely by general imputation without foundation. Words tended to be used dramatically and imprecisely whilst the Church was gripped by fear of anti-trinitarian heterodoxies. Anyone stepping out in the tradition of Herbert of Cherbury, of Locke, of Tillotson, anyone seeking a religion free of mystery and contrivance, free of revelation, full only of reason, was on the road to perdition in the eyes of his contemporaries in the late seventeenth century; he was liable to be accused of denying the Trinity, of furthering Socinianism, of being a crypto-deist.

Philocles in Shaftesbury's *Philosophical Rhapsody* remarked on the growingly common view that the idea of three-in-one is ludicrous: Berkeley's minute philosophers put forward difficulties over the word 'person' in an attempt to make the whole doctrine look silly.[183] The way in which metaphysical doubt could undermine the notion of the Trinity was made apparent in a useful work of summary over these issues by John Clendon, taken to press in 1710 after the great trinitarian squabbles of the preceding decade and a half.[184]

Those men we have studied in this chapter arrived at a common heresy or a common perdition by markedly dissimilar routes. Newton arrived at anti-trinitarianism through his belief that he could provide as masterful an exposition of the Scriptures as he had done of the book of nature; he arrived at it through his own search for an all-powerful God, a Father, a Creator; his own craving for power, retribution, interpretation of the direct statements of God's prophecies and symbols to be found in the Revelations of St John and the Apocalypse. He arrived at it through his own universe looking back to one cause, and advancing to an imminent and impending millennium; towards a land of poetry and delight briefly glimpsed whilst he was at Cambridge, or towards a dry desert of arid scripturalism whilst he was Master of the Mint and President of the Royal Society.[185] Clarke imbibed it from Newton and from Whiston, from his Arian friends and from his own conscience, again approaching it from the metaphysics of *a priori* argument and the physics of the Newtonian cosmos. Bury had derived it from different sources that will remain more refractory without access to his missing manuscripts. Tillotson was less involved but heavily implicated by criticism, perhaps more for several silly chance remarks than for any thorough-going irreligious or anti-establishment bent.[186] Chubb imbibed it from the excesses of the later deists, and from scriptural enquiry; Whiston derived it from his own researches into the Bible and other sacred texts, and from his discovery of the *Apostolic Constitutions*.

Something was probably owed by all these men and their colleagues like Locke, to the anti-trinitarian traditions that were disseminated from Holland across the seas, and patiently catalogued by Herbert MacLachlan. Some took the impetus from Hobbes's attack upon senseless and insignificant language, some from the new metaphysics of the being and attributes of God. Many were connected with the rich Londoner Thomas Firmin, who did more than anyone else to patronise and circulate the works of the anti-trinitarians, although Humphrey Prideaux thought that Firmin was wasting his time circulating books to the Norfolk gentry as they rarely read tracts.[187] Firmin's fortune was used not merely to perform good works for the poor and needy, but also for propagating a particular brand of religious heresy.[188]

Firmin made his money in trade, working up from humble beginnings with a capital of £100,[189] to the point in 1676 where he is thought to have possessed money and assets worth £9,000. This fortune was squandered in putting the poor on work,[190] supporting publishers and pamphleteers opposed to James II and his Declaration of Indulgence,[191] and in propagating Bidle's unitarian creed.[192] Firmin, an early patron of Bidle,[193] accepted his modified view of the anti-trinitarian position.[194] Firmin felt that this view should prevail: Tillotson, on the request of the Queen, attempted according to Nye to dissuade him: but he met with no success.[195] Firmin, instrumental in provoking the Sherlock disputes, was an important influence in the spread of unitarian ideas and controversies.[196] It was exceptionally difficult for the Church to respond when the greatest scientist, Newton, the greatest philosophers of two generations, Locke and then Clarke, the greatest latitudinarian divine, Tillotson, and a host of lesser men, a number of deists, and probably a growing number of reasonable clerics could not accept a crucial doctrine or were thought to be in error over it. It fell, therefore, to the lot of pusillanimous pamphleteers like John Edwards to sniff out Socinianism in works as important as Locke's *The Reasonableness of Christianity*, and seek to expose them.[197] The Church ultimately succeeded in driving unitarians away from the established Church, but ultimately had to give up Athanasius, who was to become another casualty of the new biblical and historical scholarship, which could undermine texts, authors and authorities, and remodel the Church's established position. But the battle joined in the late seventeenth and early eighteenth century was the great testing ground for Christianity; great energies were expounded on the nature of a person and the plausibility of the Trinity; only to alienate some of the finest brains of the kingdom, and to make their clerical careers difficult if not non-existent.

It is a general complaint that this nation of late years is grown more numerously and excessively vitious than heretofore; Pride, luxury, Drunkeness, Whoredom, Cursing, Swearing, bold and open atheism every where Abounding.

John Milton, *Haeresie, Schism,*
Toleration, and best means may be
used against the growth of Popery
(London, 1673), p. 16

They declared against superstition on the one hand, and enthusiasm on the other. They loved the constitution of the Church, and the liturgy, and could well live under them: but they did not think it unlawful to live under another form. They wished that things could be carried with more moderation. And they continued to keep a good correspondence with those who had differed from them in opinion . . . And upon this men of narrower thoughts and fiercer tempers fastened upon them the name of Latitudinarians.

Bishop Burnet's History of his own
time (Oxford, 2nd ed., 1833),
Vol. I, p. 342: cited in Ravitch,
Sword and Mitre (Paris, 1966),
p. 93

We do hereby renew our express commands, that the most proper and effectual methods be taken for the suppression of vice by a faithful and impartial execution of all our laws, which are now in force against irreligion, blasphemy, profane swearing, cursing, profanation of the Lord's day, excessive drinking, Gaming, lewdness, and all other dissolute, immoral and disorderly practices.

The Letters and Diplomatic
Instructions of Queen Anne ed. by
B. C. Brown (London, 1968 ed.),
p. 351: Queen Anne to Lord
Harcourt, the Lord Keeper,
October 22nd 1711

Pray, madam, let this farce be played: the Archbishop will act it very well. You may bid him be as short as he will. It will do the Queen no hurt, no more than any good; and it will satisfy all the wise and good fools, who will call us all atheists if we don't pretend to be as great fools as they are.

Lord Hervey, *Memoirs of the court*
of George II (London, 1848)

Chapter Eight

THE CHURCH IN DANGER
Ridicule Runs Riot

Most of those who attacked neo-atheists and deists so strongly believed implicitly that the views of atheists and deists were leading their contemporaries astray in the practical details of life as well as in the doctrinal. Most contemporaries shared the views of the atheist-hunters when they alleged that the nation had become more vicious than before, and when they alleged that drunkenness, whoring, luxury, cursing, swearing, and all kinds of sin were much more manifest in society after 1660 than they had been in some bygone golden age. Whilst there were numerous laws in force aimed against irreligion, blasphemy, and all those practices which were their consequence, most felt that they were ineffectively enforced and needed strengthening, both by a better policing system, and by certain amendments to their more freely worded clauses. It was this relationship between beliefs and practices that most worried contemporary commentators, and it was the association of the one with the other that intensified the disputes and made them disputes about practical politics and the constitution of society as well as disputes about theoretical and philosophical problems.

When Wake took over the Archbishopric of Canterbury it seemed to some too late for religion to be saved or the drift to social deism to be arrested. There were many reactionaries, both clerical and lay, who had felt that the case of Dr Sacheverell had been the last opportunity for the Church in danger, and that with the passing of the initiative from the Tories at the Hanoverian succession the fate of religion had been decided.[1] As they looked around them all was sadness and debauchery; the effect of deism and of irreligion was sadly manifest in the life of their contemporaries. Freedom was all very well, it was the holy principle which justified a wide range of heresies and malpractices; but it was not enough. There were many who wished to impose a more draconian, a more puritan discipline in life and manners; there were still some, suspected as Jacobites or hounded as reactionaries, who wished to reaffirm clerical power and return to the two-ox theory of the Church and State, away from the tepid and pragmatic erastianism that had settled over the early Hanoverian Anglican establishment. Men like Penton recommended an education for the children of gentlemen screened from the debauchery of the life around them,[2] in an effort to combat decline.

Wake was not convinced that the last chance had been missed, but nor did he underestimate the seriousness and difficulty of the situation that faced him. His correspondents alone did not allow him to forget. They were busy writing to him to tell him of the activities of the Hell-fire Club and other less well known or precisely defined groups of drinkers, blasphemers and mockers of religion.[3] All around him satiric or ridiculing pamphlets and journals found in the Church as ready a target as any other. Meanwhile even his own bench of bishops was likely to desert him in crucial votes in the Lords, for the political wind blew so strongly that everyone would trim to it as politicians; men of principles were almost men of folly, and few would be counted on any day of judgement in the Hanoverian House of Lords. The Archbishop found himself faced with a country out of sympathy, a political situation far from malleable to his aims to free the Church from danger that had hovered over it since the days of Sacheverell, in effect since the days of Laud.

There had been, it is true, certain signs of an independent revival furthered by the latitudinarians themselves; for they had fostered the joint missionary projects for England and abroad and had attempted to disprove the common High Church attitude that they were misleading the country. Both High and Low Churchmen regarded the others as the main apostates in the battle for men's souls: the contemporary attitude to Sacheverell was that here at last was a man standing for right and dignity. Broadsheets circulated showing his opponents reading Hobbes, disapproved in the later seventeenth and early eighteenth century.[4] Hoadley was pictured seated at the desk beneath many evil influences; as the rhyme remarked underneath:

> *View here the pourtrait of a factious priest,*
> *who (spight of Proverbs) dares defile his nest:*
> *And where he shou'd defend the Church's cause,*
> *Barely deserts her, and arraigns her laws.*

The Sacheverell case was a last fling to reverse the policy of toleration, of occasional conformity, of lax discipline and laxer manners.[5] It suffered from the allegation that it was bred of Rome and nurtured on the Canons of the Catholic Councils:[6] it was condemned for its strong Tory pose and for its irrepressible right-of-centre rage.[7]

Social deism was increasingly manifest in all walks of life, both high and low, into the eighteenth century. The puritan programmes against playhouse and bawdy house, against liberty of speech and promiscuity of act faded as a rising standard of living, a lessening of restraints, a growing toleration, and the idyll of Reason crept again through society.[8] For social deism was a phenomenon apparent in coffee-house debates, apparent in the proliferation of early eighteenth-century news-sheets and periodicals, apparent in the very prose and pose of the writings of the time. Social deism found its Bible in Shaftesbury's *Characteristicks*, its support in the deists and their books, its patronage amongst the aspirant wits of city society, its apogee in the replies of satirists and commentators, its nemesis in the promiscuity, rape and murder of dark London alleys.[9]

Social deism was to some extent no new phenomenon, nor is it entirely fair to counterpoint the Commonwealth and the rule of the Major-Generals as a chaste era of military efficiency and strict moral enforcement, with the decadent laxity of the Carolingian or Georgian courts. Court life under the early Georges was noted for its parsimony and lack of social engagement, whilst courts before under Elizabeth or James had not been beds of married love alone.[10] What was new in social deism was the living proof of the connections between writing, satire, attitudes, manners and morals, all of which to the propagandists of the day amounted to no less or no more than growing atheism. This had been feared before and seen before, but never to the extent, and never so openly avowed by the upper ranks, as it was in the period 1660–1740.

The new government in 1660 had been aware of the extent of the problem, and early royal proclamations had attempted to stem the tide of filth and evil-living in the early days of the restored King. Rebels and royalists of low life were to be treated with equal severity.[11] The churches were to become the seminaries of morality, and the proclamations against vicious people were to be read regularly to attentive congregations. The whole was connected with the proper observance of the Lord's Day, for immorality on Sundays was still more heinous a crime than immorality during the normal course of the week.[12] Later governments continued the legislative pressure: Anne crusading for 'piety and virtue',[13] William condemning blasphemy and profanity;[14] even Charles II had in his later years urged the better observance of the Lord's Day.[15] Under George I letters were sent to the archbishops and bishops to tighten controls over ordinations, enforce residence, control pluralism and to catechize widely.[16] Of all the monarchs, Anne was the one who was most concerned:[17] she was worried about deists' propaganda as well as by a looseness of morals.[18]

It was fear of the disintegrating moral ethos that prompted clerical and legislative action; the Commons had petitioned the King on this issue in 1697[19] and it was fear of these traits of English society that led to Wake's Blasphemy Bill in 1721,[20] which he urged upon the second reading on the grounds that the new enormities weakened State as well as Church: 'But when the offences tend not only to the weakening, but to the utter subversion of a constitution; policy, as well as pietie, require our utmost endeavour to prevent it.'[21]

Wake's defeat over this Bill reflected the lukewarm support his bench of bishops were willing to give him; it does not detract in any way from the eloquence of his conviction, or from the contemporary consternation at the seriousness of the problem.[22]

Wake himself had been the author of a pamphlet against swearing and cursing, and in favour of maintaining the solemnity of promissory oaths, at the time of the Glorious Revolution, and the author of a tract against swearing.[23] This book was thought a timely reminder for undergraduates at University College in 1719, when Charlett wrote to Wake reminding him of the book, saying that he had been using it amongst his undergraduates, and suggesting that it be reprinted.[24] What the archbishop was to prove unable to do by his legislative and political skills, he could do by his pen. There were plenty of laws to enforce to help him, but laws could only be aimed against specific wrong-doing, and could only be enforced if justices, juries and informers were prepared to do so.[25]

It was not high life alone that caused so much disruption. It was rather ridicule that caused havoc. Ridicule even dared to challenge the authority of tradition, that pillar of respectability in the Anglican Church that supported the whole structure of bishops and Church government. Mr Bowman's sermon, preached in Wakefield in 1731, was subsequently printed. It began by setting out its argument:

> *In which is prov'd that all Tradition*
> *Is the destruction of Religion;*
> *'Tis likewise shown by dint of reason*
> *Episcopacy is high Treason*[26]

The work of all priests, whatever their religion, was the same; it was the work of impostors.[27] The Anglican Church was as bad as the Catholic,[28] the need was to return to the pure Church of the Apostles, which did not need bishops or their cheats.[29]

Ridicule was often supported by more serious remarks. Bowman's views were defended shortly after their publication by an attack upon the bishops' claim that their powers were granted Jure Divino.[30] The attacks upon priestcraft often amounted to more than idle remarks aimed at an easy target. They could be serious arguments against pretended miracles and revelations, against special powers in the priesthood, against all those attributes of Catholic priests which in some measure shaded into an attack upon the Anglican clergy.[31]

The urge for comparison and for wide historical coverage led men to detect similar quirks and follies in Greek and Roman priests,[32] Brahmins,[33] Bonzees,[34] Sadducees[35] and Papists:[36] but the same urge to abuse free-thinkers and attack them with their own weapons led to Bowman being called the chaplain of the sect of free-thinkers.[37]

Against these assaults, the bishops tried to preserve their authority and some agreement over doctrine.[38] The Bishop of London in 1699 warned his clergy that atheists were using Socinianism as a cloak[39] and that they had to preserve the dignity of their calling.[40] Bishop Kidder asked his clergy to set good examples as well as to teach,[41] and to concentrate on the main and unquestionable elements of the Christian faith.[42]

One of the court circle who personified the traits of contemporary irresponsibility fully was the infamous John Wilmot, 2nd Earl of Rochester.[43] His conversion was in some way an affair of greater significance to the Church than was the stream of apologia and the later Boyle lectures, for it represented the admission by an open and avowed atheist that he had been wrong to pursue the riotous life that he and his friends revelled in. Bishop Burnet, who attended the bed-side of the dying libertine, wrote an account of the miraculous change of view on the part of his charge.[44]

Both Mr Tansham and Dr Radcliffe gave testimony to the effect that Rochester had changed his mind in his last hours.[45] This was recorded by William Thomas following a conversation with Dr Radcliffe at Lord Oxford's in 1702, when Thomas was Speaker of the House. The story was also confirmed in the *Verney*

Memoirs, the Verneys having connections with the Rochesters.[46] The Church made much of his conversion over the ensuing years.

They had some reason to do so, for Rochester's poems and publications had expressed the spirit of court vice they were struggling against. An early biographer remarked upon his indulgence in pleasures of court and town.[47] By 1679, this commentator felt, the continual round of drinking had broken his constitution.[48] His final conversion, it was argued, showed the eventual triumph of his reason, before occluded by love and wine.

Rochester held a view of the world entirely in keeping with his way of life. He had a mordant wit, a cynical vision of all women and most men, and a conception of life as a game played by bawds and cheats. He thought statements were merely a way of furthering men's interests, and agreed with Hobbes in supposing reason to be a means of furthering desires. His wit sought pleasure in sensual delights, and his vision thought of Charles's court at times as the bounds of human wisdom, at other moments as a manifesto of human folly. From these precepts and opinions Rochester concluded that the play of life was a farce, and that it was therefore better to play hard for enjoyment, than to become the slave of any ideology peddled by priests or politicians. Man was born of fear: he was therefore a fool if he tried to masquerade as anything more than a beast of his passions.

Rochester represented most of his philosophical views, such as they are, in his poem *A Satyr against man*. He scorned the arguments of natural religion, by inflating them and then attacking them with his own view of the nature and role of reason:

> *Bless'd, glorious man to whom alone kind heaven,*
> *An everlasting soul has freely given . . .*
> *Reason, by whose aspiring influence*
> *We take a flight beyond material sense;*
> *Dive into mysteries, then soaring, pierce*
> *The boundless limits of the Universe;*
> *Search Heav'n and Hell, find out what's acted there . . .*
>
> *And 'tis this very Reason I despise*
> *This supernatural gift, that makes a mite,*
> *Think he's the image of the Infinite.*[49]

Rochester thought prelates indulged in a pompous priestcraft which covered a thorough-going hypocrisy. He decided that he would not contemplate religion seriously until he could find a churchman who lived according to his principles.[50] To Rochester, reason was not an agent permitting men to aspire beyond themselves, it could only allow them to follow their lusts more fruitfully.[51]

> *Our sphere of Action is life's happiness;*
> *And he who thinks beyond, thinks like an ass . . .*
>
> *I own right Reason, which I would obey;*
> *That Reason that distinguishes by sense,*
> *And gives us rules of good and ill from thence;*

> *That bounds desires with a reforming will,*
> *To keep 'em more in vigour, not to kill.*
> *Your reason hinders, mine helps to enjoy . . .*

The egoism of Rochester's pursuit of happiness was explicit. He professed to a lady accusing him of inconstancy that he centred everything in his dear self:[52] he exemplified the atheist's self-regard, pride in his own wit, and belief that wit was merely a tool to advantage himself of yet another woman for the night. When Rochester used the Scriptures, it was only to bring in Eve to help further denigrate the female sex in his poem *The nature of Woman*.[53]

When Rochester finally left the court, he wrote in the vein of a debauched Jacques:

> *Tir'd with the noysom folly of the age*
> *And weary of my part, I quite the stage;*
> *For who in life's dull farce would bear,*
> *Where rogues, Whores, Bawds, all the chief actors are?*[54]

His life's achievement on his death lay in a number of poems that in the words of one critic brought 'a kind of elevation to lewdness'. He bequeathed some fine love lyrics, animated more by desire than affection, and the story of his regret at the wasting of his life. It was Rochester, who to many atheist-hunters, along with his colleagues Savile, Sedley and the rest, represented the evils of the age. The pledge Rochester made not to deny God's Being and Providence further was therefore an important one.[55]

From the maze of writing and social events certain themes stand out. There is the theme of the nature and function of wit in a civilized society, connected to the uses and abuses of satire in contemporary works. Attitudes towards this problem helped to define to what extent a man was a free-thinker: for if he endorsed the use of satire against even the Christian religion there was something of the atheist in him. Connected to this is the virulent strand of anti-clericalism so long a feature of English life, both before the Reformation[56] and following it,[57] when it became more closely connected with political causes opposing the Catholic retrenchment, Spain, and later France. Connected as it demonstrably was with the fight against French absolutism, and with Whiggish politics in the later seventeenth century, there remained a residuum of fears that more was intended than anti-popery: that some men overstepped the bounds, and argued cases which brought into doubt all priests wheresoever they were, whatsoever they might be doing. Ridicule was often an important weapon in the hands of those posing as anti-clericals: its impact could be severe.

Anti-clericalism and the rise of ridicule and reason animated a whole cultural ethos: it both reflected and encouraged contemporary social life. If it were fashionable to be witty, if facetious comment and satirical exegesis were admired if not always cultivated, the position of the sceptic was eased. Those who fumed against this growing distinction in society saw the bad implications for life and manners if the trend were allowed to continue.

The controversy that raged around the Bangorian Sermon of Sunday 31 March 1717, was another facet of the disputes about the control of religion and society, and the relationship between secular laws to keep men in order, and religious revelations.[58] His critics, like Snape, were worried lest an application of his principles led to a dissolution of the whole frame of the Church,[59] and lest he successfully called into doubt all Councils, decrees and authorities.[60] The dispute rumbled on, re-appraising the whole role of the State and of the Church in the administration of religion in the country. This debate, studied in relation to the problems of settling the constitution, and in relation to the perennial question of Church–State relations, has also to be seen against a background of the atheist scare.[61] William Law took up this point when he accused Hoadley of arguing that it mattered not what a man's religion was, as long as he were sincere in his profession of it. This made Quakers, Jews, Turks and deists as good as the sincerest Christian in the eyes of God.[62] Law also thought he could substantiate the charge that Hoadley was an anti-trinitarian.[63]

The vexed question of playhouses and other institutions of pleasure and enjoyment[64] was thought to reflect other social and intellectual changes. The trouble with society permeated the whole of it; it was reflected in the fashions of the greatest lady through to the pertness of the street girl; it captured the philosophical Hobbism of Rochester's loves and pranks through to the unthinking carouser walking the London streets. There were many who sought a puritan revival.[65]

What perhaps is interesting is not so much the evil-living itself which has been long documented and well known, but the reactions to it. For a long tradition of literature preserves the Christian restraints to the full, and decries the excesses around the author from an almost puritanical position. There was still a large body of opinion which thought in the late seventeenth century that the licensing laws on books should not be relaxed, and only Blount's making fun of the Censor, Bohun, finally decided the case.[66] Similarly a large body of opinion regretted the ridicule of religious subjects, and others grieved to see the progress of profligacy in the world. Few could with Mandeville comment on how vice made the world go round, even allowing for Mandeville's own puritan streak which nevertheless thought it dreadful that it should be so.

If we analyse this general puritan spirit manifest in so many written works of the period, we can perceive that at least at the commencement of the period it is connected vitally to political lobbies surrounding the great issues of the future of Anglicanism, the possibility of comprehension, and the relative aims of the presbyterians, the independents, the Catholics, and the varying shades of Anglican opinion. John Milward, one of the few parliamentary diarists in the Commons of 1668 gives us insights into the use of the fear of the growth of atheism in political debate. Here the statements of tract writers, and the casual observations of MPs were transmuted into a reason against comprehension. The allayment of splits within the Church was thought to offer a way of preventing the further spread of atheism,[67] when Pepys wrote of the growing sympathy for the cause of comprehension early in 1668, yet by the debates of 8 April, even by those of 11 March,[68] opinion was swinging again to the more normal position that toleration helped rather than hindered atheism.[69]

Atheism was a live political issue, connected as it was to the general question of settling the religious establishment after the upheavals of the Interregnum. It came up for discussion whenever toleration, comprehension, reform, or re-alignment in Church and State relations and in clerical policies were discussed, for clearly a wrongly formulated policy in matters of Church administration and dogma could make an atheist of everyman.

It was discussed equally whenever plays, players and playhouses came up for consideration. The playhouse had suffered badly in the Interregnum, after its flowering as a court and city entertainment during the Jacobean period. Well into the eighteenth century the lower end of the acting profession, the strolling players, were to be hounded as part of the ever-present vagrancy problem,[70] and connected with beggars and thieves. The upper end of the profession that played to aristocrats in packed fashionable theatres in Drury Lane, and could even aspire to be mistresses of a King, were less persistently spurned, for obvious reasons. Nevertheless puritans and their attitudes were still to be found, and many saw the playhouse as the adjunct of the coffee house spreading atheism amongst the upper and middling sort of people.

The content of the plays was in part to blame for the offence which severe puritans found in the playhouse, but the whole idea of representation, of lewd-ness, of free love was indissolubly connected with theatre. Night after night bawdy and farce was acted out at Haymarket; men were daily cuckolded, and social satire became one of the fashionable sports of light-headed audiences in search of pleasure. The puritanical and the serious-minded objected to the whole spirit of the play; for the play usually intended to entertain, rather than to en-courage deep thought and mature reflection for harassed social consciences.

John Henley, the famous orator, laughed at the laughter when he came to write his *Oration on Grave conundrums, and serious bufoons*. His long title-page pointed the way to the gist of his argument: it described how its task was the

> . . . justifying Burlesque teaching, in its turn, by philosophy and Reason, Divinity, Logic, Ethicks, Rhetoric, Law, the Burlesque of Wisemen, Fathers, Poets, Drs, Popes, Bishops, Deans, High and Low Churchmen, Preachers celebrated, controversial writers, dissenters of all sorts, Professors, Kings, Emperors, magistrates, Peers, Commons, Courts of all kinds, Schools, Colleges, conversations, and all the most solemn persons, on the most solemn subjects and occasions, as one forcible way to discover truth, and engage the virtue.[71]

The whole was a great parody of Shaftesbury and his school who defended the art of satire. The Oratory recited a long list of those who had used this method of wit in Classical and modern times, and ended up praising the method in facetious tones, and suggesting how it was conducive to the finding of truth. The style was flippant, and the references damaging to the advocates of wit: 'The Greeks were always burlesquing one another, hence, as merry as a Greek was a pro-verb: Epicurus, Ennius, Lucretius, Tully, derided the Religion of others severely; all professions to this day agree one creed, which is to laugh at one another.'[72]

Henley himself caused great offence. His Oratory used the primitive liturgy from Clement's constitutions,[73] and his whole scheme seemed to one critic to be more of a money-making venture than a religious ceremony of educational and pious value.[74] To this critic 'the place was more like a theatre than a place of worship'.[75]

Henley's lectures interfered in many areas of secular and religious policy: he felt no compunctions in making his opposition to the Hanoverian policy towards Spain and the privateers apparent.[76] He was fascinated by the question of marriage,[77] by the problems of law and order:[78] he felt that political manoeuvrings impeded men grasping his truths: 'At present ye truth is kept from men, by private counsels, votes of credit, ye secret service and Intrigues of state.'[79] He used his gilded tub to harangue the German policy of the government, the corruption of the court, and the obfuscations of the bishops and their Church.[80]

Henley's work satirized many of the debates of his contemporaries: he even resorted to satirizing their satire. His mood cultivated the ridiculous, his Oratory was thought to foster the profane. He could laugh at Mother Whiston's Prophecies of Earthquakes and Jew-Quakes:[81] he spoke of comets,[82] Berkeley's tar water, the immortal soul, and of all the other crucial questions of his age.[83] Henley both condemned the growth of irreligion, and fomented it. His Oratory was a scene of great contemporary interest, an eccentric exemplar of new departures and worrying innovations. To many it boded ill for the future.

Henley did, however, write in support of revelation,[84] and the list of subjects on which he lectured[85] shows that he had a conception wider than merely wishing to implement the primitive liturgy which he favoured.[86] He was industrious enough to manage disputes over the administration and aims of his Oratory[87] at the same time as disputing with Whiston and printing his lectures.[88]

In his famous *Characteristicks* Shaftesbury had taken as one of his most pointed themes the question of the role of wit. The whole of his second essay in the collection was a defence of the 'freedom of wit and humour' written 'in defence of raillery'.[89]

Here are penned those delightful phrases reflecting Shaftesbury's idea of Whiggism, liberty, politeness and civilization, phrases which gradually ceased to be the phrases of a radical and almost cynical thinker, and became the phrases of a man summing up all that was best in English civilization and thought, stressing beauty, truth and other major civilized virtues. This change took time: for when Shaftesbury published many felt his cynicism to be Hobbist, his realism to be unpalatable, and his idea of civilization decadent.

Shaftesbury felt that 'All politeness is owing to liberty. We polish one another, and rub off our corners and rough sides by a sort of amicable collision.'[90] Shaftesbury's idea of society seemed rather like the random atoms of the atheists' universe, rubbing against one another and out of their perpetual pointless motions producing by chance the polite virtues he so much cherished. But there was more than random wanderings behind Shaftesbury's idea; there was also an idea of the kind of knowledge and the kind of society that can be created by different rhetorical and conversational standards. As he himself stated, a 'freedom of raillery, a liberty in decent language to question everything, and an allowance of unravelling or refuting any argument, without offence to the arguer, are the terms which can render such speculative conversations any way agreeable'.[91] This he contrasted with orations, which 'are only fit to move the passions; and the power of declamation is to terrify, exalt, ravish, or delight, rather than falsify or instruct.'[92]

Shaftesbury echoed the great liberal plea for rational and free discussion. He rightly apprehended that the freedom of oratory and demagoguery swayed crowds on emotional questions, and swayed them in a way favourable only to the person exercising that power. To him the origins of fanaticism were a style of prose, and fanaticism and enthusiasm were expressed through particular forms, of which oratory was one, that were therefore objectionable. Shaftesbury's great hope was that free enquiry and discussion would lead to reconciliation; enthusiasm and frenzy whipped up religious, social and moral differences, leading to dispute and conflict, therefore free enquiry and civilized debate should lead the other way through the mediation of common sense.[93]

The liberal cry, just as it often seems correct to the rational mind, often seems to miscarry in practice. Emotions and oratory cannot be detached from politics, and scepticism, that greatly hated monster of the later seventeenth century, was rightly feared from what Shaftesbury was saying. Men could perceive that the same rules which Shaftesbury applied to the connections between a certain kind of prose, a certain kind of expression, a certain kind of debate, which led to enthusiasm, applied to his own system: and his own free enquiry, where reconciliation was worked towards equally by all sides was tantamount to stating that there were no rights or wrongs. Many feared with Wotton that ridicule against the Church was too high a price for freedom.[94]

Moral prevarication could therefore be charged against some of Shaftesbury's passages: but so could direct incitement to a society to become dissolute and free in its manners and morals. For to free wit, to make it a paradigm for social converse, was allowing scoffers, anti-clericals, despisers of belief, creeds, and even of the Bible, to appear as the heroes of the peace. They were those that permitted a toleration; they were the true irenicists: to Shaftesbury, as to all those with liberal views, it therefore seemed obvious that to them should be given the kingdom. To his colleagues this was not so obvious. Raillery meant laughter, laughter meant the erosion of forms of authority; the erosion of authority meant the end of respect for ancient traditions, rites and institutions: amid this laughter what might happen to the Church of England, to the political system, to the social fabric? Laughter was dangerous to politicians and dangerous to clerics: it was the centre of much of the argument over the licensing laws, through to Walpole's struggle with the caricaturists and the satirical news-sheets of the 1730s. It was fundamental that men should not be given such freedom, the freedom to scorn: out of this irenicism might arise, but it would be irenicism after scepticism had triumphed, the Church had been dismantled, the lengthy volumes of apologia brought to nothing, and philosophy all but debunked. All that would remain would be the purest form of social deism: even perhaps the Hobbist State.

Shaftesbury was not unaware of the implications of what he was saying, and he hastened to justify it fully. He commented on how

. . . the reason why men of wit delight so much to expose these paradoxical systems, is not in truth that they are so fully satisfy'd with them; but that they may better oppose some other systems, which by their fair appearance have help'd, they think, to bring mankind under subjection. They imagine that by this general scepticism, which they wou'd introduce, they shall better deal with the dogmatical spirit which prevails in some particular subjects.[95]

This kind of statement was not couched in a way which allayed men's fears: it rather underlined them. Shaftesbury shows us one extreme of the contortions which the combined evils of scepticism and enthusiasm forced upon men. Like so many they feared that toleration would give way to Catholicism, and Catholicism meant political repression as well as idolatory and atheism: at the same time some wished to tolerate the sects, whilst others had no such intention. Also men feared reason, yet saw it had to strengthen their case otherwise their cause was lost: at the same time reason must not be allowed to take men into ataraxy. Shaftesbury decided that emotional millenarianism was far more of a threat both to liberty and religion than scepticism was: it was this judgement that aroused antagonism. Shaftesbury's friends and acquaintances underlined the fears many had of his works. He had met and talked with Bayle,[96] and had granted a pension to John Toland.[97] In his letters he revealed his great sympathy for Bayle,[98] and spoke of the beneficial effects of his scepticism.[99]

These attitudes dominated the eighteenth century for much of its duration, and not only in England. The world that Voltaire described scathingly in his Encyclopaedia was not so far from the world of Shaftesbury as all that: the very subjects chosen illustrate the continuity in crucial words and concepts between the England of the early century, and France after the mid century with the flowering of the deistical *philosophes*. Voltaire's first edition of the *Philosophical Dictionary* wrote about the Flood, the Chain of Being, historical research into Christianity, atheism and atheists, the human understanding, folly, toleration, prejudices and superstition: it was overwhelmingly theological in its origins, but philosophical and rational in its tone, running like other encyclopaedic authors across the full gamut of scholarly disciplines and debates. Voltaire's faultless levity of tone, his rhetorical flourish, captured the essence of the man of wit and letters, that peculiarly eighteenth-century creation that was so much feared by the stalwart sons of the Church; feared not only for his anti-clericalism, or even for his scepticism, but also for his brilliant and scathing prose.

As the world of the sword became the prerogative more and more of large states with expensive and elaborate machinery, and as in France and England the dangers of revolt seemed to recede, the revolt of the pen and the fight over the presses became of increasing moment. Publishers like Edmund Curll, renowned for publishing suspect books, were brought to court in an effort to suppress their activities.[100] Curll was convicted on 30 November 1725 for publishing several obscene and immoral books. The debate about the liberty of the press was part of the fear about the revolt of the literate through the presses, whether it were discussed in an explicitly political context as it was in relation to the activities of the *Craftsman*[101] and in the age of L'Estrange,[102] or whether it were more consciously concerned with religious and moral matters. Similarly, with the growing laxity of manners and the freeing of conversation, came that great fear. Men perceived that where before their predecessors would always have made saving remarks about the wonders of theology, have strengthened their remarks with a cry to the saints or to God, or would have taken seriously all matters of higher import, they were now tossing God about the logic of the drawing-room with gay abandon. It is difficult for a historian to penetrate the exact atmosphere or conversation of diverse groups, without imagination and guesswork. Those multiple manifestations of a past life, of the quality of mind and matter that passes in every English salon or every English meeting during the early years of the eighteenth century, are difficult to evidence or to generalize. All that remains for us is the imperfect insight which letters, diaries, books and pamphlets give us, when read in quantity, of the way men feared the world was moving, and the way in which such literate men knew the world was moving. This has to suffice for our purposes, inadequate as it may be, for no historian can write the aggregate lives of men in a community over a space of some hundred years.

The playhouse and the bawdy house recur constantly in the moralizing literature of the time, as they had done for a century or more before the advent of the restored King. We can understand their animus when expressed in such ephemeral works as the *Maxims and Reflections upon plays* of 1699 and *Some considerations about ye danger of going to plays* of 1704. These like other such works present the puritan case, the argument that plays and players were leading country and Commonwealth to destruction.[103] The playhouse was to such writers an unmitigated evil:[104] certainly men were not recommended to go there at all if they wished to preserve their chastity, their virtue or their hopes of salvation. William Law in 1726 similarly attacked playhouses[105] and recommended prayer and devotion in their stead.[106] Law was attacked in turn for adopting the old puritanical position that no one should ever be merry.[107] There was no particular text of Scripture which condemned playhouses, his critic contended.[108] The playhouse was never to be advised in the homiletic literature of the time: a small treatise trying to show men what they were to do in one Christian day made frequent mention of the need to improve the mind, to pray, to encourage pious devotions, and to restrain desires by acts of self-discipline, but it never hinted that the playhouse had any moral role![109] Advocates of the religious societies urged instead the virtues of religious conversation.[110]

As the *Maxims* reasoned, plays were of no use to Christian morality, for 'charming the senses is but a very awkward and unlikely way of reforming the mind, and introducing the sentiments and love of severe virtue'.[111]

There had been a time when divines had had no hesitation, when they for a long while 'set themselves against publick shews, and in particular manner against those of the theatre'.[112]

Some then began to think that perhaps the theatre could be converted into a forum for moral elevation and discussion: perhaps something could be made of its great drawing powers, to persuade and interest the masses in virtue. The author of the *Maxims* felt this experiment had been most unsuccessful, that the whole project was absurdly utopian. As he pointed out so accurately, and so much in accord with the better reactionary thinking of his day: 'It is the fondest

Imagination in the world to hope for any mighty reformation, or true improvement, from a method, where matters are managed so, as to make a Mens Vices a jest, and his virtue an amusement.'[113]

To another author the stage had represented an easy defilement.[114]

The argument of the *Maxims* may be taken as a well-researched example of the case that could be made against plays and players. It was scholarly, looking back to the Fathers and to the Ancients for arguments from authority: it was perceptive, in its analysis of the impact of atmosphere, form and message upon impressionable people assembled as a social group for the observing of a single often dissolute spectacle; it was well argued in the long tradition of a pamphlet invective, able to make its debating points well, being aimed against the pamphlet produced on the other side in favour of plays, entitled *Of the Lawfulness and Unlawfulness of plays*. Its combination of these three characteristics, shared in part or whole by a host of other tracts, merits attention.

Classical scholarship brought the philosophy of Plato to bear against the theatre. The author pointed out that the Ancients had not allowed women on the stage, and had maintained higher moral standards in their serious tragedies than moderns did in their slight comedies. Plato, despite this ancient superiority, had nevertheless condemned plays as unworthy of virtuous men.[115] Aristotle had not endorsed the theatre, and the Ancient Fathers of the Church had roundly condemned it.[116] Aquinas, Ambrose, Jerome, and the Bible[117] itself all disliked wit and acting: as Ambrose suggested, 'Non solum profusos sed omnes etiam jocos declinados arbitor.'[118]

Here in a Father of the Church was that very association between wit, laxity of manners, and the theatre, which all late seventeenth-century thinkers could recognize.

The legal aspects to be debated were mainly concerned with the actors, and whether they fell under royal dispensation through a licence, or whether they were subsumed by the Vagrancy Laws. A typical controversy over legal and moral matters came to the fore late in the 1720s, when a gentleman took up the case of the theatre established in Goodman's Fields, London, by an impresario called Odell. The author of a pamphlet against Odell's house tried to use the infringement of the King's prerogative to strengthen his case against the prevailing times, 'when luxury, and a taste for the lightest amusements, have overspread the British world'.[119]

The arguments brought against the particular house in Goodman's Fields were conventional puritan remarks. Plays wasted time and money; they were the resort of lewd women, such that Goodman's Fields had already become a whores' den like Covent Garden and Drury Lane; the plays enacted took their heroes out of Bridewells, and often ridiculed traders and merchants: and finally, plays drew away the attentions of honest-working merchants and businessmen leading to the ruination of their personal fortunes, and of the nation's economy.[120] The downfall of the Commonwealth was the most likely end of all this activity.

These allegations deserve longer discussion than our pamphleteer was prepared to devote to them and have to be weighed against those made by contemporaries in favour of drama.[121] The claim that plays made men profligate by virtue of the subject matter, and that low comedies made fun of the industrious and upright members of society, is one that can be supported by the large number of plays published and produced at the time that were either mediocre social satire, parading wit in the form of late-night review-type laughter, or were comedies of love, promiscuity and cuckoldry. Any catalogue published at the time reveals the same long list of seamy titles, and any reading amongst these works reveals the same predominant themes of ribaldry, amorous adventure and the pleasures of wine, women and song. Anonymous plays appeared entitled *The Costly Whore, Cupid's Whirligig,* and *Amorous Old Woman.*[122] The Duke of Newcastle wrote *Humerous Lovers,* and the Duchess, *Wits Cabal:*[123] Henry Clapthorn found *Wit in a Constable,* Sir Francis Fane *Love in the Dark,* and Lord Viscount Faulkland chose *Marriage Night* for one of his pieces.[124] Repetition characterized these somewhat tedious entertainments: repetition of those very vices and techniques the pamphleteers decried.

Court entertainment was far from edifying. In 1680 three farces were acted before the King at Newmarket. *The Merry Milkmaid of Islington or the Rambling Gallants defeated,* which started a pamphlet war all of its own; *Love lost in the dark, or the Drunken couple* which was a bawdy burlesque; and *The Politick Whore or the Conceited Cuckold.*[125] Typical of so many was this latter, where caricature figures like Sir Isaac Jealousie, his friend Fido, and Innocentia revealed in their names their whole caricature, and their appointed role in the disreputable plot. Policia caused a scandal, being pregnant of another man, and the play dragged on through fears and realities of cuckoldry and buffoonery.

The metaphors which sprang most readily to the late seventeenth-century mind were the metaphors of pollution, and social disease. The theatre was a great contagion, wrote a man in 1704, summarizing opinions of a century of propaganda.[126] To this author the essence of theatre was fiction and show: this would denigrate men preserving 'anything real within'.[127] The combination of promiscuous content, bad influence, and the unpleasant vanity of audiences, would lead men to atheism. For plays influenced men profoundly:

> They [men] are now taught how they might be without a Creator; and how, now they are, they may live best without any dependence on his Providence. They are call'd to doubt of the existence of God. . . . His wise Providence at every turn is charged with neglect. . . . They make very bold with the Grace of God, and crave inspiration to serve the ends of lust and revenge.[128]

These were strong claims, and not entirely without foundation, just as they were not entirely accurate. As the author himself acknowledged in his strong conclusion, 'some have suggested other causes of our horrid declension', 'yet most considering people have the fairness to own, that the stage has gone further in running us down to this low and almost brutal condition'.[129]

Others saw even more direct and dire consequences for religion itself. A writer in 1698 thought that the educative influence of the theatre was great and far from benign:

> They appear to have study'd all the arts of an easie defilement. . . .
> They are now taught how they might be, without a Creator; and how,

now they are, they may live best without any dependence on his Providence. They are call'd to doubt of the Existence of God, or if that be allow'd them, 'tis only to question what motive he takes: His wise Providence at every turn is charg'd with neglect.[130]

The stage gave a bad idea of marriage, full of rows and turmoils, of cuckoldry and deceit. The theatre furnished men with ammunition against matrimony as an institution and encouraged other less respectable sexual liasons.[131] It brought men to that same condition, and in the same phrase, that we had arrived at in our author of 1704.[132]

This brutal condition at which men had arrived was more than echoes of Hobbist man: it was social reality. Men were well aware of the low ebb of social manners, of the threat to good Christian souls lying in the plackets and thieving hands of whores and pickpockets.[133] None was more all-embracing in its treatment of these than a short pamphlet published soon after the Restoration, which promised to make

> . . . a full discovery of the whole trade of Pads, Pimps, Cheats, Trappans, Hectors, Bawds, Whores, Fyles, Culls, Mobs, Budges, Galsses, Mills, Bulkers, Kidnappers, Thief-catchers, and all other artists, who are, and have been students of Whittington College.[134]

The first passages of the work presented a conversation between Jezebel, a crafty bawd, Isobel the wandering whore, Pimp Whiskin, Ruth, two noble culls, Gusmond, and Hazard, a grand cheat. They relayed to the reader details of the difficulties of a whore's trade and the methods deployed by wandering ladies of leisure. The poem at the end included little rhymes to summarize the trade, practice and characters of all those other miscreants mentioned on the title-page. Another book suggested new laws to encourage matrimony and curtail prostitution,[135] whilst one author was worried because the bawds paid the magistrate to permit them to stay in business.[136]

These manifestations of practical atheism bore out everyman's pet theory. It could be playhouses alone that caused it all: for they provided meeting places in the neighbouring area, and men weakened by sensual frivolities of the play would readily pay some woman for a few minutes of pleasure. Lord Hervey remarked on the need to curb both the irreligion and the opposition to the government manifested in the playhouse. Alternatively the numbers of cheats and rogues could prove any theory of social decay, of impending rupture of the Commonwealth, or it could argue any particular cause of atheism which the author believed most fervently.

Whitelocke Bulstrode felt that a masquerade, especially where transvestism was encouraged, carried more Christians away from the Christian faith than raising ten men from the dead would have kept in the faith.[137] John Lacy explained the problem in terms of immoral justices who gave a bad example to the rest of the nation.[138] He went on to request an alliance between Anglicans and dissenters against the major threat of immorality to both.[139] Roger L'Estrange thought knavery and sedition had political origins, when he drew a parallel between the reformers of 1677 and those of 1641.[140] All that was accepted was the persistent and growing threat to moral men and manners by the great laxity of the times, and by the noticeable prospering of cheats and evil-livers. It was activities which reversed the true Providential scheme that most annoyed many writers against irreligion.

One of the most interesting movements of the last decade of the seventeenth century, in full force some ten years later, was the movement for the reformation of manners. It was fashionable to attempt reform by the means of private enterprise societies, although as White Kennett warned, little progress could be made if these societies alienated both Church and State.[141] This movement managed to publicize itself to the full with a wide range of tracts which gave, if somewhat prejudiced, a nevertheless informative account of the vices and bad habits of upper and lower society.[142] Drunkenness, promiscuity, idleness, folly, gaming and plays were all part of that same world of wasted opportunity which grieved the heart and even the pocket of the man who believed that the way to heaven was the way of toil, industry and honesty. Often lust and debauchery were linked with Catholicism and the horrors of Rome.[143] These great vices were flourishing now as they never had been before, and they all reciprocated on each other to the worsening of the disease.[144] It was the Society for the Reformation of Manners in general, and their avid protagonist the Rev. Josiah Woodward in particular, who hated these desultory emanations of high and low society alike. Their greatest fear was that the evils of some would lead to the downfall of the whole kingdom and social framework: their hope was that men would confess their sins and benefit from an awakened conscience.[145]

Josiah Woodward was an indefatigable if unoriginal pamphleteer. His seminal ideas of impending doom, and the evil social and moral consequences of bad living, were recited whatever the subject of his particular concern. His printer in Bartholomew Close by Smithfield, one Mr Downing, was kept constantly busy, in the early eighteenth century, putting out tract after tract. There was one against gaming, which stressed the theme that 'no person in the short space of this probational life, can have much space to spare for Diversion'.[146] He reasoned that carding and gaming were a waste of time, and that 'it too often sacrifices good company, good humour, and a good conscience together', something which not infrequently leads to broils and fights between the players and contestants.[147] There was another against drunkenness, which Woodward feared made men like beasts. It furthered their carnal desires, and removed Christian constraints more normally placed upon their actions by their conscience and sense of propriety. His main contention was that 'Man, as he is rational and wise, bears the image of God; but intemperance blots out that divine resemblance',[148] and his sense of the Great Chain of Being led him to despair when men, little lower than the angels, thus rebuked God whilst the angels did but praise him.[149]

Woodward happily recited how the societies had repressed many infamous houses, and how they had 'brought to punishment many thousands of lewd persons in this city alone', that is in London.[150] He found that 'the very name of a pastime is an absurd and hateful notion', implying folly and wasted excesses.[151] He issued a warning to all who swore, drunk, or were promiscuous, warning them of the dangers in this life and the next, and the dire consequences of their actions. Drunkenness, for example, was regarded as an agency for causing quarrels and disrupting society.[152] He condemned characters like that of the town gallant, satirized in 1675.[153] He discussed the activities for the Society for the Reformation of Manners.[154]

Other anonymous penny pamphlets and broadsheets carried similar messages, and may be his work as well. *A Kind caution to prophane swearers* decried swearing, for it provokes God's severest wrath. If we continue to dishonour God in this way we harden infidels against him as well as ruining ourselves. Woodward's *An Earnest persuasive to the serious observance of the Lord's Day* argued a similar case,[155] stressing the doubly heinous nature of curses on a Sunday. One gentleman published a work explaining for even the 'meanest understanding' the nature of the holy feasts,[156] with instructions for their observance; others defended the Society for the Reformation of Manners.[157]

Much of this literature came from the endeavours of Josiah Woodward, that great champion of the cause of the Society for the Reformation of Manners. This idea was mooted in the last decade of the seventeenth century,[158] and by the following decade the societies were well advanced in their task of hunting out permissiveness and evil-living wherever it could be found and brought to punishment. The aim of the society was to effectively prosecute the criminal laws on the subjects of Sabbath observance, gaming, drinking, cursing and profanities in general;[159] the method was to persuade clerics and members to encourage informing and to persuade the magistrates to back the society in its aim of furthering draconian laws,[160] as well as to distribute edifying tracts and set a good example.[161]

The Queen, and earlier King William III, were both in favour, at least in their public proclamations. In 1702 Anne had issued a formal letter to be read in all churches four times every year[162] whilst William had enacted a Statute for the 'more effectual suppressing of blasphemy and Prophaneness'.[163] Charles II had witnessed the parliamentary passing of an 'Act for the better observance of the Lord's Day'[164] whilst the Statutes of I Car I c I and 3 Car I c I were still referred to. Despite the existence of Statutes sufficient for the task the problem of enforcement remained. There was a sense of great despondency over the condition of the country's morals at the end of the Carolingian hey-day, and there were the endless debates over the morality of informing to contend with, here as elsewhere in the enterprise of law and order. It has been said of Tudor and Stuart social and economic legislation that the Statute book was no more than the tabling of pious hopes; this judgement is severe, but the evidence of the Cursing and Blasphemy Acts suggests that enforcement and control was indeed difficult.[165]

Enforcement depended upon informing, and informers were widely disliked and in many ways discouraged by the society they served.[166] One of the constant cries of the Society for the Reformation of Manners was that the informer should be welcomed as an asset, not hounded as a miscreant.[167]

The Tower Hamlet Society were well aware of the problem. They arranged weekly meetings to plan prosecutions and receive informations,[168] and built up a fund to fight cases.[169] They elected four or more Stewards per ward in the city of London to check up on the conduct of the Constables.[170] They hired spies to locate bawdy houses.[171] Meanwhile the Constables were convinced that the lower officers were the corrupt ones who were making enforcement of the laws against debauchery difficult, and so they met at the coffee house near the Royal Exchange,[172] and worked out varied beats between them.[173] The Constables did have considerable powers to handle such cases: as Sergeant Pemberton recorded, in some cases Constables had powers to fine on the spot, and in other cases like violation of the Sabbath they could haul offenders before the Justice without a warrant.[174] At a higher level still, Franks thought that the clergy should be invested with commissions of the peace to strengthen control in the counties and aid the gentlemen on the Bench.[175] Others merely expressed concern lest atheists and debauchees sat in judgement over others.[176]

It was this problem that was to be reformed by the societies and by the indefatigable energy of Josiah Woodward. Their operation has been little studied, and the motives of this little-known cleric remain occluded. His books are almost single-mindedly concerned with the societies and their problems, and when they are not chronicling the progress of the schemes[177] they are directly exhorting young ministers, seamen, soldiers, or the public at large to take up the message of a pure and true life. Woodward was involved in writing the *Seamen's Monitor*[178] and devoted particular attention to printing and reprinting and expanding his work urging seamen to lead good lives.[179] He predictably took up the cause of poor children and suggested that their education stress the correct moral disciplines suitable to a holy life, and he too addressed himself to the question of the theatre. He is reminiscent in his operations of Mr Maryott, the tireless pamphleteer working for the erection of more and more workhouses in the 1720s, and himself deeply implicated in the economics and administration of several of them.[180]

Woodward published one of the classic answers to the accusations of those who found the system of informing immoral and corrupt in idea and practice.[181] He defended the informer on the grounds that he was a high-minded man with a social conscience, who rightly feared God and was concerned for the well-being of his neighbour, such that he informed to the magistrate. Josiah for his troubles in combatting practical atheism for so much of his life, was made Boyle lecturer in 1709–10. He gave a set of lectures which marked the apogee of his campaign, stressing as they did *The Divine origin, and incomparable excellency of the Christian religion*.[182]

The penal laws were frequently summarized to help all well-meaning citizens to clean up the streets and back alleys of their towns and villages. A movement was put afoot to inundate the country with penny and threepenny pamphlets underlining the laws, the Christian duties, and the chances of a great national reformation. Anne's proclamation had stressed the need at a time of national crisis to call on God's help: this could only be expected, reasoned the members of the society, if the great reformation were put on foot.[183]

At the same time the Societies for the Propagation of the Gospel were well underway: these were the foreign branch of the Biblical Christians, and in some ways represented the overseas counterpart to the fervour of Christianizing an atheists' paradise here at home manifest in the reformation societies. Founded by Proclamation of William III, the work had of course been going on for many years before the official inauguration of this great venture.[184] The history of the society's progress need not concern us here, interested as we are in the attitudes of the exporting society rather than in the missions and their impact, and the materials distributed by the society abroad. The history has not been recently written in full, and can best be traced through De La Mothe's *Relation de la Societé établie pour la propagation de l'évangelie dans les pays étrangers* and David Humphrey's *Historical Account of the incorporated society for the propagation of the gospel in foreign parts*.[185] All that is interesting is the concern with which men willingly tackled the problem of educating people scattered across the globe, who had been deprived of the blessings of the Gospel: how they willingly gave time and effort to these schemes. The motive may well have been mixed, and it is tempting to deride their efforts as manifestations of mere imperial rationalizations, or evidence of cultural brutality such as the Spaniards before them had practised. But to do so would be unfair: for these men earnestly believed their own faith, and thought it essential in the names of civilization and reason to bring such people the news they must be waiting to hear to lift them from barbarism. Their projects for raising money and the minute books of their proceedings are testimony to their concern.[186] These men could therefore tolerate no infidels at home, and looked upon the reform of manners as the counterpart of their own projects; for it needed a truly Christian society, to give self-confidence to those who exported the Christian message elsewhere, as part of their holy duties.

The conjoint influences of these societies, if their own propaganda is anything to go by, was considerable. They installed a system of printed orders of Sessions circulated to invite good Christians to inform against vicious and profane people, evidence of the growing printed bureaucracy emanating from local government officials at last beginning to standardize procedures in all fields from the Poor Laws to the Gaming Laws.[187] They had the backing of a large number of impressive figures of Church and State.[188] In effect their influence was less far-reaching and less benign; people seemed to be made sinners, and sinners they would remain. The Grand Juries of Middlesex, London, Southampton, Nottinghamshire, Derbyshire, Buckinghamshire and Monmouthshire might well endorse the societies' work, and the obligations of the J.P.s in this respect could be frequently stressed:[189] but the problem was intractable in the extreme, and warnings against the persistence of the bad manners and vicious habits continued. The technique of indictment by the Grand Jury was one that was much used to enforce the legislation against blasphemy and sedition. The accusations were made by the Jury against neighbours or authors of disreputable books, allowed free press after 1693, and were then referred to the Petit Jury for final judgement and sentencing. The Grand Jury was the main means available to the Justices of the Peace to get information about parochial crimes, and the county Grand Jury would usually represent the different towns and hundreds of the area concerned to ensure that truly local presentments and information were forthcoming.[190] There were occasions when the Justices instructing the

Grand Juries would give them a lead in the correct direction. Certainly the directions of Sir John Gonson in the years 1727 and 1728 were thought sufficiently full and worthwhile to warrant publication in 1728.

Gonson summarized the roles of the two Juries:

> . . . no man can be convicted, or attainted of any crime before two juries pass him, of at least 24 persons; the one a grand jury, to present the offence for trial; and the other a petit jury, to try the truth of that presentment; The Grand Jury coming from all parts of the county, city, or liberty, for which they serve, and the other, viz. the Petit Jury, from the very neighbourhood where the offence was committed.[191]

Occasions had arisen in the past when the Grand Jury had intermeddled in the tasks of the Petit Jury.[192] Sir John was keen to point out to the juries that they had a competence to prefer charges in three categories of crime. They firstly were to think of offences 'as concern Almighty God, and his holy religion established amongst us'. They were secondly to consider offences against the King, and finally against 'our neighbours, or fellow subjects'.[193] He told his first jury that

> . . . there are such books published, daily sold in shops, and advertised in the publick newspapers, that ought rather to pass the fire than the press; and are a scandal to any Christian country. If you can't find out these detestable authors, present the Printers and publishers.[194]

He returned to this same theme in his third jury speech when he remarked upon the times in which they lived:

> Therefore you are to enquire of all offences against the Act of the ninth year of King William III, for the more effectual suppressing Blasphemy and pro-phaneness; and particularly of all books and pamphlets, wrote against the Christian religion, or the divine authority of the holy scriptures; there are several late writers, who go under the names of Deists, but are really atheists, without God in the world, renouncing his Providence, and even denying the Lord that bought them; pretending indeed an enquiry after sensible ideas of the spiritual and supernatural truths of eternal life: whereas, with all their boasted reason, they are not able to give an idea of the breath of natural life, nor can tell the composition of the least pile of grass; and yet, by rational demonstration, would determine and judge of things invisible which can only be the objects of faith in the word of God.[195]

He was worried that certain authors denied the immortality of the soul and the future state of rewards and punishments; he was worried by the Hobbist theories which wished to subject mankind to the level of brutes, and to thereby dissolve the bonds of human society.[196] He went on to incite the jurors to prefer crimes not only against printers and publishers of evil doctrines, but also to consider crimes of drunkenness and debauchery, the social manifestations of all this wrong thinking.[197] He believed that the Trinity had to be defended against its detractors,[198] urged more effective enforcement of the laws, and a general tightening of moral restraints.[199] He could categorically state that

> ... we want neither good laws, nor due encouragement from our superiors, nor yet good magistrates; but many of the constables and other inferior officers, are so very negligent and remiss in their duty if informing against and prosecuting common swearers, drunkards, sabbath-breakers, etc. that they often render our pains as it were ineffectual, for the promoting a general reform of manners.[200]

He was keen to oust sodomy and other similar evils;[201] he believed that the magistrates should act as well as the society for the reformation of manners.

The situation in the sphere of moral legislation was the same as that in the related field of Poor Law regulation; law after law could be and had been passed, amended, and renewed, but the information procedures could not keep pace with the problem. Despite the pledge of support for informers by some zealots,[202] men were reluctant to prefer their neighbours for transgressions they themselves would commit; or else men would be preferred for charges as part of a private vendetta, or through malicious and ill-informed gossips, making the process of pressing a charge difficult. The legislation allowed moral regulation on the scale and intensity of the best days of Calvinist Geneva; the practice of the system allowed as much vice and ill-living for the rich as they could possibly want, and was only hard on the poorest classes over whom society had at times some degree of control.[203]

Those who sought to spread Christianity abroad were dismayed by the lack of reform at home. Despite the royal proclamation for the foundation of the Society for the Propagation of the Gospel,[204] despite the terms of its charter[205] and the earnestness of its early devotees,[206] they felt undermined at home.[207]

Cases of blasphemy and immorality were constantly before the courts and public. In 1665 the Vicar of Laxfield, William Adamson, was accused of blasphemy for allegations in a tavern concerning Sherman, who he suggested was a bastard.[208] Adamson counter-attacked by accusing Dawsing, his critic, of being an immoral and debauched person, and went on to slur the characters of William Weeke and Thomas Sherman.[209] Early in 1678 the Master of Dulwich College complained to the Visitor about Mr James Allen, Senior Fellow and Minister of his institution. He maintained that Allen was a quarrelsome drunkard, 'a notorious whoremaster', and that he had made Elizabeth Oxley, a servant of the College, pregnant.[210] In 1681 Mr Ashenden was accused of writing an infamous pamphlet, and pressure was applied to make him recant in church on Sunday.[211] There were occasions as with the dismissal of Mr Alexander from his lectureship in Ipswich when a town feud was fomented between the faction who alleged that he had been improperly dismissed, and those who supported the decision.[212]

These cases illustrate the way in which claims and counter-claims could be generated over a tankard of ale, or could come from the abuses of those in institutions of learning and religion. It was meetings at an alehouse, where the women members of the Family of Love Circle were alleged to stay all night, that had most concerned Sir Roger L'Estrange when he wrote to Bishop Compton on 20 August 1678 concerning immoral conventicles.[213] Henry Newton had written to Compton in 1706, worried about Hickeringill's books, and Butler's work on marriage, but the Court of Arches had not upheld the case.[214] Nevertheless the Court of Arches was willing to pursue a case against William Coward.[215] Just as Compton was urged to take up such cases, so later was Wake: in May 1728 Wake received a letter enjoining him to take action against Woolston[216] for example.

Such disputes could arise out of something more prosaic than the pursuit of truth: in the case of Bernard in 1707 his drift towards primitive Christianity was related to his lack of success in pleading for augmentation to his two livings in Lincolnshire from the Bishop of Lincoln. Bernard began by requesting some increase to his two meagre livings on 4 March.[217] By 5 June he was threatening legal action against the Bishop of Lincoln, and promising to publish a book asserting, amongst other things, that the Church had lost her candlestick and that the nation was not brought up in the Christian life.[218] By 14 July 1708 Bernard was arguing that no one could answer his objections and reasons against and concerning Common Prayer written since June 1707.[219] In July 1708 Bernard asserted that the 39 Articles were often sophistical and that the Book of Homilies contained a great deal of false doctrine.[220] By this stage Bernard's attempts to put pressure on to the bishops to give him an extra £100 a year had clearly not been very successful, and his belief that he had merely to become more and more abusive and heretical to receive his deserts did not seem well-founded. The next move came from Sharpe, Bernard's curate at Kelsterne, who read a sequestration saying he had taken the parish over: the salary from Ludford Parva, Bernard's other parish, was also cut off.[221] Bernard therefore evicted Sharpe from the curacy of Kelsterne. In a letter of 31 July 1708 to the Bishop of Lincoln Bernard was taking a more defensive tone, saying that his previous propositions did not intend to reject the Common Prayer approved by Parliament, and that he, Bernard, was not to be thrown out of his entitlement by a curate, whose life and morals he thought extremely questionable.[222] Bernard's case is an important one: it demonstrated the way in which a cleric would drift towards primitive Christianity in an effort to force the clerical authorities to silence him by paying him more, only to find instead he had jeopardized what he already had as clerics lower down the ladder attempted to exploit his drift to what they considered to be irreligion. Legal proceedings were also adopted against authors and publishers of books as well as against men of immoral inclinations. The Grand Jury of Middlesex presented Tindal's *Rights of the Christian Church asserted*[223] as a seditious work liable to cause scandal, and pamphleteers endorsed the Grandy Jury's concern that the points relating to government were conducive to anarchy and confusion, whilst those with respect to the Church would lead to schisms and immoralities.[224] In Boston, New England, a publisher was even fined £50 for publishing Leslie's *Short and easy method with the deists*[225] on the grounds that that work called the King's title into doubt,[226] and was a false and scandalous libel. It was the search for legal remedies after the lapsing of the Press Act that led Harley to write to Gibson over the draft of a Bill to make printers and authors liable for everything they published.[227]

The Whig-inspired societies to reform manners, and the religious enthusiasm that inspired the rhetoric if not the profitability of the plantations men, could not remove all the causes of Wake's regret and worry in the 1720s. There were young men, of good birth, openly forming the Hell-fire Club, and associating for the purpose of mocking religion and spreading atheism. There were the inevitable drunkards and bawds, cheats and tricksters, who profited daily to the detriment of God's justice and Providence. And there appeared to be an increasing number of men willing to tolerate all this, and willing to laugh with the best of them. It was wit and cynicism, scepticism and a sense of the unimportance of a moral life that most threatened the more puritanical of the clergy and bishops. The age of reason could perhaps more eloquently and adequately be called the age of ridicule, for it was ridicule, not reason, that endangered the Church and most severely led to a seeming decay of manners.

Let others creep by timid steps, and slow,
On plain experience lay foundations low,
By common sense to common knowledge bred,
And last, to Nature's cause thro' nature led,
All-seeing in thy mists, we want no guide,
Mother of arrogance, and source of pride!
We nobly take the high priori road,
And reason downward, till we doubt of God.

Alexander Pope, *Dunciad*, Book iv
(London, 1965 ed.), pp. 386–7

. . . were there no general laws fix'd in the course of nature, there could be no Prudence or Design in Men, no rational expectation of effects from causes, no schemes of action projected, nor any regular execution.

Francis Hutcheson, *An Enquiry
into the origin of our ideas of beauty
and virtue* (London, 1725), p. 97

. . . there is nothing, that I know, hath done so much mischief to Christianity, as the disparagement of Reason, under pretence of respect, and favour to Religion; since hereby the very foundations of the Christian faith have been undermined, and the world prepared for atheism.

Joseph Glanvill, λογογσρμΣκε:A,
or, a *seasonable recommendation and
defence of reason, in the affairs of
religion against Infidelity* . . .
(London, 1670), p. 1

As it is every Man's natural right and duty to think, and judge for himself in matters of opinion; so he should be allow'd freely to profess his opinions, and to endeavour, when he judges proper, to convince others also of their truth; provided those opinions do not tend to the disturbance of society.

Anthony Collins, *A discourse of the
grounds and reasons of the Christian
religion* (London, 1724), p. vi

Chapter Nine

THE REASON OF NATURE AND THE NATURE OF REASON

Reason in the later seventeenth and early eighteenth centuries was referred to in adoring tones. It was eulogized, apostraphized, invoked and venerated: it was the means by which men could solve their problems, could understand their world, and eventually obtain that salvation that all pretended to hold dear, if they did not seem to hold it dear by their lives and activities. Yet amidst all this debate and discussion, in which the word 'reason' was never omitted and rarely defined, there were few who questioned its nature, or wondered why so many men, all applying reason to the same problems, found so many different answers. Reason was a strong, unified force; it could with the aid of sense and evidence lead men to the way of both truth and light.

It may appear to many reading the theological and natural philosophical works of the period we are concerned with, that reason did produce a surprising, or intelligible, similarity of view. It was reason, after all, by which men perceived the unity of God's design in the universe, and it was with reason that they interpreted their observations of the world as evidence on a massive scale for the beauty and goodness of God's Creation. The differences between them can appear trifling beside the premises which most of them undoubtedly shared. They all agreed that the alternative form of enlightenment through enthusiasm, through paroxysms of grief and joy, through emotional appreciation of the world of God's imagining, was a form of enlightenment that could be best cast aside, a form that produced dissension, lunacy and social disorders. In England most accepted that certain social aims should always be clearly before men. They idolized, or professed to respect the legitimate quest for social order. They agreed that political liberty, and the strength of the Protestant religion, were mutually conjoint favourable influences, that England was an especially privileged society divorced from the excesses of political absolutism and Catholic dogmatism across the Channel. They agreed that rational enquiry could produce an intelligible view of the world, a world that had been created if not sustained by God's own direct intervention. They often resembled the deists in their attitude: but some were something more, and it is in these differences that men found important cases, important areas of dispute, where differences became great if not cataclysmic.

All thought that the world was intelligible in propositions, lemmae, and arguments, recorded in plain English prose and hurried to the printer's to place it before the knowledge-hungry public; although Edwards and others at Oxford continued to defend syllogism. But what did Chubb's reason have in common with that of Wilkins? And what properties did Collins's share with Glanvill's? And how did the reason of any of these differ from that of Aquinas or the later schoolmen, whom they all attacked so roundly?

To a man like Chubb reason was the sole means of enlightenment. He saw it as a force conflicting with revelation for the role of informing men of the true nature of religion.[1] Revelation was unfair, as many millions of people had never received it,[2] how then could it be God's means of telling us what to believe? The pagans had run into vile and dangerous practices, particularly those concerned with brutality and sacrifice, and this had been for want of reason.[3] It was therefore essential that Christians avoided this danger, and in consequence reason was the bulwark against the barbarism and folly of Catholicism.[4] To Wilkins reason had an equally important role: 'The greater congruity or incongruity there is in anything to the reason of mankind, and the greater tendency it hath, to promote or hinder the perfection of man's nature, so much greater degrees it hath of moral good or evil,'[5] but Silkins would not have agreed with the severity of Chubb's attack upon revelation, or upon his vindication of the primacy of reason in all religious matters. The logic of Wilkins and his friends, working for reason in the 1670s, may well have inspired the extreme rationalism of Chubb in the 1720s: but it seems likely that they would have been horrified had they perceived the drift of ideas, just as Locke was annoyed by Toland's developments of his theories.

Similarly, Glanvill believed it essential to defend the role of reason in religion: 'Since hereby, Religion will be rescued from the impious accusation of its being groundless, and imaginary: and Reason also defended, against the unjust charge of those, that would make this beam of God, prophane, and irreligious.'[6]

But he understood that reason could not prove revelations which were of a different nature.[7] He did, however, believe that 'reason defends all the mysteries of the faith and religion'.[8] Collins saw reason as the agent of free-thought, and saw in free-thought the true means of freeing men from superstition,[9] removing tiresome disputes among the clergy,[10] advancing the sciences,[11] and leading men to enlightenment. He may have agreed with Glanvill about the nature of reason, but substantially disagreed about the extent of its competence, and the competing modes of explanation that also had a place. Glanvill believed in scepticism around certain fixed points of belief that were given;[12] Collins believed that certainty came solely from reason, and that clerical traditions, authorities, and dogmas, misled and restrained the sciences and man's intellect.

The form of reason all these men accepted had a different scope but some common features. They all agreed reason was the language of nature, although Glanvill would have included in the language of nature the agency of Providence and the intervention of a spirit world. They all agreed that certain deducibles from sense experience could be produced that represented divine and therefore human wisdom. All of them fell in varying degrees under the anthropologically centred universe of the later seventeenth- and eighteenth-century rationalists. They dissented from Aquinas and the schools in not giving pride of place to metaphysical arguments, and in not prizing the syllogism as the only or highest form of expressing an argument.[13]

They all substituted for the elaborate arguments that God existed, others equally elaborate but more firmly and exclusively based in the world of physicotheology. The work of Derham,[14] Ray and others, narrowed the range of the apologist, but seemed to strengthen the argument by making it increasingly compatible with philosophy, and reason, its language. As we have seen, in the age of Berkeley natural religion differed from that of Cudworth or even Wise in that it used a different prose and different argument; it was an age of dialogue, wit, rakish writing, an age that in Berkeley's own dialogue agreed to omit refined metaphysical argument, and hammer out the consequences and import for religion of fifty years of natural philosophy. Cudworth had been more conscious of the long tradition of metaphysical argument, and had set his own work more explicitly in the tradition of arguments for the being and providence of God that were older even than the Ancient Fathers of the Church, as old as philosophy itself.

The reactions to Clarke's *a priori* argument provide an interesting insight into the ambience that he attempted to influence. Writing after some forty years of congealed final-cause apologia, Clarke's addition of the *a priori* position to the *a posteriori* antagonized many, and impressed others.[15] To those like Gretton, it reflected Clarke's Arianism,[16] and was an otiose if not undesirable addition to the debate. As Gretton himself remarked, 'Since the argument from innate ideas[17] hath been laid aside by some, and less insisted on by others, Reasons drawn from the Works of Creation and Providence, have been chiefly used, and with great success.'[18]

The *a priori* argument demonstrated the necessity of the existence of one being prior to the universe, thereby placing God above and before Christ and the Holy Spirit.[19] There was a need, therefore, to free the debates from 'those false metaphysical principles which have already long disquiet'd the world'.[20]

In contrast, a pupil and protégé of Clarke's, John Jackson, felt that the *a priori* argument was not only useful, but also necessary to repair the defects in the *a posteriori* position. As he stated,

All my proofs run *a priori*, because I think it impossible to demonstrate the Existence (and much more the unity) of God as a necessarily existent, infinite Being, *a posteriori*. The proof *a posteriori*, or from the effect to the cause, goes no further than to demonstrate that we ourselves, or other things, being plainly dependent, we and they must depend upon a prior cause and Superior Agent which is necessarily existing; but whether that prior cause, and superior necessarily existing agent, be God in the proper, and philosophical sense, as being infinite in perfections, cannot be directly proved from the existence of *finite* things, and can only be proved by arguing from his Nature and Attributes, i.e. *a priori*.[21]

All seemed to agree that the idea of God was not innate, or that the innate ideas argument was not a good one.[22] But all also agreed that religion aided social control, and that therefore the natural religion argument conduced towards social harmony.[23] All agreed that enthusiasm was an evil.

Not all would have agreed with Thomas Morgan's statement of the position in his *Enthusiasm in distress*, however.[24] Morgan acknowledged that 'there are as many different senses and acceptations of the word *Reason* among men, as there are different and contrary opinions in the world'.[25]

Morgan's attack on the *Reflections upon Reason* defended the deists' position. He felt that any speculative pattern of belief could co-exist with a wicked life, and that it was not necessarily deism which led to profligacy.[26] He argued that the reason used by defendants against the deists was often as spurious as the reason of the minute philosophers themselves.[27] Morgan attempted to foist upon his opponent a more severe form of Cartesian dualism, arguing that reason can only judge of modes, properties and relations of material objects. Only the spirit can judge of spirits, and reason cannot extend beyond interpretation of sense evidence.[28]

This view was deprecated, as was any that suggested reason could be fallible, more limited than it should have been, or that the deists' perversion of reason was in any manner acceptable. But the attack on enthusiasm was common, and led to such works as that of Archibald Campbell, writing in 1730 to prove that the apostles were not enthusiasts.[29]

The utility of reason was related to the form of evidence which men would regard as acceptable testimony in the debates with which they were concerned. The question of the role of reason was directly related to the question of the form of evidence used and the method of sifting it. There was a predominant weighting throughout the period of this study given to the information provided by the senses, to the evidence of nature. But men did not wish to exclude other sources of information and proof. Biblical evidence had to be sifted and criticized. The Fathers and the ancient philosophers were all much canvassed, as we have seen in everyone from Cudworth to Crito, from Clarke to Whiston. Evidence of revelations, witches, apparitions, poltergeists, dreams, fancies and spirits would also be regarded as important, but this latter category of testimony was probably the most in doubt throughout the period.

To a man like Chubb the problem was easy to solve. Reason was the means by which men distinguished divine revelation from delusion.[30] Reason was the means by which miracles could be judged, to see if they conformed to the divine plan.[31] 'Divine Revelation, in this case, must accord with the nature and reason of things.'[32] God, if possessed of arbitrary will, would thereby render reason useless;[33] God therefore is equivalent to nature and reason. God is determined by good: 'If true religion is founded on the moral fitness of things, then man, by his own natural ability (consider'd as a man) is qualified to discover it.'[34] This form of association was developed in a different way by the physico-theologians. They felt that God was the Creator of the world, and that reason could appreciate his design, but that God did not force men to do good in every case, allowing apparent evil to occur only if the general scheme were moving in the correct direction. Such a work as Morgan's would attempt to bring together the work of past labourers in the field of physico-theology, and give the final result something more of a deist flavour. Morgan reviewed the mechanical powers of bodies and their properties.[35] He looked into the general laws of intelligence and sensation,[36] and decided that 'we do not find that the general establish'd laws of nature are suspended, or set aside to serve particular purposes'.[37] Morgan was sure that no particular providence of the Deity ever had been proved to have set aside the natural laws.[38] He saw himself as a protagonist of a third, moderate party,[39] neither asserting on the one hand an Epicurean atomic necessity,[40] nor on the other a providential scheme dependent upon the arbitrary will of God.[41] Morgan's irenicism could be misconstrued; but his belief in one prior general Providence, and his faith in the testimony of nature, was shared by many who had written over the preceding fifty years.

The debate over the reasonableness of miracles, aroused by Woolston and his colleagues, reflected the different approaches to nature and reason more sharply than many of the issues discussed. Morgan's *Moral Philosopher* had seemed to rule out miracles, and was reprimanded for this by Joseph Hallet.[42] Morgan replied that 'the natural and moral evidence, in the reason and fitness of things, is always the same; and beyond this, miracles can prove nothing'.[43]

The philosopher complained that he was being condemned because he could not understand the Scripture allegories in their literal sense, 'so as to turn every natural truth and fact into mystery and ridicule'.[44]

The opposing case put by his critics, reflected the more traditional clerical attitude developed over the preceding years before *Alciphron*. One put it succinctly:

> All the doctrines I can name in revelation, whether discoverable by reason or not, are agreeable to the nature and reason of things; even such as the fall of Adam, the introduction of death, the incarnation, sacrifice, and intercession of Christ, &c. but our unassisted reason could not equally discover them all.[45]

The great debate about the role of reason and natural cause explanation recalled the struggles over Hobbes's doctrines in the 1650s and 1660s. As Hobbes had written to King,

> The Doctrine of Naturall Causes hath not infallible and evident Principles. For there is noe Effect which the power of God cannot produce by many severall wayes.
>
> But seeing all effects are produced by motion, He that supposing some one or more motions can derive from them the necessity of that effect whose cause is required has done all that is to bee expected from naturall reason.[46]

This Hobbes manuscript includes a defence of *Leviathan*'s attitudes towards civil power, and argues that in *Leviathan* there was nothing against the bishops.[47] It also goes on to discuss natural problems like heat and light,[48] motion,[49] the vacuum,[50] and Toricelli's experiments.[51] Hobbes was cautiously rewording his statements to say that whilst certain phenomena could have mechanical explanations, it did not mean necessarily that they did have:[52] the mechanism of *Leviathan* was moderated slightly under critical pressure. Men would not allow anyone to suggest, without a rigid dualism of mind and body, that the world was a purely mechanical place.

As Sir Charles Wolseley argued in a little book of 1691, 'A great part of a true Christian's life, and I am sure the best part of it, is a converse with spirits; the best and noblest part of man is a spirit.'[53]

He further added that there was literal truth in the five monarchies[54] theory as there was in the theories of anti-Christ, the beasts and Satan.[55] Wolseley represented the latent tradition of old-fashioned spiritualism; it was not fanaticism, not enthusiasm, merely a belief in the literal sense of biblical passages, and an unassuming disingenuous approach to an area of concern rife with controversy and difficulty.

The more important philosophers all took Hobbes's point that the pressing problem was to define the function of natural evidence, and to see what reason could deduce from it. Wollaston for one had taken natural religion as far as it could be stretched, to the consternation of the authorities. He felt that if there were moral good and evil, then there was religion,[56] and he assumed that all men would pursue happiness,[57] defined in a Hobbist way as being a consciousness of something agreeable.[58] Reason was the means to discover truth,[59] but truth did not necessarily bring happiness.[60]

John Clarke among others was not impressed by Wollaston's ideas. He felt it silly to suggest that truth was moral and falsehood immoral by definition, for 'I doubt not but a man of invention equal to that of our author might assign to any species of vicious action or omission, as many Probable meanings, affirmative of truth, as he could for the denial of it.'[61] He preferred a distinction to be drawn between the notions of truth and of goodness, to avoid tautology, nonsense, or worse.

A number of interesting arguments concerning natural religion can be found in a large manuscript volume in the Rawlinson collection.[62] Written in a plain copyist's hand, the work includes rules for Christian meditations,[63] notes on the lives of the apostles,[64] and ends with a comparison of true religion, that is the Anglican pattern of belief, with popery,[65] proferring advice to English Catholics.[66] This work demonstrates the way in which an unfortunately unknown author could relate practical meditations to a strong belief in the orthodoxy of the Anglican establishment and doctrine, to the use of final-cause arguments taken from the substantial body of natural religious apologia.

The overriding problem in all the debates was the problem of the correlation of different kinds of evidence. How much weight should biblical testimony be given in matters of natural philosophy? How much weight should the evidence of the senses be given in interpreting the Bible? How many miracles and revelations were useful as testimony to the spirit world, and evidence of God's overbearing grandeur? What was the best way to prove any given point?

The evidence from the Bible was under attack from two directions. There were firstly those patient textual scholars working in the way of Bentley, checking each text for authenticity and accuracy against its originals. There was secondly the possibility of divergent interpretations of the texts once established, whether through allegorical as opposed to literal meanings, or through citing alternative passages from other sections of the Bible as additional or contradictory proof. Neither of these techniques were new in 1660: Lorenzo Valla's scholarship had shown the potency of textual criticism in the sixteenth century,[67] whilst an issue like Catherine of Aragon's divorce had shown the conflict that could arise between different passages in the Bible.[68] But in the second half of the seventeenth century these issues of the nature of biblical criticism were crucially important in this wide spectrum of debate concerning irreligion.

Men like Thomas Doolittle believed that the testimonies of the Fathers were of consummate importance in settling disputes about the Sabbath.[69] Byfield reaffirmed that the Scriptures came from the inspiration of the Holy Ghost,[70] whilst Leland in replying to Morgan supported the authority of the Gospels and their mutual compatibility.[71]

When Richard Bentley, the great Cambridge Classical scholar, was editing the Greek Testament of the Bible, it was rumoured that he intended to leave out 1 John V. 7. Letters were sent to Bentley urging him to retain this verse, as it was an essential part of the Church's case against the Arians,[72] and had been included in the 1550 edition of the Bible. Bentley's reply was that of the textual scholar, not the apologist: he remarked that he would settle the problem by studying all the available old texts and deciding the merit of the textual case, and would not settle it by reference to doctrine.[73] This little interchange is illustrative of the impact textual scholarship could make on convinced apologists.

A work of textual scholarship attempting to further the Arian cause in a different way was that of William Whiston and his primitive doxologies. Whiston's revival of the Apostolic Constitutions as forms useful for services and for doctrine was met with a volley of criticism. He was harangued for seeing 'fit to amuse us with vain boasts of certainty without argument, with his own wild suspicions of the forgery and interpolation of what he does not like, with partial and unnatural constructions of what he takes for genuine',[74] and some supported Sacheverell who threw him out of his church in London when Whiston came to the service.[75] Whiston wrote to Sacheverell after the incident denying that he was a true Socinian, but the damage of his writings and textual scholarship had been done.[76]

Whiston waged war against the Bishop of London, who opposed his textual innovations. He felt that Basil,[77] Origen,[78] Polycarp[79] and others of the Fathers supported his cause. He felt that the Bishop of London had himself supported Whiston in demanding that the old form of Trinity be adhered to, and not any new-fangled notion. Whiston agreed and argued that his form of doxology was the true primitive one, the Church's being a later erroneous form.[80]

Whiston supported using the three epistles of St John as part of the orthodox canon of Scripture:[81] men like Higgs attacked his whole approach to scriptural and textual criticism, seeing in it one long plot against the doctrine of the Holy Trinity.[82] Another critic, disguising himself as if he were Origen against Celsus, thought that Whiston had aroused an Arian controversy as acrimonious and important as the Bangorian disputes,[83] and argued powerfully that Christ was divine contrary to the Whistonian position, and to the heterodox interpretation of the new Whistonian Scriptures.[84] Styan Thirlby was upset because Whiston accused Athanasius of being a 'knave and an ignoramus',[85] Dr Grabe because he felt Whiston had been selective and biased in his reading and interpretation of scriptural testimony.[86] He had omitted crucial New Testament texts that favoured the Trinity,[87] had omitted important evidence from the Fathers,[88] and had wrongly assigned biblical texts where he had acknowledged them.[89]

This barrage of criticism surrounded most of Whiston's forays into the world of scriptural and textual commentary from his expulsion from Cambridge through his trial by the University authorities to the end of the second decade of the eighteenth century. He was roundly condemned, for example, for doubting that the Canticles was a sacred book.[90] The revival of the Constitutions most worried contemporaries; but their works were united by a common perception and a common fear, that Whiston's scholarship always had as its polemical aim the introduction of the Arian or anti-trinitarian creed.[91]

Whiston's position seemed deliberately provocative. In 1712 he went so far as to publish proposals for the erection of 'a primitive library' in Cross Street, Hatton Garden.[92] This library was planned as a repository for all the texts of the first four centuries, and was supported by a group of booksellers.[93] He continued his own work on Josephus and other authorities to establish his case.[94]

Some years before Whiston's Arian excesses Toland had challenged the authority of some of the Church Fathers in his *Amyntor*.[95] He had attacked the authority of the Epistle of Clemens and had harangued the work of the mighty Origen. Critics hastened to correct what they took to be Toland's dangerous and distorted vision. Clemens was defended,[96] Origen defended on the testimony of Hermas,[97] and this particular protagonist rounded off with a defence of the style of the Fathers' reasoning:

> What Mr Toland has invidiously urged about the divisions among the Fathers, and their Want of exactness in their Reasonings, I suppose will not move those, who know that truth is never the less such for being surrounded with a multitude of errors.[98]

Most of the other deists had like Whiston and Toland indulged in deviant textual exegesis: Chubb for example had extracted Old Testament prophecies from Clarke's *Discourse of the Being and Attributes of God*[99] and had discussed Christ from his own view of these sources.[100]

Just as the nature of biblical evidence was discussed, and great differences emerged between the deists and their opponents, so differences arose over how to use evidence once marshalled and established as texts, observations or authorities. A man like the Reverend E. Vernon, reading widely in scientific and theological works, would deny with Derham that Scripture had a role to fulfil in teaching men natural philosophy as well as morality and divinity. In his commonplace book Vernon remarked on how certain texts that appeared in the Scripture against the Copernican system, should therefore be discounted.[101] Acquainted with the work of Boyle on chemistry,[102] a convinced Copernican,[103] aware of the work of Bacon[104] and Willis's work on fermentation,[105] Vernon could look down on the work of the late seventeenth and early eighteenth century and show his interests in natural philosophy and religion leading him to accepting certain canons of selection and preference for certain kinds of evidence that favoured the pure natural philosopher. Vernon also gave some detailed space and attention to Clarke's *Defence of the Being and Attributes of God*.[106] Vernon's drift to natural philosophy represents the way in which the atmosphere of reason led men inexorably to the light of natural philosophy, and only then ineluctably to natural religion.

Scriptural evidence retained some of its hold, however. Edward Yardley in 1727 thought it a valuable exercise to collate scriptural testimonies and liturgies to prove the validity of the Eucharist.[107] Lukin, some thirty years earlier, had published a small volume in a very popular genre, giving evidence to people culled from a biblical passage taken from St John.[108] This book sought to 'shew you some characters whereby you may make some judgement of your spiritual state'[109] and in the manner of most sermons bolstered a biblical text and made out of it a set of recommendations for the godly life. Men like Daniel Whitby spent hours and trouble compiling new commentaries on the New Testament: biblical scholarship was not ousted by the reason of nature.[110] A tradition of sermonizing preserved the pressure for belief in the fabric of revelation brought to man through the Scriptures.[111] Men like Conybeare would defend revelation against the deist critics, although their language of 'credibility', evidence, proof and 'expediency' was itself influenced by the deist attack.

As Thomas Morgan pointed out, the truth of a revealed proposition depended upon the quality of testimony of the revealer.[112] It was therefore a thing of the highest moment to have accurate texts of the Scriptures, and to weigh their accuracy against one another, and in relation to historical information concerning the principal actors and authors in the divine drama. Thomas Chubb felt that such discreet and reasonable enquiry could cause troubles for a man's belief in revelation, and he busily refuted the common fallacy that it was a man's deeds that led him away from the truth of religion:

> I am sensible that the common cry is, that it is not men's perceiving any difficulties which attend the divinity of the Christian revelation, but it is their love to their vices which is the ground and cause of their infidelity; though this is a presumption which, I think, does not appear to be well grounded.[113]

To Chubb every being should and did seek happiness,[114] and only had to obey 'that eternal and unalterable rule of action which is founded in the reason of things'.[115] The Gospel was only an address to men to quicken their rationality, and foster their pursuit of the divine rational scheme of things and the eternal law.[116] There was therefore no real need of a religious scheme based on revelation and the testimony of witnesses of Christ. Chubb reflected the new atmosphere of deist-influenced reason when he argued that if deism and infidelity did in fact prevail then evidence from revelation would be of no use in converting these men, for they would naturally doubt all such evidence anyway.[117] Instead the Christians 'must show by arguments drawn from reason and experience, that it is their *wisdom*, their *duty*, and their *interest*, both with respect to this world, and that to come, to live good and virtuous lives'.[118]

Chubb in additional work denied that providences were at all likely. He thought that there was no proof, and many reasons to suppose that God was not continually intervening in the world,[119] and was extremely sceptical of all particular providences.[120]

Critics like Edgcumbe made their animosity towards Chubb's general position over reason and religion explicit in their refutation of his work on *The Sufficiency of Reason in Matters of Religion*. Edgcumbe devoted two sermons at St Mary's, Oxford, on 27 October 1734 and 2 February 1736 to attacking Chubb's central thesis and defending the utility of scriptural evidence and revelation.[121] His remarks had no impact upon the deist precepts of Chubb's mind, and the cause of natural religion, the cause of one great universal Providence laying down a mechanical universe, seemed to be winning, spreading insidiously through the works of its opponents as well as through its proponents.

Hallet attacked Chubb's true gospel more directly in his reply to that work.[122] Hallet disliked Chubb's emphasis upon the immutable laws of nature: he thought Christ recommended things not because they represented the patterns inhering in nature, but because they were God's will.[123] Hallet also believed in particular providences because they were taught by Christ and the apostles,[124] and felt that God's will and the spirituality and infallibility of Christ and the apostles needed stressing in contradistinction to Chubb's view.[125]

The critics of Chubb and his colleagues feared that not only had Christianity become a subject for debate and for proof or discussion, something with which they on the whole agreed, but that it had been discovered to be fictitious by false reasonings, and that this was now a belief in common currency. They feared that too many had come to feel that 'nothing remained, but to set it [religion] up as a principle subject of mirth and ridicule, as it were, by reprisals, for having so long interrupted the pleasures of the world'.[126]

Scripture and the Fathers were used not only to support the fabric of revelation and providence, but also to defend the fabric of free will, God's omnipotence and ability to intervene in the world of his creation, and the framework of the Church. Wheatley, who began writing his commonplace book on 11 September 1711, was quick to perceive the utility of the Fathers in supporting the 'Doctrine, worship, or manners' of the Christian community.[127] He found in their writings arguments to support the supremacy of bishops over priests,[128] the divinity of Christ,[129] the Anglican Eucharist,[130] and the role of the preacher.[131]

The manuscript defence of Christianity in the Rawlinson collection similarly defended the Anglican point of view, attacking Browne's *Religio Medici* for its attempt firstly to argue that there were no fundamental differences between the Anglican and the Romanist position, and then secondly for suggesting that the Anglicans should agree that the Romanists were correct in a number of fundamental respects.[132] The author recites the dogmas that

... there by more mediators than Christ, that his body is not contained in heaven, but everywhere is newly created of bread, that the Saints are the objects of our prayers, that the Pope's traditions are of equal authority with the scripture, that Apocriphal books are canonical. . . .[133]

The Protestant tone of Anglican apologia, and the episcopal form of Anglican clerical institution, was to be defended by reference to favourable Fathers and suitable Scriptures; deists attacking their value attacked the establishment that lay behind them.

The deist also attacked from the defence of liberty. Just as there were differences over the true use of reason, and the satisfactory nature of evidence, so too there were divisions over the freedoms that all apologists and deists professed to revere. To the deist any restriction upon presses or pulpits, any controls over men's thoughts, words, or even deeds, was thoroughly undesirable. Most accepted the need for some restraints particularly upon the lower classes, to keep society together; but many disagreed about how far these restraints were to go, and to what end they were being enforced. To the deist many religious dictates were devices for furthering the clericalism they detested: to their opponents, they were necessary and reasonable restraints placed upon men naturally inclined to sin.

The dispute would at times surface as a major pamphlet war, or as a political squabble over particular legislation for the Church. In the early 1720s the Waterland Arian position raised the question of subscription to the 39 Articles. John Conybeare preached to the Oxford audience at St Mary's on the subject,[134] and William Stevenson, replying to Waterland's view of the need for extreme liberalism,[135] suggested that men could permit themselves a freedom of belief if the Articles so permitted them.[136] Stevenson was worried about the rigid enforcement of a specific doctrine on a matter so difficult as the Trinity, for as he argued, if only one scheme is correct then

> All, or all but One, of those great men, Bishop Bull, Drs Wallis, South, Sherlock, Bennet & co. must have been guilty of these enormous crimes, and must have deserved the imputation of giving great scandal. . . .[137]

Others defended the 39 Articles with more vigour,[138] seeing in every clause and comma a necessary part of the faith that had to be laid down clearly by the Church. No one could forget Hare's arguments, showing how difficult it was for the individual conscience to study the Scriptures and by that means to discover the truth.[139]

On a more philosophical level, Christians sought to defend liberty of human action and free will against the incursions of deterministic theories from their deist colleagues. As Samuel Clarke stated, in response to Collins's work on human liberty,[140]

> When we say, in vulgar speech, that Motives or Reasons DETERMINE a man; it is nothing but a mere figure or metaphor. It is the man that freely *determines himself* to act.[141]

Clarke defended the notion that man has within him 'a principle or power of self-motion' which causes action, and represents man's ability to choose his own course of motion.[142] Man is distinct from the beasts to Clarke by dint of his moral consciousness: but beasts do share the same self-active principle as men have. He here attacks the Cartesian theory that all beasts are necessarily determined by physical necessity. God's foreknowledge of men's actions does not mean they are all previously determined, it merely (to Clarke) reflects upon God's great wisdom in being able to foretell the freely chosen courses of action of mankind.[143]

Clarke, however, agreed with the deists in some measure. He condemned the 'superstitious men and lovers of darkness' who 'endeavour to retrench that liberty of enquiring after truth, upon which all valuable knowledge and true religion essentially depends'.[144] Clarke believed that minds should rove freely, but that their discoveries from so roaming should be confined within certain patterns of intelligibility and decency. He, like many of his colleagues, baulked at arguing for an authoritarian Church, an episcopal tyranny, or an official and unmoveable dogma. For in such courses they would draw nearer to the Romanism which they all hated. It was a difficult balance for intelligent Protestants to find, when working from their reason, between the necessary stability of belief to guarantee order, and freedom of enquiry to guarantee individual rights and liberties. Clarke's severity against Collins was justified intellectually, and imperative socially.

Others were well aware of the importance of this debate. Chubb added a tract on the subject of liberty to a collection of his pieces in 1730,[145] and argued elsewhere that persecution and repression were themselves causes of disorder. Persecution was wrong, for no judge can be infallible:[146] dispute sprang from repression of free enquiry, not from permitting dissent.[147] Chubb extended these beliefs into the field of political theory, defending a more widespread and full liberty to each man than most would have liked. He felt that all governors derived their effective and true power from the people,[148] and thought religion was 'wholly and only personal'.[149] Religion was not necessary to social order:

> The belief of a God, a providence, and a judgement to come, doth not necessarily make them injurious and hurtful to it: men's relation to, their interest in, their dependence upon, and their obligations to society being exactly the same, whether they believe these points, or not.[150]

Chubb argued that one man's conscience could not oblige him to oppose any other man's conscience if it felt differently.[151] What to Chubb was liberty, was to others akin to anarchy in the world of the understanding, an anarchy they feared would carry across into the world of politics.

Anthony Collins was equally strong in his defence of liberty for free enquiry, but in discussing the case of Whiston's free-thought he did add a caveat concerning social order:

> As it is every Man's natural right and duty to think, and judge for himself in matters of opinion; so he should be allow'd freely to profess his opinions, and to endeavour, when he judges proper, to convince others also of their truth; provided those opinions do not tend to the disturbance of society.[152]

Collins disagreed with Whiston's views, but felt he had a right to express them, and even to attempt to persuade people to them. In this belief Collins seemed free with his own proviso concerning social control, for many of Whiston's opponents took his Arian creed to be an extremely dangerous subversive system. Collins bolstered his cause for freedom from no less a churchman than

Archbishop Wake,[153] citing the Preface to Wake's *Sure and honest means for the conversion of all hereticks*,[154] and pointed out that numerically in the world Anglicanism was a small faith.[155] Only bigots, politicians, hypocrites, enthusiasts and the ignorant to Collins's mind attempted to suppress reason because they lacked its quality themselves.[156]

Collins's dispute with Whiston, developed in the *Discourse of the grounds and reasons*, was one tempered by a mutual sense that they held principles like liberty dear against the ignorance of tyrannizing priests. But this sense of mutual support did not affect Collins's judgement, when he decided that Whiston, great mathematician and well-meaning divine that he was,[157] was sadly deficient in judgement when it came to matters of textual scholarship.[158] Collins drew on the work of Simon and Le Clerc, the most incisive of recent biblical scholars, to defend his views of the Scriptures as having a broadly allegorical meaning.[159] Whiston, in contrast, had suggested that the apostles had cited accurately and argued literally from the Greek or Septuagint translation, and that the biblical text had only been corrupted later, by the Jews. Yet, said Collins, Whiston had failed to give a single example of a prophetical quotation out of the Old Testament in the New Testament where a literal interpretation would apply.[160] The Septuagint version was not agreeable to the Hebrew text in the age of Christ,[161] while Whiston misused the sources of the Apostolic Constitutions, the Greek Psalms, several manuscripts of the Septuagint, the Chaldee Paraphrases and the works of Philo.[162]

Free-thought was therefore necessary, but free-thinkers accepted that they would often disagree, and that members of their fraternity would from time to time need reproof for stupidity. Free-thinkers could at times only agree on a negative and loosely worded programme against priestcraft and authority. Collins made his position on these matters plain when he opposed the 20th Article of the Church of England.[163] He felt that Chillingworth's *Religion of Protestants*[164] had proved the primacy of the Scriptures above the dictates of the Church, and therefore rendered false the article that 'The Church hath Power to decree rites and ceremonys, and authority in controversys of faith.'[165] But Collins, interestingly enough, was not content merely with theological argument culled from one of the great seventeenth-century sources for English Protestant apologia. He also brought historical evidence to bear, attempting to prove that the 20th Article was never in the draft approved by Parliament anyway. This was tantamount to an acknowledgement by Collins that legal and historical evidence and argument was as crucial as theological viewpoints.[166]

Collins was prepared to argue elsewhere that free-thinking was necessary for the perfection of society,[167] that only through it could the Devil's kingdom be destroyed as it had been in Holland,[168] that it remedied superstition[169] and prevented pretences to revelation gaining any credibility.[170] As early as 1713 Collins had the audacity to suggest that foreign missions put out by the Society for the Propagation of the Gospel in foreign parts would only succeed if they exported free-thought,[171] whilst he wrote that the clergy themselves agreed that the doctrines of the Church were contradictory to one another and to reason.[172]

The clergy were to Collins particularly silly because they attacked the most rational and most securely anti-Papist of the Anglican and Protestant authors for being Socinian or atheist. Such had been the fate of Cudworth, Tillotson, Clarke, Locke, Bold,[173] and Chillingworth. Meanwhile men like Leslie and Nicholls made free-thinking ever more necessary, on account of 'their daily publishing of books concerning the nature of God, and the Truth and Authority of the Scriptures, wherein they suggest the arguments of unbelievers'.[174]

Collins concluded his free-thinkers' manifesto by rebutting common prejudices against him and his colleagues. Men do have sufficient ability to think freely;[175] they do not create divisions and disorders.[176] Free-thinking does not make men atheists,[177] nor is it necessary to the peace and order of society to impose certain dogmas about it.[178] Bacon,[179] Hobbes,[180] Clarendon,[181] Tillotson, Cudworth, More, Temple and Locke,[182] Collins felt were in agreement with him.

Collins also wrote at length on the subject of reason and proof. He reflected and partly inspired the deist love of legal and historical proof for all belief and argument, and defined reason as the means 'to perceive the credibility of the witness . . . and the credibility of the thing testify'd'.[183]

He attacked with great vigour the distinction of things above and things contrary to reason, a long-standing distinction stressed by Boyle: 'For 'tis chiefly by virtue of that distinction the Divines militate in behalf of Mysterys and Contradictions, against those who say they can only believe that which they can understand.'[184] Boyle had felt that this distinction provided the middle course for the natural philosopher and man of science: denying value to contradiction, but bolstering faith through admitting that some things were truly above men's comprehension.[185] Collins would have none of this. One of the positions he considered was: 'Things are said to be *above reason*, when we are ignorant of the manner, or of the Physical Cause of their existence.'[186]

He went on to question the whole notion of the Trinity,[187] singling Gastrell out for particularly severe treatment,[188] and finally moved to considering the true nature of liberty. Collins was of the opinion that liberty was compatible with divine prescience, because 'all the liberty we have, consists in a power to do or forbear Several actions, according to the Determinations of our mind, and that liberty is perfectly consistent with that certainty of Actions before they are produc'd'.[189] Liberty is therefore consistent with necessity, and many divines had encouraged errors through holding, to Collins's mind, a false notion of liberty.[190]

Collins's style was reiterated in works like the *Tryal of Witnesses*[191] published some years later, when Christianity was on trial in a court-room drama, reflecting the ever-increasing love of legal and historical evidence tested by reason to determine faith. Nevertheless the Church fought against the new atmosphere on two levels. Increasingly it came to accept the new standards of debate, and attempted to meet them in its own style of dogmatizing, catechizing and arguing; but it came to this only after a long rearguard battle against free-thought and the weighing of evidence in such rational and secular ways.

Bishop Gibson, for example, had not been averse to influencing the publication of the *Philosophical Transactions*; he had written to Sloane:

> I prevail'd so far as to have it put in ye Philosophical Trans; presuming upon
> your favour and kindness in yis matter; and I assure myself, that cannot be
> wanting in the application of a paper, which evidently confutes a late wild
> and dangerous hypothesis that has given so much advantage to Deists and
> Atheists,

and attempted to use the periodical occasionally for correcting the damage
done by pernicious or anti-clerical authors.[192] Men like Bramton Gurdon thought
it better to meet Spinoza, Hobbes and their followers on grounds of reason, and
worked systematically through their arguments defeating them one by one.[193]
Whilst the Boyle lecturers poured out arguments against speculative atheism,
the Church attempted to block publication of deist works, or to prosecute their
authors: whilst the pamphlet controversies raged, the Church was seeking legal
action against heretics and blasphemers, seeking to limit their works, their
influence, and their control over the criteria of the debate. They did not meet
with whole-hearted support or unfailing success.

Men like John Jackson felt they had found a middle path. To them,

> . . . to bring appetite and inclination under the dominion of reason, is worthy
> of a rational and sensible being; but to make Reason subservient to pleasure,
> and its use to consist only in procuring it, is the principle of all vice, and the
> utmost corruption of all moral judgement.[194]

They accepted new standards of debate, but denied that these inevitably led
to free-thought and Hobbism. Different in tone but perhaps similar in intent
was Francis Hutcheson, striving to vindicate Shaftesbury against Mandeville.
He felt that beauty was a necessary perception, and that

> . . . supposing the deity so kind as to correct sensible pleasure with certain
> actions or contemplations, beside the rational advantage perceivable in them,
> there is a great moral necessity, from his Goodness, that the internal sense of
> men should be constituted as it is at present, so as to make Uniformity amidst
> variety the occasion of pleasure.[195]

The age of heated debate about the essentials and adiaphora of religious practice of the mid-seventeenth century had become for Hutcheson and Shaftesbury
an age of debate about the relationship between aesthetics and God. Men could
still intervene and defend long-acknowledged doctrines against the aspersions
of deists, and demand old-fashioned proof from the Bible. For example, a critic
of Chubb's views on original sin defended the idea that it was imputed and that
man's nature inherits Adam's fall, and pointed out that Chubb had produced
no biblical evidence for his case.[196] But on the whole the atmosphere for everyone
was becoming deist, for their influence over the subjects debated, the evidence
used, and the importance of reason, was spreading.

And I love the New Philosophy so much the more; for why, it sets the hand a working not a striking, and answers the noise of talking by the stilness of doing, as the Italians clam rowt and tattle into nodding and beckning.

N. Fairfax, *A Treatise of the bulk and selvedge of the World, wherein the greatness, littleness and lastingness of bodies are freely handled* (London, 1674), Epistle Dedicatory

Dieu est la support de la science, comme il est le support de la création. Omnia in ipso constant, le monde idéal, et le monde réel. Tous les êtres visibles et invisibles peuvent répéter la parole de l'Apôtre: in ipso vivimus, movemur et sumus. Tous les verbes sont l'écho du verbe être: toutes les pensées sont l'écho de la pensée par laquelle l'homme pense l'être.

E. Hello: M. Renan, *L'Allemagne et l'athéisme au XIXe siècle* (Paris, 1859) (Reprint edition Hants, 1971), p. 43

Aphorisme of Numa Pompilius, Nulla res efficacius multitudinem regit, quam superstitio: of which, if taken away, Atheisme and (consequently Libertinisme) will certainly come into its (roome) (sted).

John Aubrey, *Remains of Gentilisme and Judaisme* (London, 1881), p. 6

There's no such thing as good or evil,
*But that w*ch *do's please, or displease,*
There's no G-d, Heav'n, Hell, or a Devil,
'Tis all one to debauch, or to be civil . . .

Bodl. MS Firth C15 ff. 27–8.
Song by Lord Vaughan.

Chapter Ten

THE SIGNIFICANCE OF THE
MINUTE PHILOSOPHERS

To seek to understand the causes of these great debates in later seventeenth- and early eighteenth-century English society is almost akin to seeking the reasons for human enquiry and curiosity itself. For the most simple explanation of the debates is that they represent a conflict that arose between the free wish to pursue learning and understanding about man and the world around him, and the inherited ideas that were received by the Augustans through their Churches, Bibles, and literary heritage. Men sought to understand the world in terms that they felt appropriate to a universe of matter and motion; they sought physical and mathematical explanations of observable phenomena, and this led them ineluctably towards questioning the origin of the universe, the nature of man and reason, and the role and existence of God. The great disputes about atheism were, under this theory, merely reflections of the great tension between theological and philosophical modes of explanation, and the fear of increasing atheism both reflected an increase in near-atheist views, and perhaps helped to keep in check the opinions of all but a hardened few, keeping them on the straight and narrow path to salvation.

This view would not have been the one which contemporaries would have urged at all. They did not, after the fashion of later commentators, see any conflict between reason and religion. Most of the men we have been studying would have hastened to argue their fundamental compatibility, and eulogized over the way in which natural philosophical arguments strengthened the religious cause. This enthusiasm for the efficacy of the new learning in religion would, however, conceal inner fears. That Boyle and his colleagues wrote at length defending their scientific enterprises to the theologians and couched much of their philosophy in terms deferential to and influenced by the theologians, illustrates the contention that they were apprehensive lest natural philosophy should appear to be opposed to the Christian religion. Boyle saw the danger of allowing all things within the ambit of reason, for example, and many others wrote defending revelations and miracles, things above and beyond the compass of ordinary mathematical and physical comprehension.

The debates about the nature of reason and the reason of nature, partial and unsatisfactory as they were, were therefore crucial to the wider questions that these methodological disputes sought to resolve. If one argued that reason was so omnicompetent, and that men imbibed sufficient reason to comprehend the world about them, one was moving towards a position where God was a remote first cause, a logical necessity rather than an imminent interventionist presence in daily life. If one apostraphized science as the new light, one spoke but stintingly of the old lights of theology. The outcome was the stress placed continually upon natural philosophy and theology working together through the final-cause argument: arguments which more or less monopolized Christian apologia after the turn of the eighteenth century.

These arguments were heralded as a new rigour in the proof of God's existence, and in man's appreciation of the world; but they were arguments that lacked the metaphysical subtlety and the width and depth of earlier arguments for God and his universe, lacking even the sophistication of Cudworth's positions. It is one of those ironies that the arguments brought in to strengthen theology, that seemed to almost strangle other arguments in apologia, proved in the end to be incapable of withstanding revised scientific theory, and proved to be weaknesses rather than strengths in the Anglican position. Final causes could be used to dislodge difficult metaphysics, arguments thought too recondite to be useful with the people at large either in England or abroad in the colonial missions, but they ultimately could not be used to dislodge Darwinism. By setting themselves up as men taking account of new developments in the sciences, apologists left themselves open to the possibility that the science on which they founded their religion would one day be fundamentally and perhaps irreparably altered.

The much-vaunted rise of rationalism in the early eighteenth century should not be taken as a sufficient or even a real cause of Enlightenment questions concerning God, man and society. The argument ignores fundamental problems of definition with respect to the word 'reason', indicts by omission or implication all preceding thought as if it were not itself rational, and fails to acknowledge that the historical problem before us is why a particular group of men at a particular time should come to use the word 'reason' in a given way, and why their adoption of certain premises of enquiry should have the consequences they did. Reason for the early eighteenth century was, as we have seen, a word thought by many to represent a consensus approach to understanding, but in effect reflecting a disparate number of prejudices and preconceptions on the part of each individual.

We can, however, perceive a certain hazy unity in men's attitudes towards reason. Many felt that the new natural philosophy, thriving upon mathematics and to a lesser extent upon empiricism, was a flourishing and productive method of seeking the truth about the world. Euclidean models, so successful in mathematics and physics, were applied to morals, ethics, politics, and economics as well. Later seventeenth-century England began to quantify problems, and sought to express its views through axioms, lemmae, and deductions. Many thought that new methods had been discovered, and that these led to enlightenment. They certainly led to some fundamental revisions in the mental world shared and fostered by the average English scholar.

But these sources of atheism, the new arguments culled from nature and reason, and fears that they engendered amongst the more conservative thinkers, were by no means the only causes of a voluminous anti-atheist literature. There was also the strongly perceived threat from revival of ancient heresies. The English face of Democritus, Epicurus and Lucretius, emboldened by modern editions of their works, and fostered by the growing utility of the atomic hypothesis to natural philosophers, challenged many orthodox men into worrying lest the anti-Christian, anti-religious elements of these thinkers be revived with their scientific views. Men quite correctly wondered whether it was possible to dissociate the Epicurean view of matter from the Epicurean position over chance and the origin of the world: they wondered whether one could use Lucretius's *De Rerum Natura* as a source for natural philosophy without being tainted by the immorality of the work and by its explicit paganism. Men questioned whether all atomists were not in fact looking back to these past masters, and seeking to revive Democritean manners, politics and ethics, as well as his atomism. Similarly they disputed whether anyone could justify publishing works by such as Apollonius Tyanaeus, without implying that one's own position was hostile to Christ and his miracles.

There was a general view that a scholar probably espoused the views of those he reprinted or commented upon, and a further expectation that a scholar would take into account his moral responsibilities and his Christian views when considering the utility of ancient sources for whatever scholarly purpose. But this view was being challenged by the advocates of critical and more detached scholarship, and by those who wished to pillage the disreputable ancients for their own studies. These men either had to argue that the ancient from whom they wished to borrow was in fact a respectable Christian and an advocate of religion, or they had to hurriedly condemn his moral position, christianizing any views they happened to borrow from him by explicit statement of how these views fitted into the Christian world picture. It is wrong to suggest that this was necessarily a self-conscious process, although severe contemporary critics would have argued that there was a great plot afoot, run by able men out to undermine all true religion and order, and that these works of ancient heresy rushed to the press along with vindications heralded far worse trouble for the Church.

Nevertheless all agreed that some ancient sources were essential to true enquiry. All theologians acknowledged the value of the Ancient Fathers, although they disagreed over the interpretation they might place upon any given text, or disagreed over the authenticity and value of particular texts in the repertoire. We have seen the acrimony of the Whiston debates over the Apostolic Constitutions, and have considered the impact of the new biblical scholarship in the Simon and Bentley tradition, applying linguistic and textual considerations to the works at the expense of religious considerations. This too could lead to allegations of atheism, and disputes over the true nature of Christian testimony. Contemporaries thought of these disputes within the Christian society as fundamentally de-stabilizing: they were perhaps less damaging than they imagined, however, for most of them were still conducted in the spirit that Christianity was correct and that there was a true answer to the questions concerning salvation, and in a way they merely aroused further interest in this way to heaven.

Those who did argue strongly against toleration and dispute had a good argument, however: and one that not merely gained force from having been in common currency for so long. The view that each culture and society needed one agreed religion was inevitably bound up with the notion that religion was essential to public order and decency. If one permitted differing standards in religion and tolerated deviant sects, one ran the risk not only of declining faith and order, but even of a repeat of the civil wars. Toleration was correctly resisted for many decades, but its eventual victory in many ways represented a triumph for apathy and pragmatism.

The issue of toleration of views brought the conflict between an Englishman's liberties, and the need for law and order, to the fore. It was generally accepted as an essential canon that gentlemen had the right to political liberties, but it was not universally agreed that they had a liberty to speculate to such a point that they reached markedly different conclusions from the orthodox. It was piously assumed that men had the right to think freely, but that such true freethought would follow the uniform path of reason to similar and socially acceptable conclusions. Unfortunately this often proved to be wrong.

In the case of the dissenting sects like the Quakers, thought and faith took them away from the Anglican fold. To many upright Anglicans these men were no better than atheists, deviationists who denied many of the essential doctrines and proprieties that to their contemporaries made up true religion, that strange mixture of social medicine, reasoned reflection, and ecclesiastical indoctrination. They were scarcely preferable to Catholics, whose idolatry and clericalism damned a man's soul and his liberties at the same time. These categories of spurious atheists demonstrated the continuing force of the argument from social order, and the continuing xenophobia of the average Church, sure that it could only survive and flourish if other Churches withered away. Later events have perhaps demonstrated a measure of truth in that perception.

Some clerics of the time saw that their greatest enemies were not found within the broadly Christian framework of clerical dispute and sectarian squabbling which we have been describing. They perceived that there was a measure of half-hearted agreement over essentials amongst the Churches, and that all of them were in some measure threatened by the turn of social and economic events. It was apathy, materialism and the pursuit of worldly goals and pleasures which proved to be the strongest forces against the Church over the centuries. It was true that to lose the status of sole recognized Church within the nation, and to lose the secular arm enforcing the rudiments of religious belief and Church attendance, was to lose almost everything; but even in early eighteenth-century England where these restraints in some measure still operated, the Church was prey to errant congregations and vanishing members. An earthquake or plague, death or serious illness might return the people to Church for a brief spell, as they reeled beneath the impact of an event which reminded them of their early youths and sermons upon providential happenings: but on the whole life was becoming more comfortable for the professional and business classes in the towns and for the upper classes, and with comfort came involvement in the world of the coffee house and the salon.

One group that was nothing new, but who worried clerics and pious laymen alike, was the court circle of rakes and libertines. With the return of the King in 1660 had returned the vices of court life. It is true that the court of James I had not been a particularly pure or edifying place, and had in its day been attacked for its atheism of life: but with the return of court vices after 1660, after the puritan programmes against playhouse and bawdy house, the vices seemed to be writ large. They attracted screeds of literature condemning them, for they were regarded as an appalling example to the nation. Savile, Sedley, Rochester and their friends were thought to have gone too far for comfort.

But beneath this elevated circle of influential rakes in the public eye were the usual vices of society at all levels. Vice among the moderately affluent was less worrying to contemporaries than vice at the top or bottom of society, for it was tempered by an expedient hypocrisy that would prevent it ever having dangerous social consequences. Men only became drunk within the comfort and the cover of their own homes; they did not jeopardize the public in the streets, and their violence if it developed under the influence, would be safely and wisely confined to their servants or their family. Women who took lovers would do so discreetly in the homes of accomplices, and at times which kept their neighbours and friends unsure of their nefarious deeds. Any unfortunate offspring from such acquaintances would be provided for by the father or adopted father, and would not become chargeable to the parish. Above all their activities in vice were not normally directed against property or the safety of their fellow men.

In contrast, the moral outrage at the activities of the lower orders was the more pronounced, reflecting as it did an inner fear that their vice would lead to social disorder. The artisan or apprentice who did not know his station in life, work soberly, and keep out of trouble, was a potential drunk rioter or a potential father of illegitimate offspring to be supported by the parish. He therefore had to be taught the virtues and threatened by law and theology into eschewing the vices to which he might be tempted. He had to be at church, although he was more likely not to attend than his moderately affluent townsman neighbour, and he was the object of so much loving attention by all those tract writers urging more adequate catechizing and preaching. It was his unruliness, his swearing, cursing, rioting, drinking, whoreing, blaspheming, and disrespect for the Church that constituted much of the atheist problem facing the Augustan Church.

It must not be assumed that the atheist problem was necessarily such a real one in all its manifestations. It is naive in the extreme to take the huge literature aimed against atheism, and to take it at face value to mean that there was an equally sizeable atheist problem, without questioning the motive behind the writings, and the causes of the literature itself. Much of the problem of atheism was created by the imaginations and the writings of clerics and reactionaries upset by the age in which they lived. It was an enterprise which fed on itself. Men would read Cudworth or his continuator, and see the dangers that perhaps they had never contemplated before. They would then begin to see the world in terms of the struggle between faith and improper views: a notion encouraged by the sermons they heard and the tracts they could not fail from time to time to glance at in St Paul's churchyard or at their own local booksellers. The literature against atheism produced its own literary and argumentative tradition, and one reason for any given pamphlet is that its author had undoubtedly read another similar one which had convinced him of the dangers. Universities were especially prone to breeding voluminous and often spiteful printed controversies.

A further reason is that the later seventeenth century came to see, as a result of this literature, the debate against infidelity as in many ways the most crucial any man could contribute to, as in some respects the most important for mankind. With this spirit in the air, it was not surprising that clerics eager to make a reputation or a few pence to add to their stipends would turn to the theme that everyone seemed to acknowledge as so important. What better way could there be to obtain clerical promotion and preferment than to have hounded out atheism in one's contemporaries and even in the ancients, and in so doing affirmed one's own outstanding orthodoxy? The way was fraught with dangers, it has to be acknowledged, for, as we have seen, those that did most to attack atheists were often more likely to be attacked themselves for their deviant views, or for leaning too favourably towards the views they were refuting. But careers necessitated some form of publication, otherwise instead of being criticized for one's views one would be criticized for not having any views sufficiently reasonable to be made public. Who knew what a man was teaching or spreading to his friends if he never felt at liberty to print his impressions?

Publication was therefore desirable, and one stood as much risk of being attacked for atheism writing a book about the Trinity, the immortal soul, providence, revelation, the Bible or whatever, as one did by directly assaulting the citadel of atheism and discussing arguments for the existence of God and the arguments of natural religion: in most cases rather more danger. Allegations of atheism also tell us something concerning the psychology of disputes. The atmosphere was one in which men anticipated attacks from atheists and near-atheists, and were therefore likely to construe anything, whatever its intention, in that spirit. Writing against atheists was not only a means of clearing oneself, but also a means of discrediting others that one attacked. The whole anti-atheist movement took on the characteristics of a witch-hunt, and possibly fomented the problem in consequence.

At a more specific level the debates were part of the political controversies that punctuated Church history of the time. The High Churchmen would complain about lack of standards and accuse their Low Church colleagues of infidelity for their less hard-line views; the Low Churchmen would indict the High Churchmen for their suspected Catholicism or near-Catholicism and all that that entailed in the debates over piety. Whig would accuse Tory and Tory would attack Whig: and atheism was a term of abuse in sufficiently common currency to be a natural choice for the would-be polemicist.

The movement of minute philosophy, as Berkeley derisively termed it, was largely a Whig cause. It was certainly anti-Papist and anti-Jacobite, although its critics suggested that court life which formed an integral part of the deist's world was or had been tainted by Catholic elements. It was anti-clerical, and it attacked the conjunction of Church and State in one monolith. In some ways it was an opposition programme: an assertion of that popular eighteenth-century belief that central institutions, whether they were religious or secular, should not be strong for that was to attack the much-valued and vaunted liberties of the English gentleman in the provinces. The demand for minimum government, by no means confined to the deists, and surviving long after them, was not the product of deism, but it is true that deists often believed in the policy of curtailing government power and initiative. The deists also owed much to the movement of natural philosophy, and to the confusion that reigned over acceptable criteria of proof for any given proposition, and to the changing respect for authorities as opposed to reasoned arguments. Blount's statement against scholastic logic and rhetoric, that he left 'that to those who delight more in the study of words, than the nature of things',[1] had a family resemblance with the motto of the Royal Society and the views of Bishop Sprat. Sprat and his colleagues were convinced that their attitudes and methods strengthened religion through revealing the wonders of nature: deists could apply the techniques differently.

It is therefore impossible to understand the deists without some passing knowledge of Whig politics: impossible to understand Locke's philosophical importance without reference to his social context and his political and theological views: impossible to comprehend the fashionable style of facetious wit and grace without some social history to place the speech, dress and manners of both people and books into the scene of the drawing-room, the salon and the coffee house.

In the movement we have been describing a notable feature is the way in which the problem was reflected at all levels in society. There were the rich and fashionable rakes, libertines, courtiers and politicians in London. The circles of the court, the Royal Society, the men of learning, poetry, music and the arts, men of the professions, especially the medics of the College of Physicians, writers of biography, travel literature and curiosity seekers all intermingled with the clerics and the country clergymen who communicated one with another, and with their counterparts abroad. What we seek to explain is this movement of fashion amongst this large yet unified group of writers, courtiers, aristocrats and all those who felt it their duty to participate in the literature and culture of Augustan society: a society which stretched from London through correspondence and travel across the whole of England, Scotland and Wales, and impinged at times on life as far south in Europe as Naples, as far east as the China Seas, and as far west as the Americas.

Within the general framework of social ease, the pursuit of material comfort and civilized manners, wit and sophistication, within the framework offered by the periwig, the rich gown and the face-powder, the endless cups of chocolate and coffee, the endless round of sociability, the pursuit of reason seems a natural inclination. It is scarcely surprising to us, looking back on this age of grandeur, classicism and first empire, to find there a growing threat of atheism. As we have seen, bad manners were the root of the problem, and bad manners were encouraged to the puritan mind by the relaxation of standards of moral probity following the Restoration. This was combined with the new-found freedom of enquiry into philosophical matters, and the new idea of concern with explanations rational and comprehensible to the indomitable human intellect. Scepticism, rationalism, natural religion, deism, were the fashions of the age. They had all been present before, but they were now converted into a social model, a behaviour frowned upon yet praised, unhealthy to the Tory and the clerical, splendid to those of more moderate educational and political leanings.

To seek causes for this movement is to seek causes both for the general change of ambience in society, and for the particular growth of atheism, which was a term used to cover a multitude of speculative and practical sins. Part of the explanation lies in a return to court vices with the return of high society after the puritan banishment in the wars. That it returned with fervour is shown by the links with the clergy and the gentlemen of the counties, and by the interest the court expressed in the flowering of the sciences. Much of the problem comes to be something like the old warfare between religion and science, and offers us an explanation in terms of the collision between secondary-cause explanation, and primary-cause religion. More is the social conflict between the profit analysis of economics, the mesmerized counting of statisticians and political arithmeticians, and the self-help doctrine of some of the economic and social thinkers of the period. All these were related in a vision of the world, not so unlike the one that had passed with the passing of Charles I's court, but one a little less concerned with the paternalism of the society of the Tyranny and the Interregnum, more involved in that mixture of political corruption, interest and laissez-faire which marked the Augustan achievement.

From All Souls to the Royal Society, from the Archbishop's Palace at Maidstone to the court at St James's, men were expected, or encouraged each other, to follow curiosity, reason, and nature. These often-discussed attributes of eighteenth-century thought were the expression of the society created by the Restoration and fulfilled by the successive Settlement Acts and by the social and political life of the counties and the centre which have often been commented upon in histories of the period. This search led some of them into attitudes and manners, as we nave noted, which were to their less brazen and radical contemporaries thought to be atheistic. These friends, enemies and colleagues poured forth a hitherto little-examined flood of literature against such people who seemed to be undermining the Christian faith in their wish to study nature and the heavens with the unaided powers of their telescopes, microscopes and reasons. These, with all those who were violently anti-clerical, and with those philosophers who found in scarcely respectable ancient theories a new solution to old problems, or who found scepticism attractive and easy to defend, combined to assault the conscience of the Tory and the earnestly religious. As attendance at church remained poor, as promiscuity as always seemed to flourish, as society limped on subject to earthquakes, floods and disasters, there were those who nodded a sad and wise head, and attributed all of the sins of the age to one cause. These sins were the product of atheism, now so apparent in English life. There were Socinian clerics and deist courtiers, atheist authors and libertine free-livers. This new age was not to its people merely an age of sparkling achievement and enlightenment, which it has become to us. To many it was a godless place, an age drifting spiritually, pursuing wealth, commerce, empire, for the want of better things to pursue, forgetting its God as it assumed its own self-complacent pride in its achievement and light. Newton was to such as these a mixed blessing, Toland a renegade, Tindal an outrage, even Samuel Clarke an errant and foolish man. These people, who attempted in pamphlet after pamphlet to decry evil-living and correctly noted the tendencies of their society to express dislike of them, have gone for too long unnoticed.

The Church's case rested upon a number of crucial arguments. The ontological argument being somewhat out of fashion, apologists drew on the *a priori* and *a posteriori* positions, and stressed natural religion. They sought to defend spirit worlds, immaterial substances, presages and providences, the authority of the Church, the argument from universal consent and the Trinity in unity. All these arguments were challenged by someone during this period. The most serious complete theory against the Church was that provided by atomistic materialistic determinism. The incursions of rationalism cannot be laid solely at the door of Hobbes, but reflect rather the growing pressure of the Arminians, Socinians, and advocates of a layman's rational religion as well. The cynics who thought men were selfish and nasty attacked the Christians who strove to maintain man as a creature of morality and principle; the ridiculers sought to discredit everything and everyone.

By the time of Burke the deists seemed a thing of the past: their hey-day was over by the middle of the eighteenth century, and it is to France that we have to look to see the pressure of anti-clericalism, ridicule and reason taken further. England settled down to the conformity of natural religion, and to the enjoyment of the apologia and positions adopted during the hectic decades of the earlier eighteenth century when it had seemed that the atheists would win from force of numbers and shrillness of tongue.

This discussion has not established that atheism was an entirely new problem. It was as old as religion. There is literature of a similar tenor aimed against the Jacobean court, and such literature aimed against the Elizabethan entertainments and ideas. There were to be great outcries at the atheism of the Jacobins and Revolutionaries in the 1790s. All that is new is its volume and its persistence, its wide range, and its intimate concern with philosophy, the study of nature, and the study of the Classics. Cudworth and Wise are living testimonies to the threat of learning. With Berkeley's *Alciphron* they formed one of the ways for a fashionable gentleman to acquire all those views they sought to destroy, for they rushed uncensored from the presses, whilst the works of their contemporaries openly or subtly advocating pantheism, scepticism, the supremacy of human reason and a disbelief in miracles and priestcraft had to creep from the presses, despite the relaxation of the licensing laws in the middle of our period. The burning of books by the Middlesex juries and by the English and Irish Parliaments is a tribute to the fear that was engendered by the new thought of the advanced, the civilized and the enlightened. The fact that they killed none of these men, that they found their views influencing more and more the minds of those who lived with them in their society, and the fact that in the end the ataraxy of the sceptic, if not the outright atomism and negation of the atheist would win, was a tribute to the extent of social change, the rise of toleration, and the rise of an avowed, in place of an expedient commercial ethic. The atheist-hunters pursued their contemporaries with a force only to be equalled in the grim age of disbelief that marked the coming of the new god of social radicals, the French Revolution and the promise of heaven on earth.[2] They pursued and fought their fellows for a full seventy years and more with an unrivalled if unoriginal intensity. Their strivings helped their opponents, and their cause probably made proselytes of few. They leave us their books, their struggles, and their problems.

NOTES
BIBLIOGRAPHY
INDEX

NOTES

Introduction

1 T. Beverley, *A Solemn Perswasion to most earnest prayer for the revival of the work of God, bringing forth the kingdom of Christ, whenever it appears declining under his indignation . . . upon the late stroke of divine displeasure in the death of the Queen* (London, 1695), is one example. See also Chapter One.
2 E. Stephens, *Achan and Elymas: or, the troubles of Israel, the enemies of Righteousness, and perverters of the right ways of the Lord detected . . .* (London, 1704).
3 *Ibid.*, p. 2ff.
4 A. Egane, *The Book of Rates, now used in the Sin custom-house of the Church of Rome* (London, 1673), title-page and *passim*.
5 *An Antidote against Popery; or, an Argument whereby the meanest Protestant may overthrow the very foundations of the Romish faith necessary as a preservative against the present growth of Popery* (London, 1713).
6 *A Discourse shewing the reasons, why Protestant subjects cannot enjoy their laws, religion, liberty and property under a Popish Prince. In a Dialogue between a Romanist and an Englishman* (London, 1714).
7 *Ibid.*, p. 47.
8 Anon., *Questions and Answers concerning the two religions: viz that of the Church of England, and the other, of the Church of Rome* (London, 1727), pp. 3–5.
9 *Ibid.*, p. 17.
10 John Geree, *The Character of an old English Puritan, or Nonconformist* (London, 1682), p. 4.
11 *Ibid.*, p. 6.
12 *Statutes of the Realm* (London, 1819 folio) 14 Car. II c. 1. 'An Act for preventing the Mischiefs and dangers that may arise by certaine persons called Quakers and others refusing to take lawfull Oaths.'
13 *Ibid.*, Vol. V, pp. 350–1.
14 Charles Leslie, *Primitive heresie revived,* in the faith and practise of the people called Quakers (London, 1698).
15 *Ibid.*, p. 2.
16 *Ibid.*, p. 7.
17 *Ibid.*, p. 12.
18 *Ibid.*, p. 14.
19 *Ibid.*, p. 17.
20 William Penn, *A Key, opening the way to every common understanding* (9th edition, London, 1699), pp. 16–17.
21 *Ibid.*, p. 33ff.
22 George Whitehead, *Innocency triumphant: Our Christian testimony reaffirmed.*
23 George Fox, *Journal*, e.g. for 1694.
24 T. Hicks, *The Spirit of Enthusiasm exorcised*, Sermon given at Oxford on 11 June 1680.
25 *A Parrallel between the faith and doctrine of the present Quakers, and that of the chief hereticks of all ages of the Church. And also a parrallel between Quakerism and Popery* (London, 1700), p. 27.
26 *Ibid.*, p. 22.
27 *A Pastoral Letter from the Bishop of Bath and Wells . . .* (London, 1688), p. 3.
28 A Plebian, *An Explanation and Paraphrase of the Lord's Prayer* (London, 1726).
29 *The Plebian Prayer-book: or, devout exercises, adapted in a brief method for all sorts and conditions of men, especially those of the middle state* (London, 1726), Preface (unnumbered pp. in Bodleian edition).
30 E. Synge, *A Gentleman's Religion with the grounds and reasons of it* (London, 1693); W. Darrell, *A gentleman instructed in the conduct of a virtuous and happy life* (London, 1704).
31 Additional MS 4293 Section 4.
32 Luke Melbourne, *Psalmology Recommended in a Sermon preach'd to the Committee of Parish-clerks* (London, 1713).
33 Simon Ford, *A Plain and profitable ex-*

position of, and enlargement upon, the Church catechism by way of questions and answers (London, 1684).

34 *Ibid.*, pp. 26–7.

35 W. Claggett, *The Religion of an oath. A Discourse, proving the danger and immorality of rash and prophane swearing* (London, 1700).

36 *The Present State of England. In Several Letters from Esquire Hush* (London, 1713), p. 27.

37 *An Impartial Enquiry into the Causes of Rebellion and Civil War in this kingdom: in an examination of Dr Kennett's sermon* (London, 1704).

38 *Ibid.*, p. 42.

39 *Dr Kennett's Panegyric upon the late King James: being an extract of several passages from his Preface to an address of thanks to a good Prince* (London, 1704), Preface p. iii.

40 *Ibid.*, Preface p. iv.

41 *The Character of a thorough-pac'd Tory, Ecclesiastical or Civil* (London, 1682), p. 1.

42 *Ibid.*, pp. 1–2.

43 *Ibid.*, p. 5.

44 *Ibid.*, p. 3.

45 *The Jesuites policy to suppress monarchy ... and a dialogue ...* (London, 1678).

46 *The 2nd Character of an Informer: wherein his mischievous nature and lewd practices are detected* (London, 1682), p. 3.

47 *Ibid.*, p. 6.

48 *The hue and cry: or, a relation of the travels of the Devil and towzer, through all the earthly territories, and the infernal region, together with many of their most memorable adventures in search of the lost Heraclitus* (London, 1682), Preface.

49 *A Sermon preach'd at the internment of the renown'd Observator* (London, 1682), p. 2.

50 *An Elegy upon the Right Reverend the Observator, Guide to the Inferiour clergy* (London, 1682).

51 *The Loyal Observator: or historical memoirs of the life and actions of Roger the fiddler* (London, 1683), p. 5.

52 *Ibid.*, pp. 9–10.

53 See Sir Roger L'Estrange, *A Seasonable memorial in some historical notes upon the liberties of presse and pulpit: with the effects of Popular petitions, Tumults, Associations, Impostures, and disaffected common councils* (3rd edition, London, 1681).

54 *The Principles of the Observator examin'd, and the Queen vindicated shewing that she is a Queen of the royal succession ...* (London, 1704), pp. 19–22.

55 *Ibid.*, p. 5.

56 Nicholls Newspapers 4 (Bodleian), No. 70, *The Observator in Dialogue*, 12 November 1681, f30r.

57 *The Observator*, No. 35, Wednesday 19 August to Saturday 22 August 1702.

58 Nicholls Newspapers 4 (Bodleian), No. 68, Saturday 5 November 1681, f13v.

59 *Some Reflections on Prescience: In which the Nature of Divinity is enquired into* (London, 1731), p. 2. (Printed for J. Roberts.)

60 *Some Reflections on Prescience and the nature of beauty and morality*, pp. 2–6.

61 *Ibid.*, p. 8.

62 *Ibid.*, pp. 9–11.

63 *Ibid.*, pp. 11–16.

64 *Ibid.*, p. 18.

65 J. Asgill, *An argument, proving that according to the covenant of eternal life revealed in the scriptures ...* (no place, 1700).

66 *Ibid.*, p. 11.

67 *Ibid.*, p. 98.

68 *Ibid.*, p. 84.

69 John Turner, *A Vindication of infant baptism, from the four chief objections brought against it* (London, 1704), p. 5.

70 Charles Leslie, *The Socinian Controversie Discuss'd: wherein the Chief of the Socinian tracts (publish'd of late years here) are consider'd* (London, 1708). See Chapter Seven below.

71 George Hickes, *Spinosa reviv'd* (London, 1709), pp. 19, 22, 24.

72 *Ibid.*, p. 77.

73 *Ibid.*, p. 102.

74 *Ibid.*, p. 137.

75 *Appendix to Spinosa Reviv'd*, p. 145.

76 *Ibid.*, p. 149.

77 Thomas Woolston, *The moderator between an infidel and an apostate* (London, 1725), p. 17 using prophecies of the Old Testament to prove his own case.

78 *Ibid.*, pp. v–vi.

79 G. Hales, *Tract on Schism and Schismatics*.

80 James Foster, *An Answer to Dr Stebbing's letter on the subject of heresy* (London, 1735), p. 68ff.

81 *Ibid.*, pp. 7, 68ff.

82 Henry Stebbing, *A True State of the controversy with Mr. Foster, on the subject of heresy; in answer to his second letter* (London, 1736), p. 2.

83 M. Tindal, *Reasons against restraining the press* (London, 1704), p. 7.

84 *Ibid.*, p. 14.

85 Printed at London in 1734 (2nd ed.).

86 G. Adams, *The Deist Confuted* (2nd ed., London, 1734), p. 133.

87 *Ibid.*, pp. 64–5.

88 *The way to heaven in a string ...* (London, 1700), p. 9. Rogero refers to Sir Roger L'Estrange and his licensing activities.

89 E.g. *The history of Sin and heresie attempted, from the first war that they rais'd* *in Heaven* . . ., p. 2 and pp. 57–8 concerning pride.

90 For an uncharitable view of Tindal's anti-clericalism, see J. Turner, *A Vindication of the rights and privileges of the Christian Church* (London, 1707), p. iii and p. xxviii.

91 *Ibid.*

92 *Christianity as old as the Creation: Being an essay upon the original of divine Revelation* (London, 1730), p. 2.

93 *Ibid.*, p. 9.

94 *The Charge of Edmund, Lord Bishop of London, to the clergy of his diocese; in his Visitation* . . . *concerning the proper methods of opposing and defeating the present attempts of infidels against the Christian religion* (London, 1731), p. 12.

95 *Ibid.*, p. 18.

96 *The Charge of Edmund Gibson* . . ., p. 19.

97 Gibson MSS (Bodleian) Deposit c 233 ff116–17, 28 February 1734/5.

98 *Ibid.*, ff110–16.

99 *Ibid.*, ff65–6.

100 *Ibid.*, ff136–7.

101 *Ibid.*, f145.

102 *Ibid.*, Letter from William Stukeley, 8 April 1731, ff108–9.

103 Gibson MSS c 237 f42, 'Positions touching the rights of ye Civil Power in matters of religion'.

104 *Ibid.*, f44.

105 *Ibid.*, f46–7.

106 *Ibid.*, f47v.

107 *Ibid.*, f49.

108 Bodleian MS Eng. Misc. d. 297, W. Whiston's Commonplace book, p. 215.

109 E. Gibson, *Pastoral Letter* (London, 1728), p. 8.

110 *Ibid.*, p. 42.

111 Wildman, *Vivitur Ingenio: Being a collection of Elegant, Moral, Satirical, and comical thoughts, on various subjects* (London, 1726).

112 *Ibid.*, p. 21.

113 *Ibid.*, p. 22.

114 Tanner MS 25, f52.

115 *Ibid.*, f54.

116 *Ibid.*, f55rff.

117 *The Observator*, No. 75, attacking Jacob's thanksgiving sermon of 10 September 1702.

118 *A Letter to the Vicar of St Aldate's, Oxon. occasion'd by some passages in his sermons lately published* (London, 1731).

119 Arch. Univ. Oxon E W 3ª–19 f12v, 'A Decree for burning before the theatre . . .', 13 July 1713.

120 Bodleian MS Rawl. D 1169, 27 January 1709/10, Hearne to Woodward, f49v.

121 *The Observator*, No. 92.

122 *A Letter to Dr Snape, wherein the authority of the Christian priesthood is maintain'd;* . . . (London, 1718).

123 *The lay-clergy: or, the lay elder. In a short essay in answer to this query; whether it be lawful for persons in holy orders to exercise temporal honours. Jurisdictions and Authorities* (London, 1695), p. 35.

124 *The Observator*, No. 94.

125 *Ibid.*

126 *Ibid.*, No. 95.

127 *Ibid.*, No. 96.

128 *Ibid.*

129 *Ibid.*

130 *The Rochester–Savile letters 1671–80*, edited by John H. Wilson (Ohio State University Press, 1941), p. 44.

131 Bodleian MS Frith c 15 f29.

132 *Ibid.*, ff47–9.

133 Bodleian Eng. Misc. d. 297 p. 88.

134 *Ibid.*, p. 265.

CHAPTER ONE **Atheists assailed**

1 The dissolute life of the Court, scarcely a new problem in 1660, is reflected in works like *The lives and loves of Queens and royal mistresses* (London, 1726).

2 A view expressed in a letter to Sancroft, for example, urging him to issue a Proclamation against profanity. Bodleian MS Tanner 26 f67, 1691.

3 For Atheism as a decay of morals see *The Practical Atheist: or Blasphemous clubs taxed* (2nd ed. Edinburgh, 1721), p. 4ff. Also, *A Conference betwixt a modern atheist, and his friend* (London, 1693).

4 British Museum Add. MS 4295 Toland Papers f18.

5 *The Counter-plot or the close conspiracy of Atheism opened, and, so, defeated* (London, 1680), p. 1.

6 See e.g. *The Voice of the nation, or, an humble address to Parliament, for their just severity to repress the growing boldness of atheism* (London, 1676), folio sheet.

7 Stephen Charnocke, *Several discourses upon the existence and attributes of God* (London, 1682), pp. 47–108, reflects fears about practical atheism.

8 See e.g. W. Carroll, *Remarks upon Mr. Clarke's Sermons, preached at St Paul's against Hobbs, Spinoza, and other atheists* . . . (London, 1705).

9 S. Johnson, *A Dictionary of the English Language* (London, 1822 ed.), p. 50.

10 For the Boyle lecturers and their fight against atheism see pp. 103–108 below.

11 F. Gastrell, *The Certainty and Necessity*

of Religion in general . . . (London, 1697), p. 251.

12 *Ibid.*

13 Gastrell cites this view, p. 250.

14 Samuel Butler, *Satires & Miscellaneous Poetry and prose* (ed. René Lamar, Cambridge, 1928), p. 112.

15 *Ibid.*, p. 114.

16 *Ibid.*, p. 140.

17 Samuel Butler, *Hudibras*, ed. A. R. Waller (Cambridge, 1905), pp. 17–18.

18 William Whiston, *Historical Memoirs of the life and writings of Dr. Samuel Clarke* (3rd ed. London, 1748), p. 12ff.

19 *Ibid.*, pp. 6–7.

20 J. Swift, *Travels into several remote nations of the world* (Oxford, 1941): III To Laputa, pp. 163–70.

21 Bacon's works were edited by Spedding, Ellis and Heath, 1857–9. Bacon's scheme for the advancement of learning can be found in his *Instauratio Magna*.

22 Francis Bacon, *Essays* (The World's Classics, O.U.P. 1937 and reprints), pp. 70–2.

23 *Ibid.*, pp. 66–9.

24 Robert Boyle, *Works* (ed. T. Birch, London, 1744): of particular relevance are *A Disquisition concerning the final causes of natural things* (London, 1688), and *The Christian Virtuoso* (London, 1690).

25 Henry Power, *Experimental Philosophy, containing new microscopical, mercurial and magnetical experiments* (London, 1664), Preface.

26 John Ray, *The Wisdom of God manifest in the works of the Creation* (London, 1678): *Historia Plantarum* (London, 1686–8). Ray planned other demonstrations of God's wisdom, e.g. *Synopsis methodica animalium quadrupedum et serpentini generis* (London, 1693) and his project on insects in 1705, works designed not only to reform taxonomy but also to strengthen apologia. See C. Raven, *John Ray, naturalist* (Cambridge, 1942) and C. Raven, *English Naturalists from Neckham to Ray* (Cambridge, 1947).

27 H. More, *Enchiridion Ethicum* (London, 1668), and *An Antidote against Atheisme* (London, 1653), Preface. Descartes's precept, 'I think, therefore I am' (cogito, ergo sum) attracted considerable attention, but some thought it was a circular argument.

28 N. Durand, *The Life of Lucilio (alias Julius Caesar) Vanini, with an abstract of his writings* (London, 1730): Johanne M. Schramm, *De Vita et scriptis famosi athei Julii Caesaris Vanini tractatus singularis* (Custrini – Kustrin in Graesse's Dictionary – 1709): Mr de la Crose, *Entertainments upon divers subjects of history, literature, religion and criticism* (London, 1711): No. IV 'Atheism'.

29 L. Vanini, *Amphitheatrum Aeternae Providentiae Divino-Magicum Christiano-Physicum, nec non Astrologo-Catholicum. Adversus veteres Philosophos, Atheos, Epicureos, Peripateticos, et Stoicos* (Leyden, 1615).

30 *Ibid.*, Exercitatio Prima.

31 *Ibid.*, e.g. p. 140

32 *Ibid.*, pp. 149–66.

33 *Ibid.*, Exercitatio XXI.

34 L. Vanini, *De Admirandis Naturae Reginae Deaeque Mortalium Arcanis*, Libri Quattuor (Leyden, 1616).

35 *Ibid.*, pp. 31–7.

36 M. Mersenne, *Quaestiones in Genesim* (Paris, 1623).

37 See Note 28 above.

38 N. Durand, *The life of . . . Vanini* . . ., p. 57. The couplet argues that all time is lost that is not spent in loving.

39 Durand, p. 37 discusses the literature of Morhoff, Barleus, and Dieckmann who found nothing irreligious in Vanini, but stresses the arguments of the Mersenne-La Crose school who thought otherwise.

40 *Ibid.*, p. 38.

41 *A General Dictionary, Historical and Critical: In which a new and accurate translation of that of the celebrated Mr Bayle* . . . (eds Bernard, Birch and Lockman, London, 1739), vol. ix, pp. 675–8.

42 Durand, *La Vie et les Sentimens de Lucilio Vanini* (Rotterdam, 1707), p. 49.

43 *Ibid.*, p. 106.

44 *Ibid.*, p. 213.

45 See *Dissertation sur le Traité des III Imposteurs* (1716?), Koninklijke Bibliotheek Te 's-Gravenhage No. 12 g L 12 ff3–4.

46 Durand, *The Life of Lucilio Vanini*, p. 89, the testimony of Vanini's accuser, Franconi – hardly an unbiased source. Cf. *La Vie* . . ., p. 188.

47 *Ibid.*, pp. 73–8.

48 P. Bayle, *Dictionnaire Historique et Critique* (Rotterdam, 1697), 4 vols.

49 L. P. Courtines, *Bayle and the English* (New York, 1938), e.g. p. 70, pp. 152–3.

50 L. Moreri, *Le Grand Dictionnaire historique, ou le mélange curieux de l'histoire sainte et profane* (Lyons, 1674).

51 P. Bayle, *Pensées diverses sur le comète* (Rotterdam, 1683) was published in vol. iii of Bayle's *Œuvres* (La Haye, 1737) along with his *Addition aux Pensées diverses* and his *Continuation des Pensées diverses*. The *Pensées* circulated in England both in the French language edition, and in subsequent translation.

52 P. Bayle, *Miscellaneous Reflections* (London, 1702, 1708).

53 *Ibid.* (1708), pp. 212–25.

54 Benedict de Spinoza, *Opera Posthuma*

(no place, 1677), Pars Prima 'De Deo'.
55 P. Bayle, *Œuvres* (La Haye, 1737), vol.
iii, pp. 48–51.
56 P. Bayle, *Miscellaneous Reflections . . .*,
pp. 329-67.
57 P. Bayle, *Œuvres* (La Haye, 1737),
vol. iii, pp. 97–8.
58 *Ibid.*, pp. 86–97.
59 T. Hobbes, *The Leviathan, or the Matter,
Forme and Power of a Commonwealth Ecclesiasti-
call and Civil* (ed. Michael Oakeshott,
Oxford, 1946). The secondary literature on
Hobbes is too immense to bear summary
here. A useful bibliography of anti-Hobbist
tracts can be found in the Appendix to S. I.
Mintz, *The Hunting of Leviathan* (Cambridge, 1962), although this list ends
abruptly in 1700 and is not entirely ex-
haustive before that date.
60 Spinoza, *Opera Posthuma, Ethices* Pars
Prima (Rotterdam, 1677).
61 John Howe, *The Living Temple* (London, 1675).
62 Spinoza's *Opera Posthuma* was published in 1677 following the 1670 and 1674
publications of his *Tractatus Theologico-
Politicus*. A French translation of the *Tractatus* appeared in 1678, and an English one
in 1689. The best commentary on the reception of Spinoza can be found in L. S. Feuer,
Spinoza and the rise of Liberalism (Boston,
1958): information on 'Spinozan Quakers'
can be found on p. 58. A general treatment
of Spinoza, philosopher and man, can be
found in S. Hampshire, *Spinoza* (London,
1951). For Spinoza's attitude towards Descartes, and his modifications of the Cartesian scheme, see L. Roth, *Spinoza,
Descartes, and Maimonides* (Oxford, 1934),
especially p. 124.
63 A disciple of Spinoza, *Traité des trois
Imposteurs* (no place, after 1733) discusses
some of this literature.
64 Christian Kortholt (the elder) *De Tribus
Impostoribus magnis liber* (Kilonii, Kiel,
1680) and The Hague, Koninklijke Bibliotheek Te 's-Gravenhage Handschrift No.
12g L 12 f5 *Dissertation sur le traité des trois
imposteurs*.
65 C. Kortholt, pp. 4–92 against Herbert
of Cherbury, pp. 93–138 against Hobbes,
and pp. 139–214 against Spinoza. See p. 3
for his consideration of the conventional
impostors.
66 British Museum Add. MS 1024 R.
Smith, *Observations upon the reports of the
horrid blasphemy of the 3 Grand Impostors, by
some affirmed to have been of late years uttered,
and published in print.*
67 See R. H. Popkin, *The history of skepticism from Erasmus to Descartes* (Assen, 1960).

68 This problem being the concern of the
ensuing chapters where the relevant references can be found.
69 Bacon, *Essays*, 'Of Atheisme', pp. 66–9.
70 W. Charleton, *The darkness of atheism
dispelled by the light of nature* (London, 1652)
shows the continuity of argument from the
Civil War period to the eighteenth century.
Advertisement, and Chapter 1, Section 2.
71 See e.g. Sir William Dawes, *An Anatomy
of Atheism* (London, 1694), pp. 22–3, the
pride of sense in an atheist; Thomas Tennison, *Sermon concerning the folly of atheism*
(London, 1691) – Tillotson's other sermons
give evidence of his concern about atheism,
*The folly of scoffing at Religion, The Excellency
of the Christian Religion*, etc., and are in-
dexed in Bodleian MS Rawl. c 605 – J.
Howe, *The Living Temple* (London, 1675)
attacks the pride of atheists, p. 4.
72 See e.g. MS Eng. Misc. (Bodleian)
d. 297, p. 265. William Whiston's Commonplace book.
73 J. Edwards, *Some thoughts concerning the
several causes and occasions of atheism, especially
in the present age.* (London, 1695), p. 3.
74 William Whiston, *Primitive Christianity
revived* (London, 1711), vols i–v. In 1715
Whiston helped to found a club for the
promotion of primitive Christianity: see
*Memoirs of the life and writings of Mr William
Whiston, containing several of his friends also,
and written by himself* (2nd ed. London,
1753). The proceedings of the Society from
3 July 1715 to 28 June 1717 minuted by
Whiston as acting secretary (Dr Gale being
the first Chairman) can be seen in MS Eng.
th. (Bodleian) c 60 ff2–49. George Bull,
*Some important points of primitive Christianity
maintained and defended* (London, 3 vols,
1713).
75 Swift's attack is the most scathing – *An
Argument to prove that the abolition of
Christianity in England . . .*, in vol. ii of J.
Swift, *Works* (Oxford, 1941), pp. 27–8.
76 *Ibid.*
77 Dorotheus Sicurus, *The Origins of
Atheism in the Popish and Protestant Churches*
(London, 1684).
78 *Ibid.*, Preface to the Reader.
79 Lactantius was available in a 1684 London edition of *De Divinibus Institutionibus*,
as well as in many earlier European editions,
particularly from Paris.
80 William Law, *A Serious call to a devout
and holy life* (London, 1729), p. 482. Law
also wrote *A Practical Treatise upon Christian
Perfection* (London, 1726) and keenly urged
the proscription of stage plays to improve
public morals – see Chapter Eight.
81 Moses Amyraldus, *Traité des Religions*

contre ceux qui les estiment toutes indifférentes (Saumur, 1631), Preface.

82 *Ibid.*, pp. 1–96.

83 *Ibid.*, pp. 113–52.

84 *Ibid.*, pp. 97–112.

85 *Ibid.*, pp. 385–415. Amyraldus stressed God as Creator, and the arguments of natural religion from 'l'estude de la nature'.

86 Sir Charles Wolseley, *The Unreasonableness of Atheism* (2nd ed. London, 1669), p. 58.

87 *Ibid.*, p. 117.

88 Bodleian MS Smith 48 ff5, 6 Boyle to Smith, December 1675.

89 Henry Oldenburg, Correspondence (ed. A. and M. Hall: Madison and Milwaukee, 1963), Spinoza to Oldenburg, September 1665, vol. ii, p. 542. See also Oldenburg's plea for philosophical liberty, urging Spinoza to ignore the clergy, 12 October 1665, Oldenburg to Spinoza, vol. ii, p. 566.

90 D. Sicurus, *The Origine of Atheism . . .*, E.B.'s Preface to 1684 London ed.

91 Thomas Sprat, *History of the Royal Society* (reprint of 1667 1st ed., London, 1966), pp. 356–8.

92 *Ibid.*, pp. 358–62.

93 The Royal Society's activities can be traced from British Museum Sloane MS 244, The Journal Book (a copy of the Royal Society's archive Book); from the *Philosophical Transactions* (an index to these can be found in British Museum Add. MS 8974), and from Birch's *History of the Royal Society*. Dr Croone's experiment, 15 January 1661/2, can be found in British Museum Add. MS 4432 f1.

94 For example, in 1722 the Society of Apothecaries' lease on the botanical garden in Chelsea was renewed on condition that they sent 50 good dried specimens of distinct plants each year to Sloane. The list of those sent in 1738 can be found in British Museum Add. MS 4435 f44.

95 Bodleian MSS Locke c 41 and b 7 Herbarium.

96 An argument adduced in e.g. K. Thomas, *Religion & The decline of magic* (London, 1971). It may well be that magic was in decline, but this remains an impression rather than a documented surety.

97 Anthony Ashley Cooper, *Characteristics of men, manners, opinions, times* (London, 1711), vol. i, pp. 147–8.

98 *Ibid.*, p. 118.

99 *Ibid.*, pp. 88–9.

100 *Ibid.*, p. 119.

101 J. Swift, *Works* (Blackwell ed., Oxford, 1941).

102 Thomas Sprat, *History of the Royal Society* (reprint of 1667 ed.), pp. 417–19.

103 Swift, *Works* (Oxford, 1941), vol. iv, pp. 27–50 (1st ed. published London, 1713).

104 Mandeville, *The Virgin unmask'd* (Anon., London, 1709) and *A Modest defence of public stews* (London, 1724) reflected the views that men feared from the line of wit.

105 N. Sykes, *From Sheldon to Secker, aspects of English Church history 1660–1768* (Cambridge, 1959) provides a good treatment of the cause of Church reform in this period.

106 *The Origine of atheism in the Popish and Protestant Churches* (London, 1684), pp. 1–23, provides a full exposition of this attitude.

107 Sir Charles Wolseley, *The Unreasonableness of atheism* (London, 1669), p. 38; *The Atheist unmasked* (London, 1685), pp. 18–19; and R. Bentley, *A Confutation of Atheism from the Origin and Frame of the world* (London, 1697) are amongst those who deal with this problem.

108 Cicero, *De Natura Deorum* was printed at Paris in 1550 and 1660. It was included in the English edition of the *Opera Omnia* of 1681, and appeared in two Cambridge editions in 1718 and 1723. Joseph Hindmarch published an English translation in 1683 from London.

109 T. Creech, *Lucretius his six books of Epicurean philosophy: and Manilius his five books* (London, 1700). This edition included the parts of Lucretius previously available in English in Dryden's translation. The latin version was available (*De Rerum Natura*) in the Amsterdam edition of 1620, Frankfurt 1631, Florence 1647, Cambridge 1675 and 1686, Oxford 1695, and London 1712, 1713, and 1717.

110 J. Bury, *The Idea of Progress* (London, 1920) and R. F. Jones, *Ancients and Moderns* (2nd ed., St Louis, 1961) provide the best modern discussions of this theme.

111 P. Gassendi, *Syntagma Philosophiae Epicuri, cum refutationibus dogmatum quae contra fidum Christianam ab eo asserta sunt.* (Amsterdam, 1684). For Gassendi's reflections upon nature see Section 1 of Pars Secunda. For his treatment of the difficult problem of what Epicurus meant by happiness see pp. 419–29.

112 C. Bailey (ed.) *Fragments*, Epicurus to Anaxarchus No. 23. (London, 1926).

113 Christianus Michelmann, *Thomae Hobbesii epicureisum delineatum* (1668).

114 Du Rondel, *La Vie d'Épicure* (1686), and the later edition *De Vita et moribus Epicuri libri octo* (Lyons, 1647).

115 J. Digby, *Epicurus's Morals* (London, 1712), Dedication.

116 E.g. *La Morale d'Épicure* (1686), p. 26, Maxim V.

117 P. Bayle, *Dictionnaire Historique et Critique* (Rotterdam, 1697), vol. ii, pp. 1044–7.
118 *Ibid.*, p. 1044.
119 *Ibid.*, p. 1047.
120 *Ibid.*, p. 1047, Note F.
121 The life of Epicurus can be traced in *The Lives of the Ancient Philosophers* (London, 1702), pp. 421–500. His fellow atomist Leucippus is found on pp. 392–3.
122 Bryant Lillywhite, *London Coffee-houses* (London, 1963), p. 751, Item 2001. Lillywhite's book is the obvious point of departure for any future study of the importance of the coffee house in the literary and intellectual life of the capital. See also *Notes & Queries*, 1909 II, 10th series, p. 102.
123 Bodleian MS Wood F. 39 ff27–8, Andrew Allam to Anthony Wood, October 1680.
124 Bodleian MS Smith 45 f147, 28 May '1691', Richard Bentley to Edward Bernard.
125 Richard Bentley, Boyle lectures for 1692.
126 See for example the attributions of success to God in disputes over the Civil Wars: Alsted, *Happy News to England sent from Oxford* (1642) prophesied that God would bring the King to London.
127 Published at London in 1685.
128 See e.g. *A Short Answer to his Grace the Duke of Buckingham* (London, 1685) printed for S.G.; *An Apologie for the Church of England* (London, 1685) by E.B.; *The Antithelemite, or an Answer to certain Quaeres of the Duke of Buckingham* (London, 1685): Some defended the Duke and toleration against these critics: e.g. G.C., *A Reply to the Answer of the Man of No Name to his Grace* . . . (London, 1685); The Pensilvanian, *A Defence of the Duke of Buckingham's Book of Religion and Worship* (London, 1685); Anon., *A Defence of the Duke of Buckingham* (London, 1685).
129 *A Persuasive to an ingenious trial of opinions in religion* (London, 1685), pp. 5–11.
130 *Ibid.*, pp. 12ff. Cf. the traces of Hobbes, Bayle, and anti-clerical Whiggery in Bernard de Mandeville, *Free thoughts on Religion, the Church, and national happiness* (London 1720) showing the continuities of these debates.
131 *Ibid.*, pp. 12–13.
132 *Ibid.*, p. 18 against Hobbes, p. 29 for the defence of the Church of England constructed from reason, scripture, and the antiquity of Church practice.
133 *Ibid.*
134 *The Abuses of Christianity; being an attempt to end all controversies in religion.*

With an address to the Christian ministry, p. 2.
135 *Ibid.*, pp. 64–5.
136 Charles Blount, *Miracles, no violations of the laws of nature* (London, 1683).
137 Charles Blount, *Religio Laici, written in a letter to John Dryden* (London, 1683).
138 *The Atheist unmasked* (London, 1685), p. 18.
139 *Ibid.*, p. 19, and Robert Clavel, *An Admonition to a Deist* (London, 1685).
140 Herbert Croft, *Some animadversions upon a book intituled 'The Theory of the Earth'* (London, 1685), Preface.
141 H. Croft, *Some Animadversions* . . ., pp. 39–41 (where Croft feared that natural philosophy would make all men scoffers).
142 *Ibid.*, p. 53.
143 *Ibid.*, p. 99.
144 *Ibid.*, p. 101.
145 *Ibid.*, p. 152.
146 S. I. Mintz, *The Hunting of Leviathan* (Cambridge, 1962), pp. 24–36.
147 Humphrey Prideaux, Letters to John Ellis (Camden Society, London, 1875), p. 116.
148 N. Clagett, *The Abuse of God's grace: discovered in the kinds, causes, punishments, symptoms, cures, differences, cautions, and other practical improvements thereof* (London, 1659), Epistle Dedicatory.
149 The most recent biography is that of Pinto, *Enthusiast in wit: a portrait of John Wilmot, 2nd Earl of Rochester* (London, 1962 revised ed.).
150 G. Burnet, *The Sermon preached at the funeral of John Wilmot, 2nd Earl of Rochester* (London, 1680).
151 G. Burnet, *The Libertine Overthrown* (London, 1700 ed.).
152 British Museum Add. MS 4162 (72).
153 *Ibid.*, f255r.
154 *Ibid.*, f255v.
155 *Ibid.*
156 R. Sault, *The Second Spira* (London, 1693).
157 *Ibid.*, p. 30.
158 *A Short Way with Prophaneness and Impiety: or a sure and just method of putting a stop to public infidelity* . . . (London, 1730), pp. 1–5. Cf. *A Vindication of an undertaking of certain gentlemen, in order to the suppressing of debauchery and prophaneness* . . . (London, 1692), p. 9, discusses the move for law enforcement and its relation to manners.
159 Martin Fotherby, *Atheomastix* (London, 1622), Preface to the Reader.
160 The works Fotherby was probably referring to are Thomas Aquinas, *Contra Gentiles*; Raimonde de Sebonde, *Theologia naturali*; Bradwardine, *De Cause Dei*; Valesius, *De sacra philosophia*.

161 The works are too numerous to cite in full, and many are mentioned on ensuing pages. The list would include William Bates (Puritan divine), *Considerations of the existence of God, and of the immortality of the soul, with the recompenses of the future state* ... (London, 1677); Richard Burthogge, *Causa Dei, or an apology for God* (London, 1675); Robert Jenkin, *A brief confutation of the pretences against natural and revealed religion* (London, 1702); Matthew Poole, *A Seasonable Apology for religion* (London, 1673).

162 *A Short Way with prophaneness* ..., pp. 17–21.

163 *Ibid.*, p. 26

164 *Ibid.*, p. 10.

165 *Reflections upon the great depravity and infidelity of the times* (London, 1729).

166 'Mr Richardson', *The Infidel convicted* (London, 1731).

167 *The Infidel convicted*, pp. 1–8.

168 *Ibid.*, p. 9.

169 The following were printed at London in 1735: Dr Waterland, *The Importance of the Holy Trinity asserted; Christian Liberty asserted*, and *A Defence of Dr Waterland's book*.

170 *The Strange and religious customs, manners and religions of sundry nations* (London, 1683) savoured the idiocies of pagan, Jewish, Islamic and Muggletonian belief.

171 Jean Chardin, *The Travels of Sir John Chardin into Persia* (London, 1686). For a modern discussion of travel and its reciprocal impact on societies in the seventeenth century, see John Stoye, *English Travellers Abroad 1604–67* (London, 1952).

172 See for example, *A Sermon occasioned by a late earthquake* by Samuel Doolittle (London, 1692); W.C., *The Summ of two sermons on the witnesses, and the earthquake that accompanies their Resurrection, occasion'd from a late earthquake* (London, 1692); *A True Relation of what happened at Bedford, on Munday last* (London, 1672); *A True Relation of the terrible earthquake at Westbrummidge in Staffs* (London, 1676); *Wonders, if not miracles* ... (London, 1665).

173 R. Cressy (publisher), *Sixteen Revelations of divine love* (London, 1670) Dedication.

174 *Ibid.*, p. 58, p. 115, p. 176, etc.

175 *Ibid.*, Dedication.

176 Sir K. Digby, translation of Albertus Magnus, *A Treatise of adhering to God* (London, 1654).

177 *Ibid.*, Chapter 6 for freedom from material things, pp. 42ff. for freedom from temptations.

178 Thomas Adam, *The Main Principles of the Christian Religion in an 107 short*

articles or aphorisms (London, 1675).

179 W. Cross, *The Instrumentality of faith* (London, 1695) and others; looking back to Chillingworth, *The Religion of Protestants, a safe way to salvation* (London, 1687).

180 W. Allen, *The Christian's Justification stated* (London, 1678), Chapter 1.

181 *Ibid.*, Chapter 3.

182 *Ibid.*, Chapter 4.

183 *Ibid.*, p. 255.

184 W. Chillingworth, *The Religion of Protestants* ... (London, 1687 ed.), p. 4. For an assessment of Chillingworth, see P. Desmaizeaux, *An Historical and Critical account of the life and writings of William Chillingworth* (London, 1725).

185 *A Short and Sure Way to Grace and Salvation; being a necessary and profitable tract, upon three fundamental principles of Christian religion* by R. Young (London, 1722), p. 32.

186 *An Answer to all the Excuses and Pretences which men ordinarily make for their not coming to Holy Communion* (London, 1722), e.g. p. 18.

187 For a basic catechism see Bodleian MS Rawl. D 397 1672 f167.

188 K. Thomas, *Religion and the decline of magic* (London, 1971); for magic see pp. 209–332, witches, pp. 517–698.

189 See, for example, Glanville, *Saducismus Triumphatus* (2nd ed., London, 1682), and *A Whip for the droll, fiddler to the atheist* (London, 1682) for the defence of strange phenomena with particular reference to the case of the drummer of Tedworth. Such regional curiosities as *A Narrative of the demon of Spraigton* (London, 1683) contained reflections on drollery and atheism, and admonished those who denied spirits.

190 Arthur Bury, *The Naked Gospel* (Oxford, 1690).

191 The Racovians were unitarians who centred on the town of Rakow in the seventeenth century. Racovian and Socinian views were debated throughout Christian Europe in the seventeenth century, as the Trinity was an important part of doctrine in Catholic and Protestant Churches.

192 John Edwards, *The Socinians' Creed* ... *wherein* ... *is shewn the tendency therein to irreligion and atheism* ... (London, 1697); *Some brief Reflections upon Socinianism* (London, 1695); and *Some thoughts concerning the several causes and occasions of atheism* (London, 1695).

193 See Chapter Seven below.

194 *The Charge of Socinianism against Dr Tillotson considered* (London, 1695).

195 *Ibid.*

196 *Ibid.*, p. 2.

197 *Ibid.*, p. 2.

198 *Ibid.*, pp. 4–5.
199 *Ibid.*, p. 13.
200 *Ibid.*, pp. 13–14.
201 Dr Tillotson, *Six Sermons* (London, 1694), Sermon 3, p. 103: a much-discussed remark that harmed Tillotson's reputation amongst High Churchmen still further.
202 *The Charge . . .*, pp. 14–15.
203 In 1695 came Dr Sherlock, *Vindication of the Holy Trinity;* followed by *Tritheism charged upon Dr Sherlock's new notion of the Trinity:* this was considered in *Reflections on the Good temper, and fair dealing, of the Animadverter on Dr Sherlock;* there was a set of *Reflections on the XXVIII Propositions touching the Doctrine of the Trinity in a letter to the clergy; A short defence of the Unitarian faith;* a reply to the Socinians in *A Second Defence of the Propositions* and in a *Third Defence . . .; The Judgement of the fathers about the doctrine of the Trinity; The Doctrine of the Fathers and Schools considered . . .;* Thomas Holdsworth's attack upon the Dean of St Paul's and his *Vindication of the Trinity; Directions to our Archbishop and bishops to preserve . . . A Vindication of the sermons of the Archbishop and Bishop of Worcester* and countless other replies, contentions, and counter-assertions.
204 *Religion, the only happiness, A Poem* (London, 1694), p. 9.
205 Richard Ames, *The Rake, or the Libertine's Religion* (London, 1693).
206 *To the King's most excellent . . . the Humble Address of the atheists, or sect of the Epicureans* (London, 1688).
207 *The Atheist Unmasked*, p. 9 commenting upon Fuller's remark that such a notable physician should have died so young.
208 *Ibid.*, p. 1 stated such a view.
209 Crusading works against the Turks were still to be found. A 1684 tract argued for an English–French alliance: see J. Leake (printer), *Christian Valor Encouraged: or, the Turk's downfall.*
210 *The Counter-Plot or the close conspiracy of atheism and schism opened, and, so, defeated* (London, 1680), p. 1.
211 *The Conversion and Persecutions of Eve Cohan, now called Elizabeth Verboon* (London, 1680).
212 Richard Kidder, *A Demonstration of the Messias. In which the truth of the Christian religion is defended, especially against the Jews* (London, 3 vols, 1684, 1699, 1700) containing his Boyle lectures on the same theme.
213 J. Miller, *Popery and Politics in England 1660–88* (Cambridge, 1973) appeared after I had written this chapter, and provides a useful analysis of anti-Catholicism in political and social life before the Revolution.

Cf. Clifton, 'The Popular fear of Roman Catholics in England 1640–60', *Past & Present*, No. 52, August 1971.
214 Andrew Marvell, *An Account of the growth of Popery and Arbitrary Government in England* (London, 1678) and Bramhall, *A Preface showing what grounds there are of fears and jealousies of Popery* (London, 1672), to which Marvell replied.
215 *The Proceedings at the Sessions of the Peace held at Hicks-Hall, for the County of Middlesex, Dec. 5 1681 . . .* (London, 1682), p. 2, pp. 7–8, Sir William Smith's speech to the Grand Jury.
216 See e.g. *The Pedigree of Popery* (London, 1688). For the association of popery and political oppression, see *Father La Chaise's Project for the extirpation of heretics* (London, 1688). These views were particularly strongly canvassed at the time of the Revolution.
217 See e.g. *An account of the reasons which induced Charles II to establish Popery in England, Scotland, and Ireland* (London, 1689), and *The Character of a Protestant Jesuite* (London, 1689).
218 E.g. John Harris, *The Immorality and Impostures of Popery* (London, 1716) and Daniel Whitby, *Irrisio Dei panarii Romanensium* (London, 1716) strongly voiced anti-Catholic feeling.
219 Jones, *Ancients and Moderns* (2nd ed., St Louis, 1961) deals with theories of the decay of the world. The scholarship behind Hakewill's attack upon the notion of the decay of the world, in his *An Apologie for Providence . . . of God* (London, 1627) was often more highly thought of in the later seventeenth century than the views he was refuting.
220 N. Carpenter, *Libera Philosophia* (2nd ed., Oxford, 1622).
221 C. E. Raven, *Tolerance and Religion* (London, 1958) and W. K. Jordan, *The Rise of Religious Toleration in England*, 3 vols (London, 1932–4).

CHAPTER TWO **The encyclopaedic chroniclers of atheism**

1 E. Cassirer, *The Platonic Renaissance in England*, translated by Pettegrove (London, 1953), p. 1.
2 *Ibid.*, p. 38.
3 R. L. Colie, *Light and Enlightenment* (Cambridge, 1957), pp. xi, 7, etc.
4 See H. More, *An Antidote against atheisme* (London, 1659), and Cudworth's *True Intellectual System . . .*
5 The best extant account of the importance of the Cambridge men remains J.

Tulloch's *Rational Theology and Christian Philosophy in England in the seventeenth century* (2 vols, Edinburgh, 1872), vol. ii. F. J. Powicke's *The Cambridge Platonists* (London, 1926) is a useful introduction, as is Cassirer, *op. cit.*, and Colie, especially good on the Dutch connections of the Platonists.

6 E. Cassirer, pp. 159–60; J. A. Passmore, *Ralph Cudworth an Interpretation* (Cambridge, 1951), pp. 96–100.

7 S. P. Lamprecht, *The role of Descartes in seventeenth century England. Studies in the History of Ideas III* (New York, 1935); J. A. Gregory, 'Cudworth and Descartes', *Philosophy* (1933), pp. 454–69.

8 All Souls, Codrington W.2.12 (ult.), title page.

9 *Ibid.*, Preface to the Reader.

10 *Ibid.*, p. 2 of Preface.

11 See p. 53 above, first citation.

12 Cudworth's first edition of 1677 was followed by Wise's abridgement in 1706, published at London (hereafter *Wise*). In 1732 John Oswald reprinted the Cudworth version: Mosheim published a latin translation with notes at Leyden in 1733; and Birch issued an edition in 1743 in London. The Book was therefore available, if not a best-seller, throughout the period with which this work is concerned. Miss Colie argues, p. 117, that by 1703 Cudworth's book was rare, on the testimony of one letter to Le Clerc. This may have been the case, although there were library copies. She exaggerates the rarity of the book, however, by omitting the 1732 edition, and making Birch's the second full English edition in 1743.

13 See e.g. S. Nye, *Considerations on the Explications of the Doctrine of the trinity . . .* (London, 1698), pp. 13–19, for the view of Cudworth as a near Socinian, advocated by a flagrant heretic over the Trinity in defence of himself. For the especial difficulties for any apologist in this sphere, see Chapter Seven below.

14 R. L. Colie, *Light and Enlightenment*, pp. 117–26.

15 Cudworth, *True Intellectual System of the Universe* (hereafter *Cudworth*), pp. 6–9; *Wise*, pp. 1–4.

16 *Cudworth*, Preface.

17 They could draw upon J. C. Magnenus, *Democritus reviviscens; sive vita et philosophia Democriti* (Leyden, 1648 and London, 1658).

18 *Cudworth*, Preface and pp. 1–10.

19 *Ibid.*, pp. 11–12.

20 *Wise*, pp. 4–32; *Cudworth*, pp. 10–26.

21 *Cudworth*, p. 26.

22 *Ibid.*, pp. 40–9.

23 *Ibid.*, p. 63.

24 *Ibid.*, p. 64.

25 *Ibid.*, pp. 65–6.

26 *Ibid.*, pp. 67–8.

27 *Ibid.*, p. 69.

28 *Ibid.*, pp. 70–2.

29 *Ibid.*, pp. 73–5.

30 *Ibid.*, p. 75.

31 *Ibid.*, p. 76.

32 *Ibid.*, p. 76.

33 *Ibid.*, p. 77.

34 *Ibid.*, pp. 77–8.

35 *Ibid.*, p. 79.

36 *Ibid.*, p. 80.

37 *Ibid.*, pp. 81–3.

38 *Ibid.*, p. 83.

39 *Ibid.*, pp. 84–97: the first major explicit attack on Hobbes.

40 It is instructive to compare Cudworth's defence with Pascal working in the French and Catholic traditions: see Pascal, *Œuvres Complètes* (Pléiade ed., 1954), pp. 1315–34, *Pensées*.

41 *Ibid.*, pp. 107–8.

42 *Ibid.*, p. 123.

43 *Ibid.*, pp. 131–3.

44 *Ibid.*, p. 171.

45 *Ibid.*, p. 172.

46 *Ibid.*, p. 192.

47 *Ibid.*, p. 194.

48 *Ibid.*, p. 195 and pp. 634–48.

49 *Ibid.*, pp. 207–633.

50 *Ibid.*, pp. 634–7.

51 'Nothing can be understood that is not first perceived by the senses.'

52 *Ibid.*, pp. 637–8.

53 René Descartes, *Discourse on Method and other writings* (London, 1970, translation by Sutcliffe), pp. 53–4 e.g.

54 *Cudworth*, pp. 637–8.

55 *Ibid.*, pp. 638–9.

56 *Ibid.*, p. 640.

57 *Ibid.*, pp. 640–1.

58 *Ibid.*, p. 642.

59 *Ibid.*, pp. 654–6.

60 *Ibid.*, pp. 657–64.

61 *Ibid.*, pp. 665–7.

62 *Ibid.*, pp. 667–9.

63 *Ibid.*, pp. 691–3.

64 *Ibid.*, pp. 674–90.

65 *Ibid.*, pp. 700–6.

66 *Ibid.*, pp. 706–9.

67 *Ibid.*, pp. 710–15.

68 *Ibid.*, pp. 715–25.

69 H. More, *An Antidote against Atheisme, or, An appeal to the natural faculties of the minde of man, whether there be not a God* (London, 1653), Preface.

70 The circularity had first been noticed by A. Arnauld in *pour bien conduire sa raison, et chercher la verité dans les sciences*. See

Discours de la méthode (Leyden, 1637), particularly Sections II–V. This work was translated and published in London in 1649.

71 *Cudworth*, p. 725.
72 *Ibid.*, pp. 725–6.
73 *Ibid.*, pp. 728–9.
74 *Ibid.*, pp. 733–4.
75 *Ibid.*, pp. 738–67.
76 *Ibid.*, pp. 767–9.
77 *Ibid.*, pp. 829–30, 832.
78 *Ibid.*, pp. 831, 832.
79 *Ibid.*, pp. 817–20.
80 *Ibid.*, pp. 824–6.
81 *Ibid.*, pp. 835–6.
82 *Ibid.*, p. 836.
83 *Ibid.*, p. 837.
84 *Ibid.*,
85 *Ibid.*, p. 838.
86 *Ibid.*, pp. 839–90.
87 *Ibid.*, pp. 841–2.
88 *Ibid.*, pp. 842–4.
89 *Ibid.*, pp. 846–7.
90 *Ibid.*, pp. 846–8.
91 *Ibid.*, pp. 854–5.
92 *Ibid.*, pp. 874–5.
93 *Ibid.*, pp. 875–6.
94 *Ibid.*
95 *Ibid.*, pp. 878–9.
96 *Ibid.*, p. 886.
97 *Ibid.*, pp. 886–7.
98 *Ibid.*, pp. 887–8.
99 *Ibid.*, pp. 890–2.
100 *Ibid.*, pp. 890–8.
101 See p. 80 below.
102 *Wise*, Introduction, pp. 6–9.
103 For Charles Blount and the problem of Apollonius restated, see p. 139 below, and J. A. Redwood's article on Blount in *The Journal of the History of Ideas* (July 1974).
104 *Wise*, pp. 23–132.
105 This controversy can be traced in P. Bayle, *Œuvres* (La Haye, 1727), vol. iii, pp. 216–17, 881, 996–7: vol. iv, pp. 181, 184, 865 and 873: in Le Clerc, *Bibliothèque choisie*, Tome 5 Article 4, Tome 6 Article 7, Tome. 7 Article 7: and in P. Bayle, *L'Histoire des ouvrages des Savants* (August 1704). Article 7 (December 1704), Article 12.
106 *Wise*, pp. 138–42.
107 *Ibid.*, pp. 4–32.
108 *Cudworth*, p. 53.
109 *Wise*, pp. 33–50.
110 *Ibid.*, pp. 51–108.
111 *Ibid.*, Introduction.
112 *Ibid.*, pp. 106–8.
113 M. Nicolson, 'Early Stages of Cartesianism in England' in *Stud. Philol.* (1929); C. Webster, 'Henry More and Descartes: some new sources', *British Journal*

of the History of Science, IV (1969), pp. 359–77; H. Hervey, 'Hobbes and Descartes', *Osiris*, X (1962), pp. 67–90, give some idea of the varied response to Descartes. S. P. Lamprecht, 'The Role of Descartes in Seventeenth Century England', *Studies in the History of Ideas*, iii (1935).

114 For Towneley, see Kargon, *Atomism in England, from Hariott to Newton* (Oxford, 1966), p. 124, and for Power, see C. Webster, *Ambix* (1967).
115 J. Norris, *Theory of the Ideal World* (London, 1701–4).
116 *Wise*, p. 113.
117 *Ibid.*, pp. 176–7.
118 *Ibid.*, pp. 177–9.
119 Cicero was available in several editions, e.g. *M.T. Ciceronis opera quae extant omnia* (London, 1680) and *Opera Omnia* (Leyden, 1693).
120 G. Hakewill, *An Apologie of the power and providence of God* (Oxford, 1627).
121 Robert Boyle, *Works* (London, 1732), 'A Disquisition on final causes'; Bishop Wilkins, *Of the principles and duties of natural religion* (London, 1675).
122 C. Scheiner, *Oculus, hoc est fundamentum opticum in quo exiti anatome* (London, 1652 ed.).
123 Richard Bentley, Boyle lectures for 1692, *A computation of Atheism*, No. 7.
124 Sir Isaac Newton, 'De Philosophiae Naturalis', *Principia mathematica* (London, 1686).
125 See R. Lower, *Tractatus de corde, item De Motu et Colore sanguinis, et chyli in eum transitu* (London, 1669), p. 62ff., where he discusses Harvey's and Descartes's theories.
126 Commentary on Descartes, *De la formation du foetus* (Paris, 1664), published as *L'homme de René Descartes*. See Descartes, *Œuvres et lettres* (Pléiade ed., Paris, 1953), pp. 807ff., for the mechanist view of body.
127 London, 1664.
128 E. Stillingfleet, Bishop of Worcester, *Origines Sacrae* (London, 1662), pp. 466–70 for attack on Descartes.
129 Henry More, *Enchiridion ethicum, praecipua moralis philosophiae rudimenta* (London, 1668), pp. 149–55, e.g. about free will.
130 Henry More, *An Antidote against atheisme, or An appeal to the natural faculties of the minde of man, whether there be not a God* (London, 1653): the degree of providence in the natural religious tradition, pp. 53–104.
131 Dr John Scott, *The Christian Life from its beginning to its Consummation in Glory* (2 vols, London, 1681).

132 Published at London in 1691.
133 P. Huetius, *Censura philosophiae Cartesianae* (Paris, 1689). For Huet's life, see *Biographie Universelle* (Michaud) (Paris, 1858), vol. xx, pp. 101–5.
134 J. Keill, *An Examination of Dr Burnet's Theory of the Earth* (Oxford, 1698); see Chapter Four for a discussion of this work.
135 B. Binet, *Traité historique des dieux et des démons du paganisme avec quelques remarkes critiques sur le système de M. Bekker* (Delft, 1696).
136 William Coward, *Second thoughts concerning the human soul* (London, 1702).
137 William Coward, *The Grand Essay; or a Vindication of Reason and against impostures of philosophy* (London, 1703).
138 Printed in London.
139 Derodon, *Disputatio theologica de Existentia Dei* (Geneva, 1661): David Derodon was known to the vernacular reading public through the 1679 translation by Joshua Bonhomme (London publication) of his *L'Athéisme convaincu; traité demonstrant par raisons naturelles qu'il y a un Dieu* (Orange, 1659).
140 *Dict. Nat. Biog.*, vol. xii, p. 373.
141 John Turner, *Vindication of the Separate Existence of the Soul* (London, 1707) and John Broughton, *Psychologia, or an account of the nature of the soul* (London, 1703).
142 Dr Grew, *Cosmographia Sacra, or a discourse of the Universe* . . . (London, 1701) reiterates this view in Bk 2, Chapter 1, pp. 30–6.
143 T. Creech, *Lucretius his six books of Epicurean philosophy: and Manilius his five books* (London, 1700).
144 T. Tennison, *A sermon concerning the folly of atheism* (London, 1691); Bodleian Sermons 20 (7).
145 J. Toland, *Motion not essential to matter*.
146 *Ibid.* For an early English translation of part of Spinoza's *Tractatus*, see *Miracles no violations of the laws of nature* (London, 1683).
147 Charles Blount, *The Oracles of Reason* (London, 1693).
148 M. Mersenne, *Quaestiones in Genesim, cum accurata textus explicatiore* (Paris, 1623).
149 Boethius had been published in many editions in the late fifteenth century: fewer were published in the seventeenth. One could cite the 1655 London edition *Boethii de consolatione philosophiae, libri V a T. Pulmanno emendati*.
150 Henry Lee, *Anti-scepticism; or notes upon each chapter of Mr Locke's essay concerning humane understanding* (London, 1702).
151 Sir John Davies, *The Original, Nature*

& Immortality of the soul, a poem (London, 1697), Prefatory account.
152 John Keill, *An Examination of Dr Burnet's Theory of the Earth* (Oxford, 1698).
153 Bishop Wilkins, *Of the Principles and Duties of Natural Religion* (London, 1675).
154 Phillipe de Mornay, *De veritate religionis Christianae liber* . . . (Leyden, 1587) translated by Sir P. Sidney and others as *A woorke concerning the trewnesse of the Christian Religion* (London, 1587: 4th ed., London, 1617).
155 For a treatment of anti-Hobbist literature before 1700 see S. I. Mintz, *The Hunting of Leviathan* (London, 1962) which is reasonably complete, although it omits a work like G. Lawson, *An Examination of the political part of Mr Hobbs his Leviathan* (London, 1657). Wise cites works from the natural law tradition as well: in particular, Sharrock, *De Finibus et efficiis secundum Naturae Jus* (Oxford, 1660) – for an explanation of the scope of natural law, see pp. 37–68. Grotius, *De Jure Bellis et Pacis* (Paris, 1625) and Bishop Parker, *A Demonstration of the law of Nature*. There was an English translation by H. Evats, published at London in 1682 in folio.
156 The Cudworth manuscripts are discussed in an Appendix to J. A. Passmore, *Ralph Cudworth An Interpretation* (Cambridge, 1951), pp. 107–13. A Cudworth bibliography can be found on pp. 114–18.
157 M. Hope Nicolson, *The Correspondence of Anne, Viscountess Conway, Henry More, and their friends 1642–84* (London, 1930) comments on the activities of this circle and transcribes some of the letters from British Museum Add. MSS collections.
158 Add MS 23,216 f275 More to Lady Conway. See Nicolson, p. 243.
159 See Section I above.
160 W. Nicholls, *A Conference with a theist* (London, 1697).
161 George Berkeley, *Alciphron: or, the minute philosopher, in seven dialogues* (London, 1732), 2 vols (hereafter cited as *Alciphron*). See also, *The Moral Philosopher, In a dialogue between Philalethes a Christian Deist, and Theophases, a Christian Jew* (2nd ed., London, 1738).
162 *Alciphron*, Preface.
163 *Ibid.*, pp. 26–31.
164 *Ibid.*, pp. 7–18.
165 *Ibid.*, pp. 18–25.
166 *Ibid.*, pp. 12–14.
167 *Ibid.*, pp. 26–31.
168 *Ibid.*, p. 30.
169 *Ibid.*, p. 33.
170 *Ibid.*, pp. 33–5.

171 W. S. Howell, *Logic and Rhetoric in England* (Princeton, 1956) provides a good treatment of the Ramist and later controversies.
172 *Alciphron*, p. 35.
173 *Ibid.*, pp. 35–6.
174 *Ibid.*, pp. 37–8.
175 For Petty, see E. Strauss, *William Petty* (London, 1954); and for his use of quantitative method in economics, S. Letwin, *The Origins of Scientific Economics* (London, 1963), pp. 140–6.
176 *Alciphron*, pp. 42–3.
177 A. A. Pucelle, *Alciphron* (Paris, 1952) reviews the controversy in his Introduction.
178 *Alciphron*, pp. 70–4.
179 *Ibid.*, p. 79.
180 *Ibid.*, pp. 74–7.
181 *Ibid.*, pp. 93–4.
182 *Ibid.*, p. 94.
183 *Ibid.*, pp. 99–100.
184 *Ibid.*, p. 102.
185 *Ibid.*, p. 115.
186 *Ibid.*, p. 117.
187 *Ibid.*, p. 144.
188 *Ibid.*, pp. 149–50.
189 *Ibid.*, pp. 154–63.
190 *Ibid.*, p. 164.
191 *Ibid.*, p. 191.
192 *Ibid.*, pp. 192–9.
193 *Ibid.*, pp. 201–7.
194 *Ibid.*, pp. 208–10.
195 *Ibid.*, pp. 215–40.
196 *Ibid.*, p. 215.
197 *Ibid.*, p. 228.
198 G. Berkeley, *Essay towards a new Theory of Vision* (Dublin, 1709).
199 *Alciphron*, p. 233.
200 *Ibid.*, pp. 238–9.
201 *Ibid.*, pp. 238–44.
202 *Ibid.*, p. 245.
203 *Ibid.*, p. 249.
204 *Ibid.*, p. 251.
205 *Ibid.*, p. 256.
206 *Ibid.*, pp. 270–3.
207 *Ibid.*, pp. 282–5.
208 *Ibid.*, 286–7.
209 *Ibid.*, pp. 308–9.
210 *Ibid.*, pp. 308–11.
211 *Ibid.*, pp. 312–14; making reference to Shaftesbury, *Soliloquy or Advice to an Author* – see part 3, section ii.
212 *Ibid.*, p. 331.
213 *Ibid.*, p. 344.
214 *Ibid.*, p. 345.
215 *Alciphron*, vol. ii, p. 9.
216 *Ibid.*, ii, p. 12.
217 *Ibid.*, ii, p. 17.
218 *Ibid.*, ii, pp. 16–17.
219 *Ibid.*, ii, pp. 22–3.
220 *Ibid.*, ii, pp. 16–23.

221 *Ibid.*, ii, pp. 52–3.
222 *Ibid.*, ii, p. 54.
223 *Ibid.*, ii, pp. 67–9.
224 *Ibid.*, ii, p. 73.
225 *Ibid.*, ii, p. 74.
226 Sir John Marsham, *Chronicus Canon Egyptiacus, Ebraicus, Graecus, et disquisitiones* (London, 1672), and Joseph Scaliger, *Epistola de vetustate et splendore gentis* (Leyden, 1594).
227 *Alciphron*, vol. ii, p. 83.
228 *Ibid.*, ii, p. 89.
229 *Ibid.*, ii, pp. 89–90.
230 *Ibid.*, ii, pp. 90–2.
231 *Ibid.*, ii, pp. 102–5.
232 *Ibid.*, ii, p. 108.
233 *Ibid.*, ii, pp. 127–8.
234 John Locke, *An Essay concerning human Understanding* (London, 1690), Book 4, Chapter 7.
235 *Alciphron*, vol. ii, pp. 135–9.
236 *Ibid.*, cf. ii, p. 127 to ii, p. 145.
237 *Ibid.*, ii, pp. 147–8.
238 *Ibid.*, ii, p. 153.
239 *Ibid.*, ii, pp. 154–5.
240 *Ibid.*, ii, p. 204.
241 *Ibid.*, ii, p. 198.
242 T. E. Jessup, *Bibliography of George Berkeley* (London, 1934), gives a list of the main works published before Jessup compiled it. Berkeley's career is briefly chronicled in *D.N.B.*, vol. ii, pp. 348–56, and a lengthier study can be found in A. A. Luce, *Life of George Berkeley* (London, 1949).
243 A. A. Luce and T. E. Jessup, *The Works of George Berkeley* (London, 1948–57), vol. ii.
244 Printed at London.
245 M. Bracken, *The Early reception of Berkeley's immaterialism* (London, 1965), p. 84.
246 J. S. Mill, *Dissertations and Discussions* (London, 1875), vol. iv, p. 178.
247 E. A. Sillem, *George Berkeley and the proof of the existence of God* (Gateshead, 1957).
248 'To renew optics, geometry and infinitesimal calculus, and to strengthen pious feelings.' M. J. Gueroult, *Le Dieu de Berkeley* (Paris, 1956), p. 118. See also his chapter on 'Dieu et la grammaire de la nature'.
249 J. O. Wisdom, *The Unconscious origin of Berkeley's philosophy* (London, 1953).
250 G. A. Johnstone, *The Development of Berkeley's philosophy* (London, 1923).
251 P. J. Olscamp, *The Moral Philosophy of George Berkeley* (The Hague, 1970).
252 J. Pucelle, Introduction to *Alciphron* (Paris, 1952).
253 H. G. Alexander (ed.), *The Leibniz–Clarke correspondence* (Manchester, 1965).

CHAPTER THREE **Atheism as a political cause**

1 There is now a vast interpretative literature on Hobbes which needs little expansion here. For a general view there is L. Strauss, *The Political Philosophy of Hobbes. Its basis and its genesis* (Oxford, 1936), which considers the influence of tradition and science on Hobbes's political ideas; of particular use is M. Oakeshott, 'The Moral Life in the writings of Thomas Hobbes' in *Rationalism in Politics* (London, 1962); for Hobbes's influence, there is Q. Skinner, 'Thomas Hobbes and his disciples in France and England' in *Comparative Studies in Society and History* (London, 1966). Hobbes's works can be found in the edition of Sir William Molesworth (London, 1839–45).
2 For the reception of Hobbes's views up to 1700, see I. Mintz, *The Hunting of Leviathan* (Cambridge, 1962) and John Bowle, *Hobbes and his critics* (London, 1969). Neither of these works is complete in its treatment, but they point the general areas of criticism levelled against Hobbes. A useful corrective to the interpretation brought by many of Hobbes's contemporaries and in turn by his subsequent critics can be found in *The Divine Politics of Thomas Hobbes. An Interpretation of Leviathan* (Oxford, 1964) by F. C. Hood, who argues Hobbes's Christian concern and his materialism, e.g. p. 2; here Hood sees Hobbes as 'essentially a sincere writer', e.g. p. 253.
3 See, for example, A. Ross, *Leviathan drawn out with a hook* (London, 1653); John Bramhall, *The Catching of Leviathan;* John Eachard, *Mr Hobbes's state of nature consider'd* (London, 1672); and John Whitehall, *The Leviathan found out* (London, 1679).
4 John Milton, *Brief Notes upon a late sermon, titl'd, The Fear of God and the King* (London, 1660).
5 John Milton, *The Readie and easie way to establish a free commonwealth, and the excellence thereof compar'd with the inconveniences and dangers of re-admitting kingship in this nation* (London, 1660), p. 18.
6 *Ibid.*, p. 1ff.
7 Sir Roger L'Estrange, *No blinde guides* (London, 1660).
8 E. Ludlow, *The Plagiary exposed* (London, 1691); R. Hollingsworth, *Defence of Charles I* . . . (London, 1692); A. Walker, *A True account of the author of a book entituled* . . . (London, 1692). A most useful work for Milton's role in politics and literary life after 1660 is Masson, *The Life of Milton in connexion with the history of his time* (London, 1871), vol. 6.

9 See *Carolus II Rex Angliae Proclamations* (London, 1660) (Bodleian, f660. 84), e.g. 'Proclamation by the Council of State against Livewel, Chapman of London, for printing seditious pamphlets' (1660); 'A Proclamation for calling in, and suppressing of two books written by John Milton; the one intituled, *Johannis Miltoni Angli pro Populo Anglicano Defensio, contra claudii Anonymi alias Salmasii, Defensionem Regiam;* and the other in answer to a book intituled, *The Pourtraiture of his Sacred Majesty in his solitude and sufferings.* And also a third book intituled *The Obstructors of Justice,* written by J. Goodwin.' 13 August 1660.
10 *Evangelian Armatum. A specimen; or short collection of several Doctrines and Positions destructive to our government both civil and ecclesiastical; preached and vented by the known leaders and Abettors of the pretended Reformation* (London, 1663).
11 *Ibid.*, p. 13.
12 *Ibid.*, p. 16.
13 *Ibid.*, pp. 54–7.
14 *Ibid.*, p. 1, reference to Calamy's *Sermon to the Lords* (London, 1644), p. 9.
15 The best treatment of this one aspect of the many-sided problem of bad influences in political theory in the seventeenth century is F. Raab, *The English face of Machiavelli* (London, 1962). Raab admitted the difficulty of discovering how much of the change he noted is the influence of Machiavelli, e.g. p. 263, but perhaps overstressed the nature of the change from 1500–1700 and overestimated the decline in the importance of divine justification which he entirely excluded as an influence in the age of Halifax.
16 This is of particular relevance to Machiavelli of *Il Principe* rather than of *I Discorsi sopra la prima deca di Tito Livio.* For Machiavelli and sixteenth-century thought, see the good introductory study of J. W. Allen, *A History of Political Thought in the sixteenth century* (London, 1928), pp. 445–95. For editions of Machiavelli, see e.g. *The Discourses*, ed. L. J. Walker (London, 1950), *Il Principe*, ed. L. Burd (Oxford, 1891); and *The Prince* translated by W. Marriott (London, 1958).
17 E.g., *Il Principe* (Oxford, 1891), p. 360.
18 See Lily B. Campbell (ed.), *The Mirror for Magistrates* (Cambridge, 1938), Introduction.
19 T. Campanella, *Atheismus Triumphatus* (Paris, 1636), e.g. pp. 133–4.
20 Sir W. Molesworth, *The English Works of Thomas Hobbes* (London, 1839), vol. iii, p. 23.
21 *Ibid.*, p. 25.

22 See C. Hill, *Puritanism and Revolution* (London, 1958) and *God's Englishman* (London, 1970); L. F. Solt, *Saints in Arms*; H. N. Brailsford, *The Levellers and the English Revolution* (London, 1961); C. Hill, *Intellectual Origins of the English Revolution* (Oxford, 1962); and C. B. Macpherson, *The Political Theory of Possessive Individualism* (Oxford, 1962).

23 R. S. Bosher, *The Making of the Restoration Settlement* (London, 1957), pp. 143–218 and 278–83; Edward Hyde, Earl of Clarendon, *The History of the Rebellion and Civil Wars in England*, edited by W. D. Macray (6 vols, Oxford, 1958 reprint of 1888, 1st ed.), vol. 6, pp. 233–4, describes the joy on Charles's Restoration.

24 J. E. C. Hill, *The World Turned Upside* (London, 1972) and *Puritanism and Revolution*, Part II, pp. 199–394 (London, 1958) are good general studies of these movements, men and attitudes. Specific studies include B. S. Capp, in F. Tonnies (ed.), *Behemoth* (London, 1889). The Diggers fought for the use of the commons by the poor in the Civil War, founding communes on wasteland.

25 E. Hyde, *The History of the Rebellion* ... (London, 1702); publication was delayed. T. Sprat, *History of the Royal Society* (London, 1667).

26 G. Burnet, *History of the Reformation of the Church of England* (London, 1679–1715). Reissued in 1683 in abridged form.

27 O. Skinner, 'Thomas Hobbes and the defence of *de facto* powers', Seminar Paper given at Oxford, 1970 Trinity Term. Fussner, *The Historical Revolution* (London, 1962), pp. 170–3.

28 James Harrington, *The Commonwealth of Oceana* (London, 1656) is a clear antecedent of many theories of rising gentry and the causes of the civil war. Lawrence Stone, *The Causes of the English Revolution 1529–1642* (London, 1972) is one of the few to repay the debt. Its surreptitious influence is unequalled by that of Hobbes's *Behemoth* or *Leviathan* in modern historiography. It is strange that whilst *Leviathan* has been often reprinted, and even *Behemoth* has a standard modern edition, *Oceana* has only been reprinted from Heidelberg during this century. It is time that this and the imbalance in interest it represents was redressed. R. H. Tawney in his Ralegh lecture for 1941 attempted to explain why Harrington had been neglected after the great interest aroused by his works up to the French Revolution: see R. Tawney, *Harrington's Interpretation of his age*, p. 37, p. 10ff. Tawney also rightly points out that favourable reference can be found in Acton, *Lec-*

tures on Modern History, p. 204; in F. W. Maitland, *Collected Papers* (ed. by H. A. L. Fisher), i, pp. 21–2; and in G. P. Gooch, *English Democratic Ideas in the Seventeenth Century* (London, 1927), pp. 241–57. A good modern study of Harrington is that of C. Blitzer, *An Immortal Commonwealth, the political theory of J. Harrington* (London, 1960).

29 Thomas Hobbes, *Leviathan* (ed. Oakeshott, Oxford, 1941), p. 395.

30 *Ibid.*, p. 385.

31 R. S. Peters, *Hobbes* (London, 1967), Introduction; see also G. C. Robertson, *Hobbes* (London, 1886) and J. Laird, *Hobbes* (London, 1934).

32 D. P. Gauthier, *The Logic of Leviathan* (Oxford, 1969), pp. 1–5, discusses Hobbes's use of Galilean method and his mechanistic views.

33 Thomas Hobbes, *An historical narration concerning heresie, and the punishment thereof* (London, 1680), p. 17.

34 MS Tanner 456 f14, 4 November 1673.

35 *Ibid.* f39.

36 F. Raab, *The English Face of Machiavelli*, p. 204.

37 There are modern commentaries on Harrington to be found in *American Political Science Review*, September 1959, pp. 662–92, and in P. Zagorin, *A history of Political Theory in the English Revolution* (London, 1954), pp. 132–45. H. Russell Smith, *Harrington and his Oceana* (Cambridge, 1914) contains the fuller treatment.

38 J. Rogers, *Mr Harrington's Parallel unparallel'd – wherein it appears neither the spirit of the people, nor the spirit of men like Mr R., but the spirit of God is the fittest for the government of a Commonwealth* (London, 1689), p. 4.

39 This point is illustrated by J. Lesley's letter to Harrington in 1657, reproduced in Sir J. Harrington, *Nugae Antiquae* (London, 1769), pp. 82–5, where Lesley comments 'Fear God, and know the King, are both in one place, and support each other as the corner stones of religion and royalty.'

40 Raab, *The English Face*. . ., p. 262.

41 See, for example, the dedication of Samuel Clarke's 1704–5 Boyle lectures.

42 John Aubrey, *Brief Lives* (ed. A. Clark, Oxford, 1898), vol. i, 'The Life of Thomas Hobbes of Malmesbury'.

43 *The Oceana of James Harrington, and his other works* (ed. J. Toland, London, 1700), pp. 39–40.

44 *Ibid.*, p. 54.

45 *Ibid.*, pp. 42–3.

46 *Ibid.*, p. 83.

47 *Ibid.*, The Second Order.

48 *Ibid.*, p. 84 The Third Order.

49 *Ibid.*, p. 84 The Fourth Order.

50 *Ibid.*, pp. 87–9 The Sixth Order.

51 These views, first expressed in *Oceana* (London, 1656) are reiterated in his *Art of Lawgiving* (London, 1659) which circulated in post-Restoration London. For the idea of balance, see pp. 1–5; for superstructure theory, pp. 23–5; for the division and constitution, see Book III, pp. 19–20; for religion, and the state, see Book III, pp. 67–77 These views were again reprinted in Toland's edition of Harrington: p. 127, e.g. in 1700 ed. for the function of the Council of Religion.

52 See e.g. *James Harrington, Politicaster, or, a comical Discourse, in answer to Mr Wren's book, Intituled, Monarchy Asserted* (London, 1659), p. 5; Toland's ed. *Oceana* (1700), pp. 38, 42, 48, 52, etc. and J. Harrington, *Pian Piano. Or Intercourse between H. Ferne, Dr in Divinity, and J. Harrington, Esq. upon occasion of the Doctor's censure of the commonwealth of Oceana* (London, 1656), p. 49, for his attitude to Machiavelli. His view of Hobbes can be found in *Oceana* (Toland's edition), especially pp. 38–60.

53 J. Harrington, *The Art of Lawgiving*, Book III, pp. 6–12, is one such attempt to distance himself from anarchists and Levellers.

54 Harrington's critics included Dr Henry Ferne, the royalist author of *Conscience satisfied* (London, 1643); Matthew Wren, *Considerations on Mr Harrington's Commonwealth of Oceana* (London, 1657) and *Monarchy Asserted* (London, 1659); and Richard Baxter, *Holy Commonwealth*.

55 See H. F. Russell Smith, *Harrington and his Oceana* (Cambridge, 1914), pp. 98–109.

56 B. Lillywhite, *London Coffee Houses* (London, 1963), p. 263 item 545 and p. 166 item 263.

57 J. Harrington, *The censure of the Rota upon Mr Milton's book* . . . (London, 1660), p. 14.

58 *Ibid.*, p. 13.

59 J. Harrington, *The Rota: or, a model of a free-state, or equall commonwealth* (London, 1660), p. 1.

60 J. Harrington, *The Rota* . . ., p. 3.

61 *Ibid.*, p. 23.

62 *Ibid.*, p. 21.

63 *Ibid.*, p. 23ff.

64 J. Harrington, *Decrees and Orders of the Committee of safety* (London, 1659).

65 J. Harrington, *The wayes and meanes whereby an equal and lasting Commonwealth may be suddenly introduced* (London, 1660).

66 J. Harrington, *The benefit of the ballot* (London, 1660).

67 J. Harrington, *The wayes and meanes* . . . (London, 1660), p. 4.

68 See e.g. *A Modest Plea for an equall commonwealth* (London, 1659), an anti-monarchical work, and *A Modest Reply, in answer to the modest plea* (London, 1659): and *An Answer to a proposition in order to the property of commonwealth or democracy. Proposed by friends to the Commonwealth by Mr Harrington's consent* (London, 1659).

69 Richard Baxter, *A Holy Commonwealth, or political aphorisms, opening the true principles of government* (London, 1659).

70 R. Baxter, *A Holy Commonwealth* . . . (London, 1659), pp. 45–6.

71 *Ibid.*, p. 4.

72 *Ibid.*, p. 6.

73 *Ibid.*, pp. 18–21.

74 *Ibid.*, p. 226.

75 *Ibid.*, p. 230.

76 *Ibid.*, pp. 168–72.

77 *Ibid.*, p. 209.

78 *Ibid.*, pp. 121–8; on p. 134ff. he discusses the operation of Providence.

79 *Acta Convocatione* Univ. Oxon Arch T B 28 (1671–83) ff375–81. The text has been reprinted in an English translation in the Historical MSS Commission collections, but there it lacks the important interpolations concerning the writers thus indicted.

80 The text of the examination is reprinted by Toland in his *Life of James Harrington* prefixed to the 1700 edition of *Oceana* and his other works, pp. xxxi–xxxiv.

81 There is no full-scale history of the press in our period, and one is much needed. Useful for the activities of L'Estrange is Kitchin's biography (London, 1913). The Act can be found in *Statutes of the Realm* as 14 Car II c 33 *An Act for preventing the frequent abuses in printing seditious treasonable and unlicensed Books and Pamphlets and for regulating of Printing and Printing Presses.*

An interesting draft history written by a contemporary, John Bagford, can be found in Tanner MS 453. The work includes long bibliographical collections, the life of Caxton f39, lives of Gutenberg and Faustus f42, and the history of printing in China f44.

Useful general modern comment can be found in D. McMurtrie, *The Book*, p. 136, and in Steinberg, *Five Hundred Years of Printing*. L. Hanson, *Government and the press 1695–1763* (London, 1936) deals with the period after the lapsing of the press Acts. For details of enforcement and history of the legislation see J. Walker, in *History* (1950), pp. 219–38.

Interesting documentation of a typical dispute between the Stationers, and Oxford

University Press, can be found in Oxford Univ. Arch. B b 29 ff18–32, ff296, 350, 366, and 376. The dispute arose over the rights of the University press to print certain kinds of material.

82 *Statutes of the Realm* (London, 1819), vol. V, pp. 428ff. 14 Car II c 33.

83 For a modern account of the Plot, see J. Kenyon, *The Popish Plot* (London, 1972); and M. D. R. Leys, *Catholics in England 1559–1829* (London, 1961), pp. 98–104.

84 Charles Blount, *An Appeal from the country to the city, for the preservation of His Majesty's person, liberty, property, and the Protestant religion* (London, 1679).

85 Charles Blount (ascribed), *King William and Queen Mary conquerors . . .* (London, 1693). Commons Journals, 20–5 January 1692/3, vol. 10, pp. 783–8 (London, 1803 ed.).

86 We rely on the testimony of R. Bentley as reported by N. Luttrell, that Blount wrote this pamphlet. See All Souls College MS 158, pp. 378–9 (also available edited by H. Horwitz, Oxford, 1972, who relates the story of the case in the Commons and the burning of Blount's work).

87 Charles Blount, *A Just Vindication of Learning: or, an humble address to the High Court of Parliament in behalf of liberty of the press* (London, 1693).

88 See Macaulay, *A History of England from the accession of James II* (London, 1915), vol. v, pp. 2303–5, 2308–9 and *A Collection of the Parliamentary debates in England* (ed. Torbuck, London, 1741), vol. ii, pp. 359–60.

89 For Walpole's actions against *The Craftsmen*, see J. H. Plumb, *Sir Robert Walpole The King's Minister* (London, 1960), pp. 141–3.

90 *A Letter to the Right Rev. The Lord Bishop of Asaph* (London, 1731), p. 5.

91 M. Tindal (ascribed), *Reasons against restraining the press* (London, 1704), p. 4.

92 *Ibid.*, pp. 10–14.

93 Tanner MS 447, *Reasons offered to Sancroft for the regulation of the press*, ff171–2.

94 R. Atkyns, *The Origin and Growth of Printing: collected out of history, and the records of this kingdome* (London, 1664), Epistle to Charles II.

95 *Ibid.*, p. 16.

96 *Ibid.*, p. 17: although the plea is addressed to Parliament as well, and Atkyns envisaged new legislation to topple the Stationers and reinforce royal control.

97 J. E. Neale, *Elizabeth and her Parliaments* (London, 1953), vol. ii, pp. 376–90; M. Ashley, *England in the seventeenth century* (London, 1952), p. 44.

98 M. Cranston, *John Locke A Biography* (London, 1957), pp. 386–7.

99 Bodleian MSS Locke b 4 f75, and *House of Lords Journals*, XV, pp. 545–6, cited in Cranston, pp. 386–7.

100 Sir Roger L'Estrange, *Considerations and Proposals in order to the regulation of the press* (London, 1663).

101 *Ibid.*, pp. 11–24.

102 Philopatris, *A Vindication of Learning* (London, 1679), p. 7.

103 James Harrington (ascribed), *Reasons for Reviving and Continuing the Act for the Regulation of Printing* (London, 1692), folio sheet.

104 Tanner MS 30 f143.

105 Tanner MS 30 ff175, 185, powers to Midgeley and the College.

106 Philopatris, *A Just Vindication of Learning: Or, An humble address to the High court of Parliament in behalf of the liberty of the press* (London, 1679), Proem.

107 *Ibid.*, p. 11.

108 For the debates over George, Duke of Buckingham and his writings, see Chapter One, p. 42. The classic study of toleration is W. K. Jordan's *The Development of Religious Toleration in England* (London, 1936, 4 vols). Klibansky's Preface to the 1968 Oxford edition of John Locke's *Epistola de Tolerantia*, pp. x–xvii, provides useful comments on Anglo–Dutch ideas of toleration. Gough's Introduction to that edition, pp. 1–42, is also useful.

109 John Locke, *The First and Second Treatises of Civil Government* (London, 1689). John Dunn, *The Political Thought of John Locke* (Cambridge, 1969), pp. 47–57, and T. P. Laslett, *John Locke, Two Treatises of Civil Government* (Cambridge, 1966), pp. 45–66.

110 Dunn, pp. 58–76. But cf. Locke's earlier attitudes of a more conservative nature in P. Abrams (ed.), *John Locke, Two Tracts on Government* (Cambridge, 1967).

111 John Locke, *Epistola de tolerantia* (ed. Raymond Klibansky) (Oxford, 1968), pp. 141–9, plea for individual liberty in matters of conscience; pp. 131–41, for those groups that the magistrate is not to tolerate.

112 *Ibid.*, pp. 125–7, and pp. 131–3.

113 J. Proast, *The Argument of the Letter concerning Toleration, briefly consider'd and answer'd* (Oxford, 1690) and *A second letter to the Author of three letters for toleration* (Oxford, 1704).

114 For Locke in his contemporary background see the essays in *John Locke Problems and Perspectives* (edited by J. W. Yolton) (Cambridge, 1969). For the educational writings, see *The Educational Writings of John Locke* (ed. James L. Axtell), especially

Appendix I which reproduces Locke's letters to Edward Clarke for the period 1684–91; for the work on the laws of nature, which was also well judged, see John Locke, *Essays on the laws of nature* (ed. W. Von Leyden) (Oxford, 1954).

115 Leo Strauss, *Natural Right and History* (Chicago, 1953), Part B, Chapter 5.

116 M. Seliger, *The Liberal Politics of John Locke* (London, 1968) and H. Laski, *The Rise of European Liberalism* (London, 1936), pp. 86–160.

117 A. A. Cooper, *The Moralists, a philosophical rhapsody* (London, 1709), pp. 217–218.

118 *Ibid.*, p. 229.

119 *Ibid.*, p. 251.

120 For further discussion of this problem of reason producing more than one credible answer, see Chapter Nine below.

121 A. A. Cooper, *Characteristicks of Men, Manners, Opinions, Times* (3 vols, London, 1711).

122 *Ibid.*, i, p. 111.

123 *Ibid.*, i, p. 115.

124 *Ibid.*, i, pp. 138–9.

125 *Ibid.*, i, pp. 138–42.

126 See Chapter Eight below.

127 A. A. Cooper, *The Moralists*, p. 248 (vol. ii of *Characteristicks*).

128 A. A. Cooper, *Characteristicks*, ii, p. 257, Philocles to Theocles.

129 *Ibid.*, i, p. 262.

130 *Ibid.*

131 Francis Hutcheson, *An Inquiry into the origin of our ideas of beauty and virtue* (London, 1725), in two treatises.

132 *Ibid.*, pp. 262–78 e.g.

133 Bernard de Mandeville, *The Fable of the Bees: or, Private Vices, Publick Benefits* (London, 1714), See also *A Modest defence of public stews* (London, 1724), variously attributed to Mandeville or George Ogle.

134 J. M. Keynes, *The General Theory of Employment, Interest and Money* (London, 1967), pp. 359–62.

135 *Fable of the Bees, passim.*

136 P. Harth, *The Fable of the Bees* (Harmondsworth, 1970), p. 7.

137 *Ibid.*, p. 69, and *The Fable of the Bees* (London, 1724, 3rd ed.), p. 11.

138 *Ibid.*, p. 76, and *The Fable of the Bees* (London, 1724, 3rd ed.), pp. 23–4.

139 Bernard de Mandeville, *A Letter to Dion occasion'd by his book call'd Alciphron* (London, 1732), e.g. p. 34 where the debt is explicit and Mandeville, *Free thoughts on religion, the Church, and national happiness* (London, 1720), Preface, p. xv, and p. 93.

140 *A Letter to Dion*, p. 29.

141 *Ibid.*, p. 9.

142 B. de Mandeville, *An enquiry into the origin of honour and the usefulness of Christianity in war* (London, 1732), p. ix.

143 *Ibid.*, see Horatio's summary of Cleomene's argument, pp. 236–7. See Dialogues II and III for its full statement.

144 Machiavelli, *The Prince* (London, 1961).

145 For Mandeville's irenicism, see the arguments of almost any chapter of B. de Mandeville, *Free thoughts on religion, the Church, and national happiness* (London, 1720).

146 *Ibid.*, p. 66.

147 *Ibid.*, p. 214ff.

148 *Ibid.*, pp. 146–79.

149 See Chapter Ten below.

150 The literature aimed against Mandeville is vast, and can be approached through Kay's edition and Introduction to the *Fable*. Some of the better-known are: *Vice and luxury, publick mischiefs: or, remarks on a book intituled . . .* (London, 1704); R. Fiddes, *A general Treatise of morality form'd upon the principles of natural reason only* (London, 1724); G. Blewitt, *An Enquiry whether a general practice of virtue sends to the wealth or poverty, benefit or disadvantage of a people?* (London, 1725); B. de Mandeville, *The True Meaning of his Fable of the Bees* (London, 1726) – an attempt to answer some of his critics; and A. Campbell, *An Enquiry into the false notions collected by the author of the Fable of the Bees* (London, 1728).

151 Matthew Tindal, *The Rights of the Christian Church* (London, 1709).

152 *Spinoza reviv'd; or a Treatise proving the book entitled, The Rights of the Christian Church & C. to be the same with Spinoza's Rights of the Christian clergy* (London, 1709), p. 53.

153 *Ibid.*, p. 61.

154 *Ibid.*, p. 73.

155 *Ibid.*, p. 18.

156 *Ibid.*, p. 112.

157 *Ibid.*, p. 123.

158 *Ibid.*, p. 121.

CHAPTER FOUR **Theories of matter and the origin of the world**

1 See R. Hahn, *Laplace as a Newtonian Scientist* (Los Angeles, 1967), W. A. Clark Memorial Lecture; and P. Simon, Marq. de Laplace, *The System of the world*, tr. by J. Pond, 2 vols (London, 1809).

2 M. Hesse, in *Models and Analogies in Science* (London, 1963), gives a general treatment of the problem of analogy in science. *The Scientific Papers of James Clerk Maxwell*

(New York, 1965), ed. W. D. Niven. For atoms and attraction see pp. 445–91.

3 D'Alembert and Diderot (*inter alia*) *Dictionnaire Encyclopédique des Mathématiques* (Paris, 1789–97), Tome II, p. 150.

4 *Four Letters from Sir Isaac Newton to Dr Bentley containing some arguments in proof of a deity* (London, 1756), p. 1.

5 Richard Bentley, Boyle lectures for 1692–3, *The Folly and Unreasonableness of Atheism demonstrated* (London, 1693).

6 Sir Isaac Newton, *Principia Mathematica* (2nd ed., London, 1713), Preface.

7 Dr Samuel Clarke, *A Discourse on the Being and Attributes of God* (London, 1706) being the Boyle lectures for 1704–5.

8 Samuel Clarke, *The Leibniz–Clarke papers* (London, 1717).

9 William Derham, *Physico-theology* (London, 1712, 3rd ed., 1714) and *Astro-theology* (London, 1715).

10 James Thomson, *To the Memory of Sir Isaac Newton* (1727) in the edition of Thomson's works edited by J. Logie Roberton (Oxford, 1965 reprint), p. 438.

11 R. Blackmore, *Creation. A Philosophical Poem. Demonstrating the Existence and Providence of God*, e.g. pp. 14–16 (London, 1715).

12 J. Desaguiliers, *The Newtonian System of the World, the best model of government. An allegorical Poem* (London, 1728).

13 R. Blackmore, Preface, pp. xxi–xxiii, xli–xxii, pp. 107–38.

14 *Four Letters*, Letter 3, p. 28ff.

15 *Ibid.*, Letter I, Cambridge, 10 December 1692, Newton to Bentley, pp. 1–4.

16 *Ibid.*, p. 10.

17 *Ibid.*, Letter II, Cambridge, 17 January 1692–3, pp. 14–15.

18 Derived from Wallis, *Arithmetica Infinitorum* (*Opera Mathematica*) (Oxford, 1656–7).

19 *Four Letters*, Letter II, pp. 16–17.

20 *Ibid.*, p. 20. Reference is made to Blondel, *Book of Bombs*, i.e. François Blondel, *L'Art de jetter les bombes* (Amsterdam, 1690).

21 *Ibid.*, Letter III, Cambridge, 25 February 1692–3, pp. 24–6.

22 *Ibid.*, p. 26.

23 William Whiston, *Sir Isaac Newton's mathematik philosophy more easily demonstrated: with Dr Halley's account of comets illustrated* (London, 1716).

24 Sir Isaac Newton, *De Mundi Systemate* (London, 1728) and *A Treatise of the system of the world* (London, 1728), *vide* Preface, pp. i–iv.

25 William Whiston, *Sir Isaac Newton's corollaries from his philosophy and chronology in his own words* (London, 1729).

26 *Ibid.*, pp. 1–7.

27 *Ibid.*, p. 7.

28 *Ibid.*, p. 19.

29 *Ibid.*, pp. 24–5.

30 G. Berkeley, *The Works . . .* (ed. Fraser, Oxford, 1871), vol. i, pp. 220–6 (*A Treatise Concerning the Principles of human knowledge* (London, 1710)); and vol. iii, pp. 290–8 (*The Analyst . . .* (1734)).

31 G. Berkeley, *The Analyst: or a discourse addressed to an infidel mathematician* (London, 1734).

32 George Berkeley, *The Works . . .* (ed. A. C. Fraser, Oxford, 1871), vol. iii, Query 60 p. 297.

33 *Ibid.*, Query 59 p. 297.

34 The controversy begun by Berkeley's *Analyst* included Dr Jurin, *Geometry no Friend to Infidelity; or a Defence of Sir Isaac Newton & the British Mathematicians . . .* (London, 1734): Geo. Berkeley, *A Defence of Free-thinking in Mathematics* (London, 1735); Dr Jurin, *The Minute Mathematician: or the Free-thinker no Just thinker . . .* (London, 1735). J. Walton, *Vindication of Sir Isaac Newton's Fluxions* (London, 1735), and *Catechism of the Author of the Minute Philosopher* (London, 1735); Geo. Berkeley, *Reasons for not replying to Mr Walton's Full Answer* (London, 1735); J. Walton, *Answer to the Reasons for not replying . . .* (London, 1735).

35 Other authors also contributed: e.g. B. Robins, *A Discourse concerning the Nature & certainty of Sir Isaac Newton's Methods of Fluxions . . .* (London, 1735); T. Bayes, *Introduction to the Doctrine of Fluxions, & Defence of the Mathematicians against the objections of the Author of the Analyst . . .* (London, 1736); and *The Harmony of the Ancient & Modern Geometry asserted: in answer to the Call of the Author of the Analyst . . .* (London, 1742 to Royal Society).

36 For Newton's God, and his austere beliefs in the will of a Calvinist master, see Manuel, *The Religious belief of Sir Isaac Newton* (lectures presented to the University of Oxford, 1973).

37 See Chapter Seven below.

38 M. Fontenelle, *Eloge de M. Neuton.* This was printed as an Appendix to Sir Isaac Newton, *The Chronology of Ancient Kingdoms Amended* (London, 1728), p. 22.

39 *Eloge*, p. 5. Descartes had excluded the vacuum and attraction from Physics, but Newton reintroduced them in a novel way.

40 Two principles dominate Newton's work, that of centrifugal forces, and that of resistance of a medium to movement. Both were almost entirely new, and handled with the geometrical mastery of the author.

41 *Eloge*, p. 12. The fundamental discovery of the Treatise is the different refractivity of red, yellow, green, blue and violet rays.

42 P. M. Rattansi and J. E. McGuire, *Newton and the Pipes of Pan* in Records of the Royal Society, 1966, pp. 108–38. On p. 138 the authors rightly conclude that all of Newton must be seen in the context of problems crucial to his generation which transcended disciplinal divisions between 'theology' and 'science'.

43 J. Wallis, *A discourse of gravity & gravitation, grounded on experimental observations* (London, 1675), p. 2.

44 *Ibid.*, pp. 33–4.

45 Sir Isaac Newton, *Observations upon the prophecies of Daniel and the Apocalypse of St John* (London, 1733), p. 276ff.

46 Sir Isaac Newton, *The chronology of ancient kingdoms amended* (London, 1728).

47 *Ibid.*, Dedication to the Queen, p. viii. Queen Caroline was an equally enthusiastic supporter of Newton, and the lavish state funeral was a tribute to Newton's fame and grandeur within the realm.

48 For Newton and the occult, see F. Yates, *The Rosicrucian Enlightenment* (London, 1972), pp. 200–5; Manuel, *Isaac Newton historian* (Cambridge, Massachusetts, 1968).

49 For the partial scepticism of the English tradition, see Popkin, *History of Skepticism*; for Neo-Platonism, see Powicke, *The Cambridge Platonists*. For 'the cool candle of the Lord', see Powicke on Whichcote, and other biographies, e.g. Jackson Cope, *Glanvill, Anglican Apologist*.

50 Lord King, *The Life of John Locke* (London, 1830), vol. i, p. 417, letter from Newton to Locke, 6 September 1693.

51 *The Correspondence of Isaac Newton* (ed. H. W. Turnbull, Cambridge, 1961), vol. III, pp. 71–6, a letter from Newton to Locke expounding themes from the *Principia*, March 1689/90.

52 *Ibid.*, pp. 76–7, Note 6, citing *Works of John Locke* (2nd ed., 1722), p. 89.

53 John Locke, *Works* (3 vols, 6th ed., London, 1759), vol. i, *Essay concerning Human Understanding* (1st ed., London, 1690), p. 96.

54 *Ibid.*, p. 167, pp. 228–37, Book 3 Chapter 10.

55 Thomas Hobbes, *Leviathan* (London, 1651), Preface; and J. Locke, *Works* (6th ed.,), Book 4, Chapter 3, p. 257.

56 For a modern consideration of scepticism and methods of refuting it, see A. J. Ayer, *The Problem of Knowledge* (Harmondsworth, 1966), pp. 68–82.

57 J. Locke, *Works*, pp. 299–303.

58 *Ibid.*, vol. i, Book 1, Chapter 1.

59 *Ibid.*, vol. i, p. 330.

60 *Ibid.*, vol. i, p. 257.

61 *Ibid.*, vol. i, p. 259.

62 *Ibid.*, vol. i, p. 267.

63 *Ibid.*, vol. i, p. 330.

64 *Ibid.*, vol. i, pp. 293–9.

65 *Ibid.*

66 *Notes and Records of the Royal Society*, December 1965, James Axtell, 'Locke's Review of the Principia', pp. 152–61.

67 *Acta Eruditorum*, June 1688, pp. 303–15.

68 *Philosophical Transactions*, Vol. XVI, No. 186, March 1687.

69 Sir Leslie Stephen, *A History of English Thought* (London, 1876), vol. i, pp. 93–119. E. Crous, *Die Grundlagen der Religionsphilosophischen Lehren Lockes* (Halle a. S., 1909), who also considers Locke's belief in Jesus as the Messiah, p. 45ff.

70 S. G. Hefelbower, *The Relation of Locke to English Deism* (Chicago, 1918).

71 John Edwards, *The Causes of Atheism* (London, 1695), which attacked Locke's *Reasonableness of Christianity* (London, 1695); and J. Leland, *The Principal Deistical Writers* (London, 1754) who (p. 380) recognized certain differences but also implied certain connections between Locke and the deists.

72 J. Harrison and T. P. Laslett, *The Library of John Locke* (2nd ed., Oxford, 1971), p. 76.

73 *Ibid.*, p. 238.

74 *Ibid.*, p. 84.

75 *Ibid.*, p. 238. F. Lany, *Le Nouvel Athéisme renversé* (Paris, 1696).

76 J. Locke, *A Vindication of the Reasonableness of Christianity* (London, 1695), against Edwards, *Some thoughts concerning the several causes and occasions of atheism, especially in the present Age*.

77 First published at London in 1690 though written in part many years earlier. Reprinted by Everyman, London, 1961.

78 Paolo Mattia Doria, *Difesa della metafisica degli antichi filosofi contro Giovanni Locke ed alcuni altri moderni autori* (Venezia, 1732), p. 201.

79 J. Locke, *The Reasonableness of Christianity, as delivered in the Scriptures*, in *Works* (London, 1759), vol. ii, pp. 511–88.

80 Romeo Crippa, *Studi sulla conscienza etica e religiosa del siecento; esperienza e libertà in J. Locke* (Milano, 1960), p. 152.

81 *Ibid.*, pp. 133–4.

82 J. Locke (tr.), *Discourses on the Being of a God and the immortality of the soul; of the weakness of man; and concerning the way of* *preserving peace with men: being some of the essays written in french by some Messieurs du Port Royal* (London, 1712).

83 *Port Royal Discourses*, p. 1.

84 *Ibid.*, pp. 5–8.

85 *Ibid.*, pp. 10–12.

86 J. Edwards, *Some thoughts concerning the several causes and occasions of atheism, especially in the present age* (London, 1696).

87 J. Locke, *The Reasonableness of Christianity, as delivered in the Scriptures* in *Works* (London, 1759), vol. ii, p. 570.

88 *Ibid.*, p. 585.

89 *Ibid.*, p. 586.

90 *A Vindication of the Reasonableness of Christianity, &c. From Mr Edwards Reflections* . . . in *Works*, vol. ii, pp. 589–98 and *A Second Vindication of the Reasonableness of Christianity* in vol. ii, pp. 601–719.

91 See F. H. Anderson, *The influence of contemporary science on Locke's methods and results*, Univ. of Toronto Studies: Philosophy, vol. 2 (Toronto, 1923).

92 Boyle's will bequeathed £50 a year to a lecturer who was to refute some aspect of anti-Christian thought, but was not to descend to inter-sectarian wrangling.

93 G. S. De Beer (ed.), *The Diary of John Evelyn* (Oxford, 1959), vol. v., p. 94.

94 R. White, *Richard Bentley, a study in academic scarlet* (London, 1965).

95 J. H. Monk, *Richard Bentley* (2nd ed., London, 1853). White has added little to our knowledge of Bentley, save to modify Monk's criticism that Bentley spent too much of his time on classical scholarship and not enough on religion. See also C. Wordsworth (ed.), *The Correspondence of R. Bentley* (London, 1842–3).

96 R. Bentley, *A Confutation of Atheism from the origin and frame of the world* (London, 1693).

97 See Bailey (ed.), Lucretius, *De Rerum Natura* (Oxford, 1966), for a statement of these views in vol. i, the text.

98 Bentley, sermons, *The folly of Atheism, and (what is now called) Deism* (London, 1693), p. 14.

99 Bentley, sermon II, *Matter and Motion cannot think, or, a Confutation of Atheism from the faculties of the soul* (London, 1693).

100 *Ibid.*, p. 3.

101 Cotes's Preface to Newton's *Principia* (2nd ed., Cambridge, 1713).

102 See pp. 113–114 above.

103 For Descartes and his early training see H. L. Roth, *Descartes' Discourse on Method* (Oxford, 1937).

104 Descartes invited criticism of his work and published some replies; see Arnauld.

105 Bentley, sermon VI, p. 13.

106 *Ibid.*, p. 25 following a long attack on intellectual atomists.

107 *Ibid.*, pp. 29–30. In part a defence and in part a veiled attack on the Cartesians.

108 *Ibid.*, p. 35.

109 Bentley, *A Confutation* . . . *from the origin and frame of the world* (London, 1693).

110 See pp. 94–9 above.

111 Bentley, *A Confutation* . . . *from the origin and frame of the world*, p. 22.

112 Thomas Hobbes, *3 Papers presented to the Royal Society against Dr Wallis* (London, 1671), and replies (available in Bodleian Savile E.e.1), Wallis 2nd Answer, p. 1.

113 Hobbes's 3rd Paper.

114 J. Locke, *Works* (6th ed., London, 1759), vol. i, p. 92.

115 *Ibid.*

116 *Ibid.*, pp. 31–2.

117 *Ibid.*, Part II.

118 *Ibid.*, Part II, p. 8.

119 *Ibid.*, Part II, pp. 28–9.

120 As in F. Gastrell, *The Certainty and Necessity of Religion in General, or, The First Grounds and Principles of Humane Duty established* (Boyle lectures, London, 1697).

121 *Ibid.*, pp. 26–8.

122 *Ibid.*, p. 48.

123 *Ibid.*, pp. 50–5.

124 Dr John Harris, Boyle lectures for 1697/8.

125 *Ibid.*, Sermon II, *The Atheist's Objection, that we can have no doubt of God, refuted*, p. 11ff.

126 *Ibid.*, Sermons IV–V, *The Atheist's Objections, against the immaterial nature of God, and Incorporeal Substance refuted*, p. 17, citing Locke, *Essay on Human Understanding*, p. 143.

127 Boyle lecturer for 1706–7.

128 Dr John Williams, Boyle lectures for 1695–6.

129 Samuel Bradford, *The Credibility of the Christian Revelation, from its intrinsick evidence* (London, 1699).

130 Offspring Blackall, Boyle lectures for 1699–1700, *The Sufficiency of the Scripture-Revelation*.

131 J. R. Partington, 'The Origin of the Atomic Theory', *Annals of Science*, 4 (1939), p. 245. A. G. Van Melsen, *From Atomos to Atom* (New York, 1960). M. Boas, 'The Establishment of the mechanical philosophy', *Osiris*, 10 (1952), pp. 412–541.

132 T. S. Hall, *Ideas of life and matter. Studies in the History of General Physiology 600 BC–1900 AD*, p. 279ff.

133 *Ibid.*, pp. 312ff.

134 E. McMullin, *The concept of matter in Greek and medieval philosophy* (Notre Dame, 1963).

135 R. Boyle, *Works* (ed. Birch) (London, 1744), vol. i, pp. 450 and 459.
136 *Ibid.*, vol. i, p. 451.
137 *Ibid.*, vol. i, p. 435.
138 *Ibid.*, vol. i, pp. 130, 282, 448–52.
139 J. Gay, Freedom and matter in the thought of Samuel Clarke, *Journal of the History of Ideas* (1963), p. 85ff.
140 J. E. McGuire, 'Atoms and the Analogy of nature: Newton's third rule of philosophising', in *Studies in the History and Philosophy of Science* (May 1970, vol. i, no. i). See also Tillyard, *The Elizabethan World Picture* (London, 1943) and A. O. Lovejoy, *The Great Chain of Being* (Cambridge, Massachusetts, 1966), e.g. pp. 99–143.
141 *Ibid.*, p. 1ff.
142 *Ibid.*, p. 46.
143 F. H. Anderson, *The Philosophy of Francis Bacon* (Chicago, 1948), e.g. pp. 70–80 – especially p. 77 – and pp. 118–20. Anderson also considers the influence of Hero on Bacon, pp. 70–80.
144 It was during this period of interest that Burton dedicated his *Anatomy of Melancholy* to Democritus Junior.
145 Published in London in 1654.
146 R. Boyle, *Works* (ed. Birch) (London, 1744), and H. Fisch, 'The scientist as priest: a note on Robert Boyle's theology', *Isis*, xliv (1953).
147 For the reaction of Newton, Whiston and others to the Cartesian scheme, see J. Herivel, *The Background to Newton's Principia* (Oxford, 1965), e.g. pp. 65–76 concerning gravitation and the break with Descartes.
148 J. E. McGuire, 'Boyle's Conception of Nature', in *Journal of the History of Ideas*, 1972, p. 542: for comment on Boyle's conception of matter.
149 R. H. Kargon, *Atomism in England from Hariott to Newton* (Oxford, 1966), pp. 5–17, 63–76.
150 S. Toulmin and J. Goodfield, *The Architecture of matter* (London, 1962), pp. 194–222.
151 Francis Gastrell, *The Certainty and Necessity of Religion in General or The First Grounds and Principles of Humane Duty established* (London, 1697).
152 *Ibid.*
153 J. Harris, Boyle lectures (London, 1698), *The Atheist's Objections against the immaterial nature of God, and Incorporeal Substance refuted*, pp. 35ff.
154 See Spinoza, *Opera Posthuma* (no place, probably Amsterdam, 1677).
155 S. Bradford, *The Credibility of the Christian Revelation* (London, 1699).
156 S. Clarke, *A Discourse of the Being and Attributes of God* (London, 1705).

157 William Derham, *Physico-theology; or, a demonstration of the being and attributes of God, from his works of creation* (London, 1713), note on pp. 312–13.
158 J. Leng, *Natural Obligations to believe the principles of religion and divine revelation* (London, 1719), e.g. p. 88ff.
159 *Ibid.*, p. 69, note C, citing Cicero, *De Naturae Deorum*, cap 43.
160 G. D. Hadzsits, *Lucretius and his Influence* (New York, 1963), pp. 62–78, deals generally with Lucretian atomism in seventeenth-century science.
161 See e.g. D. P. Mellor, *The Evolution of the Atomic Theory* (Amsterdam, 1971), pp. 9–33. Mellor shows how atomism was connected with alchemy in Newton and Boyle.
162 C. Maclaurin, *An Account of Sir Isaac Newton's Philosophical Discoveries* (London, 1748), pp. 64–90.
163 For Newton's criticisms of Descartes and Epicurus, see e.g. *Unpublished Scientific Papers of Isaac Newton* (ed. by A. R. and M. B. Hall) (Cambridge, 1962). *De Gravitatione et Aequipondio Fluidorum*, pp. 150–1.

CHAPTER FIVE **The origin of the earth**

1 Some writers analysed Genesis in great detail: e.g. *A Cabbalistical Dialogue in Answer to the Opinion of a learned Dr in Philosophy and Theology, that the world was made of nothing . . .* (London, 1677), pp. 18–30.
2 Fossil collections had been started by Aldrovandi (1522–1605) and Ole Worm (1588–1654): see H. K. Butler, unpublished University of Oklahoma Ph.D. thesis, 1968, 'The Study of Fossils in the last half of the Seventeenth century', p. 41.
3 John Ray, *The Wisdom of God manifested in the works of the Creation* (London, 1691). For Ray's work see Chas. E. Raven, *John Ray Naturalist, His life and works* (Cambridge, 1942), and the publications of the Ray Society: e.g. R. W. T. Gunther, *Further Correspondence of John Ray* (London, 1928), and C. Raven, *English Naturalists from Neckham to Ray* (Cambridge, 1947). Important work was also underway in Europe: see for example G. W. Leibniz, *Protégé ou de la formation et des Revolutions du globe* (ed. Bertrand de Saint-Germain) (Paris, 1859).
4 See Sloane MS cited below.
5 British Museum Sloane MS 3529 ff3–4.
6 Additional MS 4019 f16v and 17r.
7 Sloane MS 4015, a catalogue of plants, e.g. f5r, 'Alsine aquatica media . . . locus in ulginosis'.
8 *Ibid.*, f19 with colour-wash drawing.

9 Sloane MS 3323 f45r and v.
10 Sloane MS 4015 f120.
11 Sloane MS 4019 f46.
12 *Ibid.*, f51.
13 Sloane MS 3323 f59.
14 *Ibid.*, ff77–80.
15 *Ibid.*, f325.
16 *Ibid.*, f259.
17 See Sloane MS 4019 for a list of contributions to Sloane's collection given by Mr John Bell, f48.
18 See Sloane MS 4019 f69 for a list of Indian rarities in the galleries of that garden. Sloane MS 1142 ff55–148 describes the botanical garden.
19 K. G. Ponting (ed.), *Natural History of Wiltshire* (London, 1969).
20 Available in a Folk Lore Society publication (ed. James Britten, London, 1881).
21 R. Boyle, *Works* (ed. Birch, London, 1744), vol. iv, pp. 515–50. John Ray, *The Wisdom of God manifested in the works of the creation* (London, 1691), Preface.
22 *Psalms*, xix, 19.
23 Bishop of Chester, *A Treatise of Natural Religion* (London, 1691).
24 See Chapter Four, above.
25 Charles Blount, *Oracles of Reason* (London, 1693) and Thomas Burnet, *Telluris Theoria Sacra; orbis nostri originem et mutationes complectens* (London, 1681).
26 Dr John Woodward, *An Essay towards a natural history of the earth and terrestial bodies, especially minerals . . . with an account of the universal deluge . . .* (London, 1695). William Whiston, *A New Theory of the Earth* (London, 1696).
27 For the career of Edward Lhwyd, Keeper of the Ashmolean Museum, Oxford, see Joseph Foster (ed.), *Alumni Oxonienses* (Oxford and London, 1891), vol. ii, p. 913ff.
28 Edward Lhwyd, *Archaeologia Britannica, giving some account of the languages, histories and customs of the original inhabitants of Great Britain* (Oxford, 1707): for a comparative vocabulary of British and Irish languages see Tit. II; for an Irish dictionary see Tit. X.
29 *Ibid.*, and J. L. Campbell, *Edward Lhwyd in the Scottish highlands.* Lhwyd's work on fossils can be found in his *Lythophylacii Britannici Ichnographia* (ed. Oxon, 1760), which divided fossils into different categories, e.g. Class V Bivalvia, pp. 25–43.
30 John Ray, *The Wisdom of God manifested in the works of the Creation* (London, 1691), Preface.
31 *Ibid.*, pp. 3–4.
32 *Ibid.*, pp. 20–40.
33 More, *An Antidote against atheism* (London, 1659), 1. 2. c 10 cited in Ray, p. 102.
34 *Ibid.*, pp. 93–102, 135ff.
35 John Ray, *Three Physico-theological discourses concerning 1. The Primitive Chaos 2. The Deluge 3. The dissolution of the world* (London, 1693), pp. 62–80.
36 *Ibid.*, p. 163.
37 *Op. Cit. Dictionary of National Biography*, vol. iii, p. 409.
38 Thomas Burnet, *The Sacred Theory of the Earth* (ed. B. Willey, London, 1965) (Centaur Classics), Introduction, pp. 5–14. A view of Burnet as a misdirected writer can be found in B. Willey, *The Seventeenth Century Background* (London, 1934). Willey also stresses the harmony of religion and science at the expense of perceiving the reaction against scientific determinism, mechanism, and ancient heresies. See Willey, *The Eighteenth Century Background* (London, 1948), pp. 32–5.
39 For the role of Burnet in English thought see Allen, *The Legend of Noah* (Urbana, 1949); K. B. Collier, *Cosmogonies of our Fathers* (New York, 1934); S. C. Greene, *The death of Adam, evolution, and its impact on western thought* (Ames, 1959), pp. 38–42; F. C. Haber, *The Age of the world, Moses to Darwin* (Baltimore, 1959), pp. 71–83; F. D. Adams, *The Birth and Development of the Geological Sciences* (Baltimore, 1938); C. Gillespie, *Genesis & Geology* (Cambridge, 1951); and Sir Archibald Geikie, *The Founders of Geology* (New York, 1962 reprint of 1905 2nd ed.), pp. 66–7 for a hostile view.
40 The theory can be found in Thomas Burnet (ed. by Foxton), *Archaeologiae Philosophicae: or the ancient doctrine concerning the originals of things. To which is added, Dr Burnet's Theory of the Visible world, by way of commentary on his own theory of the earth* (London, 1681–9). A useful modern edition is that of Willey (London, 1965): for the surface of the globe before the Flood see Chapter V, pp. 53ff.; for proof of the universal deluge being caused by a rupture in the abyss see pp. 68–71.
41 Thomas Burnet, *Sacred Theory . . .* (London, 1965). The two last books, 'Concerning the burning of the world', and 'Concerning the new heavens and the earth', p. 213ff.
42 For some criticisms of Burnet see Sir H. Sheers, *Essay on the causes of the earth's motion* (London, 1698); T. Robinson, *Anatomy of the earth* (London, 1694); *De Situ Telluris Paradis Burnetiano* (Hamburg, 1695); Mr Beaumont's *Considerations on Dr Burnet's Theory of the earth* (London, 1693); A. Lovell, *Summary of Heads in answer to Dr Burnet* (London, 1696); T. Baker, *Reflec-*

tions on learning (London, 1708); Philosophical Transactions from the year 1710 to the year 1733, abridged: E. Halley, 'Some considerations about the causes of the universal deluge'; E. Warren, *Geologia; or a discourse about the earth before the deluge . . . it is made to appear that the Dissolution of the Earth was not the cause of the universal deluge* (London, 1690). Pepys was in favour of Burnet, see e.g. in his letter to Evelyn in *Samuel Pepys, Private Correspondence and miscellaneous papers* (ed. J. R. Tanner, London, 1926), I, pp. 23–4. For modern discussions of the Burnet controversies see D. C. Allen, *The Legend of Noah, Renaissance rationalism in art, Science and letters* (Urbana, 1949), pp. 91–112, and M. H. Nicolson, *Mountain gloom and mountain glory: the development of the aesthetics of the infinite* (New York, 1959), pp. 225–70.

43 A letter to the bookseller Mr E. Curll, prefixed to Foxton 1736 edition. The defence is parallel to that in a letter from Blount to Gildon, reprinted in Blount's *Oracles of Reason*: for comment see pp. 122–3 below.
44 *Pensioner of the Charterhouse: A summary of Material Heads which may be enlarged and Improved into a Compleat Answer to Dr Burnet's Theory of the Earth* (London, 1696), p. 14.
45 *Ibid.*, p. 23.
46 *Sacred Theory*, p. 30ff. for volume of water necessary for universal deluge; p. 31ff. for quantity of water in rainfall for 40 days; for argument that antediluvian earth must have been better see p. 42ff.
47 *Ibid.*, p. 81.
48 Thomas Burnet, *Archaeologiae Philosophicae: sive Doctrina Antiqua de rerum Originibus* (London, 1692).
49 *Ibid.*, p. 202. Burnet lists the errors of Aristotle on p. 184: the first he cites is 'Mundum Aeternum esse statuit, ex utraque parte: Ingenitum et incorruptibilem'.
Burnet criticizes Aristotle's idea that the world is eternal, and comments on the traditions that believe the world was formed from the chaos.
50 *Ibid.*, Book I Chapter XIII 'De Platonicis, Aristotelisis, et Epicureis, pp. 185–6.
51 Foxton's ed., p. 30.
52 Thomas Burnet, *Archaeologiae Philosophicae* (London, 1736), Preface p. x.
53 H. Croft, Bishop of Hereford, *Some Animadversions upon a book Intituled the Theory of the Earth* (London, 1685), pp. 40–1.
54 Charles Blount, *Oracles of Reason* (London, 1693), Preface.
55 *Ibid.*, pp. 2–8.
56 *Ibid.*, pp. 15–51.

57 For Blount's other heresies see Chapters Three and Four above, for political theories and theories of matter, Chapter Six below.
58 For the contributions of Burnet, Whiston and others to geology, see Sir Arthur Geikie, *The Founders of Geology* (London, 1897), a work that has scarcely been superseded. F. D. Adams, *The Birth and development of the geological sciences* (Baltimore, 1938) is also useful, as is C. Schneer's article, 'The Rise of historical geology in the seventeenth century' in *Isis*, xlv (1954), pp. 256–68. H. Meyer, *The Age of the world, a chapter in the history of enlightenment* multigraphed at Muhlenberg College, Allentown, 1951, I am told is valuable although I have not used it myself.
59 For the career of William Whiston see *Dict. Nat. Biog.*, vol. LXI, pp. 10–14; and William Whiston, *Memoirs of the life and writings of Mr William Whiston containing several of his friends also, and written by himself* (London, 1749).
60 Whiston was deeply involved in popularizing and adapting Newtonian theories: see W. Whiston and Hauksbee, *A Course of mechanical, optical, Hydrostatical, and Pneumatical experiments* (London, 1713).
61 John Keill, *An examination of Dr Burnet's Theory of the Earth, together with some remarks on Mr Whiston's New Theory of the Earth* (Oxford, 1698), p. 177.
62 *Ibid.*, p. 178.
63 E.g. William Whiston, *Primitive Christianity Reviv'd* (London, 1711) (see Chapter Nine below).
64 It is surprising that he has escaped a biographer, seeing that his own Autobiography and the testimony of friends and rivals, court records about his trials, and letters from and to friends all survive to sustain one.
65 William Whiston, *A New Theory of the Earth* (London, 1696), p. 3.
66 *Ibid.*, p. 26.
67 *Ibid.*, pp. 14–15.
68 *Ibid.*, p. 26ff.
69 *Ibid.*, pp. 52–3.
70 William Whiston, *A Short Review of the Chronology of the Old Testament, and of the harmony of the four evangelists* (Cambridge, 1702), Proposition 17, p. 65.
71 John Ray, *The Wisdom of God manifest in the wonders of the Creation* (London, 1691). See also C. E. Raven, *John Ray Naturalist, His life and works* (Cambridge, 1942); C. E. Raven, *English Naturalists from Neckham to Ray* (Cambridge, 1947); and R. W. Gunther, *Correspondence of John Ray* (London, Ray Society).

72 J. Ward, *Lives of the Gresham Professors* (London, 1740), p. 283.
73 *Dict. Nat. Biog.*, vol. xxi, p. 894.
74 Dr John Woodward, *An Essay towards a natural history of the earth* (London, 1695).
75 *Ibid.*, Preface.
76 *Ibid.*, p. 3.
77 *Ibid.*, p. 86.
78 *Ibid.*, pp. 73–5.
79 *Ibid.*, pp. 100–1.
80 *Ibid.*, pp. 158–62.
81 *Ibid.*, p. 163.
82 Tanner MS 25 f229r.
83 J. Woodward, *An Essay* . . ., p. 180.
84 *Ibid.*, p. 191.
85 *Ibid.*, pp. 208–10.
86 *Ibid.*, p. 212.
87 *Ibid.*, p. 217.
88 *Ibid.*, p. 247.
89 *Ibid.*, e.g. p. 256 concerning the pre-existence of mountains.
90 *Ibid.*, pp. 274–6.
91 Woodward's long correspondence with Hearne can be found in the Rawlinson manuscripts (Bodleian). For his letters to Moore, see e.g. Tanner xxv 193 (Bodleian).
92 Woodward shared the popular anthropocentrism in his treatment of final causes. See *An Essay* . . ., p. 238.
93 *The State of Physic and of diseases: with an inquiry into the causes of the late increase of them* (London, 1718); answered by John Quincy, *An Examination of Dr John Woodward's State of Physic* (London, 1719). This was followed by *An Account of De Quincy's Examination.*
94 Rawlinson Letter 12 f44.
95 *Ibid.*, f439.
96 John Arbuthnot, *An Examination of Dr Woodward's account of the Deluge, and c. with a comparison between Steno's philosophy and the Dr's in the case of marine bodies dug out of the earth* (London, 1697). These remarks were answered by John Harris in *Remarks on some late papers relating to the universal deluge* (London, 1697).
97 *Museum Woodwardianum, in duas partes distributum* (London, 1728), being a sale catalogue of his library. Bodleian copy in Mus. Bibl. III has interpolated prices in hand.
98 For the history of trades project see T. Birch, *History of the Royal Society* (London, 1755–7), I, pp. 55, 65, 83, etc. For collections of providences see K. Thomas, *Religion and the Decline of magic* (London, 1971), especially pp. 90–132.
99 J. Woodward, *Fossils of all kinds, digested into a method suitable to their mutual relation and affinity* (London, 1728), p. 120.
100 J. Woodward, *An Attempt towards a natural history of fossils of England* (London, 1729), Preface pp. xiii–xiv.
101 Cf. Descartes, *Discourse on Method* (London, 1968), p. 45ff., and Robert Hook, *Micrographia* (London, 1665), Preface.
102 J. Woodward, *Fossils of all kinds, digested into a method suitable to their mutual relation and affinity* (London, 1728), Letter No. 5, p. 54.
103 *Ibid.*, pp. 55–6.
104 Agostino Scilla, *Lettera circa i corpi marini, petrificati* (Naples, 1670).
105 J. Woodward, *Fossils of all kinds* . . ., Letter No. 3, pp. 25–37.
106 *Ibid.*, Letter No. 6, pp. 58–75.
107 *Ibid.*, Letter No. 7, pp. 77–86.
108 *Ibid.*, p. 85.
109 Dr Buttner, *Corollographia Subterranea.*
110 In 1692 Woodward was Gresham Professor of Physic: see J. Ward, *Lives of the Gresham Professors* (London, 1740), pp. 283–301; and *Dict. Nat. Biog.*, vol. 21, 894–6.
111 J. Woodward, *Fossils of all kinds* . . ., p. 113.
112 *Ibid.*, p. 107: referring them to a long-standing dispute about whether minerals were still being produced through organic processes or not.
113 *Ibid.*, p. 124.
114 J. Woodward, *Fossils of all kinds* . . ., pp. 39–43.
115 Genesis, iv v. 22.
116 For further interest in this subject, see e.g. 'An Account of the Abbot Charmoy's book . . . called L'Origine des Nations', *Philosophical Transactions*, 1699–1700, pp. 274–80.
117 J. Woodward, *Fossils of all kinds* . . ., pp. 43–4 (and facing illustration of arrow types).
118 *Auction Catalogue of Dr Woodward's Library* (London, 1728), p. 32; for his copy of Thomas Burnet, see p. 6.
119 Sir H. Sheers, *Essays on the causes of the earth's motion* (London, 1698). T. Robinson, *Anatomy of the Earth* (London, 1694).
120 *Philosophical Transactions*, January and February 1696, *passim*.
121 *Auction Catalogue*, p. 59.
122 *Ibid.*, p. 110.
123 *Ibid.*, pp. 134, 136.
124 *Ibid.*, p. 77.
125 John Harris, *Lexicon Technicum: or, an universal English dictionary of Arts and Sciences* (London, 1704–10), 2 vols: vol. i, Article on 'Fossils'.
126 *Ibid.*, Article on 'Deluge'.
127 *Ibid.* He had some sympathy for Whiston's approach – see article on 'Chaos'.

128 Harris published one volume of a planned five-volume *The History of Kent* (London, 1719). He also published a collection of travel curiosities, reprinted as *Navigantium atque itinerantium bibliotheca: or a collection of voyages and travels, consisting of above 600 writers*, revised and continued by J. Campbell, 2 vols (London, 1764). Cf. John Ray, *A Collection of Curious Travels and Voyages, in 2 tomes. Added, 3 Catalogues of such trees, shrubs, and herbs as grow in the Levant* (London, 1693); and Robert Plot, *The Natural History of Oxfordshire* (Oxford, 1677).

129 For a treatment of the controversies as a literary enterprise, see M. H. Nicolson, *Mountain gloom and mountain glory: the development of the aesthetics of the infinite* (New York, 1959). For the Scriblerians see C. Kerby Miller (ed.), *The Memoirs of Martinus Scriblerus* (New Haven, 1950); Martinus set out to show 'a mechanical explication of the formation of the universe, according to the Epicurean hypothesis'. Also useful is K. B. Collier, *Cosmogonies of our Fathers* (New York, 1934).

130 R. Plot, *The Natural History of Oxfordshire* (Oxford, 1677), p. 82; M. Lister, *Historiae Animalium Angliae* (London, 1678).

131 F. C. Haber, *The age of the world, Moses to Darwin*, gives the best treatment of the way all these thinkers worried at the problem of fossils and earthquakes, although his treatment of the reception of Burnet is perforce limited, and his analysis sometimes suffers from wishing to see more revolutionary changes than there were, p. 7.

132 T. Burnet, *Sacred Theory*, Book II, p. 173; also cited in Haber, p. 74.

133 *Dict. Nat. Biog.*, vol. xxi, pp. 10–11.

134 Locke, Letter to Molyneux, 22 February 1696, also cited in *Dict. Nat. Biog.*

135 William Whiston, *Memoirs of the life and writings of Mr William Whiston . . . written by himself* (2nd ed., London, 1753), p. 257ff.

136 E. G. R. Taylor, 'English World makers of the seventeenth century, and their influence on the earth sciences', *Geographical Review*, pp. 104–12.

137 Robert Hooke, *The Posthumous Works* (London, 1705), pp. 424–33.

138 *Ibid.*, pp 371–84.

139 R. Hooke, *Earthquakes and Subterraneous Eruptions* (London, 1668).

140 R. Hooke, *The Posthumous Works* (London, 1705), p. 411ff.

141 These problems were perceptively noted by H. K. Butler's thesis, *op. cit.*, p. 181.

142 *Nicolai Stenonis de solido intra solidum naturaliter contento dissertationis podromus* (Florence, 1669), p. 67; translated by H. Oldenburg as *The Podromus to a dissertation concerning solids naturally contained within solids laying a foundation for the rendering a rational accompt both of the frame and the several changes . . .* (London, 1671).

143 F. Redi, *Experimenta circa generationem insectorum* (Amsterdam, 1671). Swammerdam, *The Book of Nature: or, The History of Insects* (London, 1758), p. 10ff.

144 L. E. Orgel, *The Origins of life: Molecules and Natural Selection* (London and New York, 1973, p. 5ff.).

CHAPTER SIX **Witches, apparitions and revelations**

1 J. W. Packer, *The Transformation of Anglicanism* (Manchester, 1969), pp. 45–87 discusses the Hammond circle and their attitude to reason. See also H. Hammond, *Of the Reasonableness of Christian Religion* (London, 1650); and Packer, pp. 186–99.

2 K. Thomas, *Religion and the decline of Magic* (London, 1971) gives the most comprehensive treatment. See pp. 517–18 of 1973 (Harmondsworth ed.) for a bibliography of witchcraft. H. C. Lea, *Materials towards a history of witchcraft* (ed. A. C. Howland, Philadelphia, 1959), remains an important collection.

3 Dr A. Macfarlane, *Witchcraft in Tudor and Stuart England* (London, 1970), based on Essex materials.

4 An interesting list of contemporary works on magic compiled by Francis Douce can be found in Bodleian MS Douce e 48.

5 D. P. Walker, *The Decline of Hell, Seventeenth-Century Discussions of Eternal Torment* (London, 1964), pp. 3–70 contains a general discussion about the arguments for and against eternal punishments. These arguments will not be restated here.

6 For 'The place of miracles in English thought', see J. S. Lawton's D.Phil. thesis, deposited in the Bodleian Library. This work surveys the changing attitudes, and includes a short section on the period of the Boyle lecturers, of whom there is no printed study.

7 Dr Samuel Bradford, *The Credibility of the Christian Revelation, from its intrinsick evidence* (London, 1699), p. 1.

8 For Blackall, and Gastrell see below, pp. 136–9

9 Bradford, *The Credibility*, Sermon II, pp. 14–16.

10 *Ibid.*, Sermon III, p. 26.

11 *Ibid.*, Sermon III, p. 4.

12 *Ibid.*, Sermon IV.
13 *Ibid.*, Sermon V, e.g. p. 4 and p. 26.
14 *Ibid.*, Sermons VI and VII.
15 *Ibid.*, Sermon VIII, p. 27.
16 Samuel Bradford, Boyle lectures 1700, Appendix.
17 Offspring Blackall, *The Sufficiency of the Scripture Revelation, as to the proof of it* (London, 1700), pp. 3–4, Part I, summarizing previous 2 lectures.
18 *Ibid.*, p. 4ff.
19 *Ibid.*, p. 10 of Sermon III.
20 *Ibid.*, p. 14.
21 *Ibid.*, Lecture I, pp. 10–14, pp. 15–19, pp. 20–3.
22 *Ibid.*, p. 23.
23 *Ibid.*, pp. 21–2.
24 *Ibid.*, Sermon II, p. 17.
25 *Ibid.*, Sermon II, pp. 25–6, following a discussion of the decline of Hell, and the drift of people in England into irreligion.
26 *Ibid.*, Sermon IV and V.
27 *Ibid.*, Sermon VI, pp. 6–9.
28 *Ibid.*, Sermon VI, pp. 10–13.
29 *Ibid.*, Sermon VI, pp. 13–26.
30 *Ibid.*, Sermon VII.
31 *Ibid.*, Sermon VIII.
32 *Ibid.*, Sermon VII, p. 19.
33 *Ibid.*, Sermon VII, p. 29.
34 *Ibid.*, Sermon VIII, p. 49.
35 It is interesting to note that Blackall's sermon before the Commons in January 1699 attacked Toland strongly: see Desmaizeau, *An Historical Account of the Life and Writings of the late Eminently Famous Mr John Toland* (London, 1722), pp. 8–14.
36 See e.g. Bodleian Rawl. MS C936 f43r.
37 *Ibid.*, f44r.
38 *Ibid.*, f46r and v.
39 Blackall, *The Sufficiency . . .*, Sermon II, p. 17.
40 Alexander Pope, *Poetical Works* (ed. H. Davis, Oxford, 1966), pp. 86–109.
41 *The Freethinker* (London, 1711–21), 24 October 1718, No. 62.
42 *Ibid.* (London, 1722–3), No. 34, pp. 246–7.
43 *Ibid.*, pp. 247–8.
44 *Ibid.*, No. 47, p. 337.
45 *Ibid.*, No. 48, pp. 347–9.
46 *Ibid.*, No. 54, p. 397.
47 See Chapter Eight below.
48 William Coward, *Second Thoughts concerning the human soul* (London, 1702).
49 *Ibid.*, title page.
50 *Ibid.*
51 *Ibid.*, *passim*.
52 *Dict. Nat. Biog.*, vol. iv, pp. 1298–9.
53 William Coward, *Optithalmoiatria*, (London, 1706).
54 Anon., *A Just Scrutiny: or, a serious*

enquiry into the modern notions of the soul (ascribable to W. Coward of Merton College B.D.).
55 W. Coward, *The Grand Essay, or a Vindication of Reason and Religion against the impostures of Philosophy, proving, according to those Idea's and conceptions of things, Human understanding is capable of forming to itself* (London, 1704).
56 Broughton, *Psychologia*.
57 Coward, *Second Thoughts . . .*, p. 37. For his difficulties with materialism see his attempt at a distinction on p. 40 in contrast with the criticism of Dodwell and Clarke.
58 *Ibid.*, p. 53ff.
59 British Museum Add MS 4041, vol. VI, letters of Coward.
60 See H. Dodwell's views in *An epistolary discourse, proving the soul is a principle naturally mortal; but immortalized actually by the pleasure of God* (London, 1706).
61 E. E. Worcester, *The Religious Opinions of John Locke* (Leipzig, 1889), pp. 120–2. This view is received in J. D. Mabbott, *John Locke* (London, 1973), p. 123.
62 British Museum Add MS 4295 f71r.
63 J. Toland, *Letters to Serena* (London, 1704), pp. 2–4.
64 *Ibid.*, p. 4.
65 *Ibid.*, p. 9.
66 Bodleian Ashmole MS 423 f189. Cf. the year of eclipses mentioned in B. de Fontenelle, *A Plurality of Worlds* (London, 1688), translated by J. Glanvill, pp. 46–7.
67 Toland, *Letters to Serena*, p. 22.
68 *Ibid.*, p. 28.
69 *Ibid.*, p. 40.
70 *Ibid.*, pp. 72–3.
71 *Ibid.*, p. 78.
72 *Ibid.*, p. 90ff.
73 *Ibid.*, p. 113.
74 *Ibid.*, p. 122 note. The great majority of things flowing from God through reason and natural philosophy gave the poets stories and filled the lives of men with every type of superstition.
75 J. Toland, *Pantheisticon* (London, 1721).
76 Giordano Bruno, *On the Infinite Universe and worlds* (London, 1584). For the world Bruno was attacking, see A. O. Lovejoy, *The Great Chain of Being* (Cambridge, Massachusetts, 1950), and E. M. W. Tillyard, *The Elizabethan World Picture* (London, 1958 ed.). For general comments upon the reception of Democritus in England, see R. Kargon, *Atomism in England* (Oxford, 1966). For general observations on the revolution in the world picture from a scientific point of view, see A. Koyre, *From the Closed World to the Infinite Universe* (Baltimore and London, 1970).

77 John Toland, *De Genere, Loco, et tempore Mortis Jordani Bruni Nolani* in *The Miscellaneous Works of Mr John Toland* (London, 1747), vol. i, pp. 304–15; and *An Account of Jordano Bruno's Book . . .*, ibid., pp. 316–49.
78 B. de Fontenelle, *A Plurality of Worlds* (London, 1688), translated by J. Glanvill. E.g. pp. 35–9, men in the moon.
79 *The Signs of the times* (London, 1681).
80 *Strange news from the East, or, a sober account of the comet, or blazing-star, that has been seen several mornings of late* (London, 1673), p. 8.
81 William Knight, *Stella Nova* (London, 1680), appended to *Momento's to the world; or, an Historical collection of divers wonderful comets and prodigious signs in Heaven* (London, 1680).
82 *The blazing star; or a discourse of comets, their natures and effects* (London, 1665), pp. 42–4, for reasons of its influence. Interesting is the comment written on the title page of the Bodley edition: 'This was wrote by some fool or knave – who understood nothing of astrology or Cometal influences.'
83 *Mirabilis Annus secundus Or, the second year of Prodigies* (London, 1662), p. 43 for a strange birth, p. 13 for the blazing star.
84 *Ibid.*, p. 67.
85 *The petitioning-comet; or, a brief chronology of all the famous comets and their events, that have happened from the birth of Christ* (London, 1681), pp. 3–4.
86 *Ibid.*, p. 1.
87 *Ibid.*
88 *Coma Berenices; or the hairy comet; being a prognostick of influences from the many blazing stars*, Periwig, pp. 6–17; quotation, p. 1.
89 E.g. *A narrative of the Demon of Spraiton. In a letter from a person of Quality in the county of Devon, to a Gentleman in London, with a Relation of an apparition or spectrum . . . with reflections on Drollery and Atheism: and a word to those that deny the existence of Spirits* (London, 1683).
90 *A Judgement of the comet, which became first generally visible to us in Dublin December XIII* (London and Dublin, 1680), pp. 20–1.
91 For the work of Newton on the mechanism of the universe see Dijsterhuis, *The Mechanisation of the world picture* (Oxford, 1961), pp. 463–91. But cf. works like *Prophetical Observations occasion'd by the new comet* (London, 1723).
92 See *Philosophical Transactions* (London, 1699 1700), p. 79 discussing the French Royal Observatory observations of new comet.

93 *Ibid.*
94 See e.g. British Museum Add MS 4068 f36, Sloane's letter 11 August 1702 concerning the account of the new comet.
95 Bodleian MS Ashmole 242 f137.
96 Thomas Chubb, *A Discourse concerning Reason, with regard to Religion and divine revelation* (London, 1733).
97 *Ibid.*, p. 23.
98 M. Tindal, *Christianity as old as the Creation: or the Gospel a republic of the religion of nature* (London, 1730).
99 *Ibid.*, p. 13.
100 *Ibid.*
101 *Ibid.*, p. 69.
102 *Ibid.*, p. 178.
103 *Ibid.*, pp. 232–6.
104 All Souls College Archives, Appeals and Visitors Injunctions, vol. i, f112r. Item No. 50, 9 May 1711.
105 M. Tindal, *Christianity as old as the Creation: or the Gospel a republic of the religion of nature* (London, 1730), p. 236.
106 *Ibid.*, p. 236, margin of 4° Rawl. 92 (Bodleian Library).
107 *Ibid.*, p. 353ff.
108 *Ibid.*, pp. 430–1.
109 J. Foster, *The Usefulness, truth and excellency of the Christian revelation defended . . .* (London, 1731), pp. 2–3.
110 *Ibid.*, e.g. pp. 270–315: Chapters 4, 5.
111 Thomas Chubb, *The True Gospel of Jesus Christ asserted* (London, 1738), p. 191.
112 Thomas Chubb, *A Short Dissertation on Providence* (London, 1738), appended to *The True Gospel . . .*, p. 210.
113 *The True Gospel . . .*, pp. 127–8.
114 Thomas Chubb, *Two Enquiries, one of them concerning Property . . . And the other concerning Sin* (London, 1717).
115 *The Doctrine of Original Sin, stated and defended; being an Answer to Mr Thomas Chubb's Enquiry concerning Sin* (London, 1727), p. 40.
116 *Ibid.*, p. 4ff.
117 Edward Ballard, 'There must be heresies', Sermon given at Oxford and published in London, 1734.
118 *Ibid.*, pp. 19–23.
119 Thomas Woolston, *The Moderator between an infidel and an apostate* (London, 1725), discussing William Whiston, *Discourse of the grounds and reasons of the Christian religion* (London, 1724).
120 *Ibid.*, p. 22.
121 *Ibid.*, p. 66.
122 *Ibid.*, p. 74 against Whiston's *Primitive Christianity* and p. 106 against Clarke's *A Discourse concerning the connexion of the prophecies of the Old Testament and the application of them to Christ* (London, 1725):

this latter was a publication of an extract from Clarke's Boyle lectures.

123 Thomas Woolston, *A Discourse on the miracles of our Saviour. In view of the present controversy between Infidels and Apostates* (London, 1727), 2nd ed., p. 4.

124 *Ibid.*, p. 41 citing St Augustine, Sermon xliii, paragraph 5. The quotation implies that infidels can understand as much as Christians can from God through human conjecture and dabbling in the magical arts.

125 Thomas Woolston, *A Second Discourse on the Miracles of our Saviour* (London, 1727), pp. 4–5.

126 *Ibid.*, p. 7. See also *Mr Woolston's Defence of his Discourses on the miracles of our Saviour* (London, 1729).

127 *Ibid.*, pp. 8–24.

128 *Ibid.*, pp. 48–64.

129 J. Sherlock, *The Tryal of witnesses of the Resurrection of Jesus* (4th ed., London, 1729).

130 *Ibid.*, pp. 11–12.

131 *Ibid.*, p. 21.

132 *Ibid.*, p. 107.

133 *Ibid.*, p. 102.

134 *Ibid.*, p. 87ff.

135 *The Miracles of Jesus vindicated* (London, 1729), Part II.

136 *Ibid.*, Part III.

137 *Ibid.*, Part IV.

138 Nathaniel Lardner, *A Vindication of three of Our Blessed Saviour's Miracles* (London, 1729).

139 *Ibid.*, pp. v–vi.

140 *Ibid.*, citing Sprat's *History of the Royal Society* (2nd ed.), p. 63.

141 Henry Stebbing, *A Defence of the Scripture-history so far as it concerns the resurrection of Jairus's daughter; the widow of' Nain's son; and Lazarus* (London, 1713).

142 *Mr Woolston's Defence of his Discourse on the miracles of our Saviour* (London, 1729).

143 Henry Stebbing, *A Discourse on Our Saviour's Miraculous power of healing* (London, 1730).

144 *An Expostulatory letter to Mr Woolston, on account of his late writings* (London, 1730).

145 *Ibid.*, pp. 9, 11–12.

146 Thomas Ray, *A Vindication of our Saviour's miracles* (e.g. 2nd ed., London, 1729).

147 William Harris, *The Reasonableness of believing in Christ* (London, 1729).

148 *The Bishop of London's Pastoral Letter to the people of his diocese; particularly . . . occasion'd by some late writings in favour of Infidelity* (London, 1728), p. 3.

149 *Ibid.*, p. 8.

150 *Ibid.*, p. 9.

151 *Ibid.*, p. 14.

152 Thomas Stackhouse, *A Fair state of the controversy between Mr Woolston and his adversaries* (London, 1730).

153 *Ibid.*, p. 290.

154 *Ibid.*, e.g. p. 209.

155 See Chapter One above.

156 Thomas Woolston, *An account of his trial for writing four blasphemous books on the miracles of our Saviour* (London, 1729).

157 It seemed to Stackpole that Woolston made Christ one of the three impostors.

158 Thomas Woolston: *For God or the Devil; or Just chastisement being no persecution* (London, 1728), p. 3.

159 *Ibid.*, p. 5.

160 *Ibid.*, pp. 7–8.

161 Thomas Chubb, *A Discourse on miracles* (London, 1741), p. 77.

162 *Ibid.*, p. 92ff. after rejecting Mr Cavalier's supposed modern miracle, pp. 85–92.

163 *An Appendix, containing an enquiry into this question, viz. Whether the Doctrine of a future state of Existence to men, and a future retribution, were plainly and clearly taught by Moses and the Prophets?* (London, 1741).

164 Conyers Middleton, *A Free Enquiry into the Miraculous Powers which are supposed to have subsisted in the Christian Church, from the earliest ages through several successive centuries in the Miscellaneous Works of the late Reverend and learned Conyers Middleton* (London, 1752), vol. i, p. xxxvi.

165 *Ibid.*, pp. 180–3.

166 *The Mandate of his Eminency Cardinal de Noailles, Archbishop of Paris. Upon occasion of the miracle wrought in the parish of St Margaret . . .*, translation (London, 1726), and *A letter to the Archbishop of Paris . . .*, pp. 49–51, the miracle.

167 B. Bekker, *De betoverde weereld*, four vols (Amsterdam, 1691).

168 B. Binet, *Traité historique des Dieux et des Démons du paganisme* (Delft, 1696), Lettre V.

169 *Ibid.*, p. 93. 'Pagans generally accepted that demons had a spiritual nature, albeit less pure and perfect than that of Gods.'

170 *Ibid.*, p. 112.

171 D. Derodon, *De Existentia Dei* (Geneva, 1661).

172 *Ibid.*, p. 71, 84, 426, etc.

173 *Ibid.*, p. 153ff. For criticisms of Aquinas, see pp. 204ff.

174 *Ibid.*, pp. 1–52 of *Disputatio Theologica, De Existentia Deo* (Geneva, 1661).

175 *Ibid.*, p. 15 against the eternal world, p. 23, argumento ex impossibilitate infiniti.

176 *Ibid.*, p. 86.

177 *Disputatio Theologica, Tractatus, in quo probatur existentia Dei ex eo quod Sacra Scriptura sit verbum Dei.*

178 Third Tractatus of *De Existentia* being Reliqua argumenta, p. 79.
179 *Ibid.*, Chapter II, p. 83.
180 W.H., *The Spirit of Prophecy. A Treatise to prove that Christ and his Apostles were prophets* (London, 1679).
181 *Ibid.*, Epistle Dedicatory.
182 *Ibid.*
183 *Ibid.*, p. 161ff.
184 J. Addison, *The Resurrection, a poem* (London, 1728).

CHAPTER SEVEN **The persons of the Trinity**

1 F. Gastrell, *Some Considerations concerning the trinity: and the ways of managing that controversie* (London, 1696), p. 1.
2 *Ibid.*, p. 25, 33, etc.
3 Bodleian MS Ashmole 1818 item 30 side 1.
4 J. Foster, *An Essay on fundamentals, with particular regard to the doctrine of the ever blessed trinity* (London, 1720), p. 4.
5 R. Tooll, *A Review of some steps and methods taken by modern Arians, for advancing a pretended Reformation* (London, 1722), p. 1. It is doubtful if this work was ever influential, as the present author had to cut the middle pages of the Bodleian copy.
6 William Keatley Stride, *Exeter College* (University of Oxford College histories) (London, 1900), pp. 72–9.
7 See Chapter Three above, pp. 76–8.
8 James Harrington, *The Account Examin'd: Or, a Vindication of Dr A. Bury, Rector of Exeter College, from the calumnies of a late pamphlet* (London, 1690), p. 5.
9 *Ibid.*, pp. 7–8.
10 Anon., *An Account of the Proceedings of the Right Reverend Father in God, Jonathan, Lord Bishop of Exon., in his late Visitation of Exeter College in Oxon* (London, 1690), see e.g., pp. 3–10.
11 *Acta Convocationis*, B b 29 f285. Convocation condemns in these words the propositions of *The Naked Gospel* as false and heretical, as utterly denying the divinity of Our Saviour and defiling the venerated mystery of the faith.
12 *Ibid.*, ff285–6, referring to Bury, *Naked Gospel*, p. 285 and p. 40.
13 B b 29, ff290–1.
14 Bodleian Rawl. MS D 843 f160r and v.
15 *Ibid.*, f160v.
16 *The Fire's continued at Oxford: Or, the Decree of the Convocation for burning the Naked Gospel considered, passim.*
17 *A Vindication of Mr James Colmear, Bachellor of Physick and fellow of Exeter College in Oxford from the calumnies of 3 late pamphlets* (London, 1691), e.g. pp. 7–12.
18 *A Defence of the proceedings of the Right Rev. the Visitor and fellows of Exeter College in Oxford* (London, 1691).
19 Anon., *The Case of Exeter College in the University of Oxford Related and Vindicated* (London, 1691), pp. 7–14, vindication from the depositions of local witnesses.
20 Anon., *A Copy of the proceedings of Dr Master upon the Commission of Appeal* (London, 1692).
21 A. Bury, *The Naked Gospel* (London, 1690), Preface.
22 *Ibid.*, p. 79.
23 *Ibid.*, pp. 1–103; pp. 13–19 for faith and natural religion.
24 Exeter College Register, 1619–1737 (College Archives), f85v. The passage describes how the gates of the College were barred to prevent the Bishop from entering, but the gates burst open and the crowd stopped them from being blocked up again so that the Bishop was able to enter the quadrangle and preach in the Hall.
25 *Ibid.*, letter interleaved between ff85 and 86, James Harrington to the Rector, 25 June 1691.
26 The pamphlet materials are collected in abundance in the College library at Exeter in the collections ZB24, ZB25, ZMA 55a and ZMA 57. They can also of course be found in large collections like the British Museum and the Bodleian libraries.
27 Bury's letter is copied in the Register, ff82v and 83r.
28 See William Nicholls, *An Answer to an heretical book called The Naked Gospel* (London, 1691), and Thomas Long, *An Answer to a Socinian Treatise, called The Naked Gospel* (London, 1691).
29 John Wallis published his *The doctrine of the Blessed Trinity briefly explained in a letter to a friend* (London, 1690), along with his seven letters the following year on the same subject, in a compilation of his theological works in London, 1691–2.
30 John Wallis, *Three Sermons concerning the Sacred Trinity* (London, 1691), Sermon I, p. 17 – sermon first preached at Oxford in 1664 and reissued with 1690–1 sermons.
31 *Ibid.*, Sermon II, e.g. p. 33ff.
32 *Ibid.*, p. 56.
33 *Ibid.*, Sermon III, p. 70.
34 *Ibid.*, p. 87.
35 Francis Fulwood, *The Socinian controversy touching the Son of God reduced . . . With an humble and serious caution to the friends of the Church of England against the approaches of Socinianism* (London, 1693), see especially pp. 14–21.

36 Anon., *A Parallel: wherein it appears that the Socinian agrees with the Papist* (London, 1693), *passim*.
37 George Bull, *Opera Omnia* (London, 1703), edition of *Harmonia Apostolica* (1st ed., London, 1676). See e.g. Johannis Tombes, *Animadversiones in librum Georgii Bulli cui titulum fecit Harmonia Apostolica* (Oxford, 1676).
38 See e.g. *The Works of the Right Reverend George Bull D.D. concerning the Holy Trinity* (2 vols, London, 1725).
39 G. Bull, *Some important points of Christianity maintained and defended: In several sermons and other Discourses* (3 vols, London, 1713).
40 *The Works of the Right Rev. George Bull D.D. . . ,* Translator's Preface.
41 Gilbert Clarke (or Clerke), *Oughtredus explicatus, sive commentarius in ejus clavem mathematicam. Cui additae sunt planetarum observationes et . . . horologium constructio* (London, 1682).
42 Bull's dispute with Clarke can be traced in R. Nelson, *History of his life* in vol. i of the *English Works of George Bull* (Oxford, 1827), pp. 430–6. The life written by Nelson should be prefaced to the 1713 English edition of Bull's works, but does not seem to have been so in the Bodleian copy.
43 *Judicium Ecclesiae Catholicae Trium Primorum Seculorum, de necessitate credendi, quod Dominus noster Jesus Christus sit versus Deus, assertum contra M. Simonem Episcopium . . .* (Oxford, 1694).
44 G. Clarke, *Ante-Nicenismus* (Cosmopoli, 1695).
45 See *A Review and analysis of Bishop Bull's Exposition of the Doctrine of Justification, by Robert Nelson Esq extracted from his life of Bishop Bull* (Bath, 1827) for comment on *Harmonia Apostolica* and Bull's response to Gataker and Truman in *Examen Censurae: sive Responsio ad quasdam Animadversiones . . .* (London, 1676) and in *Apologia pro Harmonia . . .* (London, 1676).
46 G. Bull, *Defensio Fidei Nicaenae* (Oxford, 1685), pp. 7–14 of 1703 reprint in *Opera Omnia*.
47 *Ibid.*, pp. 25–37.
48 *Ibid.*, pp. 173–86.
49 John Wallis, *Eight letters concerning the Trinity* (London, 1690–2), Letter 4, p. 6.
50 *Ibid.*, Letter 5, p. 3.
51 *Ibid.*, Letter 4, p. 3.
52 *Ibid.*, Letter 5, pp. 8–14.
53 John Bidle, *The Apostolical & true opinion concerning the Holy Trinity, revived and asserted* (London, 1691), p. 4.
54 *Twelve arguments drawn from the Scripture*, pp. 1, 3, etc.

55 John Bidle, *The Apostolical and true opinion . . .*, p. 5.
56 *A Confession of Faith touching the Holy Trinity, according to the Scripture* (1648, reprinted London, 1691), e.g. p. 17.
57 John Bidle, *The Apostolical and true opinion . . .*, Article 5, p. 7.
58 *The Testimonies of Irenaeus . . . Origen etc. concerning That One God, and the persons of the Holy Trinity* (London, 1691).
59 *Ibid.*, p. 16 from Tertullian, Chapter 8 of *Tertullianus Coloniae Agrippinae Editus* (1617). 'The Holy Spirit is third to God and the Son . . .'
60 William Frere, *A Vindication of the Unitarians against a late reverend author on the Trinity* (London, 1687).
61 *Brief Notes on the Creed of Athanasius*, e.g. p. 2 (title page missing on Bodleian copy).
62 J. Savage, *An Antidote against Poyson: or, an answer to the brief notes upon the creed of St Athanasius*, e.g. p. 11 re person.
63 A. Bury, *A Defence of the doctrines of the Holy Trinity, & Incarnation Placed in their due light*, pp. 6–7.
64 *Observations on the 4 letters of Dr J. Wallis, concerning the Trinity and the creed of Athanasius* (London, 1691), *passim*: and *An Answer to Dr Wallis's three letters concerning the doctrine of the trinity* (London, 1691), p. 1, p. 12, etc.
65 H. G. Rosedale, *Milton: his religion and polemics*, Milton Memorial lectures (Oxford, 1908) is a useful review of the problem of Milton's theology. P. Chauvet, *La réligion de Milton* (Paris, 1909) is another useful volume, whilst L. A. Wood concentrates on the anti-trinitarian aspects in his *The form and origin of Milton's anti-trinitarian conception* (Heidelberg, 1911). See also J. E. C. Welldon, *Theology of Milton* (London, 1912), pp. 901–18. Macaulay, *Essay on Milton* (New York and London, 1896), pp. 2–6 comments on Lemon's discovery of the Milton latin theological MSS and Milton's arianism. Milton went so far as to argue in his 1673 work *Haeresie, Schism, Toleration* that Anabaptists, Socinians, Arminians were not heretics, pp. 5–6.
66 John Milton's *Last thoughts on the Trinity* (London, 1859), extracted from his posthumous work *A Theory of Christian doctrine, compiled from Holy Scripture alone*, p. 5.
67 *Ibid.*, p. 7.
68 *Ibid.*, p. 37ff.
69 *The Bishop of Worcester's Answer to Mr Locke's letter, concerning some passages relating to his Essay of Humane understanding, Mention'd in the late Discourse in Vindication of the*

Trinity (London, 1697), pp. 3–5; and *The Bishop of Worcester's Answer to Mr Locke's Second Letter* . . . (London, 1698), p. 6.

70 *The Bishop of Worcester's Answer to Mr Locke's letter* . . ., p. 20.

71 John Milner, *An Account of Mr Lock's Religion, out of his own writings* . . . *II A brief Enquiry whether Socinianism be justly charged upon Mr Lock* (London, 1700), pp. 179–88.

72 *Ibid.*, p. 185.

73 *Ibid.*, pp. 182–4.

74 *Ibid.*, p. 186.

75 *Ibid.*, p. 188.

76 MS Locke c 43.

77 *Ibid.*, pp. 12–13.

78 *Ibid.*, pp. 26–7.

79 Much has been written about the religious attitudes of these men, so that we do not need to rehearse the evidence here. The reader can begin the search with Herbert McLachlan, *The religious opinions of Milton, Locke and Newton* (Manchester, 1941). For Milton's drift from Sabellianism to Arianism see pp. 63–4: for Locke's unitarian view see p. 107: for Newton's heterodoxy see pp. 160–1. For a psychological explanation of Newton's belief in the supremacy of the Father, see Manuel's Freemantle lectures (1973) where Newton is seen pursuing the Father to compensate for his own father who died before he was born.

80 Newton's unitarianism was not confirmed until study was made of his theological manuscripts in the nineteenth century. The extent of Milton's deviation over this similarly lay undiscovered until the Victorian era.

81 Support for Tillotson came in e.g. *A Vindication of the Archbishop Tillotson's Sermons concerning the Divinity and Incarnation of Our blessed Saviour* (London, 1695).

82 Tillotson, *Six Sermons* (London, 1694), p. 258: 1662 sermon 'Of the advantages of an early piety'.

83 E.g. Sermon I, 'Concerning resolution and steadfastness in religion', 3 June 1684, *ibid.*, pp. 10–37. Tillotson was misconstrued by his more antagonistic opponents; the question of Tillotson's real meaning and influence can best be found in Dr J. O'Higgins, 'Archbishop Tillotson and the Religion of Nature' in *The Journal of Theological Studies*, New Series, vol. xxiv, Part I (1973), pp. 123–42.

84 Charles Leslie, *The Charge of Socinianism against Dr Tillotson considered* (Edinburgh, 1695), *passim*.

85 Charles Leslie, *The Socinian Controversy discuss'd, in 6 parts* (London, 1708): see especially part II.

86 *The Doctrine of the Trinity and Transubstantiation compared, as to Scripture, Reason, and Tradition, in a new dialogue between a protestant and a papist* (London, 1687), 2nd part, p. 43.

87 *Ibid.*, p. 24.

88 William Sherlock (ascribed), *An Answer to a late dialogue between a new Catholic convert and a Protestant, to prove the mysteries of the Trinity to be as absurd a Doctrine as Transubstantiation* . . . (London, 1687), pp. 3–5.

89 E. Stillingfleet (ascribed), *The Doctrine of the Trinity and Transubstantiation compared, as to Scripture, Reason, and Tradition* (London, 1687), pp. 19–24.

90 *Ibid.*, p. 47.

91 J. Tillotson, *A Discourse against Transubstantiation* (London, 1684), pp. 37–8.

92 W. Payne (ascribed), *A Discourse concerning adoration of the host, as it is taught and practised in the Church of Rome* (London, 1685), pp. 1–2, p. 33, idolatry not commanded by Christ or the apostles.

93 Monsieur Boileau, *De Adoratione Eucharistae* (Paris, 1685).

94 William Claggett, *A Paraphrase with Notes, and a Preface, upon the 6th Chapter of St John* (London, 1686).

95 Henry More, *A Brief Discourse of the Real Presence of the body and blood of Christ in the Celebration of Holy Eucharist against the Bishop of Meaux and Monsieur Maimbourg who are in favour of transubstantiation* (London, 1686), p. 64.

96 *The School of the Eucharist establish'd upon the miraculous respects and acknowledgements, which Beasts, Birds, and Insects, upon several occasions, have rendered to the Holy Sacrament of the Altar* . . . *by F. Toussain Bridoul of the Society of Jesus* (London, 1687), Preface.

97 *Ibid.*, pp. vii–viii.

98 J. Patrick (ascribed), *Transubstantiation no doctrine of the primitive Fathers* . . . (London, 1687).

99 J. Gother, *An Answer to a Discourse against Transubstantiation* (London, 1687), pp. 27–63.

100 *An historical Treatise, written by an author of the Communion of the Church of Rome touching transubstantiation* (2nd ed., London, 1687), by Abbé Louis Dujour de Languerne (ascribed), p. 8.

101 *Ibid.*, p. 13.

102 *Ibid.*, p. 9.

103 *Ibid.*, pp. 72–3.

104 Dr Sherlock, *The Case of Allegiance due to sovereign powers stated and resolved* (London, 1691). There were many replies to this work, including *A Vindication of the present settlement, by way of animadversion on* *a late seditious pamphlet, entituled* . . . (London, 1692); see also, *An Answer to a letter to Dr Sherlock, written in Vindication of that part of Josephus's History which gives the account of Jadus's submission to Alexander, against the answer to the piece entituled, Obedience and Submission to the present government* (London, 1692); and *A Vindication of some among ourselves against the false principles of Dr Sherlock* (London, 1692).

105 *Proteus Ecclesiasticus: Or, Observations on Dr Sh–'s late Case of Allegiance, &c. In a letter to Mr P. W. Merch in London* (London, 1691), 10.

106 W. Sherlock, *The Case of Allegiance* . . . (4th ed., London, 1691), p. 1, p. 3. Replies in e.g. The Rector of St George, Botolph Lane, *Sherlock v. Sherlock: The Master of the Temple's Reasons for his late taking the Oath to their Majesties*: p. 2, no distinction in Sherlock between usurpers and legal kings.

107 He re-stated it in *A Vindication of the Case of Allegiance due to Soveraign Powers* . . . (London, 1691), p. 73.

108 R. South, *Animadversions upon Dr Sherlock's book, entitled A Vindication of the Holy and ever blessed Trinity* (London, 1693), p. xvii.

109 *Ibid.*, pp. 116–43.

110 W. Sherlock, *An Apology for writing against the Socinians* . . . (London, 1693), p. 10.

111 R. South, *Tritheism charged upon Dr Sherlock's new notion of the trinity* . . . (London, 1695).

112 *Ibid.*, pp. 46–7.

113 *Ibid.*, p. 280.

114 William Sherlock, *A Modest Examination of the Authority and Reasons of the late decree of the Vice-Chancellor of Oxford, and some Heads of Colleges and Halls* (London, 1696 ed.).

115 *Ibid.*, p. 2.

116 *Ibid.*, p. 7

117 *Ibid.*, p. 46.

118 J. Wallis, *An Answer to Dr Sherlock's Examination of the Oxford Decree: In a letter from a member of that University* . . . (London, 1699), pp. 3–9.

119 *Ibid.*, p. 2.

120 *The Doctrine of the Catholick Church, and of the Church of England, concerning the Blessed Trinity, explained, and asserted, against the dangerous Heterodoxes in a Sermon by Dr William Sherlock* . . . (London, 1697), p. 4.

121 *Ibid.*, p. 6.

122 *Ibid.*, p. 8.

123 J. Edwards, *Remarks upon a book lately published by Dr William Sherlock Dean of St Paul's &c* (Oxford, 1695).

124 *A Discourse concerning the Nominal and Real Trinitarians* (London, 1695), p. 3.

125 *Ibid.*

126 William Sherlock, *A Vindication of the doctrine of the Holy and ever blessed trinity* . . . (London, 1690), p. 47.

127 *Ibid.*, p. 199, p. 238, etc.

128 Daniel Whitby, *Tractatus de vera Christi deitate, adversus Arii et Socini haereses* (London, 1691), p. 21ff. patristic authorities, p. 2ff. other arguments for Christ as God.

129 L. Milbourn, *Mysteries in religion vindicated: or the filiation, deity and satisfaction of Our Saviour asserted, against Socinians and others* . . . (London, 1692).

130 S. Nye, *An Accurate Examination of the principal texts usually alledged for the divinity of our Saviour* (London, 1692).

131 *Ibid.*, p. 53. Cf. *The Unreasonableness of the Doctrine of the Trinity briefly demonstrated, in a letter to a friend* (London, 1692), p. 8.

132 S. Nye (ascribed), *Considerations on the Explications of the Doctrine of the Trinity, by Dr Wallis, Dr Sherlock, Dr S——th, Dr Cudworth, and Mr Hooker; as also on the account given by those that say, the Trinity is an Unconceivable and Inexplicable mystery* (London, 1693).

133 *Ibid.*, p. 18.

134 *Ibid.*, p. 18.

135 *Ibid.*, p. 32.

136 See Chapter Five above, pp. 123–4, for W. Whiston's hydrostatics. See also R. Smalbroke, *Reflections on the conduct of Mr Whiston in his revival of the Arian Heresy* (London, 1711), p. 7.

137 R. Smallbroke, *Reflections on the conduct of Mr Whiston*, p. 7.

138 *Ibid.*, p. 9.

139 *Ibid.*, pp. 13–14.

140 *Ibid.*, pp. 17–18.

141 Styan Thirlby, *A defence of the Answer to Mr Whiston's suspicions, and an answer to his charge of forgery against Athanasius* (Cambridge and London, 1713), pp. 1–4 and *passim*.

142 *Ibid.*, p. 5.

143 *Ibid.*, pp. 10–14.

144 Styan Thirlby, *A defence of the Answer* . . ., p. 35 Justin; p. 40 Athenagoras; p. 42 Tertullian; p. 45 Cyprian.

145 *Ibid.*, p. 42.

146 *Ibid.*, p. 66ff.

147 Dr Grabe, *Some instances of the defects and omissions in Mr Whiston's collections of testimonies from the Scriptures and the Fathers* (London, 1712), pp. 3–8.

148 *Ibid.*, pp. 8–18.

149 *Ibid.*, p. 27.

150 William Whiston, *A Second Reply to*

Dr Allix, with two postscripts. E.g. pp. 24–6 was one of many references of Whiston taking up the cudgels in his own defence; this case was directed against Mattair, and a tract of *Reflections on Mr Whiston's conduct* (London, 1711).

151 William Whiston, *A second reply to Dr Allix . . .*, p. 24.

152 John Edwards, *Socinianism unmask'd . . .*

153 William Whiston, *A Reply to Dr Allix's Remarks on some places of Mr Whiston's books, either printed or manuscript . . .* (London, 1711), pp. 20–3.

154 *Ibid.*, p. 20.

155 *Ibid.*, pp. 10–11.

156 *Ibid.*, p. 9.

157 *A Defense of the Ld Bishop of London: in Answer to Mr Whiston's letter of thanks to his Lordship. Address'd to his Grace the Ld Archbishop of Canterbury* (London, 1719).

158 William Whiston, *Mr Whiston's account of Dr Sacheverell's proceeding in order to exclude him from St Andrew's Church in Holbourne* (London, 1719), and Anon., *A Vindication of the Rev. Dr Sacheverell's late Endeavour to turn Mr Whiston out of his Church* (London, 1719).

159 W. Higgs, *A Letter to Mr Whiston, proving that his quotations from the Old Testament, in his letter to the Earl of Nottingham, concerning the eternity of the Son and Holy Ghost, are neither true nor fair . . .* (London, 1719).

160 T. Woolston, *Origenis Adamantij Renati Epistola Ad Doctores Whitbeium, Waterlandium, Whistonium Aliosque Literatos hujus saeculi Disputatores: circa Fidem vere orthodoxam, et scripturarum interpretationem* (London, 1720), p. 14.

161 *Ibid.*, p. 16.

162 *Ibid.*, p. 23.

163 See e.g. William Whiston, *Letter to the Right Hon. Earl of Nottingham, concerning the Eternity of the Son of God, and of the Holy Spirit* (2nd ed., London, 1721), and *The Answer of the Earl of Nottingham to Mr Whiston's letter to him, concerning the eternity of the Son of God* (8th ed., London, 1721).

164 *Mr Whiston's Letter of thanks to the Right Rev. the Lord Bishop of London for his late letter to his clergy against the use of the new doxology* (1st ed., London, 1719); *Mr Whiston's Second letter to the Right Rev. the Lord Bishop of London . . .* (London, 1719).

165 *Mr Whiston's Letter of thanks to the Right Rev. the Bishop . . .*, pp. 17–19.

166 Samuel Clarke, *A letter to Mr Dodwell about the immortality of the soul . . .* (London, 1706), a work designed to combat Dodwell's theory.

167 William Whiston, *Historical Memoirs*

of the life of Samuel Clarke (London, 1730), pp. 18–22.

168 Samuel Clarke, *The Scripture Doctrine of the Trinity* (London, 1712). The major account of Clarke's life can be found in William Whiston, *Historical Memoirs of the life of Samuel Clarke* (London, 1730), and some praise in Emlyn's *Eulogy on the death of Mr Clarke*.

169 D. Waterland, *Dissertation on the argument a priori* (London, 1719).

170 W. Van Mildert, *Preface to the works of Dr Waterland* (London, 1822), life of Waterland.

171 Voltaire, *Lettres sur les Anglais*, Letter VII.

172 See Chapter One above, pp. 46–7.

173 Wake MSS (Christchurch) CCXLII, vol. ix, f40.

174 Wake MSS (Christchurch) CCXLII, vol. ix, f38.

175 Thomas Chubb, *The Supremacy of the Father asserted* (London, 1718).

176 *Ibid.*, Dedication preceding p. 1.

177 *Ibid.*, pp. 1–3.

178 *Ibid.*, p. 7.

179 *Ibid.*, p. 9.

180 *Ibid.*, p. 12.

181 *Ibid.*, p. 20.

182 Thomas Chubb, *The Supremacy of the Father vindicated; or, observations on Mr Clagett's book, entitled Arianism anatomis'd* (London, 1718).

183 See Chapter Two above, p. 64.

184 John Clendon, *Tractatus philosophico-theologicus de persona* (London, 1710).

185 From Manuel, Isaac Newton's religion, taken from the Jerusalem MSS.

186 Replies to criticisms of Tillotson can be found in *A Vindication of the Archbishop Tillotson's Sermons* (London, 1695), especially pp. 1–57.

187 Gibson MSS, vol. II, 980, f56.

188 Gilbert Burnet, *A History of his own times* (London, 1857 ed.), pp. 648–50 (vol. ii).

189 S. Nye, *The Life of Mr Thomas Firmin* (London, 1698), p. 26. Nye cites little evidence that we can check: his testimony must be viewed in the context of his admiration for a man who amassed great riches, and then used them for charitable purposes.

190 *Ibid.*, pp. 29, 32, 34, 40 e.g.

191 *Ibid.*, p. 61.

192 *Ibid.*, pp. 16–17.

193 *Ibid.*, pp. 9–10.

194 S. Nye, *An Account of Mr Firmin's religion; and of the Present State of the Unitarian controversy* (London, 1698), p. 4.

195 S. Nye, *The Life . . .*, p. 16. See also *A*

Sermon on Luke X v.36, 37 occasioned by the death of Mr Thomas Firmin (London, 1698), p. 117 for a defence of Firmin's wrong thinking by virtue of his 'well-doing'.
196 See British Museum Add. MS 24478, 'Grounds and occasions of the controversy concerning the Unity of God' (London, 1698).
197 E.g. John Edwards, *Socinianism unmask'd; a discourse shewing the unreasonableness of a late writer's opinion concerning the necessity of only one article of faith* (London, 1696).

CHAPTER EIGHT   **The Church in danger**

1 A good modern treatment of the pamphlet and manuscript materials for the case, cause and trial of Dr Sacheverell can be found in G. Holmes, *The Trial of Dr Sacheverell* (London, 1973), p. 270ff. for a review of the Tory cause and the cry of the Church in danger: and pp. 46–50.
2 R. Penton, *The Guardian's Instruction, or the Gent's Romance: written for the diversion and service of the Gentry* (London, 1688), p. 72.
3 Wake MSS, Christchurch College, Oxford; *vide* CCXLII, vol. ix, Canterbury Documents IV 1721–4 ff37r/38r, undated letter: see next letter f38v about the Greyhound Tavern meetings.
4 Magdalen College Library, Sacheverell sermons and papers, N 2.20. The illustration is reproduced in Holmes, *The Trial of Dr Sacheverell*, but the compression has made distinguishing all the authors difficult in that copy of the print.
5 For the opposition to toleration see e.g. *The Church of England's late conflict with, and triumph over the spirit of Fanaticism* (London, 1710), pp. 7–12.
6 *The Whigs' Address: exploding their republican principles* (London, 1710), p. 3 provides one example: a picture can be found in Magd. N 2.20, *The High Church Champion and his two seconds* (London, 1710).
7 See e.g. *To the Wh . . . s 19 Queries, a fair and full answer by an honest tory* (London, 1710), p. 11. See also *The Worcester Triumph, Or a true account of Dr Sacheverell's entrance . . .* (London, 1710): *The High Church Hieroglyphick* (London, 1706): *A Sermon . . . a little after the Rebellious tumult . . .* (London, 1710) where the prolongation of the war is explained by reference to the nation's sins, p. 16.
8 The actors' view can be found in *The Actors' remonstrance or complaint: for the silencing of their profession and banishment*

from their several playhouses 1643 (London, 1869).
9 Bodleian MS Rawl. D 8 provides information on a number of cases of homicide. See e.g. 'murder in a Covent Garden tavern', f64r and 'a dispute in Middle Temple', f172v.
10 The infidelity and profanity during the reign of James I's was noted in *The representatives of the lower house of convocation of the English clergy examined* (Edinburgh, 1711), p. 14.
11 *A Proclamation against vicious, debauch'd, and prophane persons, by the King*, 30 May 1660.
12 *A Proclamation for the observance of the Lord's day, and for renewing a former proclamation against vitious, debauched and profane persons* (London, 1663).
13 Anne, Proclamation 25 February 1702 'for the encouragement of piety and virtue'.
14 9 and 10 William III c 32, 'An Act for the more effectual suppressing of blasphemy and prophaneness'.
15 29 Charles II c 7, 'An Act for the better observance of the Lord's day' – referring also to 1 Car. 1 c 1 and 3 Car. 1 c 1.
16 Lambeth Wake MS 933:14.
17 *The letter and diplomatic instruction of Queen Anne*, ed. by B. C. Brown (London, 1968), p. 311, 12 December 1710.
18 *Ibid.*, 20 August 1711. Queen Anne to the Archbishop of Canterbury.
19 John Lacy, *A Moral Test, the manifest intent in law, of the sacramental . . .* (London, 1704), p. 11.
20 Wake MSS CCXLII, vol. ix, ff40–50.
21 *Ibid.*, f50.
22 *Ibid.*, 'here I was again defeated by my brethren'.
23 W. Wake, *A practical Discourse concerning Swearing, especially in two great points of perjury and common swearing* (London, 1696).
24 Wake MSS CCLIV, Charlett to Wake, 14 January 1718/19.
25 Bodleian MS Rawl. c 719, pp. 113–26 summarizes laws against profanation, drunkenness and rape.
26 *Mr Bowman's Sermon versify'd* (London, 1731), p. 1.
27 *Ibid.*, p. 4.
28 *Ibid.*, pp. 8–10.
29 *Ibid.*, pp. 12–13.
30 *A full justification of the doctrines advanced in Mr Bowman's Visitation sermon: or, the authority claimed by Bishops not warranted jure divino, tho' supported jure humano* (London, 1731), especially pp. 4–11; p. 25 attacks the argument from antiquity in favour of the bishops. P. 16 cites Barronius,

Beza and Perkins to disprove the scriptural origins of the bishops' special powers.

31 See e.g. *The Behaviour of the clergy, as well as their traditions, destructive of religion* (London, 1731).

32 *The Behaviour of the clergy . . .*, pp. 16–23, pp. 23–7.

33 *Ibid.*, pp. 27–9.

34 *Ibid.*, pp. 29–33.

35 *Ibid.*, pp. 33–6.

36 *Ibid.*, pp. 36–47.

37 *Ibid.*, Preface p. ii.

38 *Bishop of London's 11th Conference with his clergy, held in the years 1699 and 1700 upon the King's Proclamation for immorality and prophaneness* (London, 1704).

39 *Ibid.*, p. 16.

40 *Ibid.*, p. 42.

41 *The charge of Richard, Lord Bishop of Bath and Wells, to the clergy of his diocese . . . June 2 1692* (London, 1693), pp. 3–5.

42 *Ibid.*, p. 13.

43 See T. Longueville, *Rochester and other literary Rakes of the Court of Charles II* (2nd ed., London, 1903), and V. de S. Pinto, *Enthusiast in Wit* (London, 1962).

44 G. Burnet, *Libertine Overthrown* (London, 1680).

45 British Museum Add. MS 4162 f255r and v.

46 *Verney Memoirs*, vol. ii, pp. 335–7.

47 Earl of Rochester, *Poems* (2 pts, 3rd ed., London, 1709), *Memoirs of the life of the Right Hon. John, late Earl of Rochester*, bound at the front.

48 *Ibid.*

49 Earl of Rochester, *Poems* (3rd ed., London, 1709), p. 5.

50 *Ibid.*, p. 12.

51 *Ibid.*, p. 7.

52 *Ibid.*, p. 112.

53 *Ibid.*, p. 33.

54 *Ibid.*, p. 160, 'Rochester's Farewel'.

55 *The Two noble converts; or the Earl of Marlborough and the Earl of Rochester their dying requests and remonstrance, to the atheists and debauchees of this age* (London, 1680).

56 See e.g. A. G. Dickens, *The English Reformation* (London, 1950), the early chapters.

57 For anti-clericalism after the accession of Anne see G. M. Trevelyan, *England under Queen Anne* (London, 1931), i, pp. 52–4. A literary illustration of the feeling can be found in Swift, *Poems* (Oxford, 1967 ed.), pp. 535, 536.

58 Bishop of Bangor, *A Sermon preach'd before the King* (London, 1717).

59 A. Snape, *A Letter to the Bishop of Bangor* (London, 1717), p. 4.

60 *Ibid.*, p. 35.

61 See also Hoadley, *An answer to the Rev. Dr Snape's letter to the Bishop of Bangor* (London, 1717); A. Snape, *A Second letter to the Lord Bishop of Bangor, in vindication of the former* (London, 1717); D. Whitby, *An Answer to the Rev. Dr Snape's 2nd letter to . . . Bangor* (London, 1717); A Gent, *Remarks upon the Lord Bishop of Bangor's Treatment of the clergy and convocation* (London, 1717).

62 William Law, *The Bishop of Bangor's late sermon, and his letter to Dr Snape in defence of it, answer'd* (London, 1717), 6th ed., p. 5.

63 William Law, *A Second letter to the Bishop of Bangor; wherein his Lordship's notion of Benediction, Absolutism, and Church-communion are prov'd to be destructive of every institution of the Christian Religion* (London, 1717), p. 67.

64 See William Law, *The absolute unlawfulness of the stage-entertainment fully demonstrated* (London, 1726), where a strong case is made against the theatre. .

65 A practical suggestion can be found in *The nature and designs of Holy days explain'd* (London, 1708), where even the 'meanest capacitys' are able to read of the correct observation of Sundays and Church festivals.

66 See J. A. Redwood, 'Charles Blount, Deism and English freethought', *Journal of the History of Ideas*, 1974.

67 Pepys, *Diary*, 16 February 1668.

68 *The Diary of John Milwood* (ed. Robbins, Cambridge, 1938), pp. 248–50 and pp. 214–22.

69 The issue of toleration is debated from the Tory side in Roger L'Estrange, *Toleration Discuss'd* (London, 1663).

70 D. Pickering, *The Statutes at large* (London, 1764), 17 Geo II c 5, *An Act to make more effectual the laws relating to Rogues, Vagabonds, and other idle and disorderly persons, and to Houses of correction* is one of many condemning Egyptians and strolling players amongst a long list of peripatetic undesirables conning the public.

71 John Henley, *An Oration . . .*, Being No. 11 of Oratory Transactions (London, 1729), title-page.

72 *Ibid.*, p. 5.

73 See *The Primitive Liturgy, for the use of the Oratory* (London, 1726).
A Letter to the Rev. Mr J. Henley, M.A. concerning his novel project: wherein his design is fully exposed (London, 1726), p. 10.

74 *Ibid.*, p. 13.

75 *Ibid.*, p. 19.

76 Add MS 10, 348 f144.

77 Add MS 10, 346 ff37–38, f46ff., f70, etc.

78 Add MS 10, 346 f86.

79 Add MS 10, 346 f97.
80 Add MS 10, 347 ff1–35. See also BM prints *The Christening of the Child* and *The Oratory*,
81 Bodleian MS Eng. Misc. e 1.
82 Auction Catalogue of Henley's MSS (London, 1759), Mus. Bibl. III 8°64 (Bodleian), p. 29.
83 *Ibid.*, p. 18, p. 5.
84 J. Henley, *The history and advantages of divine Revelation* . . . (London, 1725), pp. 12–13.
85 *Oratory Transactions*, No. 2, pp. 1–3. List of Subjects for Lord's Day from 3 July 1726 to 31 August 1728.
86 *The Primitive Liturgy and Eucharist for the use of the Oratory* (London, 1727), and P. Hall, *Fragmenta Liturgica* (Bath, 1848), vol. iv, p. 6ff.
87 E.g. *An Account of some conditions, of taking a limited number of Seats in the Oratory in Lincoln's Inn Fields* (no place, 1730); *The Appeal of the Oratory to the first Ages of Christianity* (London, 1727); *A Letter to the Rev. Mr J. Henley, M.A. concerning his novel project* (London, 1726).
88 *Mr Henley's letter and adverts, which concern Mr Whiston, published by Mr Whiston* (London, 1727); *Oratory Transactions*.
89 Anthony Ashley Cooper, *Characteristicks of Men, manners, opinions and times* (London, 1711), Section II. The work concerned was first published in London in 1709, as *Sensus Communis; an essay on the freedom of wit and humour*.
90 Shaftesbury's *Characteristicks*, p. 64.
91 *Ibid.*, p. 69.
92 *Ibid.*, p. 70.
93 *Ibid.*, pp. 76–80.
94 Wotton, *Bart'lemy Fair: Or, An Enquiry After Wit* (London, 1709), p. 23.
95 Shaftesbury, *Characteristicks*, p. 95.
96 PRO 30/24/21, Life of Shaftesbury, No. 266, ff261–2.
97 *Ibid.*, No. 266, f262.
98 PRO 30/24/22, 21 January 1706/7 to Monsieur Barnage, f31, and PRO 30/24/22 2 February 1708, f63.
99 PRO 30/24/22, f33 e.g.
100 *Dict. Nat. Biog.*, vol. v, pp. 327–8: and Bodleian MS Rawl. c 195.
101 See e.g. *An Answer to a late Pamphlet, intitled, Observations on the writings of the Craftsman* (London, 1731), and *The Doctrine of Innuendo's discuss'd, or the liberty of the press maintain'd: being some Thoughts upon the present treatment of the Printer and Publishers of the Craftsman* (London, 1731).
102 G. Kitchin, *Sir Roger L'Estrange. A contribution to the history of the press in the seventeenth century* (London, 1913).

103 Anon., *Maxims and Reflections upon plays* (London, 1699), and Anon., *Some considerations about the danger of going to plays* (London, 1704).
104 Cf. Anon., *Some thoughts concerning the stage, in a letter to a lady* (London, 1704), sometimes ascribed to Josiah Woodward.
105 William Law, *A practical Treatise upon Christian perfection* (London, 1726), p. 363ff.
106 *Ibid.*, p. 417ff.
107 *Law Outlaw'd: or, a short Reply to Mr Law's long declaration against the stage* (London, 1726), p. 4.
108 *Ibid.*, p. 7.
109 Anon, *Some short and plain directions for the spending of one day well* (London, 1701). E.g. p. 24, it suggests prayer and if possible the reading of good books of devotion; p. 15, it argues for the restraint of everyday desires.
110 *A Friendly letter in 3 Parts I To all young men, shewing the benefit of a Religious conversation II To masters of families III Shewing some marks of a Christian, or the character of a good man.*
111 *Maxims and Reflections*, p. 117.
112 *Ibid.*, p. 118.
113 *Ibid.*
114 *The Occasional Paper No. 9 concerning Some considerations about the danger of going to stage plays* (London, 1698), p. 7.
115 *Maxims and Reflections upon plays*, pp. 53–61.
116 *Ibid.*, pp. 110–16 for the Fathers; p. 105ff. for Aristotle.
117 *Ibid.*, p. 105ff., p. 111–12, pp. 66ff.
118 *Maxims*, pp. 111–12.
119 Anon., *A Seasonable examination of the Playhouse: the pleas and pretentions of the proprietors of, and subscribers to, playhouses erected in defiance of the royal licence* (title page missing), p. 4.
120 *Ibid.*, pp. 17–19.
121 *The Usefulness of the Stage to Religion and Government: shewing the Advantage of the drama in all nations since its first institution* (2nd ed., London, 1738).
122 Langbaine, *A New Catalogue of English Plays* (December, 1687, London), p. 29.
123 *Ibid.*, p. 18.
124 *Ibid.*, p. 10.
125 For these three published jointly, see *The Muse of New-market: or, mirth and drollery* . . . (London, 1680).
126 *Some considerations about the danger of going to plays* (London, 1704).
127 *Ibid.*, p. 5.
128 *Ibid.*, pp. 6–8.
129 *Ibid.*, p. 15.
130 *The Occasional Paper*, No. 9 (London, 1698), p. 7.

131 *Ibid.*, p. 10.
132 *Ibid.*, p. 16.
133 See D. Defoe, *Conjugal Lewdness: or, matrimonial Whoredom* (London, 1727).
134 Anon., *The Wandering Whores complaint for lack of trading* (London, 1663).
135 *Some considerations upon street-walkers* (no date, London), Letter 1, p. 7.
136 A Person of Quality, *A Project for the Advancement of Religion, and the reformation of manners* (London, 1709), pp. 37–8.
137 *The Third Charge of Whitelock Bulstrode, Esq., to the Grand Jury*, p. 21.
138 John Lacy, *A moral test, the manifest intent in law, of a Sacramental; and a due enforcement thereof evinced, the honour, the safety, and incomparable happiness of England* (London, 1704), pp. 11–13.
139 *Ibid.*, p. 30.
140 Roger L'Estrange, *An Account of the growth of knavery, under the pretended fears of arbitrary government, and popery* (London, 1678).
141 Bodleian MS Tanner 21 f146, White Kennett to G. Hicks, 26 August 1699.
142 *A Sermon preached to the Societies for Reformation of Manners, at St Mary-le-Bow*, by Francis Bishop of St Asaph, pp. 23–4.
143 *Ibid.*, pp. 41–8. Asaph's sermon was opposed in *A Letter to the Right Revd. the Lord Bishop of Asaph: occasioned by some passages in his sermon before the Societies for Reformation of manners, concerning the method of stopping the progress of infidelity* (London, 1731), for attacking freedom of the press.
144 See e.g. *A letter from a Gentleman in Germany, touching the discovery of a strange murder, committed there by a person of quality, upon a lustfull fryer for endeavouring to corrupt his lady* (London, 1684).
145 *Directions to an Awaken'd conscience; under the form of religion* (London, 1726), e.g. p. 52.
146 Josiah Woodward (attributed), *A Dissuasive from gaming* (London, early eighteenth century, printed under no date and no place on title page). I would attribute this pamphlet to Woodward on grounds of internal evidence alone. The style, arguments, format, printer and whole stance of the tract are all similar to Woodward's own work.
147 *Ibid.*, p. 3.
148 Josiah Woodward, *A Dissuasive from the sin of Drunkenness* (London, 1701), p. 9.
149 Anon. (probably Josiah Woodward), *A Kind caution to prophane swearers* (London, 1706), pp. 1–2. Cf. *A friendly discourse concerning prophane cursing and swearing* (London, 1701).
150 Josiah Woodward (ascribed on internal evidence), *A Short Dissuasive from the*

sin of uncleanness (no place, no date, presumably London, first decade of eighteenth century).
151 Josiah Woodward (ascribed), *A Dissuasive from gaming*, p. 3.
152 *A dissuasive from the horrid and beastly sin of drunkenness* (London, no date), p. 1. Cf. *Charge to the Grand Jury of the Royalty of the Tower of London*, 16 July 1728 (London, 1728), p. 94.
153 *The Character of a town-gallant* (London, 1675).
154 *An Account of the Societies for the reformation of manners in England and Ireland*.
155 Published at London, in 1709.
156 Anon., *The Nature and designs of Holy days explained, or short and plain reasons and instructions for the observances of feasts and fasts of the . . . Church of England* (London, 1708).
157 E.g. *A Letter to a Minister of the Church of England, concerning the Societies for the Reformation of manners* (London, 1710).
158 Anon., *Proposals for a national reformation of manners* (London, 1694).
159 *An Account of the Societies for the Reformation of manners in England and Ireland*, pp. 21–5.
160 *Ibid.*, pp. 19–20, etc.
161 *An Account of the Progress of the Reformation of manners, in England, Scotland and Ireland* (London, 1704), pp. 50–1.
162 Proclamations, Queen Anne, 25 February 1702, 'for the encouragement of piety and virtue'.
163 *Statutes at large* (London, 1786), vol. iii, pp. 689–90, 9 and 10 William III c 32.
164 *Ibid.*, 29 Charles II c 7.
165 The best extant discussion of Tudor practice and of the informing system, which persisted into the eighteenth century, can be found in Beresford, 'The Common Informer and the Penal Statutes', *Economic History Review*, 1957–8. These were defences of the Informing System – see *A Short Answer to the objections that are made against those who give informations of the breaches of the laws made against prophaneness and debauchery* (London, 1704). The role of the Societies in encouraging prosecutions can be traced in e.g. *The Sixth and thirtieth account of the progress made in the cities of London and Westminster, and places adjacent, by the Societies for Promoting a Reformation of manners; by furthering the execution of the laws against prophaneness & immorality* which lists prosecutions, 1 December 1729–1 December 1730.
166 *The Character of an informer, wherein his mischievous nature and lewd practises are detected* (London, 1675), and *The Second*

Character of an informer (London, 1682).
167 E.g. *A Sermon preached to the Societies for the Reformation of Manners*, pp. 15–20 – especially p. 19.
168 Bodleian MS Rawl. D 129, p. 18.
169 *Ibid.*, pp. 18–19.
170 *Ibid.*, p. 22.
171 *Ibid.*, pp. 24–5.
172 *Ibid.*, f8.
173 *Ibid.*, f30.
174 *Ibid.*, ff32–4.
175 Wake MS 933, f34.
176 E. Hickes, 'The test or tryal of the goodness and value of spiritual courts, in 2 Queries' in E. Hickeringill, *Miscellaneous tracts, essays, satyrs, etc* . . . (London, 1707), p. 53.
177 As in his *An Account of the rise and progress of religious societies in the City of London* (2nd ed., London, 1698).
178 *The Seamen's Monitor: wherein particular advice is given to seafaring men, with reference to their behaviour, with some prayers for their use* (London, 1703).
179 E.g. *An Address to the Officers and seamen in her Majesty's royal navy* (London, no date).
180 Both Josiah Woodward and Maryott would repay further study as men who did more than make polite noises about two important social movements for 'improvement' in the early eighteenth century. A general study of the programmes of the Societies for the Reformation of Manners, and for the Propagation of the Gospel, would also be useful.
181 Josiah Woodward, *A Short Answer to the objections made by ill or ignorant men against those pious and useful persons.*
182 Josiah Woodward, Boyle lectures for 1709–10 (London, 1710).
183 *A help to a national reformation: an abstract of the penal laws against prophaneness and vice* . . . (London, 1700) was one such that gave extracts from, and commentary upon, the laws of the land: see also *An Abstract of the Penal laws against Blasphemy, Immorality, & Prophaneness.*
184 *A Proclamation by William III founding the Society* (London, 1702), and *An Abstract of the Charter of the Society with a short account of what hath been and what is designed to be done by it* (London, 1702). Boyle had been instrumental in distributing Bibles and Christian knowledge in colonial parts before this official recognition.
185 The history of the Society can also be traced through its sometimes eulogistic but nevertheless informative reports, e.g. *The First Report issued by the society for the propagation of the gospel* (London, 1704),

reprinted 1851; and the yearly abstracts, e.g. *An Abstract of the most material proceedings and occurrences within the last year's endeavours of the Society* . . . *from 18 Feb. 1714–17 Feb. 1715* (no place, no date).
186 Bodleian MS Rawl. D 843 ff185, 188–92.
187 *An Account of the progress of the Reformation of manners* (London, 1705), pp. 53–4.
188 *Ibid.*, pp. 25–53.
189 *Presentments of the Grand Juries of* . . . *praising societies for law enforcement and asking all officers to aid this* . . . (London, 1705), and *The Obligations of J.P.s to be diligent in the execution of the penal laws against prophaneness and debauchery, for the effecting of a national Reformation* (London, 1705).
190 There is no detailed study of the operation of the Constables and Grand Juries in this period; Morrell's on Cheshire in the mid-seventeenth century is the nearest we have.
191 Sir John Gonson, *3 Charges to the several Grand Juries*, p. 15.
192 See an account of Shaftesbury's treason trial in Bodleian MS Rawl. c 719, ff219–24.
193 *The 2nd charge of Sir John Gonson to general quarter sessions of the peace for Westminster* (London, 1728).
194 *The 1st charge*, pp. 26–7.
195 *The 3rd charge*, pp. 91–2.
196 *Ibid.*, p. 92.
197 *Ibid.*, p. 94.
198 *Ibid.*, p. 57.
199 *Ibid.*, p. 59.
200 *Ibid.*
201 *Ibid.*, pp. 76–7.
202 Bodleian MS Rawl. D 129, *An agreement of divers gentlemen* . . ., ff1–13.
203 For the difficulties in one sphere of policy see *An Account of the endeavours that have been used to suppress gaming-houses and the discouragements that have been met with* (London, 1722).
204 *A Proclamation by William III founding the Society* . . . (London, 1702).
205 *An Abstract of the charter granted to the society with a short account of what hath been and what is designed to be done by it* (London, 1702).
206 D. Humphreys, *An historical account of the incorporated society for the propagation of the gospel in foreign parts to the year 1728* (London, 1730), and De la Mothe, *Relation de la société établie pour la propagation de l'évangelise dans les pays étrangers par les lettres patentes du roi Guillaume III* (Rotterdam, 1708).
207 See *Proposals for a national reformation of manners* (London, 1694).

208 Bodleian MS Tanner 137, f175r.
209 *Ibid.*, f175v.
210 *Ibid.*, 159, ff91–3.
211 *Ibid.*, 36, f33.
212 *Ibid.*, 137, f79, and Bodleian MS Tanner 138, f98.
213 Bodleian MS Rawl. c 983, Letters to Bishop Compton, 1676–1710, f18.
214 Bodleian MS Rawl. c 983, f174r and v.
215 *Ibid.*
216 Bodleian MS Rawl. A 275, f108.
217 *Ibid.*, f2.
218 *Ibid.*, f22r and v.
219 *Ibid.*, f32.
220 *Ibid.*, f33.
221 *Ibid.*, f35.
222 *Ibid.*, f37.
223 *An Answer to a letter to a friend, occasion'd by the presentment of the Grand Jury for the County of Middlesex, of the Author, Printer and Publisher of a book entitled . . .* (London, 1708).
224 *Ibid.*, p. 24.
225 *John Checkley's speech on trial for publishing Leslie's short and easy method . . .* (London, 1730), p. 40.
226 *Ibid.*, p. 63.
227 Gibson MS, vol. II, 930, f25.

CHAPTER NINE **The reason of nature and the nature of reason**

1 Thomas Chubb, *A Discourse concerning Reason, with regard to Religion and Divine Revelation* (London, 1733), a response to Gibson's 2nd *Pastoral Letter.*
2 *Ibid.*, pp. 12–13.
3 *Ibid.*, p. 23.
4 *Ibid.*, p. 30.
5 John Wilkins, Bishop of Chester, *Of the Principles and duties of natural religion . . .* (London, 1675), p. 20.
6 Joseph Glanvill, *A seasonable recommendation and defence of reason in the affairs of religion* (London, 1670), p. 1.
7 *Ibid.*, p. 11.
8 *Ibid.*, p. 12.
9 A. Collins, *Discourse of freethinking* (London, 1713), p. 35ff.
10 *Ibid.*, p. 56.
11 *Ibid.*, pp. 6–12.
12 Glanvill, *The Vanity of Dogmatizing or confidence in opinions* (London, 1661). *Philosophia Pia, or a discourse of the religious temper and tendencies of the experimental philosophy . . .* (London, 1671).
13 For the assault upon the logic and rhetoric of the schoolmen in England, see W. S. Howell, *Logic and Rhetoric in England, 1500–1700* (Princeton, 1956).

14 W. Derham, *Physico-theology* (London, 1713).
15 Samuel Clarke, *Defence of the Being and Attributes of God* (London, 1705). See also Gretton, p. 98ff. for extracts from friends' letters about *a priori* argument.
16 Phillips Gretton, *A Review of the argument a priori, in relation to the being and attributes of God* (London, 1726), pp. vii–xi.
17 Locke's attack upon innate ideas having left them unpopular.
18 Gretton, *A Review . . .*, p. iii. See pp. 83–8 for Limborch and Locke's view of the *a priori* position.
19 *Ibid.*, pp. v–vi.
20 *Ibid.*, p. xiii. See pp. 36–41 for handling of *a posteriori* argument.
21 John Jackson, *Calumny no conviction; being a Vindication of the Plea for Human Reason; against the aspersions of a book under the name of John Browne &c. called A Defense of the Bishop of London's 2nd Pastoral Letter* (London, 1731), p. 56.
22 See Brampton Gurdon, *Probabile est animam non semper cogitare. Idea Dei non est innata* (Cambridge, 1696).
23 Gurdon noted on p. 60 that even Hobbes accepted that religion aided social control: B. Gurdon, *The Pretended difficulties in natural or reveal'd religion no excuse for infidelity* (London, 1723).
24 Thomas Morgan, *Enthusiasm in distress, Or, An Examination of the Reflections upon Reason* (London, 1722).
25 *Ibid.*, p. 7.
26 *Ibid.*, p. 15.
27 *Ibid.*, p. 8.
28 *Ibid.*, p. 67.
29 Archibald Campbell, *A Discourse proving that the Apostles were no enthusiasts. Wherein the nature and influence of religious enthusiasm are impartially explain'd* (London, 1730); this work was a response to Matthew Tindal's *Christianity as old as the Creation* and to Woolston's remarks on the Resurrection.
30 Thomas Chubb, *The Previous Question with regard to Religion; humbly offer'd, as necessary to be consider'd, in order to the settling and determining all other questions on this subject* (London, 1725), p. 18.
31 *Ibid.*, pp. 19–22.
32 *Ibid.*, p. 23.
33 *Ibid.*, pp. 26–7.
34 *Ibid.*, p. 14.
35 Thomas Morgan, *Physico-theology* (London, 1741), pp. 1–29.
36 *Ibid.*, pp. 63–102.
37 *Ibid.*, p. 296.
38 *Ibid.*, p. 297.

39 *Ibid.*, p. 304.

40 *Ibid.*, pp. 305–6.

41 *Ibid.*, p. 307.

42 Joseph Hallet, *The Immorality of the Moral Philosopher* (London, 1737), p. 69.

43 *A Defence of the Moral Philosopher; against a pamphlet, entitled 'The Immorality of the Moral Philosopher'* (London, 1737), p 39.

44 *Ibid.*, p. 1.

45 *A Letter to The Moral Philosopher: Being a Vindication of a pamphlet entitled, The Immorality of the Moral Philosopher* (London, 1737), p. 37.

46 Additional MS 3930, 'Natural Causes of events' by Thomas Hobbes, f1.

47 *Ibid.*, f1v.

48 *Ibid.*, f12r–16r.

49 *Ibid.*, f27vff.

50 *Ibid.*, f7vff.

51 *Ibid.*, ff11r–12v.

52 *Ibid.*, f1v.

53 Sir Chas. Wolseley, *The Mount of spirits, that glorious and honourable state to which believers are called by the gospel* (London, 1691), Preface.

54 *Ibid.*, pp. 33–7.

55 *Ibid.*, p. 40.

56 W. Wollaston, *The Religion of Nature delineated* (no place, 1722), p. 18, Section 1, Proposition X.

57 *Ibid.*, p. 27, Section II, Proposition IX.

58 *Ibid.*, p. 23, Section II, Proposition I.

59 *Ibid.*, p. 29ff., Section III.

60 *Ibid.*, p. 27, Section II, Proposition XI.

61 John Clarke, *An Examination of the notion of moral good and evil; advanced in a late book . . .* (London, 1725), p. 19.

62 MS Rawl. B 211 Arguments against atheism drawn from the products of natural causes. (Bodleian.)

63 *Ibid.*, ff150r–170r.

64 *Ibid.*, ff126r–136v.

65 *Ibid.*, ff282–301.

66 *Ibid.*, f266ff.

67 E.g. Laurentius Valla, *De falso oedita et emerdita constantini M donatione dedamatio* (Leyden, 1620).

68 J. J. Scarisbrick, *Henry VIII* (London, 1968), pp. 163–97.

69 Bodleian MS Lat. th. e 27, *Speculum historico-geographico Theologian.*

70 T. Byfield, *The Christian Examiner* (London, 1720), p. 18.

71 J. Leland, *The divine authority of the Old and New Testament asserted: with a particular Vindication of the Characters of Moses . . .* (2nd ed., London, 1739), pp. 391–425.

72 *2 Letters to the Rev. Dr Bentley, Master of Trinity College Cambridge, concerning his intended edition of the Greek Testament* (London, 1721), p. 4.

73 *Ibid.*, p. 25.

74 *A Seasonable Review of Mr Whiston's account of Primitive Doxologies* (London, 1719), mounts an equally vindictive attack: see p. 42.

75 See e.g. *A Vindication of the Rev. Dr Sacheverell's late endeavour to turn Mr Whiston out of his Church* (London, 1719). Whiston defended himself in *Mr Whiston's account of Dr Sacheverell's Proceedings in order to exclude him from St Andrew's Church in Holborn* (London, 1719).

76 *Ibid.*, pp. 10–13.

77 *Mr Whiston's second letter to the Right Rev. the Lord Bishop of London concerning the Primitive Doxologies* (London, 1719), pp. 22–3.

78 *Ibid.*, p. 25.

79 *Ibid.*, p. 31.

80 *Mr Whiston's Letter of thanks to the Right Rev. the Lord Bishop of London for his late letter to his clergy against the use of the new form of doxology &c.* (London, 1719), pp. 17–19.

81 W. Whiston, *A Commentary on the Three Catholic Epistles of St John: in agreement with the ancientest Records of Christianity now extant* (London, 1719).

82 W. Higgs, *A Letter to Mr Whiston proving that his quotations from the Old Testament, in his letter to the Earl of Nottingham, concerning the eternity of the Son and Holy Ghost, are neither true nor fair . . .* (London, 1719).

83 *Origenis Adamantij Renati Epistola Ad Doctores Whitbeium, Whistonium Aliosque Literatos hujus saeculi Disputationes: circa Fidem vere Orthodoxam, et scripturarum Interpretationem* (London, 1720), p. 16.

84 *Ibid.*, p. 23.

85 Styan Thirlby, *A Defense of the Answer to Mr Whiston's suspicions, and an answer to his charge of forgery against St Athanasius* (Cambridge, 1713), p. 5.

86 Dr Grabe, *Some instances of the defects and omissions in Mr Whiston's collection of testimonies from the Scriptures and Fathers, against the true Deity of the Son, and the Holy Ghost; and of misapplying and mis-interpreting divers of them* (London, 1712).

87 *Ibid.*, pp. 3–8.

88 *Ibid.*, pp. 8–18.

89 *Ibid.*, e.g. p. 27, re Tit. ii 13.

90 W. Whiston, *A Supplement to Mr Whiston's late Essay, towards restoring the true text of the O.T.* (London, 1723).

91 For comment on the Constitutions see Dallee, *De Pseudepigraphis Apostolicis*, p. 9 and pp. 10–11 for comment on the manuscript sources of the Constitutions.

92 Bodleian MS Rawl. D 373, 29 July

1712, William Whiston, *Proposals for erecting a primitive library.*

93 *Ibid.*

94 Bodleian MS Eng. th. c 60, Minutes of Society for promoting primitive Christianity; notes at rear.

95 J. Toland, *Amyntor; or, a defence of Milton's life* (London, 1699).

96 *Some Reflections on that part of a book called Amyntor . . . which relates to the Writings of the Primitive Fathers and the canon of the New Testament*, p. 10.

97 *Ibid.*, p. 21.

98 *Ibid.*, p. 46.

99 Samuel Clarke, *A Discourse . . .* (London, 1705).

100 Chubb, *A Discourse concerning the connexion of the prophecies in the Old Testament . . .* (London, 1727).

101 British Museum Stowe MS 1013, f9r.

102 *Ibid.*, f9v.

103 *Ibid.*

104 *Ibid.*, ff39r–49r.

105 *Ibid.*, ff14v–15r.

106 *Ibid.*, f35–42v.

107 Edward Yardley, *An Eucharistical office for the devout and profitable receiving of the body and blood of Christ* (London, 1727).

108 H. Lukin, *A Remedy against trouble: in a discourse on John xiv i* (London, 1694).

109 *Ibid.*, p. 83.

110 Daniel Whitby, *A Paraphrase & Commentary on the New Testament* (London, 1718).

111 See e.g. John Conybeare, *The Mysteries of the Christian Religion credible* (2nd ed., London, 1725), given to University of Oxford; (London and Oxford, 1728/9) given at St Paul's Cathedral, February 1728/9.

112 Thomas Morgan, *Four Letters concerning assent to a revealed proposition, the scriptural sense of heresy, and remarks upon some of Mr Chubb's writings* (London, 1725), p. 4, Letter I.

113 Thomas Chubb, *The true gospel of Jesus Christ asserted* (London, 1738), The Author to his Readers, p. ix.

114 *Ibid.*, p. 15.

115 *Ibid.*, p. 18.

116 *Ibid.*, p. 81.

117 *Ibid.*, p. 191.

118 *Ibid.*

119 Thomas Chubb, *A Short Dissertation on Providence* (London, 1738), p. 210, appendix to *The True Gospel . . .*

120 *Ibid.*, p. 207ff.

121 James Edgcumbe, *Human Reason an insufficient guide in matters of Religion and morality* (London, 1736).

122 J. Hallet, *The Consistent Christian; being a confutation of the errors advanced in Mr Chubb's late book, intituled, the true gospel of Jesus Christ asserted* (London, 1738).

123 *Ibid.*, p. 5.

124 *Ibid.*, p. 34.

125 *Ibid.*, pp. 39–42.

126 *The Analogy of Religion, natural and revealed, to the constitution and course of nature* (London, 1736), Advertisement.

127 St John's College, Oxford, MS 220, f1. A Commonplace book to the primitive writers.

128 *Ibid.*, p. 11.

129 *Ibid.*, p. 50.

130 *Ibid.*, pp. 91–2.

131 *Ibid.*, p. 20.

132 Rawlinson MS 211, f302ff.

133 *Ibid.*, f304r.

134 John Conybeare, *The Case of Subscription to the Articles of Religion consider'd* (Oxford, 1725).

135 Waterland, *Christian liberty asserted . . .* (London, 1734), Preface.

136 William Stevenson (ascribed), *The Case of Subscription to the 39 Articles considered* (London, 1721), p. 49, referring to Dr T. Bennet's *An Essay on the 39 Articles of religion with an epistle to Anthony Collins* (London, 1715).

137 W. Stevenson, *The Case of Subscription . . .*, p. 5.

138 E.g. *A Reply to Dr Waterland's Supplement to the Case of Arian Subscription. Being a defense of the Case of subscription to the xxxix articles* (London, 1722).

139 Dr Hare, *The difficulties and discouragements which attend the study of the scriptures . . .* (8th ed., London, 1721).

140 A. Collins, *A Philosophical Enquiry concerning Human Liberty* (London, 1717).

141 Samuel Clarke, *Works* (vol. iv), p. 723 (London, 1738), *Remarks upon a book entitled, A Philosophical Enquiry concerning human liberty.*

142 *Ibid.*, p. 728.

143 *Ibid.*, pp. 732–3.

144 *Ibid.*, pp. 734–5.

145 Thomas Chubb, *A Collection of tracts, on various subjects* (London, 1730), Treatise XX, *A Vindication of God's moral character . . . Wherein the case of liberty and necessity is considered, with regard to human actions.*

146 Thomas Chubb, Treatise XXII, *A Discourse concerning persecution, wherein the grounds upon which Christians afflict and grieve, and bereave each other of life, for their different opinions in matters of religion are examin'd*, p. 291.

147 *Ibid.*, p. 296.

148 Thomas Chubb, Treatise XXVIII

Some short reflections on the grounds and extent of authority and liberty, with respect to civil government, p. 458.

149 *Ibid.*, p. 461.

150 *Ibid.*, p. 467.

151 *Ibid.*, p. 471.

152 A. Collins, *A Discourse of the grounds and reasons of the Christian religion in 2 parts* (London, 1724), 'Preface to the Reader: containing an Apology for Mr Whiston's liberty of writing', p. vi.

153 A. Collins, *A Discourse on the grounds and reasons . . .*, pp. xxxv–xxxvi.

154 Wake's book was published at London in 1688, and was a 'translation' from a Popish author.

155 Collins, *Discourse . . .*, p. xx.

156 *Ibid.*, p. lvii.

157 *Ibid.*, pp. 273–6.

158 *Ibid.*, p. 278.

159 *Ibid.*, p. 46.

160 *Ibid.*, pp. 120–30.

161 *Ibid.*, pp. 162–84.

162 *Ibid.*, pp. 217–24.

163 A. Collins, *Priestcraft in perfection: or, a detection of the fraud of inserting and continuing this clause . . . in the 20th article . . .* (London, 1710).

164 W. Chillingworth, *The Religion of Protestants a safe way to salvation* (Oxford, 1638), Cap. 6 Sect. 56.

165 A. Collins, *Priestcraft . . .*, p. 48.

166 *Ibid.*, pp. 33–7.

167 A. Collins, *Discourse of Free-thinking, occasion'd by the rise and growth of a sect call'd freethinkers* (London, 1713), pp. 6–12.

168 *Ibid.*, pp. 27–8.

169 *Ibid.*, p. 35.

170 *Ibid.*, p. 40.

171 *Ibid.*, pp. 41–2.

172 *Ibid.*, p. 76.

173 *Ibid.*, pp. 85–6.

174 *Ibid.*, p. 91.

175 *Ibid.*, p. 100.

176 *Ibid.*, p. 101.

177 *Ibid.*, p. 104.

178 *Ibid.*, p. 111.

179 *Ibid.*, pp. 169–70.

180 *Ibid.*, pp. 170–1.

181 *Ibid.*

182 *Ibid.*, pp. 171–7.

183 A. Collins, *An Essay concerning the use of reason in propositions, the evidence whereof depends upon human testimony* (London, 1707), p. 16.

184 *Ibid.*, p. 23.

185 Robert Boyle, *Works* (London, 1744): *A Discourse of things above reason*, vol. iv, pp. 39–54.

186 A. Collins, *An Essay concerning the use of reason*, p. 29.

187 *Ibid.*, pp. 33–8.

188 F. Gastrell, *Defence of the notion of a trinity in unity* (London, 1694).

189 A. Collins, *A Discourse of freethinking . . .*, pp. 49–50.

190 *Ibid.*, pp. 45–50.

191 Published at London in 1729.

192 British Museum Sloane MS 4037, f346, Edmund Gibson to Dr Hans Sloane, 24 October 1699.

193 Brampton Gurdon, *The Pretended difficulties in natural or reveal'd Religion no excuse for infidelity* (London, 1723), in the long tradition of the Boyle lectures.

194 John Jackson, *A Discourse concerning Virtue and Religion: occasion'd by some late writings* (London, 1732), pp. 5–6.

195 Francis Hutcheson, *An Enquiry into the origin of our ideas of beauty and virtue* (London, 1725), p. 95.

196 Anon., *The doctrine of original sin, stated and defended* (London, 1727), p. 40.

CHAPTER TEN **The significance of the minute philosophers**

1 C. Blount, *Anima Mundi*. To the Reader.

2 See e.g. J. Priestly, *Observations on the increase of infidelity* (London, 1796); W. Richards, *Reflections on French atheism & on English Christianity* (2nd ed., Lynn, 1795); J. Reeve, *Thoughts on the importance of religion, addressed to the poor . . . to preserve them from the . . . effects of certain publications* (Maidstone, 1796); W. Lewelyn, *An Appeal to men against Paine's Rights of Man*, 2 parts (Leominster, 1793); J. P. Estlin, *The nature and the cause of atheism . . . (and) remarks on a work, entitled Origine de tous les cultes* (London and Bristol, 1797).

BIBLIOGRAPHY

A   MANUSCRIPT SOURCES

British Museum, London: Additional MSS; Sloane MSS

Bodleian Library, Oxford: Ashmole MSS; MSS Eng. th.; MSS Eng. Misc.; MSS Locke; Rawlinson MSS; MSS Smith; Tanner MSS

College Archives, Oxford: All Souls College Archives; Christchurch Wake MSS; Exeter College Archives – the College Register 1619–1737; St John's College Archives

Lambeth Palace, London: Gibson MSS; Wake MSS

PRO, London: Shaftesbury Papers

Koninklijke Bibliotheek – The Hague

B   CONTEMPORARY PRINTED BOOKS

Anon. *Brief Notes on the creed of Athanasius; Maximus and reflections upon plays* (London, 1699); *Some considerations about ye danger of going to plays* (London, 1704); *The Character of a town-gallant* (London, 1675); *The Character of an informer* (London, 1675); *The Counter-Plot* (London, 1680); *The Lives of the Ancient Philosophers* (London, 1702); *The Lives and Loves of Queens and royal mistresses* (London, 1756); *The Practical Atheist* (Edinburgh, 1721); *The Voice of the nation* (London, 1676)
R. Ames, *The Rake* (London, 1693)
M. Amyraldus, *Traité des Religions* (Saumur, 1631)
J. Aubrey, *Remains of Gentilisme and Judaisme* (London, 1681); *Brief Lives* (ed. A. Clark, Oxford, 1898)

F. Bacon, *Works* (ed. Spedding, Ellis & Heath) (London, 1857–9)
P. Bayle, *Dictionaire Historique et Critique* (Rotterdam, 1697); *Oeuvres* (La Haye, 1737)
R. Baxter, *A Holy Commonwealth* (London, 1659)
R. Bentley, *Boyle Lectures* (London, 1693)
J. Bidle, *The Apostolical & true opinion concerning the Holy Trinity* (London, 1691)
B. Binet, *Traité historique des Dieux* (Delft, 1696)
T. Birch, *History of the Royal Society* (London, 1756)
O. Blackall, *The Sufficiency of the Scripture Revelation* (London, 1700)
C. Blount, *Miracles, no violations of the laws of nature* (London, 1683); *Religio laici* (London, 1683)
R. Boyle, *Works* (ed. T. Birch, London, 1744)
S. Bradford, *The Credibility of the Christian Revelation* (London, 1699)
J. Broughton, *Psychologia* (London, 1703)
G. Bull, *Opera Omnia* (London, 1703); *Some important points of primitive Christianity* (London, 1713)
G. Burnet, *The Libertine Overthrown* (London, 1700); *The Sermon preached at the funeral of John Wilmot* (London, 1680)
T. Burnet, *Archaologiae Philosophicae* (London, 1692); *The Sacred Theory of the Earth*, ed. B. Willey (London, 1965)
A. Bury, *The Naked Gospel* (Oxford, 1690)
S. Butler, *Hudebras* (Cambridge, 1905); *Satires* (Cambridge, 1928)
T. Campanella, *Atheismus Triumphatus* (Paris, 1636)
N. Carpenter, *Libera Philosophia* (2nd ed. Oxford, 1622)
W. Carroll, *Remarks upon Mr Clarke's Sermons* (London, 1705)
S. Charnocke, *Several Discourses upon the existence & attributes of God* (London, 1682)

W. Charleton, *The darkness of atheism* (London, 1652)

W. Chillingworth, *The Religion of Protestants* (Oxford, 1638); *The Religion of Protestants . . .* (London, 1687)

T. Chubb, *A Discourse concerning reason* (London, 1733); *A Discourse on miracles* (London, 1741); *The Supremacy of the Father asserted* (London, 1718); *The True Gospel of Jesus Christ asserted* (London, 1738)

N. Clagett, *The Abuse of God's grace* (London, 1659)

W. Claggett, *A Paraphrase with Notes . . . upon the 6th chapter of St John* (London, 1686)

S. Clarke, *A Discourse of the Being and Attributes of God* (London, 1706); *Defence of the Being and Attributes of God* (London, 1705); *The Scriptural Doctrine of the Trinity* (London, 1712); *Works* (London, 1738)

A. Collins, *A discourse of the grounds and reasons of the Christian religion* (London, 1724); *A Philosophical Enquiry concerning human liberty* (London, 1717); *Discourses of freethinking* (London, 1713)

J. Conybeare, *The Case of Subscription* (Oxford, 1725)

A. Cooper, *Characteristics of men, manners, opinions, times* (London, 1711); *The Moralists* (London, 1709)

W. Coward, *Second Thoughts concerning the human soul* (London, 1702); *The Grand Essay* (London, 1703)

T. Creech, *Lucretius* (London, 1700)

H. Croft, *Some Arian adversions* (London, 1685)

W. Cross, *The Instrumentality of faith* (London, 1695)

R. Cudworth, *The true Intellectual System of the Universe* (London, 1677)

W. Derham, *Physico-theology* (London, 1713)

D. Derodon, *Disputatio theologica* (Geneva, 1661)

R. Descartes, *Oeuvres* (Pleiade ed.) (Bruges, 1963)

P. Desmaizeau, *An historical Account of the life and writings of the late eminently famous Mr John Toland* (London, 1722)

J. Digby, *Epicurus's Morals* (London, 1712)

Sir K. Digby, *A Treatise of adhering to God* (London, 1654); *A Short way with Prophananess* (London, 1730); *A Whip for the droll* (London, 1682); *The Atheist Unmasked* (London, 1690); *The behaviour of the clergy* (London, 1731); *The Pedigree of Popery* (London, 1688)

N. Durand, *The Life of Lucilio Vanini* (London, 1730)

J. Edwards, *Socinianism Unmask'd* (London, 1696); *Some Brief Reflections upon Socinianism* (London, 1695); *Some thoughts concerning the several causes and occasions of atheism* (London, 1695); *The Socinians' Creed* (London, 1697)

The Freethinker

P. Gassendi, *Syntagma Philosophiae Epicuri* (Amsterdam, 1684)

F. Gastrell, *Some Considerations concerning the Trinity* (London, 1696); *The Certainty & necessity of religion* (London, 1697)

J. Glanville, *Saducismus Triumphatus* (2nd ed. London, 1682)

Sir J. Gonson, *3 charges to the several Grand Juries* (London, 1728)

Dr N. Grew, *Cosmographia Sacra* (London, 1701)

Grotius, *De Jure Bellis et Pacis* (Paris, 1625)

H. Hakewill, *An apologie of the power and providence of God* (Oxford, 1627)

J. Harrington, *Complete Works*, ed. Toland (London, 1704)

W. Harris, *The reasonableness of believing in Christ* (London, 1729)

Lord J. Hervey, *Memoirs of the reign of George II* (London 1848)

John Henley, *Oratory Transactions* (London, 1729); *The history and advantages of divine Revelation* (London, 1725)

W. Higgs, *A letter to Mr Whiston* (London, 1719)

T. Hobbes, *The English Works*, ed. Molesworth (London, 1839)

J. Howe, *The Living Temple* (London, 1675)

F. Hutcheson, *An Enquiry into the origin o, our ideas of Beauty and Virtue* (London, 1725)

J. Keill, *A Examination of Dr Burnet's Theory of the Earth* (Oxford, 1698)

R. Kidder, *A Demonstration of the Messias* (London, 1684–1700)

Lactantius, *De Divinibus Institutionibus* (London, 1684)

J. Lacy, *A moral test* (London, 1704)

W. Law, *The Bishop of Bangor's late sermon* (London, 1717)

H. Lee, *Antiscepticism* (London, 1702)

C. Leslie, *The Socinian Controversy discuss'd* (London, 1708)

Sir R. L'Estrange, *An Account of the growth of knavery* (London, 1678)

Leibniz-Clarke Correspondence, ed. Alexander (Manchester, 1965)

J. Locke, *An Essay concerning human understanding* (London, 1690); *Works* (6th ed., London, 1759)

B. Mandeville, *A modest defence of public stews* (London, 1724)

A. Marvell, *An Account of the growth of Popery* (London, 1678)

C. Middleton, *A Free Enquiry* (London, 1752)

J. Milner, *An Account of Mr Locke's Religion* (London, 1700)

J. Milton, *Last Thoughts on the Trinity* (London, 1859)

H. More, *An Antidote against atheism* (London, 1653); *Enchiridion Ethicum* (London, 1668)

L. Moreri, *Le Grand Dictionaire historique* (Lyons, 1674)

T Morgan, *Enthusiarm in distress* (London) 1722); *Four letters* (London, 1725); *Physico-theology* (London, 1741)

Sir I. Newton, *Principia Mathematica* ed. Cotes (London, 1713); *The Chronology of Ancient Kingdoms Amended* (London, 1728)

W. Nicholls, *A Conference with a theist* (London, 1697)

J. Norris, *Theory of the Ideal World* (London, 1701–4)

S. Nye, *An accurate examination of the principal texts usually alleged for the divinity of our saviour* (London, 1692); *An account of Mr Firmin's religion* (London, 1698); *Considerations of the Explications of the Doctrine of the Trinity* (London, 1698)

The Observator

H. Oldenburg, *Correspondence* (ed. A. and M. Hall) (Madison, 1963)

B. Pascal, *Oeuvres completes* (Pleiade ed. 1954);

Philosophical Transactions

D. Pickering, *Statutes at large* (London, 1764)

H. Power, *Experimental Philosophy* (London, 1664)

J. Ray, *The Wisdom of God* (London, 1678); *Historia Plantarum* (London, 1686–8)

G. Scheiner, *Oculus* (London, 1652)

Sir H. Sheers, *Essays on the causes of the earth's motion* (London, 1698)

Dr Sherlock, *Vindication of the Holy Trinity* (London, 1695)

J. Sherlock, *The Case of allegiance due to sovereign powers* (London, 1691); *The tryal of witnesses* (4th ed. London, 1729)

W. Sherlock, *A Vindication of the doctrine of the Holy & ever blessed Trinity* ... (London, 1690)

D. Sicurus, *The Origins of Atheism* (London, 1684)

R. Smalbroke, *Reflections on the conduct of Mr Whiston* (London, 1711)

R. South, *Animadversions upon Dr Sherlock's book* (London, 1693); *Tritheism charged upon Dr Sherlock's new notion of the Trinity* (London, 1695)

B. de Spinoza, *Opera Posthuma* (no place, 1677)

T. Sprat, *History of the Royal Society* (London, 1667)

H. Stebbing, *A defence of the Scripture-history* (London, 1730); *A Discourse on Our Saviour's miraculous power of healing* (London, 1662)

J. Tillotson, *A Discourse against Transubstantiation* (London, 1684); *Sermon concerning the folly of atheism* (London, 1691)

M. Tindal, *Christianity as old as the Creation* (London, 1730)

J. Toland, *Letters to Serena* (London, 1704); *Pantheisticon* (London, 1721); *The Miscellaneous Works of Mr Toland* (London 1747)

J. Turner, *Vindication of the separate existence of the soul* (London, 1707)

L. Vanini, *Amphitheatrum* (Leyden, 1615); *De Admirandis Naturae* (Leyden, 1616)

J. Wallis, *The doctrine of the Blessed Trinity* (London, 1690)

Dr Waterland, *The Importance of the Doctrine of the Holy Trinity* (London, 1735)

W. Whiston, *A New theory of the Earth* (London, 1696); *Historical Memoirs ... of Dr S. Clarke* (3rd ed. London, 1748); *Memoirs of the life ... by himself* (London, 1753); *Primitive Christianity revived* (London, 1711)

Bishop J. Wilkins, *Of the Principles & Duties of Natural Religion* (London, 1675)

J. Wilmot, *Poems* (3rd ed. London, 1709)

T. Wise, *Abridgement of Ralph Cudworth's True Intellectual System* (London, 1706)

W. Wollaston, *The Religion of nature delineated* (1722)

Sir C. Wolseley, *The Unreasonableness of Atheism* (London, 1669)

J. Woodward, *A dissuasive from gaming; A dissuasive from the Sin of Drunkenness* (London, 1701); *An account of the rise and progress of religious societies in the City of London* (2nd ed. London, 1698)

T. Woolston, *A Discourse on the miracles of our Saviour* (London, 1727); *For God or the Devil* (London, 1728); *The Moderator between an infidel and an apostate* (London, 1725)

C SECONDARY WORKS

F. Adams, *The Birth & Development of the Geological Sciences* (Baltimore, 1938)

R. S. Bosher, *The Making of the Restoration Settlement* (London, 1951)
J. Bowle, *Hobbes & his critics* (London, 1969)
M. Bracken, *The Early reception of Berkeley's Immaterialism* (London, 1965)
J. Bury, *The Idea of Progress* (London, 1960)

E. Cassirer, *The Platonic Renaissance in England* (London, 1953)
P. Chauvet, *La Religion de Milton* (Paris, 1909)
R. L. Colie, *Light & Enlightenment* (Cambridge, 1957)
K. B. Collier, *Cosmogonies of our Fathers* (New York, 1934)

J. Dunn, *The Political Thought of John Locke* (Cambridge, 1969)

D. P. Gauthier, *The Logic of Leviathan* (Oxford, 1969)

C. Hill, *Puritanism & Revolution* (London, 1958)
G. Holmes, *The Trial of Dr Sacheverell* (London, 1973)
F. C. Hood, *The Divine Politics of Thomas Hobbes* (Oxford, 1964)
W. Howell, *Logic and Rhetoric in England 1500–1700* (2nd ed. St Louis, 1961)

R. F. Jones, *Ancients & Moderns* (2nd ed. St. Louis, 1961
W. K. Jordan, *The Development of Religious Toleration in England* (London, 1936)
R. H. Kargon, *Atomism in England* (Oxford, 1906)
G. Kitchin, *Sir Roger L'Estrange* (London, 1913)
A. Koyre, *From the Closed World to the Infinite Universe* (London, 1970)

J. Laird, *Hobbes* (London, 1934)
H. Laski, *The Rise of European Liberalism* (London, 1936)
H. C. Lea, *Materials towards a history of witchcraft*, ed. A. C. Howland (Philadelphia, 1959)
B. Lillywhite, *London Coffee Houses* (London, 1963)
A. A. Luce, *Life of George Berkeley* (London, 1949)

A. Macfarlane, *Witchcraft in Tudor & Stuart England* (London, 1970)

C. B. Macpherson, *The Political Theory of Possessive Individualism* (Oxford, 1962)
F. Manuel, *Isaac Newton, Historian* (Cambridge, Mass., 1968)
H. McLachlan, *The religious opinions of Milton, Locke and Newton* (Manchester, 1941)
J. Miller, *Popery & Politics in England 1660–88* (Cambridge, 1973)
S. I. Mintz, *The Hunting of Leviathan* (Cambridge, 1962)

M. Nicholson, *Mountain gloom and mountain glory* (New York, 1959)

J. W. Packer, *The Transformation of Anglicanism* (Manchester, 1969)
J. A. Passmore, *Ralph Cudworth, an Interpretation* (Cambridge, 1951)
R. S. Peters, *Hobbes* (London, 1967)
V. de S. Pinto, *Enthusiast in wit* (London, 1962)
R. Popkin, *The history of skepticism* (Asser, 1960)

F. Raab, *The English face of Machiavelli* (London, 1962)
C. Raven, *English naturalists from Neckham to Ray* (Cambridge, 1947); *John Ray, naturalist* (Cambridge, 1942)
N. Ravitch, *Sword & Mitre* (Paris, 1966)
L. Roth, *Spinoza, Descartes and Maimonides* (Oxford, 1934)
H. F. Russell Smith, *Harrington and his Oceana* (Cambridge, 1914)

E. O. Sillem, *George Berkeley & the proof of the existence of God* (Gateshead, 1957)
E. Strauss, *William Petty* (London, 1654)
N. Sykes, *From Sheldon to Secker* (Cambridge, 1959)

K. Thomas, *Religion and the decline of magic* (London, 1971)
G. M. Trevelyan, *England under Queen Anne* (London, 1931)

D. P. Walker, *The Decline of Hell* (London, 1964)
B. Willey, *The Seventeenth Century Background* (London, 1934)

J. Yolton (ed.), *John Locke problems & perspectives* (Cambridge, 1969)

P. Zagorin, *A History of political theory in the English Revolution* (London, 1954)

INDEX